Making It Work

COLLEGE READING IN CONTEXT

Making It Work

COLLEGE READING IN CONTEXT

Robert DiYanni

The College Board

BEDFORD/ST. MARTIN'S   Boston ◆ New York

For Bedford/St. Martin's
Developmental Editors: Aron Keesbury and Ellen M. Kuhl
Production Editor: Arthur Johnson
Senior Production Supervisor: Dennis Conroy
Marketing Manager: Brian Wheel
Editorial Assistant: Jeffrey Voccola
Production Assistant: Tina Lai
Copyeditor: Barbara G. Flanagan
Text Design: Claire Seng-Niemoeller
Cover Design: Laura Shaw and Claire Jarvis
Cover Art: Bruce Baughman, *Out West,* reverse acrylic painting on Lucite. By courtesy of the Bruce Baughman Studio and Gallery.
Composition: Stratford Publishing Services, Inc.
Printing and Binding: R.R. Donnelley & Sons Company

President: Joan E. Feinberg
Editorial Director: Denise B. Wydra
Editor in Chief: Karen S. Henry
Director of Marketing: Karen Melton
Director of Editing, Design, and Production: Marcia Cohen
Managing Editor: Elizabeth M. Schaaf

Library of Congress Control Number: 2002112257

Manufactured in the United States of America.

8   7   6   5   4   3
f   e   d   c   b   a

For information, write: Bedford/St. Martin's, 75 Arlington Street, Boston, MA 02116 (617-399-4000)

ISBN: 0–312–13688–9 (Student Edition)
            0–312–24788–5 (Instructor's Annotated Edition)

Acknowledgments

Eric Alterman, "A Trip to Cell Hell" from MSNBC.com. Copyright © MSNBC.com. Reprinted by permission.

Maya Angelou, "Living Well. Living Good." from *Wouldn't Take Nothing for My Journey Now* by Maya Angelou. Copyright © 1993 by Maya Angelou. Reprinted by permission of Random House, Inc.

As a student it is highly unethical + morally wrong to penalize me + put me against an employee of... in which you supress my separate desires! because I refuse to take part in utilizing an + employer for her low for mistakes

Extensive review of my progress + work ethics AOL.com /

Preface for Instructors

■ A New Series for the Reading Classroom

There has long been a need for a book series that blends the best of traditional developmental reading pedagogy with new approaches. *Making It Work,* like the first book in my series, *Putting It Together,* has been carefully designed to fill this need by providing a useful tool to help students become confident readers through a realistic application of the fundamental skills of college reading. Setting out to create these books, I collaborated with the talented editors at Bedford/St. Martin's. From the beginning, our goal was to address concerns of the developmental reading classroom that other books have addressed only partially or not at all. Throughout the process, we were fortunate to receive substantial feedback, through interviews and extensive review programs, from a dedicated cache of developmental reading teachers throughout the country. Though their comments were broad and comprehensive, the concerns of those teaching developmental reading consistently highlighted three major areas of need, generally unfulfilled by other books. *Putting It Together* and *Making It Work* are built to address those needs.

First, instructors of developmental reading tell us that, while other books successfully help students isolate and learn the individual skills of college reading, in doing so they often oversimplify the complex process of reading. Too often, the result is that students learn how to read fragmented or isolated passages and to take standardized tests based on using a loose collection of skills — often at the expense of learning to read realistically.

Second, instructors tell us that, even when developmental reading books *do* include whole essays or textbook passages, they don't offer a process, or systematic program, to help students apply their skills to whole-reading proficiency. Having practiced their skills only on short excerpts, students risk becoming intimidated when confronted with a

I am very confident I would like to Address my concerns. about my Clinical Eval. first, the feedback is highly exaggerated and untrue. It is unfair to me + discouraging to accept that documents were falsified and retaliation

complete and often complex reading selection. Discouraged, they often simply put the book down.

Finally, instructors overwhelmingly report that one of the most difficult obstacles they face teaching developmental reading is student motivation. Other books have tried with varying degrees of success to attack the problem head-on by offering students encouragement or metacognitive frameworks for understanding their motivational barriers. And while instructors acknowledge that these measures sometimes persuade students of the importance of reading, they report that the selections included in most textbook readers do not sufficiently engage students in the follow-through.

To address these concerns, I blend a traditional learning model with a new, three-pronged approach. First, *Making It Work* teaches students to identify and master the distinct but interrelated skills of college reading. Second, it provides them with an innovative program of readings and activities that guides them step-by-step through the often challenging process of applying those skills to whole readings. And third, the reading program in *Making It Work* (like the program in *Putting It Together*) uses high-interest, topical essays and thematically linked textbook passages that will engage students' native interest, motivate them to practice reading, and — perhaps most important — show them the relevance of reading.

■ The Fundamental Skills of College Reading

In creating a new approach, I have not abandoned the ideas and methodologies that have for many years proved successful in developmental reading classrooms all over the country. Rather, as the table of contents shows, I have built on the best of what has come before, developing the series' innovations around the familiar skills-based model.

- **Comprehensive coverage of fundamental reading skills.** From learning vocabulary to understanding a writer's point to practicing critical reading, the twelve skills-based chapters in *Making It Work* teach step-by-step the discrete skills and strategies that prepare students for successful reading in college and in life.

- **Numerous and varied exercises offer constant reinforcement.** Throughout the skills instruction are practice activities that isolate particular skills and give students a chance to succeed at simpler tasks before moving on to more complex ones. These exercises, on perforated pages, can be used for self-study and practice or they can be submitted to instructors as homework. Additional interactive online quizzes are available on the book's companion Web site, bedfordstmartins.com/makingitwork.

- **Critical thinking activities keep students involved.** Every chapter begins and ends with a unique apparatus especially designed to get students thinking critically about their own learning—both in and out of the classroom. At the beginning of every chapter, a chapter overview and Focusing Questions ask students to reflect on how the chapter is relevant to them. An Everyday Reading feature follows, inviting students to tie their in-class experience to their out-of-class lives. At the end of every chapter, Recall/Remember exercise questions and a chapter summary actively reinforce their learning.

- **Standardized-test practice in the context of real readings.** Within a unique Reading the Parts essay segment at the end of every skills-based chapter, fifteen questions—designed to resemble the kinds of questions asked on standardized tests—allow students to practice for statewide or schoolwide exams while they engage with high-interest readings.

- **Writing activities encourage further application of reading skills.** A Reading/Writing Connection feature—new to *Making It Work*—follows each Reading the Whole essay with brief writing suggestions that invite students to think about reading from a writer's perspective, broadening their understanding of what they read.

■ A Unique Method That Transforms Skills into Whole-Reading Proficiency

To help students integrate the various skills of reading into a realistic reading experience, both *Putting It Together* and *Making It Work* conclude each chapter with a step-by-step program of readings. This method has four major components.

- **Reading the Parts** sections present engaging readings, divided into manageable two-to-three-paragraph parts. Each part is followed by five practice questions referring specifically to those paragraphs. By "reading the parts," students are able to work their way successfully through a whole essay bit by bit, practicing their skills and receiving constant reinforcement.

- **Reading the Whole** sections reassemble the Reading the Parts readings and reprint them in their entirety. Students then reread with a higher level of confidence and a greater degree of success in both comprehension and critical thinking. Integrated Skills questions follow, encouraging students to put their newly learned skills together into an integrated and realistic approach to reading.

- **Reading Textbooks** sections guide students into academic texts. Every chapter features a textbook passage that provides students with an opportunity to apply their newly acquired abilities to the kinds of reading they will encounter throughout college. Drawn from a variety of disciplines — psychology, astronomy, health, and history, for example — these textbook passages are thematically connected to other readings in the chapter, making the academic material more interesting and accessible to reluctant or intimidated students.

- **Reading the Web** screen shots — new to *Making It Work* — expand student skills for today's world. Thematically linked to the chapter's other readings, these reproductions of actual Web pages do more than provide opportunities for students to practice transferring their skills to different genres. Taken from government resources, personal pages, and even a band's official fan site, these Web examples help students to develop Internet literacy while demonstrating that reading skills can be applied to many aspects of students' lives.

■ Readings to Engage and Motivate Students

Students' motivation to read opens the door to practice and is ultimately at the heart of their success. *Making It Work,* like *Putting It Together,* provides interesting readings from current sources to motivate students by engaging their native interest.

- **Current, high-interest essays actually engage students in reading.** All of the non-textbook readings are drawn from contemporary sources such as newspaper editorial pages, student publications, and magazines like *Time* and *Newsweek*. On today's most compelling topics — sports, immigration, alcohol, and the Internet, for example — these essays channel student interest into the practice of reading. Appropriate to students' ability (according to readability tests), the essays are nonetheless exciting, engaging, and respectful of students' intelligence.

- **Thematic links to textbook readings and Web pages motivate students to read.** The textbook passage and Web page example in each chapter are carefully selected for their direct topical connection to other readings in the chapter. Explicit Thematic Connections beginning each textbook passage ask students to consider the relevance of the reading to the topics that interest them—and show how college reading can apply to their lives. Questions that follow the textbook selection and the Web example emphasize the thematic connection as well.

- **A mini-anthology of essays provides additional reading practice.** Taken from recent books and periodicals, these ten selections cover subjects that will actually get students reading by capturing their interest. Each essay is followed by ten Integrated Skills questions that help reinforce students' learning by encouraging them to combine their skills as they contemplate the overall meaning of the whole essay.

■ Supplements

A comprehensive ancillary package complements and supplements the pedagogy and practice provided in *Putting It Together* and *Making It Work*. Bedford/St. Martin's has made available this impressive package with today's students and teachers in mind.

FOR INSTRUCTORS

- **Instructor's Annotated Edition.** Available for teachers, this easy-to-use edition provides answers to all of the book's exercises, printed in a different color and typeface.

- **Test Bank and Assessment Package.** Offered in addition to the online quizzes, the printed test bank booklet provides three separate ten-question tests (with answer keys) for every chapter of *Making It Work*. A diagnostic test with an answer key and assessment guide helps instructors determine where their students need the most help.

- **Overhead Transparency Masters** of the Reading the Parts readings and activities make it easy for instructors to go over these specially "chunked" readings and practice tests in class.

- *Teaching Developmental Reading: Historical, Theoretical, and Practical Background Readings.* Compiled by Norm Stahl of Northern Illinois University and Hunter Boylan of the National Center for Developmental Education at Appalachian State University—the leaders in the field of developmental education and reading—this collection of thirty-eight essays provides instructors with seminal historical, theoretical, and practical essays on developmental reading.

FOR STUDENTS

- **A companion Web site,** at bedfordstmartins.com/makingitwork, includes abundant resources for students as well as instructors, such as links to the interactive online quiz bank (see below) and access to Bedford/St. Martin's extensive resources for students.

- **Interactive Online Quizzes.** With hundreds of questions, this quiz bank produces practice exercises specifically keyed to the parts of *Making It Work.* Students get immediate feedback and their results are collated automatically; the quizzes thus save instructors' time and allow them to easily follow students' progress online.

- *The Bedford/St. Martin's Textbook Reader* reprints five chapters from introductory college textbooks in their entirety, giving students the opportunity to practice their skills on exactly the types of reading that college requires. Each chapter is preceded by an introduction that identifies the chapter's particular reading and learning features. Three sets of questions following each chapter guide students in applying their reading skills to textbook materials, help them gauge their comprehension of the chapter's content, and prompt them to think about thematic links

■ Acknowledgments

From the beginning, *Making It Work* has been a collaborative project. I have had the good fortune to profit from the wise counsel of many reviewers, who read each draft with scrupulous care. Thanks to the following for their assistance: Bonne August, Kingsborough Community College; Ellen H. Bell, Manatee Community College; Jane Brackett, Spartanburg Methodist College; Helen R. Carr, San Antonio College; Elaine Fitzpatrick, Massasoit Community College; Lynna Geis, Rose State College; Connie Gulick, Albuquerque Technical Vocational Institute; Karen Haas, Manatee Community College; Kevin Hayes, Essex County College; Michele E. Jones, Valencia Community College, East; Doreen Kaller, Rio Hondo College; Susie Khirallah-Johnston, Tyler Junior College; Nancy Kreml, Midlands Technical Community College; Shuli Lamden, Santa Fe Community College; Patricia McDermott, Northern Essex Community College; Janice McIntyre, Kansas City Kansas Community College; Judith Y. McNeill, Portland Community College; Marilyn Sandidge, Westfield State College; Robert Zweig, Manhattan Community College.

My work on the book as author has benefited tremendously from the support provided by Bedford/St. Martin's. Among the many who deserve my appreciation and thanks are Barbara Heinssen, who convinced me to begin work on the book more than five years ago, and Karen Allanson, the acquisitions editor who signed me to write the book. The then-president of St. Martin's College Division, Ed Stanford, also lent the project his authoritative support. I would like to thank Barbara, Karen, and Ed for their confidence in my ability to turn a good idea into an excellent book. Thanks also to Meg Spilleth, the book's first developmental editor, for her outstanding assistance.

I would also like to thank the now-retired publisher of Bedford/St. Martin's, Chuck Christensen, and the current president, Joan Feinberg, who both were willing to renew the company's confidence in the book midway through its development at a point where I had hit a roadblock. They generously sent the manuscript out for a new set of reviews and then provided me with the support I needed to complete the book. I am grateful to both of these outstanding professionals for the chance to complete *Making It Work* under their direction. Among the reasons for my thanks to Chuck, Joan, and Editor in Chief Karen Henry is their decision to assign Aron Keesbury and Ellen Kuhl to the book as project editors. Their contributions to the development and final form of *Making It Work* have been critical, extending beyond offering ideas, suggesting readings, and helping the book to evolve. Ellen contributed to the writing and textual editing in too many ways to count. Without their work, *Making It Work* would not exist as the book you now hold in your hands. I also had the good fortune of having two freelance editors help me further advance the project. My warm thanks and deep appreciation go to Marilyn Weissman and Maggie Barbieri for the outstanding editing they did to make *Making It Work* the book it has now become.

In addition, Bedford/St. Martin's provided an outstanding staff of professionals who offered the first-rate assistance they are known for. Thanks are due to the production editor, Arthur Johnson, for his careful and painstaking work in bringing *Making It Work* through the production process. His good-natured demeanor and professionalism made that process as pleasant as it was effective. Thanks to Jeff Voccola, the editorial assistant, who took on and handled myriad tasks with great aplomb. Director of New Media Nick Carbone, New Media Project Editor David Mogolov, and New Media Coordinator Coleen O'Hanley conceived of and created an amazing companion Web site. Thanks as well to Julia G. Berrisford for her work in clearing permissions and to Barbara Flanagan, the most meticulous of copyeditors. It was a privilege to work with this outstanding group.

Finally, I would like to thank my wife, companion, and best friend—Mary Hammond DiYanni. Mary has been with me on this project and on many others for more than thirty years, every one of them memorable and beautiful. I treasure her steadfastness and love, and I thank her with all my heart for helping me, throughout our married life, to make it all work.

Contents

7. Examining a Writer's Language   229

9. Practicing Critical Reading   297

11. Enjoying and Interpreting Literature   387

Introduction:
Using *Making It Work*

■ The Need for Reading

The single most important skill necessary for success in college is reading
with understanding. Reading is necessary not only in school but also on
the job and in the world at large. If you want to make your way in the
world, you will need to read with competence and confidence. And if you
want to succeed in your college courses, you will need not only to read
with understanding but also to become a good critical reader. *Making It
Work* can help you succeed in becoming that kind of reader.

■ What Is Critical Reading?

But just what is critical reading? And how do you go about doing it—
reading critically? It is important to know that critical reading is not
simply being "critical" of everything you read. Critical reading does not
mean always disagreeing, always finding something to criticize. Instead,
critical reading is a process of reflective, thoughtful reading. It is a kind
of reading in which you think carefully about what a writer is saying.
You give the writer's ideas a chance—you consider them. You evaluate a
writer's ideas in terms of your own experience. You think about how
those ideas relate to what you have learned in school and in everyday
life.

Critical reading involves asking questions about what a writer is saying. It involves extending a writer's ideas by adding ideas and examples of your own in support. Critical reading is active, engaged reading. Critical reading is the kind of reading you do when you care, when what is being said matters to you.

When you read critically, you do a number of things at the same time. First, you make observations. You notice what the author is saying and how he or she is saying it. Second, you make connections between different details of the author's writing, and you make further connections with what you already know about the subject. Third, you make educated guesses, also called *inferences,* based on your observations and connections. That is, you "fill in" and "read between the lines." This is one of the most exciting and challenging aspects of reading. And fourth, you figure out exactly what the author is saying, and then you form your own opinion about it—you develop a point of view about what you read.

Making It Work helps you become this kind of critical reader, active and engaged by what you read. First, you will be introduced to all the different skills that make up the process of becoming a critical reader. And second, you will be given a chance to practice those skills separately and then—most important—all together.

■ Learning the Skills of College Reading

Every chapter in *Making It Work* is designed to help you focus on a particular skill of college reading. For example, in one chapter you will focus on increasing your vocabulary by figuring out the meanings of words based on their *contexts* and by breaking them down into parts, or analyzing them. In another chapter, you will focus on learning to identify a writer's main point and how, exactly, a writer makes that point.

Every chapter begins with three elements that will help you prepare to learn the skill that chapter presents. First, a Chapter Overview will let you know what skill, or skills, the chapter will cover. Next, a set of Focusing Questions will show you why that skill is important for reading. Third, an exercise called Everyday Reading will get you looking for the kinds of reading you do outside of college.

After these three introductory elements, the chapters in *Making It Work* explain the different skills involved in college reading. Clear explanations of each skill are followed by brief examples of readings for you to practice on. After the instruction and the examples, you will find useful, clear exercises especially designed to help you learn that skill through more extended practice.

■ The Skills of College Reading in Context

At the end of every chapter is a special set of essays, textbook passages, and Web pages. This set of readings is carefully designed to help you practice the different skills of critical reading. What's special about these readings is that they will also help you learn to put the different skills of college reading back together to read whole essays realistically.

READING THE PARTS

The first reading in the series of readings, called Reading the Parts, is usually an article from a newspaper or magazine on an interesting topic, such as the dangers of fast food or the colonization of Mars. The Reading the Parts essay is divided into small sections with questions following each section. After reading each section, you will answer the questions about that section and then move on to the next section, practicing throughout.

READING THE WHOLE

The next reading in the series is called Reading the Whole. It is the same essay or article that you read in Reading the Parts, but this time it is not divided, so that you can read the whole article without being interrupted. Rereading the essay or article will give you a better, fuller sense of what the author is saying. More important, it will give you a chance to succeed at putting your new skills together into a real reading experience. At the end of the selection are questions that will help you integrate the skills you just learned and applied as well as questions that encourage you to read from a writer's point of view.

READING TEXTBOOKS

The third reading in the series is called Reading Textbooks. As you can probably tell from its title, the Reading Textbooks selection is a passage taken from a college-level textbook. Since the purpose of your college reading class and *Making It Work* is to help you hone and practice the skills of college reading, every chapter gives you a chance to practice your reading skills on one of the many kinds of readings you will encounter in college. And because the textbook reading is on the same topic as the Reading the Parts/Reading the Whole selection, you will already have some familiarity with the material it presents, increasing your understanding of it.

READING THE WEB

The final reading in the series is called Reading the Web. A sample Web page at the end of each chapter gives you an opportunity to practice transferring your reading skills to the Internet. Each Web example is on a topic that is thematically connected to the chapter's Reading the Parts/Reading the Whole and Reading Textbooks readings, so it will give you more insight into the topic they address. Questions following each example highlight the connection between reading printed materials and reading the Web.

■ Practicing on Interesting Readings

The articles, textbook passages, and Web pages in *Making It Work* are special in another way—they are interesting and relevant to your world today. The Reading the Parts and Reading the Whole essays were first published in popular books, student newspapers from around the country, and magazines like *Time, Newsweek,* and *Discover.* Since critical reading involves actively thinking about what you are reading, it's best to begin by reading selections that are interesting. The Reading the Parts and Reading the Whole essays are not only the kinds of readings you will do on your own, outside of class, but they are also well written and will give you a lot to think about—so active critical reading should come more easily.

The Reading Textbooks and Reading the Web readings are interesting, too, but in a different way. Every Reading Textbooks and Reading the Web selection is connected directly to the other readings in the chapter. With Thematic Connections before them, the Reading Textbooks readings will actually teach you something useful—or will answer important questions—about the Reading the Parts and Reading the Whole essays. An essay about zero-tolerance policies in schools, for example, is followed by a passage from a child psychology textbook that talks about how children respond to extreme punishments. An essay complaining about cell phone companies is followed by a passage from a business textbook about customer service. The textbook passages *inform* the chapter's other essays.

The sample Web pages bring the topic of the readings into the everyday world. An essay about discarding family heirlooms, for example, is connected to the home page for Goodwill. And a scientific description of the violin-like noise some lobsters make is followed by a page from the Dave Matthew's Band site. Rather than simply practicing your reading skills on college textbooks and Web sites, you will also learn something useful about the world—and you'll find that reading is not only relevant and useful, but can sometimes even be fun.

■ The Essential Elements of Learning College Reading

Along with the editors at Bedford/St. Martin's, I've worked hard to make this book as good as it can be—and as useful to you as possible. But no book by itself can make you into a better, more competent, and confident reader. This book is one of three critical elements in that process. A second essential element is your instructor. Your reading instructor will guide you and coach you and coax you along the way. With his or her assistance, you will make progress.

The third and most important element of all, however, is you. You must *want* to succeed in improving your reading skills. This desire is fundamental and critical to your success. If you want to improve, and if you are willing to do the work to succeed, your instructor and *Making It Work* can help you achieve your goal.

If you are ready to tackle the job of learning to read well and to become a critical reader, here are a few preliminary suggestions to help you get started on realizing your dream.

1. Make reading a habit—in school and out. Read a little every day.

2. Read different types of things, like newspapers, magazines, and books.

3. Read about things that interest you—sports, music, food, love and sex, people and places, animals, cars, clothes. Read about anything you care about.

4. Find a consistent time or place to read a little each day—before bedtime, riding the subway, at breakfast or lunch, or whatever works for you.

5. Talk about what you read with friends, classmates, and family.

6. Keep a log of your reading—a simple list of what you read each day and week and month. You'll be surprised at how it adds up and how much you learn.

7. Purchase and use a dictionary to look up and learn the new words you encounter in your reading.

8. Make a reading plan—something like an exercise plan—for yourself.

By using *Making It Work* faithfully and thoughtfully, by working with your reading instructor, and by being faithful to your reading plan, you can succeed in improving your reading ability. Your competence as a reader will increase dramatically. From this improvement in your reading competence will come confidence in your reading ability. You can do it—if you really want to and if you are willing to do the work necessary to achieve your goals. And in the end, you will be happy you did.

Making It Work

COLLEGE READING IN CONTEXT

Becoming an Active Reader

Getting Ready

This book invites you to become an active reader—to ask questions about reading and to think carefully about what you read. **Active reading** requires an attentive mind for thinking and a busy hand for taking notes while you read. This chapter will get you thinking about the different kinds of reading you do in your everyday life and will offer an approach to help you read more effectively.

Becoming an active and confident reader is truly important: Not only will it help you to be successful in your college classes, but it will also enable you to get more out of your everyday reading. You may have developed or picked up some beliefs about reading that can interfere with your reading success and enjoyment. This chapter examines the most common myths and explains the benefits of reading. It also arms you with specific strategies to become an active reader: (1) making **connections** among a passage's details and sentences; (2) making **predictions** as you read; (3) asking yourself **questions** about an author's intention and attitude; and (4) considering the **implications** or the significance of what you read.

This chapter will give you plenty of opportunities to practice active reading. You will learn how talking, thinking, and writing about what you read can help you understand it better. You will also have a chance

Chapter Overview

to learn to **annotate**—or take notes—while you read. After you work through this chapter, you will have a better understanding of what academic reading involves and you will know how to become an active reader.

Focusing Questions

Why do you read, or why do you avoid reading?

What do you usually read? Why?

Describe your reading habits. Where and when do you read? Do you read quickly or slowly? Do you do anything special before you read? While you read? After you read?

How can your feelings and reactions affect your reading?

What was the best reading experience you remember having? What did you read? Why was it a "good read"?

What are your goals when reading a newspaper, a magazine, or a Web site?

What are your goals when you read a textbook?

What are some ways you can be active when you read?

Everyday Reading

Among the many things you probably read in the normal course of a day are advertisements. Ads appear on billboards and in subway cars, on bulletin boards, in school hallways, on some Web pages, and in newspapers and magazines.

Select an advertisement with a lot of words that you can photocopy. Circle or underline what interests you, draw arrows or lines between things that relate, and keep a separate page for notes. As you mark up the advertisement and write down your thoughts, think about how you might explain it to your teacher, your classmates, or a friend. What is being sold? How does the ad try to convince you to buy or use its product? What tricks does it use? How is it similar or dissimilar to other advertisements you have seen? Be prepared to talk about why you are or aren't convinced by what the advertisement has to say.

Learning the Skills

▇ Reasons for Reading

Especially in a world where television and the Internet are so important, people often ask "Why read?" One answer may simply be because you have to, because it's required. That kind of answer carries considerable weight. But there are other answers, other reasons for reading, as well.

Reading allows you to discover ideas, to develop your opinions, to see familiar things in new ways. Reading also allows you to connect with the minds and hearts of others. In reading, you come to know what others think and how they feel about things important to them, things that may also be important to you. Finally, reading can be enjoyable. These are some of the pleasures of reading:

Learning something new

Making the acquaintance of other people

Talking about your reading with others

Being entertained

To suggest that reading can bring pleasure is not to deny that reading often also requires hard work. You know from experience that reading can be frustrating as well as enjoyable. Very likely, you have encountered some of the pains and pleasures of reading already.

One of the goals of this chapter is to help you find ways to increase your pleasure in reading. Another is to minimize your frustration and disappointment with difficult or challenging assigned reading for your college courses.

▇ Overcoming Myths about Reading

Some people think that reading is not as important as it once was. Others disagree. Some people also have attitudes about reading based on ideas that aren't necessarily right. Here are a few common myths about reading. Each is followed by a response. You might wish to discuss (and debate) some of these ideas with your friends, classmates, family, or teachers.

Myth #1 *Reading isn't really necessary in today's world of rapidly developing technology. Movies and television, cameras and computers, telephones and other kinds of electronic communication have made reading obsolete.*

If computers are making reading obsolete, why are so many books, magazines, and manuals about computing being published? To take full advantage of today's wonderful technologies, reading is necessary. It is necessary for understanding how the technology works. It is necessary for using it. It is also necessary to interpret the written language that appears on computer screens, whether in a Help menu, in e-mail, from interconnected computer networks, or on your own computer.

Myth #2 *Speed reading is better than slow reading; faster is somehow better.*

There is no question that reading quickly has its uses. You use speed reading to skim news articles, to survey textbook chapters, to obtain a quick overview of the basic idea of an essay, article, or book. But speed reading also has its limitations. It does not suit all reading purposes and occasions. In addition to fast reading, you'll also need to develop a more reflective type of reading that proceeds at a more leisurely pace and that gives you time to weigh and consider what you are reading. Readers sometimes need to read slowly, carefully, thoughtfully—reflectively—to absorb and remember what they read.

There are dangers, however, in reading too slowly. If you read so slowly that you lose interest or lose your concentration and focus, you will not benefit from reading. If you read everything slowly, you will not read very much, perhaps not enough to complete your assignments. Your goal is to develop *different reading speeds for different kinds of reading materials* and for different purposes.

Myth #3 *Printed materials should never be questioned or challenged. If it's in print—especially in a book or journal—it must be right.*

Just because something appears in print doesn't necessarily mean it's true. Newspapers sometimes get facts and stories wrong in their rush to publication. Print advertisements are less concerned with revealing the truth than with selling a product. A person who creates a home page on the Web may be misinformed. Books are often more about expressing opinions than about presenting truths. Don't be afraid to question something you see in writing. Your ideas and opinions are valid too.

Myth #4 *Reading is a passive experience and cut off from reality.*

Reading is just as active as writing or speaking, mowing the lawn, or doing the week's shopping. The work of reading is mental and intellectual rather than physical: Its product is thought. Reading is also an important connection to the real world because reality is as much internal as external—a matter of what occurs inside your head as much as outside your body. Time spent reading is as valuable as time spent doing other pleasurable things, such as watching television, socializing, or exercising. Reading stimulates your powers of thought and imagination, inviting you to respond actively to ideas.

   Myth #5 *Reading is a solitary activity. You read by yourself, isolated from others, off in a world of your own.*

   While it is true that reading usually begins as a private act, it is also true that people often share what they read with others. They tend to do this not only in class discussions in school but with reading about sports and entertainment, reading of political and social news, reading of advertisements, and reading about many other "everyday" matters. Reading is not a solitary act at all; it is, when you think about it, a very social activity.

■ Reading Actively

Active reading is engaged and attentive reading. When you read actively, you *do* the following things:

- Ask yourself questions
- Underline key terms and ideas
- Jot notes and questions in the margins
- Try to understand the writer's point
- Think about what you read

   Perhaps you argue against the writer's idea; perhaps you think of additional evidence that supports it. Perhaps you partly agree and partly disagree. You may wish, that is, to qualify or modify an author's idea.

   In some ways, this entire book is about active reading. But what is involved in active reading? How can you begin right now to become a more active (and a more effective) reader? You can use the key elements of active reading: making connections, making predictions, asking questions, and considering implications.

MAKING CONNECTIONS

When you read actively you make **connections** among observations. You look to see how one sentence relates to another. You notice how an author's details and facts support his or her main point. By connecting details and thinking about their relationship to each other, you arrive at meaning—you understand what you read.

   Use a paragraph about beer (and soda) cans to try doing some active reading. The paragraph is from a 1964 essay called "Beer Can" by John

Updike. It is printed one sentence at a time with questions and comments between the sentences. This arrangement invites you to slow down and read each sentence thoughtfully. As you read this way, you will make connections among the sentences. In other words, you will be reading actively.

One of the pleasures of reading can be learning new things. So as you read through this paragraph, don't worry if you find things you've never heard of. Continue reading. Once you have finished working your way through the paragraph, things will begin to make sense.

> (1) This seems to be an era of gratuitous inventions and negative improvements.

This first sentence proposes an idea: that this is an age, or "era," of inventions the writer thinks are not improvements at all. (A "negative improvement," in fact, seems like a contradiction.) This is a fairly large claim. To be convincing, the writer needs to supply evidence in the form of one or more examples. This Updike does in his second sentence:

> (2) Consider the beer can.

What does Updike mean? Consider the beer can in what way? To understand the writer's point, you need to think about the relationship between his first two sentences. For one thing, you can guess that he means that the beer (or soda) can is an example of a "negative improvement" referred to in the opening sentence. Now look at Updike's next sentence:

> (3) It was beautiful—as beautiful as the clothespin, as inevitable as the wine bottle, as dignified and reassuring as the fire hydrant.

Notice how this sentence splits into two main sections—a short part before the dash and a longer part after it. Take the short part first: Updike says that the beer can "was beautiful," emphasizing the way it used to be. The second and longer part of the sentence compares the beer can's former beauty to three things: clothespins, wine bottles, and fire hydrants. What do these things have in common? All three are ordinary and all are useful. Their beauty is a result of their usefulness and their ordinariness. But how are they like the old-style beer can? The writer continues:

> (4) A tranquil cylinder of delightfully resonant metal, it could be opened in an instant, requiring only the application of a handy gadget freely dispensed by every grocer.

How does Updike's fourth sentence relate to his third? It describes what was "beautiful" (and useful) about the old-style can. In his next sentence (5), Updike elaborates on the pleasure of opening a can that did not have a pull tab and needed to be opened with a simple can opener. He even describes the sound of the can being opened:

> (5) Who can forget the small, symmetrical thrill of those two triangular punctures, the dainty *pffff*, the little crest of suds that formed eagerly in the exultation of release?

Look carefully at the paragraph's sixth sentence:

> (6) Now we are given, instead, a top beetling with an ugly, shmoo-shaped "tab," which, after fiercely resisting the tugging, bleeding fingers of the thirsty man, threatens his lips with a dangerous and hideous hold.

Here Updike notes that in place of the old-fashioned can "we are given, instead," something he objects to: a newfangled beer can that is opened with a tab. This new, "improved" can (although not really improved in Updike's opinion) can cut a person's fingers. Consider how the words in this sentence convey Updike's attitude toward the newer beer can. He calls its tab opener "ugly" and "shmoo-shaped." (Even if you don't know what a "shmoo" is shaped like, you can tell it's not very attractive.) By describing this tab as "fiercely resisting the tugging, bleeding fingers of the thirsty man," Updike suggests that opening the can is difficult and dangerous as well as frustrating.

Now turn to the first word of the next sentence (7): "However." Notice how this word sets up a **contrast** or a shift—a change to something different. In this case, it's a change from the problem to a solution.

(7) However, we have discovered a way to thwart Progress, usually so unthwartable.

What is this new "way to thwart Progress"? Read the paragraph's next sentence:

(8) *Turn the beer can upside down and open the bottom.*

There is more to Updike's paragraph. You have to read it carefully to make the connections among its sentences and details if you want to follow the main idea. Exercise 1-1 will help you complete your reading of Updike's paragraph. Notice how by relating each sentence to the one before and after it, you see the writer's meaning unfold. Notice, too, how in looking carefully at the words Updike uses to describe the new-style beer can, you get a clear sense of what he thinks about it. Finally, pay attention to how active reading helps you to understand things you may never have encountered before—like the old-fashioned beer can. Here is the rest of Updike's paragraph:

(9) The bottom is still the way the top used to be. (10) True, this operation gives the beer an unsettling jolt, and the sight of a consistently inverted beer can might make people edgy, not to say queasy. (11) But the latter difficulty could be eliminated if manufacturers would design cans that looked the same whichever end was up, like playing cards. (12) What we need is Progress with an escape hatch.

Exercise 1-1

Answer questions about connections in sentences 9–12 of Updike's paragraph.

Example:

What word connects sentence 9 with sentence 8?

the word "bottom" (of the beer can)

1. What is the point of sentence 9? That is, why is it important that the bottom of the can is designed the way the top of the can used to be?

    The bottom can be punctured in the same satisfying way in which the

    top used to be punctured ("the dainty 'pffff,' the little crest of suds").

2. The word *True,* which begins sentence 10, signals that the writer is aware of some objections people might make to turning over the can. What are those objections?

    The beer gets an "unsettled jolt." Some people will get nervous or even

    nauseated.

3. Which word in sentence 11 indicates that Updike is going to argue against the objections that were stated in the previous sentence?

    the word "but"

4. If manufacturers designed cans that looked the same no matter which end was up ("like playing cards"), what difficulty would be eliminated?

    People would not get upset when they saw an overturned can.

5. If manufacturers designed cans that looked the same no matter which end was up, how would the newer cans differ from the older ones that Updike was so happy with?

    They would differ from the older ones because one end would have a pull

    tab and the other end would not.

MAKING PREDICTIONS

Another strategy of active reading is making **predictions.** You anticipate where a piece of writing is going based on your experience from reading other works. Or you predict what is coming based on the words and sentences you are reading at a given moment.

To see how a reader makes predictions, look at another paragraph, the first paragraph from a 1984 essay by feminist Gloria Steinem. First, consider the title of her essay: "The Importance of Work." What does that suggest to you? Where might the writer be headed? By the way, it's not important whether you are right or wrong when you anticipate a writer's intention, direction, or attitude. Making a "wrong" prediction, in fact, is useful because it allows you to change your mind and because it helps you see what an author has decided *not* to focus on. The important thing is to begin reading actively. Making predictions is one way of doing that.

Here is the opening sentence of the paragraph:

> Faced with the determination of women to find a little independence and to be paid and honored for our work, experts have rushed to ask: "Why?"

Once you identify the writer's **topic** (women wanting to work and to become independent), you can see what the writer has to say about it. In this case she notes that "experts" (probably male experts) want to know "why" women want to be "paid and honored" for their work. Based on this sentence, what do you predict about the next one?

Answers will vary.

_____

_____

Here is Steinem's second sentence:

> It's a question rarely directed at male workers.

Does this sentence fulfill the expectations you had after reading the title and the first sentence? Why or why not? How is the second sentence related to the first? Based on these first two sentences, where do you think Steinem is going in this paragraph? What do you think she will write about in the rest of it?

Answers will vary.

_____

_____

Here now is Steinem's complete paragraph:

> Faced with the determination of women to find a little independence and to be paid and honored for our work, experts have rushed to ask: "Why?" It's a question rarely directed at male workers. Their basic motivations of survival and personal satisfaction are taken for granted. Indeed, men are regarded as "odd" and therefore subjects for sociological study and journalistic reports only when they *don't* have work, even if they are rich and don't need jobs or are poor and can't find them.

Now that you have read the entire opening paragraph of the essay, you can make another prediction about the direction of the author's thinking. What do you think she might talk about in the rest of the essay? Again, it's not so critical to be right about what comes next. It's more important to practice making predictions, to become actively involved in your reading.

Answers will vary.

_____

_____

Here is the second paragraph of "The Importance of Work":

> Job interviewers and even our own families may still ask salaried women the big "Why?" If we have small children at home or are in some job regarded as "men's work," the incidence of such questions increases. Condescending or accusatory versions of "What's a nice girl like you doing in a place like this?" have not disappeared from the workplace.

Does this paragraph satisfy your sense of where the writer is going? Did you need to revise your idea of the writer's intentions? These and similar questions should help you focus on your reading **process** — the act of making sense of a piece of writing *while* you are reading it.

At this point, ask yourself how the second paragraph relates to the first one. That is, even though you are now practicing the technique of **making predictions,** you should not abandon what you learned about **making connections.** In fact, in reading all of paragraphs 1 and 2, you have been making connections as you progressed from one sentence to another.

Exercise 1-2

Answer questions about connections between Steinem's first and second paragraph on page 11 — and make a prediction about the third.

Example:

Both the first and second paragraph refer to people who question women's work. Who are the "questioners" mentioned in the first paragraph?

"experts" (although it isn't clear exactly who the "experts" are, which is

probably part of Steinem's point)

1. Who are the questioners mentioned in the second paragraph?

    job interviewers and women's own families

2. What does Steinem say about men in the first paragraph?

    They don't get asked about why they work; their motivations are taken

    for granted. Men are considered "odd" if they don't work.

3. How does Steinem bring men into the second paragraph, explicitly and implicitly?

    explicitly, in connection with women who are doing "men's work";

    implicitly, as the questioners

4. Both paragraphs emphasize one question about women's desire to work. In fact, that question is put in quotation marks both times. What is the question?

   "Why?"

5. Make a prediction about the next paragraph of Steinem's essay. (That paragraph is not in this book. The important thing is your prediction, based on your active reading.)

   Answers will vary.

. . . .

ASKING QUESTIONS

One of the most important strategies of active reading is to ask yourself **questions** about what you are reading *while you are reading.* (You can also ask questions after you're finished, of course.) What can you ask questions about while you read? Here are the kinds of things you can ask questions about:

- The meaning of words
- The details and their connections to each other
- The writer's intention
- Your relationship to what you are reading
- Your attitude toward what you are reading

When you were reading John Updike's "Beer Can," you may have wondered about the meanings of the words *gratuitous, exultation,* and *queasy.* In Gloria Steinem's "The Importance of Work," you may have asked yourself about the meanings of *incidence* and *condescending.* You may also have asked yourself how each writer's selection of details helps you understand what the writer is saying.

In asking yourself about writer's intentions, you are asking how they want their readers to respond. Does Updike want readers to boycott beer cans (and perhaps soda cans) and buy bottled beverages instead? Does Steinem want readers to believe that women shouldn't work? Does either writer want you to smile as you read or to become upset or angry? What do they expect from you?

On a more personal level, you can ask how you relate to what these two writers are saying. To what extent does your experience correspond to what the writers are saying? To what extent does it differ? Finally, how do your attitudes about the subjects of beer cans and working women compare with the attitudes expressed by Updike and Steinem? Have either of the writers changed your views? Why or why not?

Exercise 1-3

Ask and answer questions about the passages by John Updike and Gloria Steinem on pages 6–8 and 11. (Reread the passages as necessary.)

Example:

Why does Updike capitalize the word *progress* whenever he uses it in the paragraph?

The capitalization helps Updike make fun of so-called progress by

drawing attention to it (the word "progress" is not usually capitalized)

and by overemphasizing its importance.

1. Choose one word that is unfamiliar to you in Updike's paragraph. Ask and answer a question about it.

   QUESTION: *Questions and answers will vary.*

   ANSWER:

2. What is Updike's real reason for writing the paragraph? What point(s) is he trying to make?

   His reason is to show that progress is not always progress. He also

   conveys a sense of importance about and appreciation for an item

   (the beer can) that people might not have seen in the same way before.

3. Choose one word that is unfamiliar to you in Steinem's passage. Ask and answer a question about it.

    QUESTION: _Answers will vary._ _____

    _____

    ANSWER: _____

    _____

4. How does Steinem's point about working women correspond with your own experience? Is her point of view dated (the essay was written almost twenty years ago), or do women today still have to justify why they work?

    Answers will vary. _____

    _____

    _____

    _____

5. Which writer, Updike or Steinem, asks the reader to smile and to appreciate the subject more fully? Which writer probably wants the reader to take action?

    Updike asks the reader to smile and appreciate; Steinem probably wants

    the reader to take action. _____

    _____

    _____

    _____

. . . .

CONSIDERING IMPLICATIONS

As you get used to making connections, making predictions, and asking questions about your reading, you'll begin to understand what an author is *not* saying. Through their choices of language, examples, and tone, writers provide hints about their attitudes. Ideas that are not stated directly are called **implications** — suggested meanings that you can figure out with the help of the writer's clues. By considering the writer's words, details, and sentences and by looking closely at the connections between sentences in a passage, you make **inferences** — or educated guesses — about the work's meaning.

Think again about Gloria Steinem's passages about working women that you read earlier in this chapter (page 11). Steinem does not say specifically that people are wrong to question a woman's decision to work. But look closely at what she *does* say. The passage begins with her description of women's desire to work as an effort "to find a little independence and to be paid and honored for [their] work." People don't look for something they already have, so you can reasonably infer that Steinem believes that women lack independence, pay, and honor. You can further infer that Steinem believes that women have a right to these things. Therefore, you can guess that she does, in fact, believe that the questions asked of working women are unfair.

Exercise 1-4

Consider the implications of the passages by John Updike and Gloria Steinem. Answer the questions by making inferences. (Reread the passages as necessary.)

Example:

Updike says that we live in a time of "gratuitous [unnecessary, unwanted] improvements." What inference can we make about Updike's reaction to electric hand-drying blowers instead of paper towels in public restrooms?

Updike would probably consider the blowers unnecessary and

unwanted — not an improvement at all.

1. Does Updike's essay imply that he is against *all* progress? Explain your answer.

   We cannot infer that Updike is against all progress. The last sentence

   of the paragraph suggests that he just wants us to be able to modify

   gratuitous progress.

2. Give three examples of recent inventions or new products. Based on Updike's reaction to beer cans with tabs, try to infer what his opinion of these new "improvements" would be. Give your reason(s).

   a. EXAMPLE: _Answers will vary._ _____

      UPDIKE'S POSSIBLE REACTION: _____

      _____

   b. EXAMPLE: _____

      UPDIKE'S POSSIBLE REACTION: _____

      _____

   c. EXAMPLE: _____

      UPDIKE'S POSSIBLE REACTION: _____

      _____

3. Steinem says that "men are regarded as 'odd' and therefore subjects for sociological study and journalistic reports only when they *don't* have work, even if they are rich and don't need jobs." What does this imply about society's expectations of men?

   It implies that men are supposed to work whether or not they need the

   money.

   _____

4. Does Steinem imply that men and women should be treated equally in the workplace? __Yes__

5. In Steinem's view, are men's (and society's) attitudes toward working women reasonable, or are they unfair?

   Steinem implies that the attitudes are unfair.

   _____

. . . .

ANNOTATING

One way to practice active reading is by **annotating.** When you annotate a reading passage you make notes about it. In general, your annotations should zero in on key details and central or main ideas of a passage. You will usually make your notes in the margins: For example, you may want to write down the questions you ask as you read. You can also make annotations in the body of the passage. You can underline or highlight key words, phrases, and sentences. You can put check marks and asterisks beside important words or passages. You can also draw lines and arrows to make connections.

Annotating helps you concentrate and keep your focus while you read. It can also help when you need to study or review for a test or when you need to write about your reading.

Here is an example of annotations based on a reading selection from *Sociology,* a textbook by Ian Robertson:

Who is Birdwhistell?
[Questioning]

gesture + content
= meaning
[Restating]

urinating(!) and
power transfer
[Restating]

Is this true?
[Questioning]

posture not as
noticeable as facial
expressions
[Restating]

unconscious
signals —
sounds suspicious
[Challenging]

Gestures, then, can be understood only by people of similar cultural background who attribute the same symbolic meaning to them. As Birdwhistell (1970) points out, a gesture cannot stand alone; it has meaning only in a particular context. The American gesture of "giving the finger" is meaningless in Britain, where the same message is conveyed by holding up the middle finger and forefinger with the palm facing inward. An American who was urinated upon by another person would not take the gesture kindly, but in parts of Africa the act symbolizes a welcome transfer of healing powers. Staring at a stranger does not have the same meaning in many other parts of the world that it does for Americans. American travelers to Latin America, for example, often have great difficulty in adapting to the experience of being openly scrutinized at close quarters by complete strangers.

Other forms of body language, such as posture, positioning of legs, or inclination of the body toward or away from another person, are not as readily noticed as facial expressions and overt gestures, nor do we have the same degree of control over them. Yet these signals can convey powerful messages even when neither participant in an encounter is consciously aware of them. Sexual interest on the part of one person, for example, causes the pupils of his or her eyes to dilate. The other person may well sense the nature of the message without being able to pinpoint its source.

Four Main Types of Annotations
1. Restate the point of the passage.
2. Ask questions about the passage.
3. Challenge the ideas of the passage.
4. Compare or contrast the passage with what you already know.

Exercise 1-5

The following passage is taken from the textbook *Economics* by Timothy Tregarthen and Libby Rittenberg. As you read the passage, annotate it. Be sure to make at least three or more annotations per paragraph.

There are many reasons for studying economics. One is the desire to discover explanations for the things we observe. Why, for example, do professional baseball players earn far more, on average, than professional football players? Why do airlines charge lower prices to customers who book flights two weeks in advance than they charge to customers who book flights two days in advance? Why is unemployment, on average, much higher in Germany than in the United States?

Another reason for studying economics is a concern that the choices we make might not be appropriate ones. Why do some groups suffer from discrimination in the marketplace? Why are our highways often heavily congested? Why do we choose to dump so much pollution in the air and water? Understanding why the choices we make are not always good ones may help us to find ways to correct the problems that grow out of inappropriate choices.

A third reason for studying economics is to predict the outcomes of those choices. How will a proposed tax measure affect interest rates? How will the expanded use of robots in manufacturing affect employment? Will decreased federal spending for education promote or hinder economic growth?

A fourth reason for studying economics is that we may gain insights that will allow us to do a better job in managing a firm or some other organization. Many firms, foundations, and government agencies employ economists because these organizations have found that the insights economists offer can help them to achieve their goals.

. . . .

Throughout this book you will have opportunities to write about your reading. In the remainder of this chapter you will practice active reading with two selections: a famous essay by Malcolm X about the importance of reading and writing and a selection from a psychology textbook that explores how language can influence meaning.

As you read these selections (and the other selections throughout this book), be sure to use the techniques of active reading you have learned in this chapter. Use writing and annotating to help you focus on the following: (1) making connections; (2) making predictions; (3) asking questions; and (4) considering implications.

Applying the Skills

Reading the Parts

Malcolm X was a radical activist of the 1960s whose controversial ideas about black power and resistance continue to affect how people in the twenty-first century think about race and civil rights. (Watch any Spike Lee movie to see how his ideas continue to influence American culture.) A powerful speaker, Malcolm X had not learned how much reading and writing could influence others until he taught himself an advanced vocabulary while in jail. As you read his essay, originally published in *The Autobiography of Malcolm X* (1964), use the strategies for active reading you learned in this chapter, including making connections, making predictions, asking questions, considering implications, and taking notes. After reading each section of the essay, answer the questions and move on to the next section. You will have a chance to read the whole essay when you finish.

MALCOLM X
Coming to an Awareness of Language

1   I've never been one for inaction. Everything I've ever felt strongly about, I've done something about. I guess that's why, unable to do anything else, I soon began writing to people I had known in the hustling world, such as Sammy the Pimp, John Hughes, the gambling house owner, the thief Jumpsteady, and several dope peddlers. I wrote them all about Allah and Islam and Mr. Elijah Muhammad. I had no idea where most of them lived. I addressed their letters in care of the Harlem or Roxbury bars and clubs where I'd known them.

2   I never got a single reply. The average hustler and criminal was too uneducated to write a letter. I have known many slick sharp-looking hustlers, who would have you think they had an interest in Wall Street; privately, they would get someone else to read a letter if they received one. Besides, neither would I have replied to anyone writing me something as wild as "the white man is the devil."

3   What certainly went on the Harlem and Roxbury wires was that Detroit Red was going crazy in stir, or else he was trying some hype to shake up the warden's office.

During the years that I stayed in the Norfolk Prison Colony, never did any official directly say anything to me about those letters, although, of course, they all passed through the prison censorship. I'm sure, however, they monitored what I wrote to add to the files which every state and federal prison keeps on the conversion of Negro inmates by the teachings of Mr. Elijah Muhammad.   4

But at that time, I felt that the real reason was that the white man knew that he was the devil.   5

Later on, I even wrote to the Mayor of Boston, to the Governor of Massachusetts, and to Harry S. Truman. They never answered; they probably never even saw my letters. I handscratched to them how the white man's society was responsible for the black man's condition in this wilderness of North America.   6

It was because of my letters that I happened to stumble upon starting to acquire some kind of homemade education.   7

1. What reason does Malcolm X give for the fact that he didn't receive any responses from the letters he sent to his former colleagues in the "hustling world"?

    a.   He says that they don't have time to write.

    b.   He figured most of them must be in jail.

    c.   He says that the "average hustler and criminal was too uneducated to write a letter."

    d.   He says that most of them "got jobs on Wall Street."

2. To what man does Malcolm X express devotion while an inmate at Norfolk Prison Colony?

    a.   Jumpsteady

    b.   John Hughes

    c.   Sammy the Pimp

    d.   Elijah Muhammad

3. According to Malcolm X in this selection, what is the "white man's society" responsible for?

    a.   "slavery"

    b.   "oppression of women"

    c.   "black man's condition in this wilderness of North America"

    d.   "the genocide of little children"

4. What was the result, according to Malcolm X, of his letter-writing campaign?

   a.   He began to see better.

   (b.) He began to acquire an education.

   c.   He began to read the dictionary.

   d.   He began to read the great classics of literature.

5. Of the following, which political figure is *not* one that Malcolm X wrote to during his stay in prison?

   (a.) Dwight Eisenhower

   b.   Harry S. Truman

   c.   the mayor of Boston

   d.   the governor of Massachusetts

I became increasingly frustrated at not being able to express what I wanted to convey in letters that I wrote, especially those to Mr. Elijah Muhammad. In the street, I had been the most articulate hustler out there—I had commanded attention when I said something. But now, trying to write simple English, I not only wasn't articulate, I wasn't even functional. How would I sound writing in slang, the way I would *say* it, something such as, "Look daddy, let me pull your coat about a cat. Elijah Muhammad—"   8

Many who today hear me somewhere in person, or on television, or those who read something I've said, will think I went to school far beyond the eighth grade. This impression is due entirely to my prison studies.   9

It had really begun back in the Charlestown Prison, where Bimbi first made me feel envy of his stock of knowledge. Bimbi had always taken charge of any conversation he was in, and I had tried to emulate him. But every book I picked up had few sentences which didn't contain anywhere from one to nearly all of the words that might as well have been in Chinese. When I just skipped those words, of course, I really ended up with little idea of what the book said. So I had come to the Norfolk Prison Colony still going through only book-reading motions. Pretty soon, I would have quit even these motions, unless I had received the motivation that I did.   10

I saw that the best thing I could do was get hold of a dictionary—to study, to learn some words. I was lucky enough to reason also that I should try to improve my penmanship. It was sad. I   11

> couldn't even write in a straight line. It was both ideas together that moved me to request a dictionary along with some tablets and pencils from the Norfolk Prison Colony school.

6. Malcolm X becomes "increasingly frustrated" by an aspect of himself while in prison. What is it that frustrates him?

   a. It frustrates him that he is a prisoner.

   b. It frustrates him that he is unable to express himself in writing.

   c. It frustrates him that he does not have a formal education.

   d. It frustrates him that he is not a good reader.

7. At the time that he wrote this selection, many years after he had been released from prison, Malcolm X discovered that many people had a false impression of him. What was that false impression?

   a. Many people thought that he had never been in prison.

   b. Many people thought that he was married.

   c. Many people thought that he had had a formal education beyond the eighth grade.

   d. Many people mistakenly thought that he was Bimbi.

8. To what did Malcolm X attribute this mistaken impression that people had of him? Refer to paragraph 9 for the information, if necessary.

   a. The impression was due to the fact that he had finished college while in prison.

   b. The impression was due to the fact that he had finished high school while in prison.

   c. The impression was due entirely to his prison studies, in which he took the initiative to learn.

   d. The impression was due to the fact that he told people he had a doctorate.

9. Of the following, which is *not* an item that Malcolm X requested from the Norfolk Prison Colony school to further his academic studies?

a. tablets

b. pencils

c. a dictionary

(d.) an atlas

10. What were two goals that Malcolm X set for himself while in the Norfolk Prison Colony? If you need help, refer to paragraph 11.

a. He set goals of learning to speak proper English and to do arithmetic.

(b.) He set goals of improving his penmanship and learning new words through the use of a dictionary.

c. He set goals of learning French and learning to read in English.

d. He set goals of learning calculus and biology.

I spent two days just riffling uncertainly through the dictionary's pages. I'd never realized so many words existed! I didn't know *which* words I needed to learn. Finally, just to start some kind of action, I began copying.   **12**

In my slow, painstaking, ragged handwriting, I copied into my tablet everything printed on that first page, down to the punctuation marks.   **13**

I believe it took me a day. Then, aloud, I read back, to myself, everything I'd written on the tablet. Over and over, aloud, to myself, I read my own handwriting.   **14**

I woke up the next morning, thinking about those words—immensely proud to realize that not only had I written so much at one time, but I'd written words that I never knew were in the world. Moreover, with a little effort, I also could remember what many of these words meant. I reviewed the words whose meanings I didn't remember. Funny thing, from the dictionary's first page right now, that "aardvark" springs to my mind. The dictionary had a picture of it, a long-tailed, long-eared, burrowing African mammal, which lives off termites caught by sticking out its tongue as an anteater does for ants.   **15**

I was so fascinated that I went on—I copied the dictionary's next page. And the same experience came when I studied that. With every succeeding page, I also learned of people and places and events   **16** from history. Actually the dictionary is like a miniature encyclopedia. Finally the dictionary's A section had filled a whole tablet— and I went on into the B's. That was the way I started copying what eventually became the entire dictionary. It went a lot faster after so much practice helped me pick up handwriting speed. Between what I wrote in my tablet, and writing letters, during the rest of my time in prison I would guess I wrote a million words.

I suppose it was inevitable that as my word-base broadened, I could for the first time pick up a book and read and now begin to understand what the book was saying. Anyone who has read a great deal can imagine the new world that opened. Let me tell you something: from then until I left that prison, in every free moment I had, if I was not reading in the library, I was reading on my bunk. You couldn't have gotten me out of books with a wedge. Between Mr. Muhammad's teachings, my correspondence, my visitors . . . and my reading of books, months passed without my even thinking about being imprisoned. In fact, up to then, I never had been so truly free in my life.

17

11. What is the first thing Malcolm X does in his quest to increase his knowledge?

   a.   He begins to draw maps.

   b.   He begins to read the great classics, such as *Oliver Twist*.

   c.   He begins to copy words from the dictionary he acquired.

   d.   He begins to write longer, more detailed letters about Elijah Muhammad.

12. What is the one word that Malcolm X recalls from his dictionary exercise?

   a.   anaconda   c.   albacore

   b.   aardvark   d.   acquire

13. To what does Malcolm X compare the dictionary that he works with in prison? Refer to paragraph 16 for help, if necessary.

   a.   a map of the world

   b.   a thesaurus

   c.   an index of knowledge

   d.   a miniature encyclopedia

14. Reread paragraphs 16 and 17. Which of the following is *not* one of the things Malcolm X mentions as something he learned from using the dictionary?

    a. He learned of people in history.

    (b.) He learned word roots.

    c. He learned of places and events in history.

    d. He picked up handwriting speed.

15. What was the ultimate result of Malcolm's studying and his learning to read? Refer to paragraph 17 for a hint.

    (a.) He found himself "truly free."

    b. He found himself "truly imprisoned."

    c. He found himself aware of the fact that he was "locked in a cage."

    d. He found himself aware of the days that he had left in prison.

Reading the Whole

Now that you've had a chance to read Malcolm X's "Coming to an Awareness of Language" in its parts and to practice active reading, you are prepared to reread it. As you read the whole essay reprinted here, continue to use your active reading strategies, this time asking different questions of the text as they occur to you. Continue to take whatever new notes will help you put the parts together while you look at the essay from a broader perspective.

MALCOLM X
Coming to an Awareness of Language

I've never been one for inaction. Everything I've ever felt strongly about, I've done something about. I guess that's why, unable to do anything else, I soon began writing to people I had known in the hustling world, such as Sammy the Pimp, John Hughes, the gambling house owner, the thief Jumpsteady, and several dope peddlers. I wrote them all about Allah and Islam and Mr. Elijah Muhammad. I had no idea where most of them lived. I addressed their letters in care of the Harlem or Roxbury bars and clubs where I'd known them.   1

I never got a single reply. The average hustler and criminal was too uneducated to write a letter. I have known many slick sharp-looking hustlers, who would have you think they had an interest in Wall Street; privately, they would get someone else to read a letter if they received one. Besides, neither would I have replied to anyone writing me something as wild as "the white man is the devil."   2

What certainly went on the Harlem and Roxbury wires was that Detroit Red was going crazy in stir, or else he was trying some hype to shake up the warden's office.   3

During the years that I stayed in the Norfolk Prison Colony, never did any official directly say anything to me about those letters, although, of course, they all passed through the prison censorship. I'm sure, however, they monitored what I wrote to add to the files which every state and federal prison keeps on the conversion of Negro inmates by the teachings of Mr. Elijah Muhammad.   4

But at that time, I felt that the real reason was that the white man knew that he was the devil.   5

Later on, I even wrote to the Mayor of Boston, to the Governor of Massachusetts, and to Harry S. Truman. They never answered;   6 they probably never even saw my letters. I handscratched to them how the white man's society was responsible for the black man's condition in this wilderness of North America.

It was because of my letters that I happened to stumble upon starting to acquire some kind of homemade education.   7

I became increasingly frustrated at not being able to express what I wanted to convey in letters that I wrote, especially those to Mr. Elijah Muhammad. In the street, I had been the most articulate hustler out there—I had commanded attention when I said something. But now, trying to write simple English, I not only wasn't articulate, I wasn't even functional. How would I sound writing in slang, the way I would *say* it, something such as, "Look daddy, let me pull your coat about a cat. Elijah Muhammad—"   8

Many who today hear me somewhere in person, or on television, or those who read something I've said, will think I went to school far beyond the eighth grade. This impression is due entirely to my prison studies.   9

It had really begun back in the Charlestown Prison, where Bimbi first made me feel envy of his stock of knowledge. Bimbi had always taken charge of any conversation he was in, and I had tried to emulate him. But every book I picked up had few sentences which didn't contain anywhere from one to nearly all of the words that might as well have been in Chinese. When I just skipped those words, of course, I really ended up with little idea of what the book said. So I had come to the Norfolk Prison Colony still going through only book-reading motions. Pretty soon, I would have quit even these motions, unless I had received the motivation that I did.   10

I saw that the best thing I could do was get hold of a dictionary—to study, to learn some words. I was lucky enough to reason also that I should try to improve my penmanship. It was sad. I couldn't even write in a straight line. It was both ideas together that moved me to request a dictionary along with some tablets and pencils from the Norfolk Prison Colony school.   11

I spent two days just riffling uncertainly through the dictionary's pages. I'd never realized so many words existed! I didn't know *which* words I needed to learn. Finally, just to start some kind of action, I began copying.   12

In my slow, painstaking, ragged handwriting, I copied into my tablet everything printed on that first page, down to the punctuation marks.   13

I believe it took me a day. Then, aloud, I read back, to myself,   14 everything I'd written on the tablet. Over and over, aloud, to myself, I read my own handwriting.

I woke up the next morning, thinking about those words— immensely proud to realize that not only had I written so much at one time, but I'd written words that I never knew were in the world. Moreover, with a little effort, I also could remember what many of these words meant. I reviewed the words whose meanings I didn't remember. Funny thing, from the dictionary's first page right now, that "aardvark" springs to my mind. The dictionary had a picture of it, a long-tailed, long-eared, burrowing African mammal, which lives off termites caught by sticking out its tongue as an anteater does for ants. `15`

I was so fascinated that I went on—I copied the dictionary's next page. And the same experience came when I studied that. With every succeeding page, I also learned of people and places and events from history. Actually the dictionary is like a miniature encyclopedia. Finally the dictionary's A section had filled a whole tablet— and I went on into the B's. That was the way I started copying what eventually became the entire dictionary. It went a lot faster after so much practice helped me pick up handwriting speed. Between what I wrote in my tablet, and writing letters, during the rest of my time in prison I would guess I wrote a million words. `16`

I suppose it was inevitable that as my word-base broadened, I could for the first time pick up a book and read and now begin to understand what the book was saying. Anyone who has read a great deal can imagine the new world that opened. Let me tell you something: from then until I left that prison, in every free moment I had, if I was not reading in the library, I was reading on my bunk. You couldn't have gotten me out of books with a wedge. Between Mr. Muhammad's teachings, my correspondence, my visitors . . . and my reading of books, months passed without my even thinking about being imprisoned. In fact, up to then, I never had been so truly free in my life. `17`

Integrated Skills

1. How did Malcolm X remedy his inability to read? What do you think of his unorthodox approach?

2. Why is reading so important to him? How does he demonstrate his need to read?

3. Identify three or four words Malcolm X uses in his essay that reveal how well he learned his dictionary's words and their meanings.

4. What advice do you think Malcolm X would give you about learning to improve your reading ability?

5. How do you respond to Malcolm X's desire to educate himself through reading?

6. What do you think of Malcolm X after reading this selection?

Reading/Writing Connection

One thing that Malcolm X mentions in "Coming to an Awareness of Language" is how he used the dictionary. To build up his vocabulary, he copied words and their definitions. Choose at random a page of your own dictionary. Select five words. Copy out the words as they appear with their definitions. Then write a paragraph in which you use at least three of your words in different sentences.

Reading Textbooks

Thematic Connections. In "Coming to an Awareness of Language" Malcolm X describes how an expanded vocabulary helped him to better articulate his ideas and, more important, how his new skills made it possible for him to communicate his arguments to people in power and to society at large. In the following excerpt from the textbook *Psychology* by David G. Myers, the author explores how people's thoughts and experiences are, to some extent, influenced by the language they speak. If you think of street slang and formal speech as two different languages, how does this textbook passage enhance your understanding of what Malcolm X discovered about the power of language?

Vocabulary Preview

linguist (para. 1): a person who studies language (n.)

contended (para. 1): argued (v.)

linguistic (para. 1): of or related to language (adj.)

relativity (para. 1): a connection or comparison between two or more things (n.)

hypothesis (para. 1): theory (n.)

bilinguals (para. 2): people fluent in two languages (n.)

determines (para. 3): causes, decides (v.)

perpetuated (para. 3): caused to continue (v.)

generic (para. 3): relating to more than one thing at the same time, not specific to one or another category (adj.)

conjure (para. 4): raise, bring up as if by magic (v.)

ambiguous (para. 4): unclear (adj.)

Language Influences Thinking

Linguist Benjamin Lee Whorf contended that language determines the way we think. According to Whorf's **linguistic relativity** hypothesis, different languages impose different conceptions of reality: "Language itself shapes a man's basic ideas." The Hopi, Whorf noted, have no past tense for their verbs. Therefore, he contended, a Hopi could not so readily *think* about the past. 1

Whorf's relativity hypothesis would probably not occur to people who speak only one language and view that language as simply a vehicle for thought. But to those who speak two dissimilar languages, such as English and Japanese, it seems obvious that a person thinks differently in different languages. Unlike English, which has a rich vocabulary for self-focused emotions such as anger, Japanese has many words for interpersonal emotions such as sym- 2 pathy. Many bilinguals report that they even have a different sense of self, depending on which language they are using. After immigrating from Asia to North America, bilinguals may reveal different personalities when taking the same personality test in their two languages. Learn a language and you learn about a culture. When a language becomes extinct—the likely fate of most of the world's 5000 remaining languages—the world loses the culture and thinking that hangs on that language.

It is too strong to say that language *determines* the *way* we think. A New Guinean without our words for shapes and colors nevertheless perceives them much as we do. But our words do influence *what* we think. We therefore do well to choose our words carefully. When people referred to women as *girls*—as in "the girls at the office"—it perpetuated a view of women's having lower status, did it not? Or consider the generic use of the pronoun *he*. Does it make any difference whether I write "A child learns language as *he* interacts with *his* caregivers" or "Children learn language as *they* interact with *their* caregivers"? Some argue that it makes no difference because every reader knows that "the masculine gender shall be deemed and taken to include females" (as the British Parliament declared in 1850). 3

But is the generic *he* always taken to include females? Twenty studies have consistently found that it is not. For example, Janet Hyde asked children to finish stories for which she gave them a first line, such as "When a kid goes to school, _____ often feels excited on the first day." When Hyde used *he* in the blank, the children's stories were nearly always about males. "He or she" in the blank resulted in female characters about one-third of the time. Studies with adolescents and adults in North America and New Zealand have found similar effects of the generic *he*. Sentences about "the artist and his work" tend to conjure up images of a man. Similarly, ambiguous actions taken by a "chairman of the board" seem to reveal an assertive and independent personality. The same actions taken by a "chairperson of the board" seem to reveal a more caring and warm personality. 4

Consider, too, that people use generic pronouns selectively, as in "the doctor . . . he" and "the secretary . . . she." If *he* and *his* were truly gender-free, we shouldn't skip a beat when hearing that "a nurse must answer his calls" or that "man, like other mammals, nurses his young." That we are startled indicates that *his* carries a gender connotation that clashes with our idea of *nurse*. 5

The power of language to influence thought makes vocabulary   6
building a crucial part of education. To expand language is to
expand the ability to think. In young children, thinking develops
hand in hand with language. What is true for preschoolers is true
for everyone: *It pays to increase your word power.* That is why
most textbooks, including this one, introduce new words—to
teach new ideas and new ways of thinking.

Thinking about the Textbook Selection

1. What does linguist Benjamin Lee Whorf say about the power of language?

2. How does the example of the Hopi language clarify Whorf's ideas about language?

3. What language experience of bilingual people does the author describe? Why is that bilingual experience so important?

4. What is the difference between saying that language "determines" how we think and language "influences" how we think?

5. Do you agree with the author's examples of gendered language—referring to adult females as "girls" rather than women and using the generic pronoun "he"? Why or why not?

6. How does the last paragraph of this selection add to your understanding of what Malcolm X writes about in "Coming to an Awareness of Language"?

Reading the Web

You can apply the skills you learned in this chapter to all kinds of reading, even to Web pages. You know that when you search for information on the Internet, you can't possibly read everything. You make judgments about what's worth looking at closely—and you save time—by making predictions, making connections, asking questions, and considering implications.

Take this opening page from a Web site as an example. The English-only movement in the United States is a controversial effort to make English the official language of the country. Some people believe that requiring all Americans to speak a common language and to learn in English-only classrooms will bring people together and improve immigrants' standard of living; others argue that denying nonnative speakers public use of their native tongues puts them at a disadvantage and robs them—and everybody else—of vibrant cultures. You can figure out which position U.S. English takes by reading the opening page actively.

Thinking about the Web Page

1. Why is the image on this Web page divided in half? What do the two sides of the image have in common? How do they differ?

2. What would you expect to find when you click on each side of the Web site image? Why?

3. Which point of view in the English-Only movement debate does this Web page favor? How do you know?

Reviewing

**Recall /
Remember**

1. Identify some common beliefs about reading that are at least partly wrong. Explain why these beliefs are inadequate.

2. Identify the four elements of active reading and explain why each is important.

3. How can you practice active reading?

4. Explain why you did or did not find the readings on the beer can and women at work helpful.

5. What is the most important thing you learned from working through this chapter?

**Chapter
Summary**

Through reading and doing the exercises in this chapter you have begun the work of becoming an active reader. You know from the chapter's preliminary discussion of myths about reading that reading remains important for success in today's world and that careful and active reading is necessary for understanding challenging selections.

You have also had a chance to practice some of the key components in active reading: making connections, making predictions, asking questions, and considering implications. You will have many more opportunities to develop your skill using these active reading strategies in later chapters.

Developing a College Vocabulary

Getting Ready

Chapter Overview

Reading well depends, largely, on a strong vocabulary. If you don't understand the words you read, it's unlikely you'll be able to understand the reading. Luckily, you don't need to follow Malcolm X's example of copying the entire dictionary to build a better vocabulary. You already have what is called a "sight"—or recognition—vocabulary. Your sight vocabulary includes words whose meanings you understand when you read them even though you may not be able to define them or feel confident enough to use them yourself when you write. And contrary to what you may believe, you don't have to go to a dictionary every time you find an unfamiliar word.

This chapter introduces some very helpful strategies you can use to figure out the meaning of unfamiliar words and to develop your reading vocabulary. **Word analysis**—breaking words into parts—will help you to determine definitions. By memorizing a few common word parts, you'll be able to figure out the meanings of literally hundreds of new words without looking them up. Another strategy is using **context**—the words and phrases immediately surrounding unfamiliar words—to determine a word's meaning. This chapter will give you plenty of opportunities to practice. When you're done, you'll know many more words and their meanings than you might imagine.

Focusing Questions

How would you describe your reading vocabulary? Are you familiar with enough words to be able to understand most of what you read?

Are any of your courses especially challenging for you because of their vocabulary?

What do you do when you come across a word whose meaning you don't know?

What steps can you take now to expand your vocabulary? How important is this to you?

What kind of dictionary do you own? Where do you keep it? How often do you consult it?

How often do you read? Do you discuss your reading with other students, your friends, or family members?

Everyday Reading

If you pay attention, you constantly discover new words as part of your daily life. You don't have to read books and articles to expand your vocabulary. For example, you probably read labels on food packages at the supermarket, at least occasionally. And you've probably read some of the warnings and other information labels that accompany the various products you buy—from coffee to electronics to clothing. In reading recipes from a cookbook, you read special cooking terms, such as *braise* or *baste*.

In the next couple of days, find two new words from everyday sources such as these. Try to pick words that you can imagine yourself actually using (it's unlikely you'll ever say "ribonucleic acid" in a casual conversation, but you might want to ask a friend how you could cut back on "sodium"). Write down your new words and be sure to look up their dictionary definitions. See if you can incorporate them into your active speaking vocabulary.

Learning the Skills

■ Word Analysis: Roots, Prefixes, and Suffixes

Words are not all alike. Some consist of multiple parts. You can determine the meaning of a lot of unfamiliar words by using **word analysis**—that is, by breaking down words and thinking about their smaller parts. Those smaller parts include the **root**, or central element, of a word; the **prefix**, a group of letters that appears before a root; and the **suffix**, a group of letters that is attached to the end of a root. Not all words have any or all of these parts: Some may have only a prefix and a root, like *preview*, which means "to view before" (*pre*). Others might have a root and a suffix, like *truthful*, which is made up of *truth* and *ful*—"full of truth."

In this chapter, you will study word parts and learn a number of common roots, prefixes, and suffixes that will help you understand many new words when you come across them.

SOME COMMON ROOTS

It's a good idea to become familiar with as many word roots as you can. The reason, simply, is that knowing the root of a word gives you an excellent clue to its meaning, even when you are unsure about the meaning of the entire word. The word *geology*, for example, contains the root *geo* ("the earth") and the suffix *logy* ("the study of"). Related words will contain the same root but use a different suffix: Examples include *geography* and *geothermal*. You may not know exactly what these words mean, but because you know the meaning of the root *geo*, you can assume that both of these words also have something to do with the earth. The word *scripture* is built on the word root *script*. If you know that *script* and *scrib* are roots that suggest "writing," you can understand that *transcript, superscript, subscription, description, inscribe,* and *scripted* all have something to do with writing.

Here is a list of important words and roots. Try to memorize them. They can increase your vocabulary enormously.

COMMON WORD ROOTS

Root	Meaning	Example
aster, ast	star	**asterisk:** a star-shaped mark
audi	hear	**audiology:** the study of sound

COMMON WORD ROOTS

Root	Meaning	Example
auto	self	**autodidact:** a self-taught person
bene	good, well	**beneficial:** having positive effects
biblio	book	**bibliography:** a list of books
bio	life	**biosphere:** an environment that sustains life
chrono	time	**chronological:** in order of time
dict	speak	**contradict:** to say the opposite of
fer	bear, carry	**ferry:** to take passengers from one place to another
gen	birth, race	**genealogy:** family history of marriages, births, and deaths
geo	earth	**geography:** the study of features of the earth's surface
graph	write	**monograph:** a written account on a single topic
greg	herd, flock	**congregate:** to gather together
jur, jus	law	**jury:** a group of people who decide whether someone is innocent or guilty of breaking the law
log, logue	thought, word	**dialogue:** words spoken between two people
luc	light	**elucidate:** to clarify, to make it possible for someone to "see the light"
manu	hand	**manumit:** to deliver by hand
meter, metr	measure	**hydrometer:** a device that measures water
mit, mis	send	**transmit:** to send across
omni	all	**omnipotent:** all-powerful
op, oper	work	**operate:** to use, as in machinery
path	feel, suffer	**sympathy:** a shared feeling with another
phil	loving	**philosopher:** one who loves wisdom
phon	sound	**phonics:** a teaching method that emphasizes the sounds made by letters and word parts

photo	light	**photosynthesis:** the process by which plants use light to generate energy
port	carry, bear	**portable:** capable of being carried
psych	mind, soul	**psychosis:** a severe mental disorder characterized by loss of contact with reality
scrib, script	write	**manuscript:** a document written by hand
sent, sens	feel	**sensation:** feeling
soma	body	**psychosomatic:** a bodily manifestation of a mental activity
tele	far off	**telephone:** a device that enables one to hear words spoken by someone far away
ter, terr	earth	**extraterrestrial:** a being from another planet
therm	heat	**thermometer:** a device that measures temperature
verb	word	**verbose:** wordy

Exercise 2-1

Determine the meaning of the following words by working with their word roots.

Example:

benefit   ROOT: _bene_   ROOT MEANING: _good; well_

WORD DEFINITION: If something *benefits* you, it _is good for you._

1. *diction*   ROOT: _dict_   ROOT MEANING: _speak_

   WORD DEFINITION: If I praise his *diction*, I compliment him on _the way he speaks._

2. *generate*   ROOT: _gen_   ROOT MEANING: _birth; race_

   WORD DEFINITION: If someone is good at *generating* ideas, that person is able to _bring new ideas to life._

3. *manual*　ROOT: _manu_　　ROOT MEANING: _hand_

WORD DEFINITION: If her car has a *manual* shift, she changes gears by _hand._

4. *asterism*　ROOT: _aster_　　ROOT MEANING: _star_

WORD DEFINITION: In astrology, an *asterism* is _a group of stars_

that is smaller than a constellation.

5. *lucid*　ROOT: _luc_　　ROOT MEANING: _light_

WORD DEFINITION: If the scientists give a *lucid* report of their findings, the report is _easy to understand; very clear; sheds light._

. . . .

PREFIXES

A prefix is a group of letters that is attached to the beginning of a root and alters its meaning in some way. Every prefix has a set meaning. If you know those meanings and you know common word roots, you have an excellent chance of determining the meanings of many new words. If you know that the prefix *tri* means "three," you can probably guess that *tripartite* refers to something that has three parts and that *triannual* events take place every three years. As you can see, learning prefixes will help you expand your vocabulary quickly.

Here is a list of commonly used prefixes.

NUMBER AND QUANTITY PREFIXES

Prefix	Meaning	Example
uni, mono	one	**unicycle:** a vehicle with one wheel
du, bi	two	**bipolar:** having two extremities (or ends)
tri	three	**tripartite:** containing three parts
quadr, tetra	four	**quadriplegic:** a person paralyzed in both arms and both legs
quint, penta	five	**quintuplets:** five babies all born at the same time from the same mother
sex, hexa	six	**sextet:** a group of six
sept, hepta	seven	**heptagon:** a geometric shape with seven sides

octo, oct	eight	**octopus:** a sea creature with eight tentacles
nov, non	nine	**nonagenarian:** a person in his or her nineties
dec, deca	ten	**decade:** a period of ten years

NEGATIVE PREFIXES

Prefix	Meaning	Example
a	without	**amoral:** not having morals
anti	against	**antifreeze:** a substance that prevents freezing
contra	against	**contradict:** say the opposite of
de	from, remove	**dethrone:** to remove from power
dis	apart, away	**disbar:** to take away a lawyer's right to practice law
il, im, in, ir	not	**irreparable:** unfixable
mal	bad, wrong	**malcontent:** an unhappy person
mis	wrong, bad	**misconstrue:** mistake the meaning of
non	not	**noncommittal:** giving no clear indication of attitude or feeling

PREFIXES OF TIME

Prefix	Meaning	Example
ante	before	**antebellum:** existing before a war
fore	before	**foreword:** preface
post	after	**postpone:** to put off until later
pre	before	**premonition:** previous notice or warning
re	again	**revise:** to see again, to change
syn	the same time	**synchronous:** happening simultaneously

PREFIXES OF SPACE, DIRECTION, POSITION

Prefix	Meaning	Example
ad	to, for	**adhere:** to stick to something
circum	around	**circumnavigate:** go around

PREFIXES OF SPACE, DIRECTION, POSITION

Prefix	Meaning	Example
co, col	with	**cooperate:** to do together
com, con, cor	with	**converse:** to talk with another
e, ex	out of	**extract:** a piece taken from a larger work or thing
hetero	other	**heterogeneous:** consisting of diverse parts
homo	same	**homonym:** a word that sounds the same as another word
hyper	over, more	**hyperactive:** overactive
hypo	under, less	**hypothermia:** low body heat
inter	between	**interview:** conversation between two people
intra	within	**intramural:** related to interaction of groups or people within a larger group
sub	under	**submarine:** underwater
super	above	**supersonic:** faster than the speed of sound
trans	across	**transnational:** going across national boundaries

Exercise 2-2

Fill in each blank, using the meaning of the prefix of the italicized word to determine the correct answer.

Example:

A *triathlon* is an athletic competition that has ____three____ events.

1. A *pentagon* is a figure with ____five____ sides.

2. If we *misunderstand* the directions, we will take the ____wrong____ turn.

3. The *posthumous* award was given seven years ____after____ the poet's death.

4. The *subbasement* of this building is a surprisingly beautiful story
   beneath; below the basement.

5. *Interstate* highways run ____between____ states; *intrastate* highways
   run ____within____ states.

. . . .

SUFFIXES

In the same way that you can figure out the meanings of words from
knowing their prefixes and roots, you can also make a start toward
understanding a word's overall meaning from knowing the meaning of
its suffix. If you know that the suffix *cide* means "killing," you can guess
that *insecticide* is something that kills bugs and that *fratricide* refers to
the killing of a brother. So too with phobias. If you know that a phobia
is a fear, then you have an inkling as to the meaning of *hydrophobia*
(fear of *hydro*—*water*).

Here is a list of common suffixes and their meanings.

VERB SUFFIXES

Suffix	Meaning	Example
ate	cause to become	**regulate:** make regular
en	cause to become	**brighten:** make bright
ify	cause to become	**horrify:** frighten
ize	cause to become	**idolize:** worship as a god

NOUN SUFFIXES

Suffix	Meaning	Example
acy, icy	state or quality	**hypocrisy:** the state of behaving differently from one's stated beliefs
al	process of	**betrayal:** the process of betraying
ant	one who	**defendant:** the person being defended in a trial
cide	killing	**fratricide:** the killing of a brother
er, or	one who	**advisor:** a person who advises others

NOUN SUFFIXES

Suffix	Meaning	Example
ion	process of	**subtraction:** the process of reducing a number
ism	doctrine, belief	**Buddhism:** the philosophy of Buddha
ist	one who	**Buddhist:** one who practices Buddhism
ty, ity	quality	**cruelty:** quality of being cruel or unkind
ment	condition	**amusement:** something that amuses, or the condition of being amused
ness	state of being	**sleepiness:** the state of being sleepy
phile	love	**bibliophile:** a person who loves books
phobia	fear	**hydrophobia:** fear of water
sion, tion	state of being	**revulsion:** state of being revolted

ADJECTIVE SUFFIXES

Suffix	Meaning	Example
able, ible	capable of being	**adorable:** cute, lovable
al	pertaining to	**presidential:** having to do with a president
esque	reminiscent	**Chaplinesque:** like Charlie Chaplin
ful	full of	**playful:** full of play, frolicsome
ic, ical	pertaining to	**comedic:** pertaining to comedy, funny
ish	having the quality of	**foolish:** having the quality of a fool, silly
ous, ious	characterized by	**pretentious:** having pretense, showy
ive	having the nature of	**festive:** like a festival, happy, upbeat
less	without	**spiritless:** without energy, limp
y	characterized by	**witty:** having wit, clever

Exercise 2-3

Turn the italicized words into words with slightly different meanings by adding or removing suffixes as indicated.

Example:

Change the suffix of the verb *interrogate* to make a noun meaning "one who asks questions." ___interrogator___

1. Add a suffix to the noun *cheer* to make an adjective meaning "without cheer." ___cheerless___

2. Change the suffix of the noun *dentistry* to make a noun meaning "one who is trained and medically licensed to care for teeth." ___dentist___

3. Change the suffix of the verb *hesitate* to make a noun meaning "the state of hesitating." ___hesitation___

4. Change the suffix of the verb *dramatize* to make an adjective meaning "pertaining to a drama or to the theater." ___dramatic___

5. Change the suffix of the verb *validate* to make a noun meaning "the quality of being valid." ___validity___

■ Using Context Clues

The **context** in which a word appears—the words, sentences, and paragraphs before and after it—provides clues to its meaning. You already make use of context clues instinctively, without being aware of them. If the word *lunar* appears while you are reading about the moon, you understand from the context that it has something to do with the moon. In the same way, in reading about football, if you come across the words *stunt* and *bomb* you don't expect that they refer to movie stunts or to weapons. Instead, you use your sense of the surrounding sentences to try to determine the meanings of the words—in the context of the discussion.

You can become more methodical in your use of these clues to help determine meaning as you read. A number of different kinds of context clues can help you understand what you read. Three types are most common and most useful: restatement, contrast, and exemplification.

RESTATEMENT

Writers want to be sure that their readers understand what they have written. Therefore, when they use an important term, phrase, or idea, they may formally or informally define it for their readers. In **restatement,** a word or phrase whose meaning you probably know provides the meaning of a word you are unfamiliar with. For example, in the following sentence the word *madrigal* is defined in a restatement.

> In Monteverdi's *madrigals,* or vocal compositions on secular themes, love is a frequent topic.

Exercise 2-4

Underline the words that restate the italicized term. Then define the term.

Example:

Tai chi, <u>an ancient Chinese system of movements for self-defense and meditation</u>, has been embraced in the Western world as a form of gentle and healing exercise.

Tai chi means   *an ancient Chinese system of movements for self-defense and meditation*

1. The *apex,* or <u>highest point</u>, of Mount McKinley in Alaska is usually covered by clouds.

   Apex means   *highest point*

2. A *heliocentric* model of the solar system — that is, a model <u>that has the sun as its center</u> — was first proposed by the Greek astronomer Aristarchus.

   Heliocentric means   *having the sun as a center*

3. Ever since *spreadsheets* (<u>tables of numbers, words, and graphics arranged in columns and rows</u>) have become computerized, more people have been finding that household budgets and income tax forms are easier to prepare.

Spreadsheets are *tables of numbers, words, and graphics*

arranged in columns and rows

4. A mineral or group of minerals from which something valuable — usually a metal — can be mined is known as *ore.*

   Ore means *a mineral or group of minerals from which something*

   valuable can be mined

5. Try to avoid *clichés* when you write a paper. *Clichés* — for example,
   "He roared like a lion" or "The ice was as clear as glass" — are old,
   tired, overused expressions. Try to come up with fresh new images.

   Clichés are *old, tired, overused expressions*

. . . .

CONTRAST

Writers sometimes use words with opposite meanings to explain a subject. By knowing differences, readers can better understand similarities.
In the following example, the phrase *rather than* indicates that a contrast clue is coming.

> We all hoped that the new president of the university would be an
> *asset* rather than a *detriment* to the continued viability of the school.

From the contrast clue, you can determine that *detriment* means "disadvantage" — the opposite of *asset,* or "advantage."

Exercise 2-5
. . . .

Underline the word or words that present a contrast to the italicized term. Then define the term.

Example:

The building's *curvilinear* form amazed those visitors who believed that
a building could be designed only with straight lines and angles.

Curvilinear means *having curved lines and angles*

1. Soil contains *organic* matter as well as <u>nonliving</u> components (like rock fragments).

   Organic means   *living*

2. A religion that is *monotheistic* differs in several ways from a religion whose followers <u>believe in many gods.</u>

   Monotheistic means   *believing in one god*

3. Although *egress* was permitted, the doors were locked so that <u>no one could enter</u> the building.

   Egress means   *leaving; exiting; going out*

4. *Matrilineal* societies are not as numerous as societies that <u>trace their families through their male ancestors.</u>

   Matrilineal means   *tracing families through female ancestors*

5. The *opulence* of the richest families in town made the <u>poverty</u> of the poorest families even more striking.

   Opulence means   *great wealth; abundance*

. . . .

EXEMPLIFICATION

On occasion, a writer will illustrate the meaning of a word or phrase with an example that makes its meaning clear. Consider the following sentence:

> Renaissance artists availed themselves of the arts of *classical antiquity* by studying the works of the ancient Greek and Roman masters of painting, sculpture, and architecture.

Although you may not at first know what *classical antiquity* is, you do know from the sentence that ancient Greek and Roman painting, sculp-

ture, and architecture are examples of its arts. So it's reasonable to conclude that *classical antiquity* refers to ancient Greek and Roman times.

Exercise 2-6

. . . .

Underline the words that exemplify the meaning of the italicized
term. Then define the term.

Example:

> Many movie advertisements in the 1950s boasted of the films' use of
> *Technicolor;* today, however, <u>the bright, rich, vibrant hues of the era's
> movies</u> seem unnatural to many viewers.
>
> *Technicolor* is   *an early color process that made movies look*
>
> *bright, rich, and vibrant*

1. Most *aquatic* sports—<u>swimming, sailing, and surfing, for example</u>—
    are kind to the environment; others, like <u>jet skiing or motorboating,</u> can
    be polluters.

    Aquatic means   *relating to water*

2. *Metamorphosis* occurs throughout nature: <u>Caterpillars turn into butter-
    flies, maggots turn into adult flies, and tadpoles turn into frogs.</u>

    Metamorphosis means   *the process of changing form from an*

    early stage of development to an adult one

3. After the climax of a fictional work comes the *denouement.* <u>The writer
    ties up loose strands of the plot, winds down the story, and brings the
    piece to a satisfying close.</u>

    Denouement means   *the events that follow the climax; the*

    conclusion; the end result

4. World War I *antedated* World War II; <u>the Beatles *antedated* Madonna;
    the Fourth of July</u> *antedates* Labor Day.

    Antedates means   *comes earlier in time*

5. Many people worry that whales are headed for *extinction*—that they may go the way of the dinosaur, the dodo bird, and the passenger pigeon.

    Extinction means ___the state of no longer living or existing___

Applying the Skills

Reading the Parts

Henry Louis Gates Jr. is W. E. B. Du Bois Professor of the Humanities, chair of the Afro-American Studies Department, and director of the W. E. B. Du Bois Institute for Afro-American Research at Harvard University. Although he is a well-known and highly respected academic figure, he frequently writes articles for the popular press about issues of race in America. As you read his essay, originally published in the September–October 1995 issue of *The American Enterprise,* use the strategies you learned in this chapter for determining the meanings of words, especially analyzing parts and using context clues. After reading each section of the essay, answer the questions and move on to the next section. You will have a chance to read the whole essay when you finish.

HENRY LOUIS GATES JR.
On Honoring Blackness

1   I was once walking in Washington, D.C., with my two young daughters, heading for the National Zoo, when one asked if I knew the man to whom I had just spoken. I said no. My daughter Liza volunteered that she found it embarrassing that I would speak to a complete stranger on the street. It called to mind a trip I'd made to Pittsburgh with my father. On the way, I heard Daddy speak to a colored man, then saw him tip his hat to the man's wife. It's just something that you do, he said, when I asked him if he had known those people and why had he spoken to them.

2   Last summer, I sat at a sidewalk café in Italy, and three or four "black" Italians walked casually by, as well as a dozen or more blacker Africans. Each nodded his head slightly or acknowledged me by a glance, ever so subtly. When I was growing up, we always did this with each other, passing boats in a sea of white folk.

3   Some Negroes distrust this reflex—the nod, the glance, the murmured greeting. One reason is a resentment at being lumped together with thirty million African Americans whom they don't know and most of whom they never will know. Completely by the accident of racism we have been bound together with people we

may or may not have something in common with, just because we are "black." Thirty million is a lot of people. One day you wonder: What do the misdeeds of a Mike Tyson have to do with me? So why do I feel implicated? And how can I not feel racial recrimination when I can feel racial pride?

1. Using your knowledge of word roots, prefixes, and suffixes, what do you think the word *distrust* most likely means in paragraph 3, sentence 1? Break the word into two parts to determine its meaning.

   a. are unsure of

   b. have confidence in

   c. don't like

   d. don't agree with

2. Using your knowledge of exemplification in figuring out the meaning of a word, which of the following examples does Gates use to exemplify the word *reflex* in paragraph 3, sentence 1?

   a. the handshake

   b. the loud hello

   c. the pat on the back

   d. the nod

3. In the context of this passage, what does the word *misdeeds* mean, as used by Gates in paragraph 3, sentence 5?

   a. conduct

   b. bad conduct

   c. good behavior

   d. apathy

4. The verb suffix *ate* is used in the word *implicated* near the end of paragraph 3. What does the verb suffix and the word mean?

   a. The verb suffix *ate* means "to cause to become" and the word means "in the past."

   b. The verb suffix *ate* means "to cause to become" and the word means "involved."

c. The verb suffix *ate* means "state or quality" and the word means "uninvolved."

d. The verb suffix *ate* means "state or quality" and the word means "obvious."

5. By using your knowledge of context clues, particularly contrast context clues, what do you think *recrimination* means in paragraph 3, sentence 7?

a. voluntary

b. racial

c. blame

d. color

Then, too, there are Negroes who are embarrassed about *being* Negroes, who didn't want to be bothered with race and with other black people. One of the more painful things about being colored is being colored in public around other colored people who are embarrassed to be colored and embarrassed that we *both* are colored and in public together. I used to reserve my special scorn for those Negroes, but have gradually stopped trying to tell others how to be black.

I wonder if my children will remember when their mother and I woke them up early on a Sunday morning, just to watch Nelson Mandela walk out of prison, and how it took a couple of hours for him to emerge, and how they both wanted to go back to bed and, then, to watch cartoons? And how we began to worry that something bad had happened to him on the way out, because the delay was so long? And how, when he finally walked out of that prison, we were so excited and teary-eyed at Mandela's nobility, his princeliness, his straight back and unbowed head? I think I felt that there walked the Negro, as Pop might have said; there walked the whole of the African people, as regal as any king. And that feeling I had, that gooseflesh sense of identity that I felt at seeing Nelson Mandela, listening to Mahalia Jackson sing, watching Muhammad Ali fight, or hearing Martin Luther King speak, is part of what I mean by being colored. I realize the sentiment may not be logical, but I want to have my cake and eat it too. Which is why I still nod or speak to black people on the street and why it felt so good to be acknowledged by the Afro-Italians who passed my table at the café in Milan.

6. In paragraph 5, sentence 3, Gates writes, "and how, when he finally walked out of that prison, we were so excited and teary-eyed at Mandela's nobility, his princeliness, his straight back and unbowed head?" Using context clues, and in particular using your knowledge of restatement context clues, what do you think *nobility* means?

   a. princeliness

   b. fragility

   c. illness

   d. infirmity

7. What exemplification clue does Gates use in paragraph 5, sentence 4, to give the definition of the word *regal*?

   a. "the whole of the African people"

   b. "as any king"

   c. "there walked the Negro"

   d. "as Pop might have said"

8. In paragraph 4, sentence 3, Gates writes, "I used to reserve my special scorn for those Negroes, but have gradually stopped trying to tell others how to be black." Using context clues, what do you think *scorn* means? Reread the entire paragraph if necessary.

   a. happiness

   b. contempt

   c. judgment

   d. laughter

9. Which of the following words used in paragraphs 4 and 5 uses a prefix of time?

   a. identity

   b. regal

   c. reserve

   d. gradually

10. Based on your reading of paragraph 5 and the author's use of the words *regal, princeliness,* and *nobility* in conjunction with his description of Nelson Mandela, what do you think Mandela looked like when he emerged from his long prison stay?

a. He looked like he had been beaten many times.

b. He looked tearful.

(c.) He carried himself with great dignity.

d. He looked sad.

I want to be able to take special pride in a Jessye Norman aria, a
Michael Jordan dunk, a Spike Lee movie, a Thurgood Marshall
opinion, a Toni Morrison novel, James Brown's Camel Walk. I enjoy
the unselfconscious moments of shared cultural intimacy, whatever
form it takes, when no white people are around. Like Joe Louis's
fights, which my father still talks about as part of a fixed repertoire
of stories. His eyes shine as he describes how Louis hit Max
Schmeling so many times and so hard, and how some reporter
asked him, after the fight: "Joe, what would you have done if that
last punch hadn't knocked Schmeling out?" And how ole Joe
responded, without missing a beat: "I'da run around behind him to
see what was holdin' him up!"

Even so, I rebel at the notion that I can't be part of other groups,
that I can't construct identities through elective affinity, that race
must be the most important thing about me. Is that what I want on
my gravestone: Here lies an African American? So I'm divided. I
want to be black, to know black, to luxuriate in whatever I might
be calling blackness at any particular time—but to do so in order
to come out the other side, to experience a humanity that is neither
colorless nor reducible to color. Bach *and* James Brown. Sushi *and*
fried catfish. Part of me admires those people who can say with a
straight face that they have transcended any attachment to a particular community or group . . . but I always want to run around
behind them to see what holds them up.

11. In paragraph 6, which word do you think means "state or quality of being close"? Use your knowledge of noun suffixes to
help you determine the correct answer.

a. aria

b. repertoire

c. unselfconscious

(d.) intimacy

12. Using your knowledge of context clues, can you determine the meaning of the word *repertoire* as used in paragraph 6, sentence 3?

    a. collection
    b. schedule
    c. organization
    d. association

13. Which of the following words used by Gates in paragraph 7 contains a prefix of space, direction, or position that means "across"?

    a. elective
    b. transcended
    c. affinity
    d. reducible

14. Using your knowledge of verb suffixes, what do you think *luxuriate* means in paragraph 7, sentence 4?

    a. take pleasure
    b. sit
    c. stand
    d. move into

15. Using context clues and your knowledge of adjective suffixes, what do you think the word *reducible* in paragraph 7, sentence 4, means?

    a. capable of being managed
    b. notable for being managed
    c. capable of being made smaller
    d. notable for being small in size

Reading the Whole

Now that you have had a chance to read Henry Louis Gates Jr.'s "On Honoring Blackness" in its parts and have paid close attention to word parts and context clues, you should be ready to reread it. As you read the whole essay reprinted here, continue to use context strategies for determining the meanings of words, and notice how your understanding of vocabulary helps you to appreciate the larger points that Gates is making.

HENRY LOUIS GATES JR.
On Honoring Blackness

I was once walking in Washington, D.C., with my two young daughters, heading for the National Zoo, when one asked if I knew the man to whom I had just spoken. I said no. My daughter Liza volunteered that she found it embarrassing that I would speak to a complete stranger on the street. It called to mind a trip I'd made to Pittsburgh with my father. On the way, I heard Daddy speak to a colored man, then saw him tip his hat to the man's wife. It's just something that you do, he said, when I asked him if he had known those people and why had he spoken to them.

Last summer, I sat at a sidewalk café in Italy, and three or four "black" Italians walked casually by, as well as a dozen or more blacker Africans. Each nodded his head slightly or acknowledged me by a glance, ever so subtly. When I was growing up, we always did this with each other, passing boats in a sea of white folk.

Some Negroes distrust this reflex—the nod, the glance, the murmured greeting. One reason is a resentment at being lumped together with thirty million African Americans whom they don't know and most of whom they never will know. Completely by the accident of racism we have been bound together with people we may or may not have something in common with, just because we are "black." Thirty million is a lot of people. One day you wonder: What do the misdeeds of a Mike Tyson have to do with me? So why do I feel implicated? And how can I not feel racial recrimination when I can feel racial pride?

Then, too, there are Negroes who are embarrassed about *being* Negroes, who didn't want to be bothered with race and with other black people. One of the more painful things about being colored is being colored in public around other colored people who are embarrassed to be colored and embarrassed that we *both* are colored and in public together. I used to reserve my special scorn for those Negroes, but have gradually stopped trying to tell others how to be black.

I wonder if my children will remember when their mother and I woke them up early on a Sunday morning, just to watch Nelson Mandela walk out of prison, and how it took a couple of hours for him to emerge, and how they both wanted to go back to bed and, then, to watch cartoons? And how we began to worry that something bad had happened to him on the way out, because the delay was so long? And how, when he finally walked out of that prison, we were so excited and teary-eyed at Mandela's nobility, his princeliness, his straight back and unbowed head? I think I felt that there walked the Negro, as Pop might have said; there walked the whole of the African people, as regal as any king. And that feeling I had, that gooseflesh sense of identity that I felt at seeing Nelson Mandela, listening to Mahalia Jackson sing, watching Muhammad Ali fight, or hearing Martin Luther King speak, is part of what I mean by being colored. I realize the sentiment may not be logical, but I want to have my cake and eat it too. Which is why I still nod or speak to black people on the street and why it felt so good to be acknowledged by the Afro-Italians who passed my table at the café in Milan.

I want to be able to take special pride in a Jessye Norman aria, a Michael Jordan dunk, a Spike Lee movie, a Thurgood Marshall opinion, a Toni Morrison novel, James Brown's Camel Walk. I enjoy the unselfconscious moments of shared cultural intimacy, whatever form it takes, when no white people are around. Like Joe Louis's fights, which my father still talks about as part of a fixed repertoire of stories. His eyes shine as he describes how Louis hit Max Schmeling so many times and so hard, and how some reporter asked him, after the fight: "Joe, what would you have done if that last punch hadn't knocked Schmeling out?" And how ole Joe responded, without missing a beat: "I'da run around behind him to see what was holdin' him up!"

Even so, I rebel at the notion that I can't be part of other groups, that I can't construct identities through elective affinity, that race must be the most important thing about me. Is that what I want on my gravestone: Here lies an African American? So I'm divided. I want to be black, to know black, to luxuriate in whatever I might be calling blackness at any particular time—but to do so in order to come out the other side, to experience a humanity that is neither colorless nor reducible to color. Bach *and* James Brown. Sushi *and* fried catfish. Part of me admires those people who can say with a straight face that they have transcended any attachment to a particular community or group . . . but I always want to run around behind them to see what holds them up.

Integrated Skills

1. How does Gates begin his essay? Do you think that the beginning is effective? Why or why not?

2. In what sense is Gates (or anyone) "implicated" in his race?

3. What words does Gates use as alternatives to "black"? Why do you think that he uses these other words?

4. What do you think Gates means by his title, "Honoring Blackness"? Is this a good title? Why or why not?

5. Who are the following people: Nelson Mandela, Mahalia Jackson, Muhammad Ali, and Martin Luther King Jr.? Why does Gates mention them?

6. Why does Gates nod to black people on the street? Why does he say that he will continue to do so?

Reading/Writing Connection

One of the things that Henry Louis Gates Jr. discusses in his essay is the way he acknowledges the presence of other people whose skin color is like his. Have you ever done something similar? That is, have you nodded, waved, honked, or smiled at a stranger or a group of strangers because you thought you had something in common with them? What was it that made you want to connect with that person or those people? How did they respond? Write a paragraph that describes what you did, why you did it, what happened, and why. Or, if you've never done something like what Gates describes, explain in a paragraph why you haven't. Would you now? Why or why not?

Reading Textbooks

Thematic Connections. In "On Honoring Blackness," Henry Louis Gates Jr. struggles with his racial identity. In the following excerpt from the textbook *Sociology* by Ian Robertson, the author argues that the idea of race has no biological meaning but that it does have sociological implications. The passage comes from the beginning of a chapter on race and ethnicity, or cultural heritage. As you read the selection, consider it in relation to what Henry Louis Gates Jr. says about his own cultural heritage. Would he agree with the textbook author?

Since this is a textbook selection, you can expect to find key terms defined and important differences explained. Be alert for definitions and explanations of key ideas.

Vocabulary Preview

distinctive (para. 1): standing out as special or unique (adj.)

origin (para. 1): starting point, source (n.)

adaptations (para. 2): changes (n.)

evolutionary (para. 2): relating to the process of change (adj.)

traits (para. 2): characteristics (n.)

interbreeding (para. 3): reproducing with members of other populations (v.)

continuum (para. 3): progression (n.)

anthropologists (para. 4): social scientists who study human cultures (n.)

conceptual (para. 4): related to thought; theoretical (adj.)

classification (para. 4): a way of categorizing objects according to their similarities (n.)

Ainu (para. 4): a Japanese island population (n.)

aborigines (para. 4): original inhabitants (n.)

San (para. 4): an African tribe of short hunter-gatherers (n.)

ancestry (para. 4): line of descent, family history (n.)

species (para. 4): biological category (n.)

sociologist (para. 5): social scientist who studies behavior in human societies (n.)

theorem (para. 6): a part of a larger theory (n.)

consequences (para. 6): results (n.)

persecutors (para. 6): those who attack, harass, or torture others (n.)

arbitrarily (para. 6): without any logical reason (adv.)

Race

There are about 5 billion people in the world, and they display a wide variety of skin colors, hair textures, limb-to-trunk ratios, and other characteristics, such as distinctive nose, lip, and eyelid forms.

1

Although the human animal can be traced back in the fossil record for well over 3 million years, the racial differences that we see today are of comparatively recent origin—50,000 years at the most.

These physical differences have resulted from the adaptations that human groups have made to the environments in which they lived. For example, populations in tropical areas tend to have dark skin, which protects them against harmful rays from the sun. Populations in high altitudes tend to have large lung capacity, which makes breathing easier for them. Populations in very cold climates tend to have relatively short limbs, which enable them to conserve body heat. So far as is known, these evolutionary differences affect only physical characteristics. There is no convincing evidence that different groups inherit psychological characteristics, whether these be general traits such as intelligence or more specific ones such as artistic ability.

As a biological concept, the word "race" is almost meaningless. There is certainly no such thing as a "pure" race. Different populations have been interbreeding for thousands of years, and a continuum of human types has resulted. Various societies slice up this continuum in different ways, so that the same person might belong to one "race" in one society, but another "race" in a second society. In Brazil, for example, the continuum from "black" to "white" is loosely divided into several socially recognized categories, such as *branco, cabra, moreno, mulato,* and *escuro.* In South Africa, on the other hand, the same continuum is divided [. . .] into three rigid racial categories: white, colored, and black. In the United States, only two basic categories on this continuum are recognized—black and white—even though most "black" Americans actually have white ancestry. And although all Americans who are not black are never referred to as "nonblacks," all Americans who are not white are collectively referred to as "nonwhites." In short, categories of race are a creation of the observer, not of nature.

For decades, anthropologists did try to create some kind of conceptual order out of this confusion by dividing the human species into races and subraces on the basis of physical features. The number of races that was discovered, however, depended very much on who was doing the discovering: estimates ranged from three races to over one hundred. The anthropological classification that won broadest acceptance divided the human species into three major categories: the Caucasoids, with fair skin and straight or wavy hair; the Mongoloids, with yellowish skin and a distinctive fold around the eyes; and the Negroids, with dark skin and woolly hair. However, there are many people who cannot be neatly fitted into this classification. The East Indians of Asia have Caucasoid features but dark skin. The Ainu of Japan have Mongoloid facial features but Caucasoid hair and skin color. The aborigines of Australia have dark skin, but their wavy hair is often blond. The San of Africa have coppery skin, woolly hair, and Mongoloid facial features. There are also hundreds of millions of people, such as those of Indonesia, whose ancestry is so mixed that they cannot possibly be fitted into one of the main categories. Most anthropologists have now abandoned the attempt to classify the human species into races and consider the term "race" to have no scientific meaning at all.

Thus, the physical differences among human groups are no more than a biological fact. As such, they are of no particular concern to the sociologist. The intense sociological interest in race derives from its significance as a *social* fact, because people attach meanings to the physical differences, real or imagined, between human groups. If people believe that a certain group forms a biological unity, they will act on the basis of that belief. The members of the group will tend to develop a common loyalty and to intermarry with one another, and members of other groups will regard them as "different." From the sociological point of view, then, a **race** is a category of people who are regarded as socially distinct because they share genetically transmitted physical characteristics.

In Chapter 6 ("Social Interaction in Everyday Life"), we noted the important truth of the **Thomas theorem:** "If people define situations as real, they are real in their consequences." Applied to race relations, the theorem implies that it matters little whether social beliefs about race have any biological basis. It is people's *beliefs* about race rather than the *facts* about race that influence race relations, for better or worse. Many people, for example, consider the Jews a race. In biological terms, this view is nonsense. Jews have always interbred to some extent with their host populations, and many Jewish people are blond and blue-eyed in Sweden, small and swarthy in Eastern Europe, black in Ethiopia, or Mongoloid in China. Even in Nazi Germany, which attached such great importance to the distinctions between Jews and non-Jews, Jewish citizens were obliged to wear yellow stars so that their persecutors could distinguish them from the rest of the population. Yet when any group is arbitrarily defined as a race, as Jews were in Nazi Germany, important social consequences may follow.

5

6

Thinking about the Textbook Selection

1. What is a "limb-to-trunk ratio"? What is a "fossil record"?

2. Why do different groups of people exhibit different physical characteristics, such as variations in skin color? What examples does the author use to explain and illustrate those physical differences?

3. Why does the author claim that the term *race* is almost meaningless as a biological concept?

4. What do the examples of racial categories in Brazil, the United States, and South Africa show?

5. Why does the author point out the difference in American usage of the terms *nonwhites* and *nonblacks*? What larger point is he making?

6. What do the terms *Caucasoids, Mongoloids,* and *Negroids* refer to? To what extent is this a useful set of racial categories? Why? What are the limits to this racial classification system?

7. What is the sociological perspective on race, and why is it important?

8. Why are beliefs about race sometimes more important than facts about race?

Reading the Web

In the textbook *Sociology*, Ian Robertson argues that *race* is a meaningless concept, at least as far as biology is concerned. Yet Henry Louis Gates Jr. ponders, in his essay "On Honoring Blackness," why he feels compelled to acknowledge the presence of other African Americans and why he gets such a feeling of satisfaction when he is acknowledged. Regardless of these theoretical questions, however, racial identity does come into play for many Americans, and quite often the experience is not a positive one like Gates's.

Consider this example from the Web site civilrights.org, a collection of civil rights information and resources put together by the Leadership Conference on Civil Rights (LCCR). Arguments—and those about legal and policy issues especially—are most productive when everybody involved has a clear understanding of exactly what issues are being discussed. Accordingly, this site's section on racial profiling starts with the LCCR's definition of what racial profiling is.

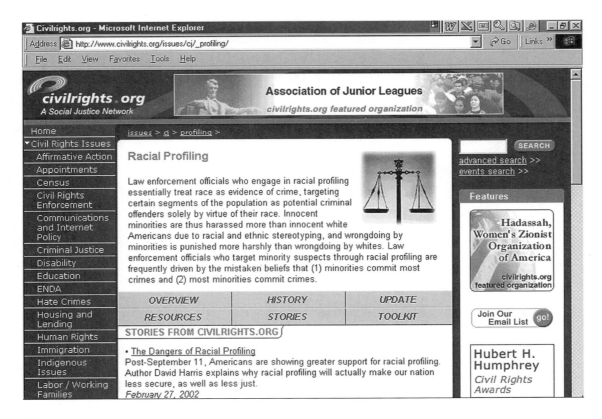

Thinking about the Web Page

1. What is the purpose of this Web page? Why do you think a pair of scales is pictured on it?

2. How is *racial profiling* defined here? Do any of the words used here help you understand the implications of this practice? How is racial stereotyping different from racial profiling?

3. According to the definition provided by the Leadership Conference on Civil Rights, does Henry Louis Gates Jr.'s practice of "honoring blackness" qualify as racial profiling? Why or why not?

4. Discuss this Web page with at least two of your classmates. What is their opinion of racial profiling? Do all agree about what it is? In talking with one another, what have you learned?

Reviewing

Recall / Remember

1. Why is it important to develop your reading vocabulary?
2. What are word prefixes, suffixes, and roots? How can recognizing them help you read more confidently?
3. Identify five prefixes and their meanings. Give a word example for each prefix.
4. Identify five roots and their meanings. Give a word example for each root.
5. Identify five suffixes and their meanings. Give a word example for each suffix.
6. Identify and explain the three types of context clues you can use to determine the meanings of words.

Chapter Summary

In this chapter you have learned how to build your vocabulary by using word analysis of prefixes, suffixes, and roots and by using context clues in reading passages. You know the importance of learning new vocabulary from other people. You know the significance of linking the words you know with new ones you are learning. And, most important, you know a number of different ways to determine a word's meaning.

Developing your vocabulary is a long-term process, but you have started in a major way through your work in this chapter. Continue reading many kinds of materials in school and outside of it, and you will continue to learn new words. Studying unfamiliar terms in your college textbooks will add to your vocabulary. Keeping a dictionary handy when you read and study and using it regularly will provide continued benefits. So too will discussing your reading with others and listening to the words and phrases they use to explain their understanding and convey their points of view.

In the following chapter you will have the opportunity to continue building your vocabulary with readings from articles from general magazines and college textbooks. Your understanding of the vocabulary in the reading selections in Chapter 3 will help you to learn the concepts emphasized there, especially to understand a writer's main idea.

Reading for a Writer's Topic and Main Idea

Getting Ready

Most of what you read contains three important elements: a topic, a main idea, and supporting details. Everything you read is "about" something. That something—the general subject of a piece of writing—is its **topic.** A writer usually has a point, something in particular he or she wants you to understand about the topic. That point, the **main idea,** is what the writer has to say *about* the topic. Writers don't expect their readers to just accept what they have to say, so they include as much information as they need to help convince readers that their main idea is valid. This additional information takes the form of **supporting details,** particular pieces of information about the topic that help prove a writer's point.

The aim of this chapter is to help you develop strategies for identifying the main points of paragraphs and of longer readings. You'll have opportunities to find the topics and main ideas of reading selections and to relate supporting details to the main ideas. By learning how to connect the details of a reading passage, you will find it easier to read with true understanding.

Chapter Overview

Focusing Questions

What is the difference between a topic and a main idea?

Why is it important to identify the main idea of what you read?

How can you determine what a writer's main idea is?

What can you do when a writer doesn't explicitly identify the main idea of a selection?

Everyday Reading

Many people read or skim through a newspaper on a regular basis. When you look at an article about your favorite sport or a new movie, you've picked a topic that interests you. But you're reading the article to find out something in particular—how the Dallas Cowboys did in yesterday's game, for example, or what a critic thinks about Ben Stiller's latest comic role. The answer to one of those queries is the article's main idea. The examples the reporter uses to back up the article's point—the Cowboys scored two touchdowns but missed a field goal attempt; a particular sight gag in Stiller's latest movie made the entire theater shake with laughter—are supporting details. Get a copy of your local or school newspaper and find two or three articles that interest you. While you're reading, try to determine what the topic, main idea, and supporting details are for each of the articles. You'll find that it gets easier with practice.

Learning the Skills

■ Main Ideas in Paragraphs

IDENTIFYING THE TOPIC SENTENCE

In much of the reading you do for school, especially in textbooks, you will find a paragraph's main idea spelled out in a sentence. This stated main idea expresses the author's key point about the topic; it is usually called the **topic sentence** but is sometimes referred to as the **main idea statement** because an author may use more than one sentence to express the main idea. In either case, the topic sentence or main idea statement best answers the question "What is the most important thing being said about the topic in this passage?"

One way to identify the main idea in a paragraph is to look for the most general opinion or point of view being expressed. The most general opinion is the broadest one, the viewpoint that covers or includes all the narrower or more specific ideas. Take a look at this example from *Lives on the Boundary,* a 1989 memoir by English teacher Mike Rose:

Students will float to the mark you set. I and the others in the vocational classes were bobbing in pretty shallow water. Vocational education has aimed at increasing the economic opportunities of students who do not do well in our schools. Some serious programs succeed in doing that, and through exceptional teachers—like Mr. Gross in *Horace's Compromise*—students learn to develop hypotheses and troubleshoot, reason through a problem, and communicate effectively—the true job skills. The vocational track, however, is most often a place for those who are just not making it, a dumping ground for the disaffected. There were a few teachers who worked hard at education; young Brother Slattery, for example, combined a stern voice with weekly quizzes to try to pass along to us a skeletal outline of world history. But mostly the teachers had no idea of how to engage the imaginations of us kids who were scuttling along at the bottom of the pond.

The author starts this paragraph by saying that students will rise to a teacher's expectations and gives a few examples of vocational education programs that try to make a difference. But then he says that those programs are the exception. In this paragraph, the most general statement is that "the vocational track . . . is most often a place for students who are

Checking for the Topic Sentence

When you are uncertain about the main idea of a paragraph, ask yourself the following questions:

1. Does the sentence contain the topic of the paragraph?

2. Does the sentence state the most important point about the topic?

3. Is the sentence more general than other sentences in the paragraph?

4. Do the other sentences in the paragraph provide more information about the main idea sentence?

just not making it, a dumping ground for the disaffected." The sentences that follow it offer examples that support this point. Notice that the topic sentence is the only one that can be connected to every other statement in the paragraph.

Be aware that not every paragraph contains a topic sentence. Some paragraphs in a reading may simply develop the idea of a previous paragraph. Other paragraphs may serve as bridges or transitions between different parts of the selection.

Exercise 3-1

Identify the topic of each paragraph and underline the topic sentence.

Example:

Before the twentieth century, women had a single role, that of wife and mother. Occasionally accidents of royal succession placed a woman in a position of great power, and the eighteenth century saw two amazingly long-lasting cases: Catherine the Great, Empress of Russia, who ruled from 1762 to 1796, and Maria Theresa, de facto [in fact] empress of the Austrian Empire from 1740 to 1780. But what we now think of as "careers" were simply not open to women, with very few exceptions. (Joseph Kerman and Gary Tomlinson, with Vivian Kerman, *Listen*)

TOPIC OF THE PARAGRAPH: *the role of women before the twentieth century*

1. An amoeba can do an unusual mathematical trick: It multiplies by dividing. After it has grown to a certain size, the amoeba's single cell divides in half to produce two amoebas. In about a day, the two amoebas have grown to the point at which they are ready to divide and form four; the day after that, there are eight amoebas, and so forth. How many amoebas will there be at the end of the week? (Harold R. Jacobs, *Mathematics: A Human Endeavor*)

   TOPIC OF THE PARAGRAPH: *amoebas*

2. The great development in your near future is the portable electronic library—a library not only of books, but of films and music. It will be about the size of an average book and will probably open in the same way. One half will be the screen with high-definition, full-color display.

The other will be a keyboard, much like one of today's computer consoles, with the full alphabet, digits, basic mathematical functions, and a large number of special keys—perhaps 100 keys in all. It won't be as small as some of today's midget calculators, which have to be operated with toothpicks. (Arthur C. Clarke, "Electronic Tutors")

TOPIC OF THE PARAGRAPH: *the portable electronic library*

3. Drama languished in Europe after the fall of Rome during the fifth and sixth centuries. From about A.D. 400 to 900 almost no record of dramatic productions exists except for those of minstrels and other entertainers, such as acrobats and jugglers, who traveled through the countryside. The Catholic church was instrumental in suppressing drama because the theater—represented by the excesses of Roman productions—was seen as subversive. No state-sponsored festivals brought people together in huge theaters the way they had in Greek and Roman times. (Michael Meyer, *The Bedford Introduction to Literature*)

TOPIC OF THE PARAGRAPH: *drama in Europe after the fall of Rome*

4. One form of distraction is *imagery*. Creating a vivid mental image can help control pain or other unpleasant physical symptoms. Usually people create a pleasant and progressive scenario, such as walking along the beach, hiking in the mountains, or enjoying a gathering of friends. Aggressive or arousing imagery can also be useful, such as imagining a heated argument, fighting off an enemy, or driving a race car at high speeds. Whatever imaginary scenario you use, try to visualize all the different sensations involved, including the sights, sounds, aromas, touches, and tastes. The goal is to become so absorbed in your fantasy that you distract yourself from the pain sensations. (Don H. Hockenbury and Sandra E. Hockenbury, *Psychology*)

TOPIC OF THE PARAGRAPH: *imagery*

5. In 1985, scientists discovered that the high-altitude ozone layer, which shields organisms from harmful ultraviolet radiation, had thinned greatly over Antarctica. Ozone (O_3) is produced by the action of sunlight on atmospheric oxygen (O_2) in tropical regions and is transported to high latitudes, where it is destroyed. Chlorine compounds, produced

mainly by humans, appear to be the main cause of the unusually high rates of ozone destruction. <u>Ozone is now seriously depleted at very high latitudes, where conditions favor its destruction.</u> (William K. Purves et al., *Life: The Science of Biology*)

TOPIC OF THE PARAGRAPH: *ozone*

. . . .

LOCATING THE TOPIC SENTENCE

In determining which sentence in a paragraph contains the main idea, you need to make a judgment. Start by asking yourself, "What is the paragraph about?" That is the topic. Then, as you learned earlier in this chapter, look for the paragraph's most general statement about the topic. That general sentence—the topic sentence or main idea statement—might appear at the beginning, at the end, or somewhere in the middle of a paragraph.

The most common position for a topic sentence is first. The following example from Olivia Vlahos's book *Human Beginnings* (1966) illustrates this familiar pattern (the topic sentence is underlined):

> <u>Nearly all living creatures manage some form of communication.</u> The dance pattern of bees in their hive help to point the way to distant flower fields or announce successful foraging. Male stickleback fish regularly swim upside-down to indicate outrage in a courtship contest. Male deer and lemurs mark territorial ownership by rubbing their own body secretions on boundary stones or trees. Everyone has seen a frightened dog put his tail between his legs and run in panic. We, too, use gestures, expressions, postures, and movement to give our words point.

Sometimes a paragraph will build toward its statement of main idea. The topic sentence will therefore often occur toward the end of a passage. Here is an example from *Psychology in Industrial Organizations,* a textbook by Norman R. F. Maier and Trudy G. Verser:

> That money represents the satisfaction of different kinds of needs becomes apparent if we speculate a moment on what people would do if they could not obtain social position and power by

means of money. In such a case, these needs might most readily be satisfied by service to society. The success of a person then would become a matter of social, rather than financial, status. Instead of competing with one another for money chips, people would compete for other socially recognized indicators of merit. In the Bennington College Community, where liberal leanings became associated with prestige, women developed nonconservative values, the most capable leaders showing a greater degree of liberalism than the less capable ones. Prestige is not inevitably associated with wealth; rather, our culture has given money a prestige value.

In this example, the final sentence of the paragraph sums up and pulls together the content of the sentences that come before it.

Sometimes you'll find a paragraph's topic sentence in its middle. When the main idea is neither in the first sentence of a paragraph nor in its last, you might be able to find it in the second sentence. In such cases, the topic sentence usually follows a bridge or transitional sentence that links the ideas in one paragraph with the ideas in the preceding paragraph. Here is an example from the political science textbook *The American Democracy* by Thomas E. Patterson:

The television campaign includes political advertising. Televised commercials are by far the most expensive part of presidential campaigns. Since 1976, political commercials on television have accounted for about half of the candidates' expenditures in the general election campaign. In 1992 George Bush and Bill Clinton each spent more than $30 million on advertising in the general election, and Ross Perot spent even more. Perot relied heavily on "infomercials"—30-minute and hour-long commercials that emphasized substance over slogans.

In this example, the first sentence links the remainder of the paragraph with the paragraph that comes before it. That earlier paragraph is about other aspects of the television campaign. The most important point made in this example paragraph is that television commercials are the most expensive part of presidential campaigns.

Be aware that the topic sentence can be placed anywhere. In the next example, from the textbook *Essentials of Biology* by Willis H. Johnson et al., the main idea does not simply follow an opening transitional sentence. Instead, it comes much later—in the middle—of the paragraph.

> What happens when foreign materials do enter the body by breaking through the skin or epithelial linings of the digestive, circulatory, or respiratory stems and after the clotting process is complete? The next line of defense comes into action. Phagocytic cells (wandering and stationary) may engulf the foreign material and destroy it. <u>The body's primary defense mechanism is the production of specific antibody molecules. Antibodies may circulate in the blood as mentioned</u> or they may be bound to cells; less is known about these cell-bound antibodies. <u>Antibodies inactivate or destroy the activity of antigens by combining with them.</u> The reaction is a manifestation of the immune response, and the discipline primarily devoted to its study is immunology. Generally immunity is considered to be peculiar to the vertebrates, but recent evidence suggests that a form of immunity occurs in invertebrate animals also.

The main idea statement of this paragraph is long and complex. It includes more than a simple statement of idea. In fact, the idea statement contains two related ideas: (1) that the production of specific antibodies occurs and that these may circulate in the blood and (2) that antibodies combine with antigens to destroy them and produce immunity.

Exercise 3-2

Locate and underline the topic sentence of each paragraph. (One of the paragraphs has two sentences that combine to express the main idea.)

Example:

> <u>Anger is prompted by a person's reactions to frustrating or provocative situations, not by the situations themselves.</u> People make themselves angry by thinking angering thoughts. By challenging these thoughts, they can learn to turn down their anger alarm, avoid hostile confrontations, and save wear and tear on their cardiovascular systems. (Jeffrey S. Nevid, Spencer A. Rathus, and Hannah R. Rubenstein, *Health in the New Millennium*)

1. Make a loud noise and infants only minutes old will startle and may even cry. They will also turn their heads toward the source of the noise,

an indication that they perceive sound as roughly localized in space. Yet newborns' hearing is not so acute for some parts of the sound spectrum as it will be when they are older. Sensitivity to sound improves dramatically in infancy and then more slowly until the age of 10, when it reaches adult levels. (Michael Cole and Sheila R. Cole, *The Development of Children*)

2. Most mass media evolve through various stages, which are initiated not only by the diligence of great inventors, such as Thomas Edison, but by social, cultural, political, and economic circumstances. For instance, both telegraph and radio developed as new industrialized nations sought to expand their control over colonies and to transmit information more quickly. The phonograph, too, emerged because of the social and economic conditions of a growing middle class with more money and leisure time. Today, the information highway is a contemporary response to similar sets of concerns: transporting messages more rapidly while appealing to middle- and upper-middle-class consumers. (Richard Campbell, *Media and Culture: An Introduction to Mass Communication*)

3. Meditation is not easy to define. In general, **meditation** refers to a group of techniques that induce an altered state of focused attention and heightened awareness. Meditation takes many forms, and has been used for thousands of years as part of religious practices throughout the world. Virtually every major form of religion has a rich tradition of meditative practices—whether Hindu, Taoist, Buddhist, Jewish, Christian, or Muslim. However, many people practice meditation independent of any religious tradition or spiritual context. Some forms of psychotherapy also include meditative practice as a component of the overall therapy. (Don H. Hockenbury and Sandra E. Hockenbury, *Psychology*)

4. Would people work if they didn't need money? The work of Maslow and Herzberg indicates that money alone is not as strong a motivator as many people believe. Almost every study of motivation points to other factors that are more influential in inspiring people to perform better. Most people will tell you that they work for the money, and of course this is true—to a degree. But for most employees, their pay remains the

same no matter how hard they work on a given day. And people sometimes refuse to do a well-paid job, whereas at other times they may work harder than they have to for no money at all. (Kenneth Blanchard et al., *Exploring the World of Business*)

5. Factory farm animals need liberation in the most literal sense. Veal calves are kept in stalls five feet by two feet. They are usually slaughtered when about four months old, and have been too big to turn in their stalls for at least a month. Intensive beef herds, kept in stalls only proportionately larger for much longer periods, account for a growing percentage of beef production. Sows are often similarly confined when pregnant, which, because of artificial methods of increasing fertility, can be most of the time. Animals confined in this way do not waste food by exercising, nor do they develop unpalatable muscle. (Peter Singer, "Animal Liberation")

. . . .

RECOGNIZING IMPLIED MAIN IDEAS

Sometimes a writer will not state the main idea directly. In this case, the main idea is **implied,** or suggested, rather than directly stated. When no single sentence in a paragraph or passage states the main idea directly, you can usually **infer** it, or figure it out, by looking carefully at the facts and details that are provided. You will learn more about supporting details in Chapter 4 and about making inferences in Chapter 8. For now, however, use your powers of reasoning to do some thinking about implied main ideas.

Just as you did when reading paragraphs and passages with stated main ideas, ask yourself a few questions to determine an implied main idea:

- What is the topic of the paragraph or passage?
- How are the details related to one another?
- What idea do the details tell you about the topic?

Once you can answer these questions, you are ready to write out the main idea in a sentence of your own. Consider the following paragraph from the 1994 essay "Sexism in English: A 1990s Update" by Alleen Pace Nilsen:

Etiquette books used to teach that if a woman had *Mrs.* in front of her name then the husband's name should follow because *Mrs.* is an abbreviated form of *Mistress* and a woman couldn't be a mistress of herself. As with many arguments about "correct" language usage, this isn't very logical because *Miss* is also an abbreviation of *Mistress*. Feminists hoped to simplify matters by introducing *Ms.* as an alternative to both *Mrs.* and *Miss,* but what happened is that *Ms.* largely replaced *Miss* to become a catch-all business title for women. Many married women still prefer the title *Mrs.*, and some resent being addressed with the term *Ms.* As one frustrated newspaper reporter complained, "Before I can write about a woman, I have to know not only her marital status but also her political philosophy." The result of such complications may contribute to the demise of titles which are already being ignored by many computer programmers who find it more efficient to simply use names; for example in a business letter: "Dear Joan Garcia," instead of "Dear Mrs. Joan Garcia," "Dear Ms. Garcia," or "Dear Mrs. Louis Garcia."

What is missing from this paragraph, and what readers therefore need to infer, is a sentence like the following: "There is much confusion today about an acceptable way to address women." A logical place to put this sentence, were it included, would be at the beginning of the paragraph. The middle of the paragraph includes numerous examples, and the end of it carries Nilsen's argument a bit further by suggesting that the confusion she describes might lead to the abandonment of titles for women.

Exercise 3-3

Use the questions on page 78 to infer the main idea of each paragraph.

Example:

Experts are now more confident than before that global climate change is indeed in progress and that at least some of the warming is due to human action, specifically the burning of coal, oil and wood, which releases carbon dioxide into the atmosphere. Like its predecessors, the forecast depends heavily on uncertain computer simulations of the atmosphere's reponse to heat-trapping gases. (William K. Stevens, "Scientists Say Earth's Warming Could Set Off Wide Disruptions," *New York Times,* September 18, 1995)

TOPIC OF THE PARAGRAPH: *experts' opinions on global warming*

RELATED DETAILS: *They're more confident than before that climate change is in progress; the forecast depends heavily on uncertain computer simulations.*

IMPLIED MAIN IDEA: *Experts are certain neither that global warming is increasing nor that it's a result of human action.*

1. Leonardo da Vinci was the illegitimate son of Piero, a notary from the town of Vinci, and a peasant girl named Caterina. The third wife of Leonardo's father later bore a son named Bartolommeo, who idolized Leonardo although he was forty-five years younger. After the death of the legendary Leonardo, Bartolommeo attempted an amazing experiment. He studied every detail of his father's relationship with Caterina. Then Bartolommeo, himself a notary by family tradition, returned to Vinci and found another peasant wench who seemed similar to Caterina, according to all Bartolommeo knew. He married her and she bore him a son whom they called Piero. Strangely, the child actually looked like Leonardo and was brought up with encouragement to follow in the great man's footsteps. Surprisingly, the boy became an accomplished artist and was becoming a talented sculptor when he died, thus ending the experiment. (Robert Wallace, *Biology: The World of Life*)

TOPIC OF THE PARAGRAPH: *Bartolommeo's experiment*

RELATED DETAILS: *family relationships; the search for a wife like Caterina*

IMPLIED MAIN IDEA: *By deliberately choosing a wife who resembled Leonardo da Vinci's mother, Leonardo's half-brother was able to father a son who was very similar to Leonardo.*

2. Perhaps the best way to begin reading poetry responsively is not to allow yourself to be intimidated by it. Come to it, initially at least, the way you might listen to a song on the radio. You probably listen to a song several times before you hear it at all, before you have a sense of how it works, where it's going, and how it gets there. You don't worry about analyzing a song when you listen to it, even though after repeated experiences with it you know and anticipate a favorite part and know, on some level, why it works for you. Give yourself a chance to respond to poetry. The hardest work has already been done by the poet, so all you need to do at the start is listen for the pleasure produced by the poet's arrangement of words. (Michael Meyer, *The Bedford Introduction to Literature*)

TOPIC OF THE PARAGRAPH: *poetry*

RELATED DETAILS: *ways of approaching poetry that are not intimidating*

IMPLIED MAIN IDEA: *People are intimidated by poetry, but there are ways to approach it that are not intimidating.*

3. In Argentina, it is bad manners to clear your throat or blow your nose at the table. In Brazil, avoid touching your food with your fingers, and be sure to wipe your mouth before taking a drink. When dining with Muslim companions, be careful not to use your left hand for eating, touching others, giving or receiving objects, or pointing. (Kenneth Blanchard et al., *Exploring the World of Business*)

TOPIC OF THE PARAGRAPH: *table manners*

RELATED DETAILS: *table manners in Argentina, in Brazil, and with Muslim companions*

IMPLIED MAIN IDEA: *Different cultures have different table manners and require different responses by guests.*

4. In 1927 social workers in various parts of the United States contributed reports to a study on whether Prohibition was working. From Cleveland it was reported that "at first the Italian groups thought Prohibition affected only whiskey-drinkers . . . and went ahead with their wine, many times quite openly." In Buffalo it was said that "our Italian people have no conviction that they are doing anything morally wrong in making and drinking their native wines. They cannot understand why Prohibition was adopted. Generally speaking, they feel that it is an evidence of fanaticism, and while they are obliged in certain ways to conform to the law, they have no special scruples against violating it." In New York, before Prohibition, Italian-Americans bought [wine] "as they bought bread in this new America, as a matter of convenience. Now they make it as they would make bread if the bread shops were closed." (Andrew Barr, *Drink: A Social History of America*)

TOPIC OF THE PARAGRAPH: *Prohibition*

RELATED DETAILS: *reports from Cleveland, Buffalo, and New York*

IMPLIED MAIN IDEA: *Prohibition was not working (at least not among Italian-Americans in these three cities!)*

5. Hong Kong is 98% Chinese. Although the official languages are English and Cantonese, the use of Mandarin (or *Putonghua*, China's official language and the one spoken by most Chinese worldwide) is bound to rise. Many other languages and dialects are spoken here, including Hakka (the language of a group of early settlers from China), Tanka (the language of the original boat people who came here some 5,000 years ago), Shanghainese, and Chinglish (a mixture of Cantonese and English). Among the nationalities living in Hong Kong, some 30,000 Filipinos make up the largest foreign community. Most are women working as maids and nannies—called "amahs" in local parlance—many of whom socialize on their days off near the Star Ferry and at Statue Square park. (*Fodor's '98 Hong Kong: The Complete Guide with Smart Shopping, Great Dining, and Trips to South China and Macau*)

TOPIC OF THE PARAGRAPH: *Hong Kong*

RELATED DETAILS: *information on the languages spoken in Hong Kong and on the different nationalities living there*

IMPLIED MAIN IDEA: *Although Hong Kong is primarily Chinese, it is a multicultural city.*

· ·

■ Main Ideas in Longer Passages

Finding the main idea in paragraphs is good reading practice, but it is not enough. To become a competent and confident reader, you need to be able to follow the development of an author's idea in longer sections of writing.

STATED MAIN IDEAS

Being able to identify topic sentences in paragraphs will help you to better understand the main idea of a longer piece of writing. You can determine a whole reading's main idea by putting together the main ideas of all its paragraphs. Just as you analyze the relationship among the details of a paragraph to identify its topic and its main idea, so you analyze the relationship among the topic sentences of all the paragraphs to determine the main idea of a reading passage as a whole.

Read the following three-paragraph excerpt from the 1982 essay "Is History a Guide to the Future?" by the historian Barbara Tuchman. As you read, identify the topic and main idea statement (topic sentence) of each paragraph.

> The commonest question asked of historians by laymen is whether history serves a purpose. Is it useful? Can we learn from the lessons of history? 1
>
> When people want history to be utilitarian and teach us lessons, that means they also want to be sure that it meets scientific standards. This, in my opinion, it cannot do, for reasons which I will come to in a moment. To practice history as a science is sociology, 2
>
> *(continued)*

an altogether different discipline which I personally find antipa-thetic—although I suppose the sociologists would consider that my deficiency rather than theirs. The sociologists plod along with their noses to the ground assembling masses of statistics in order to arrive at some obvious conclusion which a reasonably perceptive historian, not to mention a large part of the general public, knows anyway, simply from observation—that social mobility is increas-ing, for instance, or that women have different problems from men. One wishes they would just cut loose someday, lift up their heads, and look at the world around them.

If history were a science, we should be able to get a grip on her, 3 learn her ways, establish her patterns, know what will happen tomorrow. Why is it that we cannot? The answer lies in what I call the Unknowable Variable—namely, man. Human beings are always and finally the subject of history. History is the record of human behavior, the most fascinating subject of all, but illogical and so crammed with an unlimited number of variables that it is not susceptible of the scientific method nor of systematizing.

To determine the topic and the main idea of a longer passage overall, look for things that are repeated. Reading through Tuchman's argument, you see that history as a science is her topic. The topic sentence of para-graph 1 is "The commonest question asked of historians by laymen is whether history serves a purpose." In paragraph 2, Tuchman states her main idea as "To practice history as a science is sociology." Tuchman follows up on that idea in paragraph 3's topic sentence: "History is the record of human behavior, the most fascinating subject of all, but illogi-cal and so crammed with an unlimited number of variables that it is not susceptible of the scientific method nor of systematizing." Look at these three topic sentences as a group: What do they, together, have to say about history as a science? That history cannot be a science, nor should it be. Tuchman says this directly in paragraph 2: "When people want history to be utilitarian and teach us lessons, that means they also want to be sure that it meets scientific standards. This, in my opinion, it can-not do."

Exercise 3-4

Determine the topic and the main idea of the following passages.

Example:

> Around 1930, jazz gained significantly in popularity, thanks in part to [Louis] Armstrong's recordings. With popularity came changes, not all of them to the good. Jazz now had to reach bigger audiences in ballrooms and roadhouses. This meant **big bands,** with ten to twenty players, and carefully written out arrangements of the songs played. Improvisation, which was really the rationale behind jazz, was necessarily limited under these conditions.
>
> However, big-band jazz—called **swing**—compensated for some of its lost spontaneity by variety of tone color and instrumental effects. A novel style of band orchestration was developed, based on the contrast between brass (trumpets and trombones) and "reed" (mainly saxophone) groups. Soloists cut in and out of the full-band sounds. Jazz "arrangers," who "arranged" current songs for the bands, treated this style with the greatest technical ingenuity and verve; they deserve the name of composers. Sometimes they contrived to allow for some improvisation within their arrangements. (Joseph Kerman and Gary Tomlinson, with Vivian Kerman, *Listen*)

TOPIC OF THE PASSAGE: *jazz*

MAIN IDEA OF THE PASSAGE: *As jazz became more popular, it expanded into big-band jazz, or swing, which resulted in a decrease in improvisation but an increase in the variety of tone color and instrumental effects.*

1. Just as we use calendars to keep track of time, we use maps to keep track of space. Essentially, a map is a picture of a piece of the world, presented more or less as it would be seen from the air. Although most people think of maps as unambiguous reflections of objective reality, a single place can be rendered very dissimilarly on different maps.

   The first cartographic variable arises because the earth is round and a map is flat. Consequently, it is impossible to produce a map that does not incorporate some distortion in terms of shape, size, or relative placement of landforms. The mapmaker needs to select a **projection,** a systematic mathematical formula that provides rules for drawing the two-dimensional map from three-dimensional data. When a map of a very small area, like a town or city, is drawn, what projection is chosen matters little, because all will produce very similar maps. When a larger area is mapped, though, the inherent features of each projection begin to emerge and can affect the reader's overall impression tremendously. (Lanny B. Fields, Russell J. Barber, and Cheryl A. Riggs, *The Global Past*)

TOPIC OF THE PASSAGE: *maps*

MAIN IDEA OF THE PASSAGE: *Because the earth is three-dimensional and a map is two-dimensional, mapmakers have to select a mathematical formula for drawing a map; thus, the same place (especially a large area) can appear very different on different maps.*

2. Few words have become as strongly linked in the public's perception of health risks as **cholesterol.** Just what is cholesterol? Is it bad for us?

Cholesterol is a natural, fatlike substance found in body cells of humans and animals. The body makes use of cholesterol in the formation of hormones and cell membranes. Cholesterol is found in the lean and fat of meat and in animal by-products, such as eggs, milk, and other dairy products. Egg yolks and organ meats like liver and kidney meats contain the highest concentrations of dietary sources of cholesterol. One egg yolk, for example, contains about ten times the amount of cholesterol found in one ounce of meat, poultry, or fish. Cholesterol is not found in any foods derived from plants.

The body actually makes all the cholesterol it requires on its own. We do not need to consume additional cholesterol in our diets. Herein lies the problem: Since cholesterol is present in all animal tissue, including meat, poultry, dairy products, shellfish, and, in lesser amounts, fish, we may take in far more cholesterol from our diet than we could possibly use, which can increase the level of cholesterol circulating in our bloodstream. The body also converts dietary fat into blood cholesterol. The problem is that excess blood cholesterol can result in the formation of fatty deposits on artery walls, impeding the flow of blood to vital organs and increasing the risk of heart attacks and strokes. (Jeffrey S. Nevid, Spencer A. Rathus, and Hannah R. Rubenstein, *Health in the New Millennium*)

TOPIC OF THE PASSAGE: *cholesterol*

MAIN IDEA OF THE PASSAGE: *Because we make our own cholesterol and take in cholesterol from many foods, we may have excess cholesterol, which can increase the risk of heart attacks and strokes.*

3. Consider some other assumptions which underlie various beliefs. There are some people who believe that criminals should be punished or even condemned. What is the assumption which underlies this belief? It is that human beings are free agents, that they are always capable of freely choosing to do or not do something, and hence that they are responsible for their actions. Or consider another case. There are some people who believe that the universe must have been created. What is the assumption which underlies this belief? It is that nothing can exist without a cause (and, hence, that the universe must have had a cause).

Part of what philosophers try to do, then, is to make us aware of our basic assumptions or presuppositions. Why is this important? Because as long as we are unaware of our assumptions we are not intellectually free. For if we are unaware of them, we are enslaved to them and to all of the consequences they entail. We are not free in our thinking because all that we think is confined to the limits which are set by our unrecognized assumptions. We must, then, first, become aware of them, and second, examine them critically. This is not to say that we must necessarily dismiss them. We undoubtedly will continue to hold many of them. But the manner in which they are held will be different. Here, then, is another good reason for philosophizing. (E. D. Klemke, A. David Kline, and Robert Hollinger, eds., *Philosophy: Contemporary Perspectives on Perennial Issues*)

TOPIC OF THE PASSAGE: *assumptions*

MAIN IDEA OF THE PASSAGE: *We must recognize and examine our assumptions; otherwise, our thinking is confined to the limits that are set by them.*

4. Experimental filmmakers usually work independently of the usual sources for financing and distributing films. In the United States they are largely unrestricted by censorship or a ratings system and tend to be free of outside pressures on the shape and content of their finished films, especially if they make their films for showing on the Web. Experimental filmmakers are, of course, influenced by films they have seen and inevitably imitate them, reject them, use parts of an existing film, or even rework whole films.

Frequently experimental filmmakers use the most recent advances in filmmaking, or they apply advances in other forms of human expression to experimental films. For example, once anamorphic lenses were developed, some experimental filmmakers explored their use. As computer graphics emerged and evolved, experimental filmmakers explored their uses. Once video became less cumbersome and less costly (and film stock and developing film became more expensive), many artists and experimental filmmakers rushed to experiment with video's creative possibilities. (William H. Phillips, *Film: An Introduction*)

TOPIC OF THE PASSAGE: *experimental filmmakers*

MAIN IDEA OF THE PASSAGE: *Experimental filmmakers are free of many filmmaking restrictions and often explore the most recent advances in filmmaking and other technologies.*

5. Students sometimes complain that information or concepts in a textbook chapter are hard to remember because they are simply too similar. If you occasionally confuse related terms and concepts, it may be because you're experiencing **interference** in your memories for similar information.

To minimize memory interference for related information, first break the chapter into manageable sections, then learn the key information one section at a time. As you encounter new concepts, contrast them with previously learned concepts, looking for differences and similarities. By building distinct memories for important information as you progress through a topic, you're more likely to distinguish between concepts so they don't get confused in your memory. A simple way to make text information visually distinct is by using different colored highlighters for different concepts. (Don H. Hockenbury and Sandra E. Hockenbury, *Psychology*)

TOPIC OF THE PASSAGE: *memory interference for related information*

MAIN IDEA OF THE PASSAGE: *Building distinct memories for important information helps students minimize memory interference for related information.*

. . . .

IMPLIED MAIN IDEAS

Understanding the implied main ideas of paragraphs can help you to understand the implied main ideas of longer passages, including whole essays and articles. As you read longer passages, note the details and implied main idea of each paragraph. Just as you can connect topic sentences to find the stated main idea of a passage, so can you connect implied main ideas in paragraphs to determine the implied main idea of a longer work.

Remember to practice making inferences about implied main ideas in individual paragraphs as you read. Some paragraphs will include directly stated main ideas. Others may not. As you read the following column by Ted C. Fishman from the August 23, 2001, edition of the *New York Times,* try to identify how the paragraphs that don't have directly stated main ideas are related to the paragraphs that do.

A Simple Glass of Water

Recently, on a day so blistering in Chicago that authorities issued a heat warning, telling people to stay inside when possible, I was out early with my wife and 10-year-old son, hoping to run errands before the temperature topped 90. Alas, at 9:45 A.M. we were too late, and the heat hit. We wanted water. We went into a coffee shop and ordered a latte for my wife, an iced decaf coffee for my son, and please, a glass of water for me.

1

(continued)

"I can only give you a small cup," the clerk told me. That would be fine, I told him. He came back with a thimble-sized cup with roughly one ounce of liquid in it. Was it possible to get more? I asked. "No," said the clerk. "That's all we can give out. We do sell water, though."

These days it seems that providing a simple drink of water is not so much an exercise in quenching the thirsty as in soaking them. Worldwide, bottled water is a $35 billion business. Over the next four years, the bottled water market is expected to grow at 15 percent annually. That dwarfs the growth rates for fruit beverages, beer and soft drinks, all under 2 percent. Of course, sometimes bottled water does taste better or is more convenient or safer than tap water—and is worth paying for. That's nothing new. More novel is the pervasive push by businesses to sell bottled water by depriving customers of tap water.

For the past few years, the movie theaters I frequent have been declining requests for water, pushing—at $2.50 each—the bottled product instead. Seen a water fountain at a gasoline station lately? Not likely. Bottled water is one of the highest selling items—after cigarettes—in the stations' convenience stores. In restaurants, waiters now frequently ask for your drink order before they bring you tap water, in the hope that you can be talked into buying bottled water. A waitress I asked called this the "beverage greeting" that her manager required her to say before bringing a glass of water.

During my travels nearly twenty years ago through Indonesia's coffee-growing regions, I would often stop by a bamboo-thatched lean-to for a drink. Water in the land of the coffee bean rarely comes from a tap; it has to be hauled from wells, strained and boiled. Often I was served by rail-thin old men or women in fraying sarongs who subsisted on a few dollars a week. Yet, ask for water and they brought it. At first I asked to pay, not for the water, but for the work behind it. They'd refuse even the smallest coin. The custom of sharing water was too elemental to gum up with finagling. In India, the Sarai Act mandates that an innkeeper give a free glass of drinking water to any passerby. Indeed, in most places around the world, giving strangers water is the bare minimum of humane behavior. Why is that not so here?

Exercise 3-5

Answer the following questions about the newspaper column "A Simple Glass of Water" by Ted C. Fishman.

1. The first stated main idea appears toward the middle of the article. What is the first stated main idea?

   These days it seems that providing a simple drink of water is not so much an exercise in quenching the thirsty as in soaking them.

2. In paragraph 1, what idea is not stated but is implied by the words "authorities issued a heat warning, telling people to stay inside when possible"?

   The heat in Chicago was so severe that the author's health was at risk, making a request for water reasonable. Also implied is that a reasonable person or business would provide it.

3. What stated main idea in paragraph 3 is supported by the examples provided in paragraph 4?

   More novel is the pervasive push by businesses to sell bottled water by depriving customers of tap water.

4. What is the implied main idea of paragraph 5?

   Poor people in Indonesia are more civilized than American businesses.

5. There is a significant main idea that is not stated in the column. It is implied by the examples the author provides and by the comparison he makes between Indonesian and American attitudes toward free water. What does the article imply that American businesses need to do?

Provide free water upon request rather than trying to take

advantage of people's thirst to make a profit.

Applying the Skills

Reading the Parts

The following selection was written by college student Mona Maisami when she was a junior at Franklin and Marshall College; it was published in 2002 in the *College Dispatch*, a print and online journal that focuses on issues of free speech. As you read Maisami's piece, pay special attention to the topic and main idea of each paragraph. After reading each section, answer the questions and move on to the next section. You will have a chance to read the whole selection when you finish.

MONA MAISAMI
Born in Amrika

I see the life that I could have had in the faces of my Iranian relatives. They are like ghosts of the life that my parents left behind when they moved to "Amrika," haunting us with a vision of what our lives could have been. Their lives are not reality to me—I was born in the U.S., and it is the only reality I know. My overseas relatives say that I don't even look Iranian anymore, as though it has faded out of me like the color from a pair of old jeans. I have even heard them compare my accent to that of an illiterate peasant's daughter—they say I am "de-hauty." I hear them innocently laughing at me when I say, "Salaam," hello or "Quelly-mam-noon," thank you. I smile politely or even laugh along: But in my heart, it makes me feel incomplete, as though a part of me is missing.

My cousin Nina is an "F.O.B.," which means fresh off the boat. Her family has only been in the U.S. for three months now, and she still wears a chador and scarf. She and her family are guests in our house today, and I am in charge of entertaining her. Nina is my age, so I feel comfortable around her and think that we may have some things in common. She may be the link that can help me relate to my heritage. I am anxious to be alone with her so that she can teach me how to be more Iranian.

I take her to a park that is within walking distance from my house. Nina's younger brother, Ali, comes along with us, too. It is a hot, sticky, humid August afternoon. I am wearing a tank top and the jean shorts that my mom bought me to wear for our dinner

1

2

3

party. Nina has on her traditional Islamic clothing—everything is covered except for her hands and her face. Looking at her, I begin to wonder what my friends will think if they see my cousin and me at the park. Ali, on the other hand, is wearing khaki shorts and a black Adidas t-shirt. He will be able to blend right in with the other kids at the park. Nina and I walk over to two swings that are next to each other. Ali heads over to the basketball courts where a group of boys are playing "H-O-R-S-E."

4

She appears to be shy to me, so I decide to initiate the conversation. "Don't you ever get hot wearing a scarf and robe? I'm hot right now in what I am wearing. If I were you, I'd be jealous that Ali gets to wear shorts and a t-shirt." I look over at Nina expecting her to give the obvious response, that she is in fact jealous of Ali.

5

"It's not a robe, it's called a chador. You should get your facts straight if you are going to make fun of other people's lives." She says this to me as she sharply turns her back. I can tell that she is not happy spending the afternoon with me. All of a sudden, I feel like I am not good enough for her. Her scarf is made of silk and is light pink with tiny green and purple flowers on it. The colors are pretty to me, but something inside of me screams that it is morally wrong for her to have to cover her beautiful thick brown hair. I want to tear the scarf off her head and set her free. I want her to be more like me—is there something wrong with that?

1. Which of the following best expresses the topic of paragraph 1 of Maisami's essay?

   a. overseas relatives

   (b.) the author's Iranian-American identity

   c. accents

   d. Arabic

2. Identify the topic sentence of paragraph 1, or the sentence that best expresses the main idea of that paragraph.

   (a.) I see the life that I could have had in the faces of my Iranian relatives.

   b. They are like ghosts of the life that my parents left behind when they moved to "Amrika."

   c. Their lives are not reality to me—I was born in the U.S., and it is the only reality I know.

   d. I smile politely or even laugh along.

3. What is the topic of paragraph 2?

   a. the author

   (b.) the author's cousin Nina

   c. Nina's family

   d. Iran

4. Which of the following sentences from paragraph 5 best expresses the main idea of that paragraph?

   a. She says this to me as she sharply turns her back.

   b. I can tell that she is not happy spending the afternoon with me.

   c. All of a sudden, I feel like I am not good enough for her.

   (d.) I want her to be more like me—is there something wrong with that?

5. The main ideas of paragraphs 3–5 taken together are best expressed by which of the following?

   a. Nina and the author are cousins.

   b. Nina is jealous of Ali.

   (c.) The author and Nina are different culturally, despite being the same age and related.

   d. Ali doesn't really care about anything.

I am afraid to ask Nina any more questions. We are both staring out into the distance in silence, swinging back and forth, side-by-side, listening to the sound of the other children having fun. Nina kicks her feet off the wood-chipped ground to swing faster and higher. Just then, her scarf begins to fall back, revealing her hair. She instinctively tucks her hair back and readjusts her scarf within seconds. "That was close," I think to myself. "Someone almost could have seen her hair!"

6

The sun is now going down, and it is time to go home for dinner. The walk home is silent as the tension between me and Nina builds. "Why must she be so cruel?" I think to myself. "What was preventing us from being friends?" I could not think of the answer.

7

My mom is preparing a traditional Iranian meal in honor of our guests. All day she has been in the kitchen with the other women in the family preparing chicken, fish, rice with saffron, and chopping up vegetables, nuts, and feta cheese. Nina, Ali, and I walk into a

8

house filled with the aroma of tea rose, saffron, and spices. Immediately, Nina rushes over to her mother's arms and begins whispering something in her ear. I am positive it is about me.

I feel the urge to walk over and defend myself. But my Aunt doesn't understand English well, and I might cause more humiliation if I attempt to speak in Persian. Instead, I squint my eyes and purse my lips, snarling at her when she looks my way. From the sour look on Nina's face, I can tell she got the message.   9

"Mona-joon," my mom calls out my name. "Joon" is Persian for dear, or sweetheart. My mom usually calls me Mona-joon when she wants me to do some chore around the house. I guess it's her way of coaxing me into helping—it almost always works.   10

6. Which word or phrase best expresses the topic of paragraph 7?

   (a.) the tension between the author and Nina

   b. dusk

   c. the walk home

   d. cousins

7. What is the topic of paragraph 8?

   a. Nina's chador

   b. Nina's scarf

   (c.) Nina's betrayal of her cousin

   d. the author's mother

8. Which of the following sentences from paragraph 9 best expresses the main idea of that paragraph?

   (a.) I feel the urge to walk over and defend myself.

   b. But my Aunt doesn't understand English well, and I might cause more humiliation if I attempt to speak in Persian.

   c. Instead, I squint my eyes and purse my lips, snarling at her when she looks my way.

   d. From the sour look on Nina's face, I can tell she got the message.

9. Taken together, what is the main idea of paragraphs 7–9?

   a. The author is angry.

   b. Nina is angry and a tattletale.

(c.) The cultural differences between the author and Nina have led to misunderstandings.

d. The author cannot speak Persian.

10. What is the main idea of paragraph 10?

a. The author's mother is a great cook.

(b.) The author's mother uses "Joon" as an endearment and also as a way to get the author to do certain things.

c. The author's mother speaks Persian.

d. The author knows more Persian than she thinks.

She wants me to pass out tea with sugar cubes, hard honeyed candies, and golden raisins to the guests. This is a traditional chore for a young Iranian girl. The most important task is to smile and make direct eye contact with each person you serve. I serve my grandfather first, because it is customary in Iran to respect the elders. Everyone's eyes are on me as I gracefully walk around the living room with my silver tray in hand. They all smile at me, including Nina's mom and dad, saying things like "Azizam," which means "precious one." My tray is empty when I walk back into the kitchen. 11

"Thank you, Mona-joon, you did a wonderful job. I am proud of you," my mom says with a warming smile on her face. I feel a sense of pride and happiness that only my mother can give me. Her affection extinguishes the fire that has built up inside of me since the park. 12

"Mom, am I Iranian or American?" I look up at her confused — not knowing whether I would rather be one or the other. 13

"You are the best of both, azizam." As she says this, she bends down so that we are face-to-face. "You have to look at yourself in order to find out who you are — it's not where you are from that defines you." She kisses my cheek and then hurries back to the dishes. I'm not satisfied with her answer. I would be asking myself that same question for the rest of my life. 14

But then, in the middle of the chaotic kitchen, busy with women putting the finishing touches on the Iranian feast, I hold up the silver tray to look at my own reflection. "I don't have to decide," I say to myself. I place the tray down on the counter top and walk away quietly with a smile on my face. 15

11. Of the following words and phrases, what is the topic of paragraph 11?

    a. the Iranian feast

    b. the author's grandfather

    (c.) the author's serving of the guests

    d. Nina and the author

12. Which of the following words or phrases best expresses the topic of paragraph 12?

    (a.) the affection of the author's mother

    b. Mona-joon

    c. the author's mother's smile

    d. Iranians

13. Identify the topic sentence of paragraph 14.

    a. "You are the best of both, azizam."

    b. As she says this, she bends down so that we are face-to-face.

    (c.) "You have to look at yourself in order to find out who you are — it's not where you are from that defines you."

    d. I'm not satisfied with her answer.

14. What is the implied main idea of paragraph 15?

    (a.) The author is content to be who she is.

    b. The author makes up with Nina.

    c. The author decides to be more Iranian than American.

    d. The author decides to be more American than Iranian.

15. Taken as a whole, what would you say is the topic of this entire selection by Mona Maisami?

    a. the author

    (b.) cultural identity

    c. Iranians versus Americans

    d. relationships

Reading the Whole

Now that you've had a chance to read Mona Maisami's "Born in Amrika" in its parts and paid close attention to the topic sentences and main ideas of the paragraphs, you should be ready to reread it. As you read, your understanding of the paragraphs should help you better appreciate Maisami's experience with her cousin and perhaps to understand the implications of her conclusion.

MONA MAISAMI
Born in Amrika

I see the life that I could have had in the faces of my Iranian relatives. They are like ghosts of the life that my parents left behind when they moved to "Amrika," haunting us with a vision of what our lives could have been. Their lives are not reality to me—I was born in the U.S., and it is the only reality I know. My overseas relatives say that I don't even look Iranian anymore, as though it has faded out of me like the color from a pair of old jeans. I have even heard them compare my accent to that of an illiterate peasant's daughter—they say I am "de-hauty." I hear them innocently laughing at me when I say, "Salaam," hello or "Quelly-mam-noon," thank you. I smile politely or even laugh along: But in my heart, it makes me feel incomplete, as though a part of me is missing.   1

My cousin Nina is an "F.O.B.," which means fresh off the boat. Her family has only been in the U.S. for three months now, and she still wears a chador and scarf. She and her family are guests in our house today, and I am in charge of entertaining her. Nina is my age, so I feel comfortable around her and think that we may have some things in common. She may be the link that can help me relate to my heritage. I am anxious to be alone with her so that she can teach me how to be more Iranian.   2

I take her to a park that is within walking distance from my house. Nina's younger brother, Ali, comes along with us, too. It is a hot, sticky, humid August afternoon. I am wearing a tank top and the jean shorts that my mom bought me to wear for our dinner party. Nina has on her traditional Islamic clothing—everything is covered except for her hands and her face. Looking at her, I begin to wonder what my friends will think if they see my cousin and me at the park. Ali, on the other hand, is wearing khaki shorts and a black Adidas t-shirt. He will be able to blend right in with the other   3 kids at the park. Nina and I walk over to two swings that are next to each other. Ali heads over to the basketball courts where a group of boys are playing "H-O-R-S-E."

She appears to be shy to me, so I decide to initiate the conversation. "Don't you ever get hot wearing a scarf and robe? I'm hot right now in what I am wearing. If I were you, I'd be jealous that Ali gets to wear shorts and a t-shirt." I look over at Nina expecting her to give the obvious response, that she is in fact jealous of Ali.   4

"It's not a robe, it's called a chador. You should get your facts straight if you are going to make fun of other people's lives." She says this to me as she sharply turns her back. I can tell that she is not happy spending the afternoon with me. All of a sudden, I feel like I am not good enough for her. Her scarf is made of silk and is light pink with tiny green and purple flowers on it. The colors are pretty to me, but something inside of me screams that it is morally wrong for her to have to cover her beautiful thick brown hair. I want to tear the scarf off her head and set her free. I want her to be more like me—is there something wrong with that?   5

I am afraid to ask Nina any more questions. We are both staring out into the distance in silence, swinging back and forth, side-by-side, listening to the sound of the other children having fun. Nina kicks her feet off the wood-chipped ground to swing faster and higher. Just then, her scarf begins to fall back, revealing her hair. She instinctively tucks her hair back and readjusts her scarf within seconds. "That was close," I think to myself. "Someone almost could have seen her hair!"   6

The sun is now going down, and it is time to go home for dinner. The walk home is silent as the tension between me and Nina builds. "Why must she be so cruel?" I think to myself. "What was preventing us from being friends?" I could not think of the answer.   7

My mom is preparing a traditional Iranian meal in honor of our guests. All day she has been in the kitchen with the other women in the family preparing chicken, fish, rice with saffron, and chopping up vegetables, nuts, and feta cheese. Nina, Ali, and I walk into a house filled with the aroma of tea rose, saffron, and spices. Immediately, Nina rushes over to her mother's arms and begins whispering something in her ear. I am positive it is about me.   8

I feel the urge to walk over and defend myself. But my Aunt doesn't understand English well, and I might cause more humiliation if I attempt to speak in Persian. Instead, I squint my eyes and purse my lips, snarling at her when she looks my way. From the sour look on Nina's face, I can tell she got the message.   9

"Mona-joon," my mom calls out my name. "Joon" is Persian for   10
dear, or sweetheart. My mom usually calls me Mona-joon when she
wants me to do some chore around the house. I guess it's her way of
coaxing me into helping—it almost always works.

She wants me to pass out tea with sugar cubes, hard honeyed   11
candies, and golden raisins to the guests. This is a traditional chore
for a young Iranian girl. The most important task is to smile and
make direct eye contact with each person you serve. I serve my
grandfather first, because it is customary in Iran to respect the elders. Everyone's eyes are on me as I gracefully walk around the living
room with my silver tray in hand. They all smile at me, including
Nina's mom and dad, saying things like "Azizam," which means
"precious one." My tray is empty when I walk back into the
kitchen.

"Thank you, Mona-joon, you did a wonderful job. I am proud   12
of you," my mom says with a warming smile on her face. I feel a
sense of pride and happiness that only my mother can give me. Her
affection extinguishes the fire that has built up inside of me since
the park.

"Mom, am I Iranian or American?" I look up at her confused—   13
not knowing whether I would rather be one or the other.

"You are the best of both, azizam." As she says this, she bends   14
down so that we are face-to-face. "You have to look at yourself in
order to find out who you are—it's not where you are from that
defines you." She kisses my cheek and then hurries back to the
dishes. I'm not satisfied with her answer. I would be asking myself
that same question for the rest of my life.

But then, in the middle of the chaotic kitchen, busy with women   15
putting the finishing touches on the Iranian feast, I hold up the silver tray to look at my own reflection. "I don't have to decide," I say
to myself. I place the tray down on the counter top and walk away
quietly with a smile on my face.

Integrated Skills

1. Why do you think the author spells *America* the way she does?
   Is this an effective tactic? Why or why not?

2. What conflict does Maisami describe in the opening paragraph?
   How does her use of comparison emphasize and clarify this
   conflict?

3. What are the writer's expectations about her cousin Nina? Are her expectations met? Why or why not?

4. What can you infer about Maisami's feelings about her cousin's behavior? What can you infer about the author's sense of identity?

5. Why isn't Maisami satisfied with her mother's answer to her question in paragraph 14?

6. Why does Maisami smile after seeing her reflection in the silver serving tray? What do you think she is saying to her readers?

Reading/Writing Connection

One thing that comes through in Mona Maisami's "Born in Amrika" is a concern for her identity as an immigrant living in the United States. Write a paragraph about what you think it is like to be an immigrant—to forge or establish your identity—in a foreign country. You can base your paragraph on actual experience or on imagined experience. Or you can respond to what is said in "Born in Amrika."

Reading Textbooks

Thematic Connections. In "Born in Amrika" Mona Maisami relates a story about a cultural misunderstanding she had with her cousin and the tension and discomfort it caused them both. In the following excerpt from the textbook *Competent Communication* by Dan O'Hair, Gustav W. Friedrich, John M. Wiemann, and Mary Wiemann, the authors explain how cultural backgrounds and the context of an interaction can lead to miscommunication. As you read the selection, consider it in relation to Mona and her cousin. Would it help them to understand what happened between them?

Since this is a textbook reading selection, you can expect to find key terms defined and important differences explained. Be alert for definitions and explanations of key ideas.

Vocabulary Preview

context (para. 1): setting or environment (n.)

phenomena (para. 1): things that can be observed, such as facts, events, and trends (n.)

distinguish (para. 1): differentiate (v.)

consistent (para. 3): roughly the same as (adj.)

mutually (para. 3): together, affecting each other (adj.)

generic (para. 5): categorized into general groups (adj.)

bestowed (para. 6): given (v.)

Cultural and Relational Contexts

The context in which you communicate is important. As mentioned earlier, the context helps determine which messages are seen as appropriate and effective. Your social environment is the context of both your communication and your relationships. It is composed primarily of the people with whom you associate but includes non-human aspects, such as where you live and work, your house furnishings, your pets, and the like. In your social environment, you create meanings for people, objects, and other phenomena — meanings that distinguish these things from mere physical or biological description. 1

Two types of context are especially important in communication: the **cultural context** and the **relational context**. 2

We discover much of the richness of our social environment as we are growing up. Culture carries these rich meanings; to be socialized into one's culture is to learn how to interpret the social 3 environment in a way that is consistent with other people in the culture. For example, Juan learns to show respect for his elders by not questioning their authority; his friends are raised that way, and their behaviors mutually reinforce respect and unquestioned control from adults. In Juan's culture, another sign of respect for older generations is that objects that have been in the family for years are passed down from generation to generation. Lana, by contrast, is raised in a social environment that encourages her to talk to and question her elders. Her friends, raised in similar fashion, mutually reinforce a different type of respect for elders, which includes frequently questioning the exercise of control. Lana treasures few old objects; her culture throws out the old and buys new things. Both Juan and Lana view their own behaviors as natural, but if each were to look at the other's behavior, it would seem very "different" and perhaps even odd or unnatural—and probably not respectful at all.

Culture allows us to take for granted the meanings of objects and relationships in our environment, which is both a blessing and a curse. On the positive side, the world is more predictable and more understandable than it otherwise would be. We generally *know* what to do and how to act because we learn what is "right" from our parents and peers. On the negative side, the communication difficulties and blind spots of those who socialize us are often reinvented in us. We may lose sight of the complexity of communication because it seems so natural—*it is so natural.* . . . 4

The **relational context** also has pervasive influence. It allows us to talk about generic types of relationships (between parent and child, boyfriend and girlfriend, lovers, roommates, best friends, spouses, employer and employee, work-group members, professor and class) and to generalize about communication across these types. Every aspect of our communication is evaluated in terms of the relationship we have with the person(s) with whom we are interacting. 5

Our messages are given meaning by our relationships. A kiss, for example, has a different meaning when bestowed on your mother than it does when shared with your lover. In one relational context, saying "Let's be friends" (e.g., when said to a new acquaintance) is an invitation to explore relational possibilities. The same phrase, when said to someone whom you've been dating for the last year, can have an entirely different meaning (as in "Let's *just* be friends," which some say is the coldest sentence in the English language!). 6

Thinking about the Textbook Selection

1. Why is the social environment important for effective communication? How does context influence how people communicate with others in their own culture?

2. Why do the authors include the examples of Juan and Lana? What does each example illustrate? To what extent does the reference to Juan and Lana help you understand the idea of cultural context?

3. What do you think about the authors' observation that culture can be both a blessing and a curse with respect to our environment?

4. How important is relational context for communication? Can you think of an example of a relationship that either helps or hinders our ability to communicate?

5. What point do the authors illustrate with their example of the statement "Let's *just* be friends"?

6. How is the main idea of this selection related to the idea of Mona Maisami's "Born in Amrika"?

Reading the Web

In 1998, PBS aired *Beyond the Veil,* a documentary that PBS described as examining "many of the profound cultural and political differences between Iran and America through a televised dialogue between two teachers," both of them women. As it does for many of its programs, PBS produced a comprehensive Web site to give viewers background, additional information, and an opportunity to learn more about the subject. The following page, from the PBS overview of the history of women in Iran, explains why some Iranian women wear veils (like the chador worn by Mona Maisami's cousin) and why others do not.

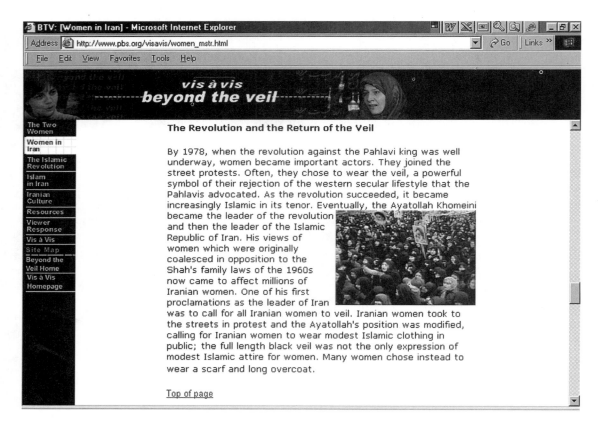

Thinking about the Web Page

1. What is the topic sentence of this Web page paragraph?

2. What is the main idea of this Web page?

3. Why do some Iranian women wear a veil? What does the veil represent?

Reviewing

Recall /
Remember

1. What is a topic sentence? What is another name for topic sentences?
2. Where can topic sentences or main idea statements be found in paragraphs?
3. How can you check for the topic sentence or main idea statement of a paragraph when you are not sure which it is?
4. Why is it useful to be able to identify the main idea of a paragraph or a longer passage?
5. What are implied ideas and how can you recognize them?

Chapter
Summary

In this chapter you have worked toward understanding the main idea of a reading selection. You have seen how details illustrate and support the main ideas of paragraphs and reading selections overall. You have practiced identifying the topic sentences and main ideas of paragraphs and of whole selections. You have learned how to infer the idea of a paragraph and passage when the main idea is implied rather than stated directly. And you have seen how writing summaries can help you better understand what you read.

In the following chapter you will look closely at supporting details—the evidence and examples that help a writer back up the main idea of a reading. You'll learn more about how these details can help you discover what the main idea of a selection is, and you'll get some practice distinguishing major supporting details from minor ones.

Recognizing Supporting Details

Getting Ready

You probably noticed in your work with main ideas that writers back up their points with evidence, examples, illustrations, specific instances, and other kinds of information to clarify or explain their point of view. Readers come to understand and, sometimes, to be convinced of writers' main ideas through their use of these **supporting details.**

Supporting details usually form the bulk of a piece of writing. Readers expect proof, and good writers provide it. A well-told story can help a writer make an argument without being repetitive. A complex idea can be clarified with an illustration such as a chart or graph. Examples and specific instances add interest and evidence to a statement of fact. In this chapter you will learn about different kinds of supporting details. Not all of them are equally important to a writer's main idea, so you will also learn to distinguish between **major supporting details** and **minor supporting details.** Finally, you will learn how supporting details convey the main idea of a piece of writing when that idea is implied rather than stated directly.

Chapter Overview

Focusing Questions

As you read a writer's main idea or see a point of view expressed, what do you expect next? Why?

Can you remember ever reading something that didn't have details to back up its claims? How did you respond to the reading? Would you have responded differently if the writer had included examples, illustrations, or other kinds of evidence? Why or why not?

Are all of the details a writer uses to support an idea of equal importance? Why or why not?

How can you determine a writer's main idea if it is not directly stated in a topic sentence?

Everyday Reading

The college registration process is an example of a situation in which you have already become good at noticing details and determining how important they are. Many aspects of registering for courses require you to pay attention to details. You fill out forms. You study course schedules and timetables. You identify teachers assigned to different class sections. If you were to try to attend to every single detail, you would become overwhelmed. So you focus on what's important to you and glance over the rest. Think back to when you registered for the classes you're in now. Make a list of the many kinds of details you sorted through in the registration process, and think about how you can apply your existing skill in noticing details to your reading.

Learning the Skills

■ Understanding Supporting Details

Writers support their topic sentences with examples, illustrations, reasons, statistics—that is, with specific details to convince readers of the validity of their main idea. Consider, for example, this topic sentence from a paragraph in *A History of the Arab Peoples*, by Albert Hourani: "The most obscure part of the life of Muhammad, as the biographers narrate it, is the early one." What kind of support would you expect to follow that statement? You would probably expect some details, some facts, about what is known (and not known) about Muhammad's early life. You would expect that the paragraph would begin chronicling Muhammad's life, starting from those early years. And Hourani's paragraph does exactly that.

IDENTIFYING MAJOR SUPPORTING DETAILS

All the supporting details we have discussed so far are **major supporting details.** Major supporting details support the topic sentence *directly.* They are essential for backing up an author's main idea. They give basic information, reasons, or evidence to convince readers of the truth or validity of the author's opinion or point. You can often identify major supporting details because the sentences that contain them refer directly to the topic sentence. These sentences will often repeat key words from the topic sentence or use synonyms—words with the same meaning—for those key words. Usually the sentences that contain major supporting details will expand on the concepts presented in the topic sentence, providing more information about them.

Look at the following paragraph, adapted from the textbook *Exploring the World of Business* by Kenneth Blanchard et al.:

(1) Advertising can be classified in a number of ways. (2) **Product advertising** creates awareness of and provides information about a type of product or a specific brand. (3) "It's AT&T's True Voice" and "Just for the Taste of It, Diet Coke" are examples. (4) In **comparative advertising,** a sponsoring company openly names its competitors and undercuts their products: "Bring Your Visa Card. Because They Don't Take American Express." (5) Some companies use **institutional advertising,** which develops and maintains a favorable image for a particular company. (6) In so doing, institutional advertising can promote the entire product line of an organization, as in Sears, Roebuck's "Come See the Softer Side of Sears" and IBM's "Solutions for a Small Planet." (7) **Professional advertising** touts the benefits offered by lawyers, doctors, consultants, therapists, and other services. (8) In the health care industry, for instance, one provider advertises "Choice Care. We Make More People Feel Better." (9) "It's Time to Make Smoking History" is an example of **advocacy advertising,** in which a particular point of view on an issue is promoted. (10) No matter what type of advertising is used, the business must manage the process of creating and executing the advertisement.

The topic sentence in this passage is the first sentence. It states the main idea of the paragraph: "Advertising can be classified in a number of ways." The major supporting details give specific examples that identify what some of those ways of classification are: product advertising (sentence 2), comparative advertising (sentence 4), institutional advertising (sentence 5), professional advertising (sentence 7), and advocacy advertising (sentence 9).

Exercise 4-1

Double underline the topic sentence and then underline the major supporting details in the following paragraphs.

Example:

Documents are written records of all sorts. They typically are divided into primary and secondary sources. <u>Primary sources are documents that have been written by a participant in the event, activity, or process described or analyzed.</u> For example, an account of the assassination of Abraham Lincoln by a witness in Ford's Theater the evening of the killing would be a primary source, as would be the diary of John Wilkes Booth, the assassin. Clearly, any primary source might include biased reporting and even untruths, but it remains a primary source because it was written by participants or direct observers. Census reports, memoirs of an officer in the U.S. Civil War, and bills of lading for ships are all primary sources. (Lanny B. Fields, Russell J. Barber, and Cheryl A. Riggs, *The Global Past*)

1. There are many reasons why people begin smoking. Some young (and some not so young) people are ignorant of the dangers of smoking. Some young people smoke because their peers smoke and they believe that smoking helps them "fit in" or is "cool" or sophisticated. Others smoke because they find it pleasurable. (Jeffrey S. Nevid, Spencer A. Rathus, and Hannah R. Rubenstein, *Health in the New Millennium*)

2. The amazing evolution of computers over the last twenty years has allowed for an equally amazing evolution in music. Today electronic music can be produced on a home computer, using sequencer software to record, edit, and reproduce digital sounds in patterns and sequences

at will. Advanced synthesizers now produce their stuff in real time (as the simpler synthesizers of popular music have been doing for years). They can interact via computer with live musicians as they perform, to produce today's cutting-edge interactive computer music. (Joseph Kerman and Gary Tomlinson, with Vivian Kerman, *Listen*)

3. There are four main modes of transporting food to one's mouth. The oldest and most widespread is the use of the hands. All peoples use the hands to some extent, but Indian, Arab, and most African traditions employ this primary mode of eating. Second, some people modify hand eating by adding an edible sheet, pieces of which are torn off and used to envelop loose food. Examples are in Ethiopia, where a supple bread called *injera* is used, and Mexico, where corn tortillas serve the same purpose. Third, some peoples use chopsticks, slender rods serving as extensions of the fingers to grasp chunks of food; their traditional use is in East Asia. Finally, the knife-fork-spoon toolkit of Europe can be used to cut, spear, and scoop food. The spoon has been used by most societies, although sometimes only as a serving implement. (Lanny B. Fields, Russell J. Barber, and Cheryl A. Riggs, *The Global Past*)

4. Economists recognize that every decision involves trade-offs. If you buy a cup of coffee for 70 cents, you are giving up other things that you could have bought with the money. Because your income is limited, whenever you choose to consume one thing, you are giving up other things. If you choose to consume coffee, you may be giving up donuts. . . . (Kenneth Blanchard et al., *Exploring the World of Business*)

5. A **conditioned reinforcer,** also called a *secondary reinforcer,* is one that has acquired reinforcing value by being associated with a primary reinforcer. The classic example of a conditioned reinforcer is money. Money is reinforcing not because those flimsy bits of paper and little pieces of metal have value in and of themselves, but because we've learned that we can use them to acquire primary reinforcers and other conditioned reinforcers. Awards, frequent flyer points, and college degrees are just a few other examples of conditioned reinforcers. (Don H. Hockenbury and Sandra E. Hockenbury, *Psychology*)

IDENTIFYING MINOR SUPPORTING DETAILS

All the details in a paragraph are not equally important. **Minor supporting details** add extra information to major supporting details. The minor supporting details may add interest to the writing, but they are not essential for understanding the author's main idea. They are less important than the major supporting details.

Minor supporting details explain, clarify, give examples, and support major supporting details. You can often identify minor supporting details because the sentences that contain them refer to the sentences containing major supporting details. Minor supporting details are often introduced with phrases like *for example* or *that is* that tell you an example or a clarification is coming up. Look again at the paragraph about advertising on page 111; each minor supporting detail gives a specific example to support the major supporting detail.

MAJOR SUPPORTING DETAIL

Product advertising creates awareness of and provides information about a type of product or a specific brand.

▶ MINOR SUPPORTING DETAIL

"It's AT&T's True Voice" and "Just for the Taste of It, Diet Coke" are examples.

MAJOR SUPPORTING DETAIL

In comparative advertising, a sponsoring company openly names its competitors and undercuts their products.

▶ MINOR SUPPORTING DETAIL

"Bring Your Visa Card. Because They Don't Take American Express."

MAJOR SUPPORTING DETAIL

Some companies use institutional advertising, which develops and maintains a favorable image for a particular company.

▶ MINOR SUPPORTING DETAIL

In so doing, institutional advertising can promote the entire product line of an organization, as in Sears, Roebuck's "Come See the Softer Side of Sears" and IBM's "Solutions for a Small Planet."

MAJOR SUPPORTING DETAIL

Professional advertising touts the benefits offered by lawyers, doctors, consultants, therapists, and other services.

▶ MINOR SUPPORTING DETAIL

In the health care industry, for example, one provider advertises "Choice Care. We Make More People Feel Better."

Sentence 9 puts both the major and minor details together in one sentence, with the minor detail followed by the major detail it supports.

MAJOR SUPPORTING DETAIL

. . . advocacy advertising, in which a particular point of view on an issue is promoted.

▶ MINOR SUPPORTING DETAIL

"It's Time to Make Smoking History" is an example of . . .

The following paragraph on Latin American music was adapted from the January/February 2002 issue of *Arrive*, the magazine for riders of Amtrak's Acela Express train. It also uses both major and minor supporting details.

Latin American music has had a powerful influence on popular music around the world. Latin rhythms, especially those from Brazil, have been popular among African musicians. They have also been discovered among some elements of Middle Eastern music. In fact, Latin rhythms have had an influence on the music used for Middle Eastern belly dancing. And in the United States, a number of forms of popular music have been much affected by Latin rhythms. American rock and roll of the last few decades, for example, shows significant rhythmic influences of Cuban music.

The first sentence is the topic sentence. The next two sentences use examples (African and Middle Eastern music) that provide major supporting details to support the claim. The fourth sentence provides a minor supporting detail whose example (about Middle Eastern belly dancing) illustrates the major supporting detail that came before it (Latin rhythms in Middle Eastern music). The last sentence, too, is a minor supporting detail that provides an example (rock and roll) for a major supporting detail (American popular music with Latin rhythms).

Exercise 4-2

You have already identified the *major* supporting details in some of the following paragraphs. Now underline every *minor* supporting detail.

Example:

> Economists recognize that every decision involves trade-offs. If you buy a cup of coffee for 70 cents, you are giving up other things that you could have bought with the money. Because your income is limited, whenever you choose to consume one thing, you are giving up other things. If you choose to consume coffee, you may be giving up donuts. . . . (Kenneth Blanchard et al., *Exploring the World of Business*)

1. Like all other mammalian hearts, the human heart has four chambers: two atria and two ventricles. The atrium and ventricle on the right side of your body are called the right atrium and right ventricle. They can be thought of as the right heart. The atrium and ventricle on the left side of your body are called the left atrium and left ventricle. They can be thought of as the left heart. (William K. Purves et al., *Life: The Science of Biology*)

2. A **conditioned reinforcer**, also called a *secondary reinforcer,* is one that has acquired reinforcing value by being associated with a primary reinforcer. The classic example of a conditioned reinforcer is money. Money is reinforcing not because those flimsy bits of paper and little pieces of metal have value in and of themselves, but because we've learned that we can use them to acquire primary reinforcers and other conditioned reinforcers. Awards, frequent flyer points, and college degrees are just a few other examples of conditioned reinforcers. (Don H. Hockenbury and Sandra E. Hockenbury, *Psychology*)

3. There are four main modes of transporting food to one's mouth. The oldest and most widespread is the use of the hands. All peoples use the hands to some extent, but Indian, Arab, and most African traditions employ this primary mode of eating. Second, some people modify hand eating by adding an edible sheet, pieces of which are torn off and used to envelop loose food. Examples are in Ethiopia, where a supple bread called *injera* is used, and Mexico, where corn tortillas serve the same purpose. Third, some peoples use chopsticks, slender rods serving as extensions of the fingers to grasp chunks of food; their traditional use is in East Asia. Finally, the knife-fork-spoon toolkit of Europe can be used to cut, spear, and scoop food. The spoon has been used by most societies, although sometimes only as a serving implement. (Lanny B. Fields, Russell J. Barber, and Cheryl A. Riggs, *The Global Past*)

4. The amazing evolution of computers over the last twenty years has allowed for an equally amazing evolution in music. Today electronic music can be produced on a home computer, using sequencer software to record, edit, and reproduce digital sounds in patterns and sequences at will. Advanced synthesizers now produce their stuff in real time (as the simpler synthesizers of popular music have been doing for years). They can interact via computer with live musicians as they perform, to produce today's cutting-edge interactive computer music. (Joseph Kerman and Gary Tomlinson, with Vivian Kerman, *Listen*)

5. **Drug misuse** is the use of a drug for the wrong reason, in the wrong way, or by the wrong person. Using sleeping pills or tranquilizers prescribed for a friend is an example of drug misuse. The drugs might be harmful for you. Popping an antibiotic for a cough without consulting the doctor is also misuse. Antibiotics combat bacteria, but the drug would be useless against a cough caused by a virus. A prescription cough syrup containing the opiate drug codeine would be misused if you used it to get high rather than to relieve a cough or if you took higher than recommended doses. (Jeffrey S. Nevid, Spencer A. Rathus, and Hannah R. Rubenstein, *Health in the New Millennium*)

■ Connecting Supporting Details to Identify Unstated Main Ideas

As you saw in Chapter 3, the main idea of a paragraph or a longer passage is sometimes unstated. In such instances the main idea is implied—it is not expressed directly but is expressed indirectly through a group of details that together suggest the writer's point.

Consider the following paragraph, which has an unstated main idea:

> Writers use words to create imaginative worlds, to convey feelings and emotions, and to explain ideas and perspectives. Politicians use words to persuade people to believe in them and vote for them. Religious ministers use words to explain the ideas and values of their religions and to encourage people to follow religious ideals. Lawyers use words to convince judges and juries to convict or acquit their clients of the charges made against them.

In this paragraph, the main idea is not stated directly in a topic sentence. Nonetheless, you can infer, or figure out, the main idea from the supporting details that are included. The unstated main idea is "Words are very important in the work of many different professions." How do you reach that conclusion? Look carefully at what is repeated in the paragraph's details. As you can see, *words* appears in each sentence: "Writers use words. . . . Politicians use words. . . . Religious ministers use words. . . . Lawyers use words." Think carefully about how these examples are related to one another. You see that each one has something in common with the others—they all explain how words are critical, or very important, in the work of each profession (and of other unnamed professions as well). That line of thinking leads you to conclude that the main idea of the paragraph is "Words are very important in the work of many different professions."

Exercise 4-3

Identify the unstated main idea of each paragraph of this selection, adapted from *Media and Culture* by Richard Campbell.

Example:

Since Thomas Paine declared government "a necessary evil," in the 1700s, Americans have had a healthy skepticism about government-funded projects. However, National Public Radio (NPR), which has been supported since 1970 by the federal government and individual donations, usually is praised for fulfilling radio's promise as a mass medium.

a. __✔__ The success of National Public Radio is a surprise.

b. _____ The success of National Public Radio is not a surprise.

1. In 1978, NPR aired the first live coverage of a Senate debate (on the Panama Canal treaties). In 1991, NPR's Nina Totenberg was the first broadcaster to report Anita Hill's sexual harassment charges against future Supreme Court Justice Clarence Thomas. NPR's many interview and news feature series are considered unrivaled in broadcast news.

a. __✔__ NPR has done better than commercial radio in some of its reporting.

b. _____ Nina Totenberg was NPR's first broadcaster.

2. So why is it that in every decade since NPR's creation, politicians have threatened to cut off its support? One reason is a perceived liberal bias. Most critics, however, regard NPR as much more even-handed than the commercial news networks. NPR's own audience studies indicate that slightly more than one-third of its listeners are conservatives, just under one-third are liberals, and the other third are moderates.

a. _____ Conservatives enjoy liberal news reporting.

b. __✔__ Politicians perceive NPR as too liberal.

3. To understand NPR's shaky status requires backtracking through radio history. By the late 1920s, corporate interests had pulled the control of radio away from the noncommercial sector: farmers, labor unions, educators, religious leaders, and other citizen groups that operated radio stations. Even prior to that time, the government had been granting favors to commercial radio, including making rules to control amateur operators and interfering with their radio signals. Radio lobbyists representing commercial interests claimed that the issues of education, religion, and labor (often represented today on NPR) were propaganda serving special interests. They also claimed that the profit motives of the networks represented the real public interest.

a. _____ Radio should be controlled by citizen groups.

b. __✔__ Negative attitudes toward NPR are partly a result of the history of radio broadcasting.

4. Based on this "logic," the newly created Federal Radio Commission (FRC) forced many nonprofit stations off the air during evening hours, turning their frequencies over to commercial stations. This limited a nonprofit station's air time and lessened its audience reach (since most radio listening occurred after dinner). Many nonprofit stations also had their daytime power severely curtailed. A signal that once traveled thousands of miles now went only a few miles.

a. _____ A new government agency was needed to control radio; thus the Federal Radio Commission was born.

b. __✔__ Those in power (the Federal Radio Commission) sided with commercial interests.

5. Slowly, commercial stations began buying up the nonprofits, which struggled to meet expenses during the Depression. During the last major battle over radio reform, 25 percent of all broadcast frequencies were going to be set aside for a wide range of nonprofit groups. The arguments of commercial lobbyists defeated the measure, however. By describing capitalism (an economic system) as a synonym for democracy (a political system), corporate interests prevailed.

a. __✔__ Politics was responsible for the success of commercial broadcasting.

b. _____ During the Depression, nonprofit radio stations suffered more severely than commercial radio stations.

. . . .

Applying the Skills

Reading the Parts

This essay by Wendy Kaminer appeared in the December 1999 issue of *The American Prospect,* a liberal "magazine of public ideas, firmly committed—however unfashionably—to a belief in public improvement." A lawyer, an editor, a much-published author, and a frequent National Public Radio commentator, Kaminer uses a number of alarming examples to argue her point about recent "zero-tolerance" policies in American schools. As you read, pay close attention to the major and minor supporting details and how, exactly, they support each paragraph's main idea and Kaminer's argument overall. After reading each section and the questions that follow, move on to the next section. You will have a chance to read the entire essay when you finish.

WENDY KAMINER
The War on High Schools

1 High school gave me my first lessons in bureaucracy: Rules were meant to be rigidly applied, not questioned; power was meant to be abused by petty functionaries. I don't mean to malign the entire faculty of my school. It included some very good teachers who encouraged curiosity and provocation and never lost their sense of humor. Because of them, high school also offered opportunities for self-expression and contained rebellion.

2 I regularly got into trouble for insubordination, but I was never suspended, much less expelled. It was the mid-1960s, a time of protest, not zero tolerance, and there was no clear rule that prohibited challenging or even insulting teachers and administrators. So the authorities simply reported me to my parents. My beleaguered mother came to expect their phone calls and made frequent visits to school, trying to placate whomever I'd offended. "You have such a nice mother," one of my teachers once said to me with wonder.

3 I doubt that my mother or any of my teachers could protect a kid from the wrath of school bureaucrats today. Fearful of violence and drugs, intolerant of dissent or simple nonconformity, public school officials are on the rampage. They're suspending and expelling even grade school students for making what might be considered, at

worst, inappropriate remarks, dressing oddly, or simply expressing political opinions. Efforts to strip students of rights are hardly new, but they have been greatly accelerated in recent months by hysteria about school violence and "terroristic threats." America's public schools are becoming increasingly Kafkaesque.°

Across the country, the American Civil Liberties Union has received hundreds of complaints about cases like this: In Ohio a third-grader was suspended after writing a fortune cookie message, "You will die an honorable death," which he submitted for a school project. (A terroristic threat? Or an innocent, well-intentioned remark by a child who watches martial-arts videos?) Eleven high school students in Ohio were suspended for contributing to a gothic-themed Web site. In Virginia a 10th-grader was suspended for dyeing his hair blue. In Missouri, high school junior Dustin Mitchell was suspended and required to perform 42 days of community service with the local police department for offering a flippant opinion on school violence in an Internet chat room (when asked if a tragedy like the Littleton shootings could happen in his school, Mitchell responded "yes"). In Louisiana a 12-year-old boy was suspended and held in juvenile detention for over two weeks after uttering a "threat" in a lunch line: "If you take all the potatoes, I'm gonna get you," the accused terrorist said.

4

Those students who dare to use their speech rights to protest such draconian° restrictions on speech are liable to be punished severely. In Texas, 17-year-old high school student Jennifer Boccia was suspended for wearing a black armband to school to protest restraints on free speech that followed the shootings in Littleton. Boccia was also reprimanded by her school principal, Ira Sparks, for daring to tell her story to the media; she was told that if she wanted to clear her record, she should refrain from speaking to the media before discussing her remarks with school officials.

5

Boccia made a federal case of it and won a settlement from her school vindicating her First Amendment rights. Sometimes schools back down when threatened with lawsuits, and many students willing to challenge their suspensions should ultimately prevail in court if their judges recognize the Bill of Rights. But repression is becom-

6

Kafkaesque: Franz Kafka (1883–1924) was an Austrian writer whose works of fiction, such as *The Metamorphosis*, are known for being surreal and tinged with a sense of doom.

draconian: Overly harsh. (The word comes from Draco, a seventh-century Athenian ruler whose punishments were excessively cruel.)

ing respectable, and some federal judges are as wary of free speech as school administrators are. Student speech rights have, after all, been steadily eroding for the past two decades. The landmark 1969 Supreme Court decision *Tinker v. Des Moines Independent Community School District* upholding the right to wear a black armband to school to protest the Vietnam War has not been overruled, but its assertion that students do not leave their First Amendment rights at the schoolhouse door has not been honored either.

1. When she was in high school in the mid-1960s, the author's punishment for her insubordination (not following the rules) was

   a.   expulsion from school.

   b.   suspension from school.

   c.   being reported to her parents.

   d.   detention.

2. Which of the following sentences from paragraph 3 is not a major supporting detail for the topic sentence, "Fearful of violence and drugs, intolerant of dissent or simple nonconformity, public school officials are on the rampage"?

   a.   I doubt that my mother or any of my teachers could protect a kid from the wrath of school bureaucrats today.

   b.   They're suspending and expelling even grade school students for making what might be considered, at worst, inappropriate remarks, dressing oddly, or simply expressing political opinions.

   c.   Efforts to strip students of rights are hardly new, but they have greatly accelerated in recent months by hysteria about school violence and "terroristic threats."

   d.   America's public schools are becoming increasingly Kafkaesque.

3. The examples in paragraph 4 are major supporting details for what stated main idea of paragraph 3?

   a.   America's public schools are becoming increasingly Kafkaesque.

   b.   I doubt that my mother or any of my teachers could protect a kid from the wrath of school bureaucrats today.

   c.   Fearful of violence and drugs, intolerant of dissent or simple nonconformity, public school officials are on the rampage.

   d.   Efforts to strip students of rights are hardly new, but they have been greatly accelerated in recent months by hysteria about school violence and "terroristic threats."

4. In paragraph 6, the author compares judges and school administrators. How are judges and school administrators alike, according to the author?

   a.   They are both wary of free speech.

   b.   They are both afraid to punish certain behaviors.

   c.   They are both out of touch.

   d.   They are both mostly old men.

5. Which of the following statements is a minor supporting detail for the sentence in paragraph 6 "Student speech rights have, after all, been steadily eroding for the past two decades"?

   a.   Those students who dare to use their speech rights to protest such draconian restrictions on speech are liable to be punished severely.

   b.   In Texas, 17-year-old high school student Jennifer Boccia was suspended for wearing a black armband to school to protest restraints on free speech that followed the shootings in Littleton.

   c.   The landmark 1969 Supreme Court decision *Tinker v. Des Moines Independent Community School District* upholding the right to wear a black armband to school to protest the Vietnam War has not been overruled, but its assertion that students do not leave their First Amendment rights at the schoolhouse door has not been honored either.

   d.   Boccia made a federal case of it and won a settlement from her school vindicating her First Amendment rights.

> Students' press rights have been severely restricted, as has their right to express themselves sartorially. Unhampered by logic, judges have ruled that clothing choices are not expressive (and so are not protected by the First Amendment), but they've given schools the power to prohibit clothing when it conveys what administrators consider inappropriate messages. In a recent Utah case, a federal

7

district court judge upheld the suspension of a high school student who wore a pro-vegan T-shirt to school and started a petition protesting a ban on vegan symbols. School officials associated veganism with the militant branch of the animal rights movement and labeled the T-shirt a gang symbol. (In Alabama and Mississippi, the Star of David has been banned as a gang symbol.) "Schools need to run, and administrators need to make rules," the judge in the vegan T-shirt case explained idiotically. "That's the only reason they exist."

Apparently. Education is becoming militarized. Teachers and administrators give orders, and students are expected to follow them. The Louisiana legislature recently passed a law treating elementary school children like little army recruits. They can no longer simply say "yes" or "no" in answer to a question in school. Under law, they are now required to address all school employees as "sir" or "ma'am," as in "yes, sir" or "yes, ma'am." **8**

The desire to regiment students is sometimes quite overt. Character First, a character education program for elementary school students, requires children to memorize this poem about attentiveness: "I will look at someone speaking / And I'll listen all I can / I will sit or stand up straight / like a soldier on command." **9**

Soldiers don't generally enjoy much autonomy, even off duty, and neither do students these days. School administrators take an expansive, totalitarian view of their own jurisdiction. They're punishing students for after-school and out-of-school activities or remarks. Numerous suspensions of students for the things they say in Internet chat rooms and other instances of cyberspeech exemplify this disturbing trend, but administrators have also targeted more traditional forms of childhood play. In a recent Massachusetts case, two 12-year-old boys were suspended for playing war with toy guns in the woods adjacent to their school after school hours. (Never mind that at the time the U.S. military was bombing Yugoslavia.) **10**

While students are being suspended for playing with toy guns, police officers armed with real guns are being deployed in some schools in order to provide security—or the appearance of it. In Houston, officers wearing bulletproof vests, trained in assault tactics, and equipped with dogs as well as guns are patrolling middle schools, high schools, and school neighborhoods. Students in the Houston schools will soon be subject to random, bimonthly searches for drugs and weapons. . . . In Georgia, an entire class of fifth-graders was strip-searched by school officials and police officers looking for a missing $26. **11**

> Why do we treat students like criminal suspects? We can't simply blame recent incidents of gun violence; minors were the victims of repressive laws and policies long before the Littleton shootings. Adults fear the sexuality of teens, or envy their youth, or worry about their judgment, or, like Dr. Frankenstein, they want to mold their little monsters instead of allowing them their freedom to develop. In any case, obsessive concern about unruly children and especially adolescents is a long-standing American tradition. . . .   12

6. Which of the following sentences from paragraph 7 is a minor supporting detail to support the major supporting detail "Unhampered by logic, judges have rules that clothing choices are not expressive . . . but they've given schools the power to prohibit clothing when it conveys what administrators consider inappropriate messages"?

   a. Students' press rights have been severely restricted, as has their right to express themselves sartorially.

   b. In a recent Utah case, a federal district court judge upheld the suspension of a high school student who wore a pro-vegan T-shirt to school and started a petition protesting a ban on vegan symbols.

   c. "Schools need to run, and administrators need to make rules," the judge in the vegan T-shirt case explained idiotically.

   d. "That's the only reason they exist."

7. What main idea in paragraph 8 is supported by the following details: "They can no longer simply say 'yes' or 'no' in answer to a question in school. Under law, they are now required to address all school employees as 'sir' or 'ma'am,' as in 'yes, sir' or 'yes, ma'am'"?

   a. how "education is becoming militarized"

   b. how the Louisiana legislature works

   c. why students call school employees "sir" or "ma'am"

   d. why elementary school children are so ill-behaved

8. Which of the following is an example of a minor supporting detail from paragraph 10?

   a. Soldiers don't generally enjoy much autonomy, even off duty, and neither do students these days.

    b. School administrators take an expansive, totalitarian view of their own jurisdiction.

    c. They're punishing students for after-school and out-of-school activities or remarks.

    (d.) In a recent Massachusetts case, two 12-year-old boys were suspended for playing war with toy guns in the woods adjacent to their school after school hours.

9. Which of the following sentences is the unstated main idea of paragraph 11?

    a. Although school administrators think that students will be better behaved around police officers, students' behavior has worsened.

    b. Although school administrators think that police officers warrant respect, students mouth off to them, too.

    (c.) Although students are prohibited from "violent" types of game playing and from using toy guns, they are surrounded by weapons and police officers.

    d. Although school administrators feel safer with police officers around, students do not.

10. Which of the following is *not* one of the reasons the author gives to answer the question "Why do we treat students like criminal suspects?" in paragraph 12?

    a. Adults fear the sexuality of teens.

    b. Adults envy the students' youth.

    (c.) Adults are envious of students' freedom.

    d. Adults "want to mold their little monsters instead of allowing them their freedom to develop."

> Juvenile crime is relatively low today. According to the Department of Justice, violent juvenile crime has declined since the early 1990s and is at its lowest point since 1986. Violence in high schools has also declined substantially; the chances of a child being shot in school are "literally one in a million," criminologist James Alan Fox recently remarked in the *New York Times*. Some may find a one-in-a-million chance of being murdered unacceptable, and random shootings naturally arouse nearly everyone's anxiety. Still, according to a *Times* survey of teenagers conducted in October, both violence and fear of violence appear to have declined among America's teens.

13

Fear of illicit drugs, however, remains high among adults, especially those who rule the schools. The war on drugs has greatly diminished students' rights (along with the rights of adults). Schools treat students like criminal suspects partly because they view nearly every student as a suspected or potential drug user. Urine testing is becoming common in schools, and courts are sometimes loathe to strike it down. In 1995 the Supreme Court upheld random drug testing for student athletes. In 1999 a federal appeals court in St. Louis held that students could be tested for drugs before participating in any extracurricular activity.[1]   14

What's the harm of drug testing? "This policy gives all kinds of people access to my private information when there isn't even any reason to think I'm doing drugs," one student challenging his school's drug-testing policy states. "It's like something out of *1984*."°   15

It's heartening to find brave students willing to challenge their schools' repressive policies. Some teenagers instinctively understand speech and privacy rights or the right to be free of unreasonable searches, despite the efforts of administrators. Others are instinctively drawn to authoritarianism. How will most students learn about freedom when schools treat censorship, surveillance, and conformity as social goods? How will they learn about democracy and the exercise of individual conscience when schools equate virtue with obedience? How did following orders become the American way?   16

1984: A George Orwell novel about a totalitarian society, ruled by "Big Brother," which keeps a close eye on its citizens to ensure they follow the society's strict rules.
[1] In 2002 the Supreme Court held that schools can subject all students who participate in extracurricular activities to drug testing, absent any reason to suspect that the students are using drugs.

11. Which of the following sentences is a major supporting detail for the topic sentence of paragraph 13: "Juvenile crime is relatively low today"?

  (a.) According to the Department of Justice, violent juvenile crime has declined since the early 1990s and is at its lowest point since 1986.

  b. Some may find a one-in-a-million chance of being murdered unacceptable, and random shootings naturally arouse nearly everyone's anxiety.

  c. Still, according to a *Times* survey of teenagers conducted in October, both violence and fear of violence appear to have declined among America's teens.

d. Fear of illicit drugs, however, remains high among adults, especially those who rule the schools.

12. The examples given in paragraph 13 support the author's contention that

(a.) juvenile crime has decreased recently.

b. violent juvenile crime has increased over time.

c. violent juvenile crime is a result of bad television shows.

d. violent juvenile crime is a result of dual-working parents.

13. Of the following sentences, which one best represents the unstated main idea of paragraph 14?

a. Handgun use is the reason for the attack on schools.

(b.) The war on drugs is the reason for the attack on schools.

c. Urine testing is a great way to find out if kids are using drugs.

d. School administrators should participate in drug testing, too.

14. "It's like something out of *1984*," a quotation by a student in paragraph 15, supports the unstated main idea that

(a.) drug testing is harmful.

b. school administrators have too much power.

c. school is becoming increasingly militarized.

d. many students are doing drugs these days.

15. Which of the following sentences from paragraph 16 is a major supporting detail for the topic sentence, "It's heartening to find brave students willing to challenge their schools' repressive policies"?

a. How will most students learn about freedom when schools treat censorship, surveillance, and conformity as social goods?

b. How will they learn about democracy and the exercise of individual conscience when schools equate virtue with obedience?

(c.) Some teenagers instinctively understand speech and privacy rights or the right to be free of unreasonable searches, despite the efforts of administrators.

d. How did following orders become the American way?

Reading the Whole

Now that you have had a chance to read Wendy Kaminer's essay in its parts and to practice looking for major and minor supporting details, you are ready to read the essay in its entirety. As you read, remain aware of how major and minor supporting details contribute to your understanding of each paragraph, but also pay attention to the essay and Kaminer's argument as a whole. You may find that you agree with Kaminer or you may decide that her point of view doesn't convince you. In either case, pay particular attention to the points she makes, and ask yourself whether or not you think they are valid and why.

WENDY KAMINER
The War on High Schools

1   High school gave me my first lessons in bureaucracy: Rules were meant to be rigidly applied, not questioned; power was meant to be abused by petty functionaries. I don't mean to malign the entire faculty of my school. It included some very good teachers who encouraged curiosity and provocation and never lost their sense of humor. Because of them, high school also offered opportunities for self-expression and contained rebellion.

2   I regularly got into trouble for insubordination, but I was never suspended, much less expelled. It was the mid-1960s, a time of protest, not zero tolerance, and there was no clear rule that prohibited challenging or even insulting teachers and administrators. So the authorities simply reported me to my parents. My beleaguered mother came to expect their phone calls and made frequent visits to school, trying to placate whomever I'd offended. "You have such a nice mother," one of my teachers once said to me with wonder.

3   I doubt that my mother or any of my teachers could protect a kid from the wrath of school bureaucrats today. Fearful of violence and drugs, intolerant of dissent or simple nonconformity, public school officials are on the rampage. They're suspending and expelling even grade school students for making what might be considered, at worst, inappropriate remarks, dressing oddly, or simply expressing political opinions. Efforts to strip students of rights are hardly new, but they have been greatly accelerated in recent months by hysteria about school violence and "terroristic threats." America's public schools are becoming increasingly Kafkaesque.

Across the country, the American Civil Liberties Union has   4
received hundreds of complaints about cases like this: In Ohio a
third-grader was suspended after writing a fortune cookie message,
"You will die an honorable death," which he submitted for a school
project. (A terroristic threat? Or an innocent, well-intentioned remark by a child who watches martial-arts videos?) Eleven high
school students in Ohio were suspended for contributing to a gothic-
themed Web site. In Virginia a 10th-grader was suspended for dyeing his hair blue. In Missouri, high school junior Dustin Mitchell
was suspended and required to perform 42 days of community
service with the local police department for offering a flippant opinion on school violence in an Internet chat room (when asked if a
tragedy like the Littleton shootings could happen in his school,
Mitchell responded "yes"). In Louisiana a 12-year-old boy was suspended and held in juvenile detention for over two weeks after
uttering a "threat" in a lunch line: "If you take all the potatoes, I'm
gonna get you," the accused terrorist said.

Those students who dare to use their speech rights to protest   5
such draconian restrictions on speech are liable to be punished
severely. In Texas, 17-year-old high school student Jennifer Boccia
was suspended for wearing a black armband to school to protest
restraints on free speech that followed the shootings in Littleton.
Boccia was also reprimanded by her school principal, Ira Sparks,
for daring to tell her story to the media; she was told that if she
wanted to clear her record, she should refrain from speaking to the
media before discussing her remarks with school officials.

Boccia made a federal case of it and won a settlement from her   6
school vindicating her First Amendment rights. Sometimes schools
back down when threatened with lawsuits, and many students willing to challenge their suspensions should ultimately prevail in court
if their judges recognize the Bill of Rights. But repression is becoming respectable, and some federal judges are as wary of free speech
as school administrators are. Student speech rights have, after all,
been steadily eroding for the past two decades. The landmark 1969
Supreme Court decision *Tinker v. Des Moines Independent Community School District* upholding the right to wear a black armband to school to protest the Vietnam War has not been overruled,
but its assertion that students do not leave their First Amendment
rights at the schoolhouse door has not been honored either.

Students' press rights have been severely restricted, as has their   7
right to express themselves sartorially. Unhampered by logic, judges

have ruled that clothing choices are not expressive (and so are not protected by the First Amendment), but they've given schools the power to prohibit clothing when it conveys what administrators consider inappropriate messages. In a recent Utah case, a federal district court judge upheld the suspension of a high school student who wore a pro-vegan T-shirt to school and started a petition protesting a ban on vegan symbols. School officials associated veganism with the militant branch of the animal rights movement and labeled the T-shirt a gang symbol. (In Alabama and Mississippi, the Star of David has been banned as a gang symbol.) "Schools need to run, and administrators need to make rules," the judge in the vegan T-shirt case explained idiotically. "That's the only reason they exist."

Apparently. Education is becoming militarized. Teachers and administrators give orders, and students are expected to follow them. The Louisiana legislature recently passed a law treating elementary school children like little army recruits. They can no longer simply say "yes" or "no" in answer to a question in school. Under law, they are now required to address all school employees as "sir" or "ma'am," as in "yes, sir" or "yes, ma'am." 8

The desire to regiment students is sometimes quite overt. Character First, a character education program for elementary school students, requires children to memorize this poem about attentiveness: "I will look at someone speaking / And I'll listen all I can / I will sit or stand up straight / like a soldier on command." 9

Soldiers don't generally enjoy much autonomy, even off duty, and neither do students these days. School administrators take an expansive, totalitarian view of their own jurisdiction. They're punishing students for after-school and out-of-school activities or remarks. Numerous suspensions of students for the things they say in Internet chat rooms and other instances of cyberspeech exemplify this disturbing trend, but administrators have also targeted more traditional forms of childhood play. In a recent Massachusetts case, two 12-year-old boys were suspended for playing war with toy guns in the woods adjacent to their school after school hours. (Never mind that at the time the U.S. military was bombing Yugoslavia.) 10

While students are being suspended for playing with toy guns, police officers armed with real guns are being deployed in some schools in order to provide security — or the appearance of it. In Houston, officers wearing bulletproof vests, trained in assault tactics, and equipped with dogs as well as guns are patrolling middle schools, high schools, and school neighborhoods. Students in the 11

Houston schools will soon be subject to random, bimonthly searches for drugs and weapons. . . . In Georgia, an entire class of fifth-graders was strip-searched by school officials and police officers looking for a missing $26.

Why do we treat students like criminal suspects? We can't simply blame recent incidents of gun violence; minors were the victims of repressive laws and policies long before the Littleton shootings. Adults fear the sexuality of teens, or envy their youth, or worry about their judgment, or, like Dr. Frankenstein, they want to mold their little monsters instead of allowing them their freedom to develop. In any case, obsessive concern about unruly children and especially adolescents is a long-standing American tradition. . . .

Juvenile crime is relatively low today. According to the Department of Justice, violent juvenile crime has declined since the early 1990s and is at its lowest point since 1986. Violence in high schools has also declined substantially; the chances of a child being shot in school are "literally one in a million," criminologist James Alan Fox recently remarked in the *New York Times*. Some may find a one-in-a-million chance of being murdered unacceptable, and random shootings naturally arouse nearly everyone's anxiety. Still, according to a *Times* survey of teenagers conducted in October, both violence and fear of violence appear to have declined among America's teens.

Fear of illicit drugs, however, remains high among adults, especially those who rule the schools. The war on drugs has greatly diminished students' rights (along with the rights of adults). Schools treat students like criminal suspects partly because they view nearly every student as a suspected or potential drug user. Urine testing is becoming common in schools, and courts are sometimes loathe to strike it down. In 1995 the Supreme Court upheld random drug testing for student athletes. In 1999 a federal appeals court in St. Louis held that students could be tested for drugs before participating in any extracurricular activity.

What's the harm of drug testing? "This policy gives all kinds of people access to my private information when there isn't even any reason to think I'm doing drugs," one student challenging his school's drug-testing policy states. "It's like something out of *1984*."

It's heartening to find brave students willing to challenge their schools' repressive policies. Some teenagers instinctively understand speech and privacy rights or the right to be free of unreasonable searches, despite the efforts of administrators. Others are instinctively drawn to authoritarianism. How will most students learn about

12

13

14

15

16

freedom when schools treat censorship, surveillance, and conformity as social goods? How will they learn about democracy and the exercise of individual conscience when schools equate virtue with obedience? How did following orders become the American way?

Integrated Skills

1. What is Wendy Kaminer's main point in this essay about American high schools? What does the title of her essay reveal about her point of view?

2. What does Kaminer say about her own high school experience? How is the information related to the overall idea of her essay?

3. What is Kaminer's purpose in mentioning the complaints that have been brought to the American Civil Liberties Union?

4. What is Kaminer's attitude toward students' rights? Where does she express her point of view most clearly and forcefully?

5. Why do you think Kaminer concludes her essay with a series of questions? How would you answer them?

Reading/Writing Connection

In "The War on High Schools," Wendy Kaminer argues that zero-tolerance policies are too extreme and that they deny students basic civil rights. Write a paragraph in which you agree or disagree with her view that we have gone too far as a society in punishing students for behaviors that just a few years ago weren't a source of serious concern. You may wish to give an example from your personal experience. Or you may wish to consider why it is or is not a good thing for school officials to take every perceived threat of violence—no matter how minor—very seriously.

Reading Textbooks

Thematic Connections. You've just read social commentator Wendy Kaminer's argument against overly strict school rules. A lawyer, Kaminer focuses on issues of civil liberties and First Amendment rights. The following passage from the child psychology textbook *The Development of Children* by Michael Cole and Sheila R. Cole doesn't expressly touch on "zero-tolerance" policies, but it does provide a perspective that adds a new dimension to Kaminer's point. As you read through it, think about whether the authors' information about children's responses to being punished for aggression complicates, undercuts, or supports Kaminer's concerns.

Vocabulary Preview

suppresses (para. 1): reduces (v.)

socialization (para. 1): the process of teaching individuals the unspoken rules and expected behaviors of their social group (n.)

punitive (para. 2): punishing (adj.)

correlational (para. 3): parallel, comparative (adj.)

causal (para. 3): constituting a reason for an action or a condition (adj.)

facilitate (para. 3): help, encourage (v.)

exasperated (para. 3): frustrated, aggravated (adj.)

corporal punishment (para. 3): physical punishment, such as spanking (n.)

ambiguous (para. 5): unclear (adj.)

in accord (para. 7): agreeing with, supporting (adj.)

begets (para. 7): causes (v.)

chronic (para. 9): unending, constant, long-lasting (adj.)

incline (para. 9): cause a tendency (v.)

perpetuate (para. 9): prolong by causing (v.)

evoke (para. 9): cause from within, make happen (v.)

Punishment

Another common belief about aggressive behavior is that it can be eliminated if it is punished whenever it occurs. This tactic suppresses aggressive behavior under some circumstances, but often it does not. If punishment is used as a means of socialization, it is most likely to suppress aggressive behavior when the child identifies strongly with the person who does the punishing and when it is employed consistently. Used inconsistently, punishment is likely to provoke children to further aggression.

Several studies have found that attempts to control children's behavior by means of physical punishment, or by threats to apply

1

2

raw power, actually increase the children's aggressiveness. Gerald Patterson and his colleagues have observed how this effect is produced under natural conditions. They observed two groups of boys age 3 to 13½ along with parents in their homes. The boys in the first group had been referred to the researchers by schools and clinics because of their excessively aggressive behavior. The second group of boys had not been referred for help. The investigators found that punitive child-rearing tactics were more frequent in the homes of the referred boys. These tactics were often associated with a higher level of aggression in the family as a whole.

Patterson's findings involve correlational data and do not isolate causal factors, but his observations suggest that punitive child-rearing tactics may facilitate the learning of aggression. Say, for example, that a younger brother hits his older sister in order to obtain a toy. His sister hits him back. He shouts at her and, while pulling on the toy, hits her again. She resists. The mother comes running to see what is the matter. She shouts at the children to stop, but they do not listen. Exasperated, she lashes out and slaps her son and roughly shoves her daughter. The boy withdraws, breaking the cycle for the moment. If matters stopped here, this would just be a case of corporal punishment. But now the mother's behavior has been modified. Since her aggressive intervention successfully stopped the children's fighting, she is more likely to be aggressive in future incidents. Observing the success of the aggression she models, her children may also learn to interact in an aggressive way. 3

Kenneth Dodge and his colleagues have conducted extensive research on the mechanisms that link parental punishment to later aggression by their children. In one study they contacted 584 boys and girls at the time of their preregistration for kindergarten. In the spring before the children entered kindergarten, a researcher went to each child's home to interview the parents about how they handled their child's misbehavior, asking specifically about whether they had ever slapped, spanked, hit, or beaten their child and whether their child had ever been physically harmed by such punishment to the point of being bruised or needing medical attention. The researchers found that 12 percent of the children had been so harmed. 4

In a separate interview, the children were shown short videos in which child actors carried out negative social actions, such as knocking over another child's building blocks or excluding another 5 child from a play group. In some cases, the videos made it clear that these negative social acts were intentional. In other cases, the negative acts were either clearly accidental or ambiguous. Immediately after seeing each video, the children were asked to recall what had happened and then to tell how they might have behaved if the same negative things had happened to them, why they thought the children in the video behaved the way they did, and what they thought the probable outcome of the situation would be.

Six months later, after the children had entered kindergarten, each child was observed for twelve 5-minute periods in the playground and in the classroom by trained observers who did not know the child's punishment history. In addition, the child's teacher and peers were asked to rate the child's aggression.   6

In accord with the belief that physical punishment begets aggression, the children who had been physically harmed when they were disciplined were rated as more aggressive by both their peers and their teachers than were the children who had not been harmed. The ratings were confirmed by the direct observations of the children in their classroom and in the playground. Children who had been severely punished were three times more likely than other children to react to either real or imagined harm by lashing out against the other child with a shove, punch, or kick.   7

An interesting finding was that the children's aggression did not seem to be the *direct* result of learning to be aggressive, as learning theory suggests. Rather, the aggression seemed to be an *indirect* result of the way the children interpreted the events that provoked them. Children who had been severely punished appeared to misread the social events depicted in the videos they were shown at the beginning of the study. They were more likely than the other children to believe that accidental and ambiguous provocations were intentionally hostile, justifying an aggressive response.   8

Dodge and his colleagues believe that these results support the idea that children who are frequently and severely punished acquire chronic patterns of processing social information that incline them to interpret unpleasant interactions as hostile and directed at them. This pattern of interpretation tends to perpetuate itself, because the children's aggressive reactions evoke hostility in their targets, falsely "confirming" their original interpretation of hostile intent. The result is the development of chronic aggression.   9

Thinking about the Textbook Selection

1. What kinds of evidence do the authors use to support their idea that physical punishment only increases aggressive behavior? Do you find their supporting evidence persuasive? Why or why not?

2. What point do the authors make with the example of the mother's reaction to her fighting children? Do you think this is a good example—a good supporting detail? Why or why not?

3. What distinction do the authors make between "direct" and "indirect" results in learning to be aggressive?

4. How does the main idea of this textbook selection relate to the point made by Wendy Kaminer in "The War on High Schools"?

Reading the Web

The following Web page is the beginning of a sample article from "This Is True," a weekly newspaper column that is also published online by its author, Randy Cassingham. The story that follows this photograph and caption includes more examples of school policies to support Cassingham's argument that "zero-tolerance" policies are silly and ineffective. As you look at the Web page, notice the use of major and minor details. They support the author's main idea, which, although not stated, is unmistakable. Take a moment, also, to think about how Cassingham's approach to making his point is different from Kaminer's. Whose style and details are more effective?

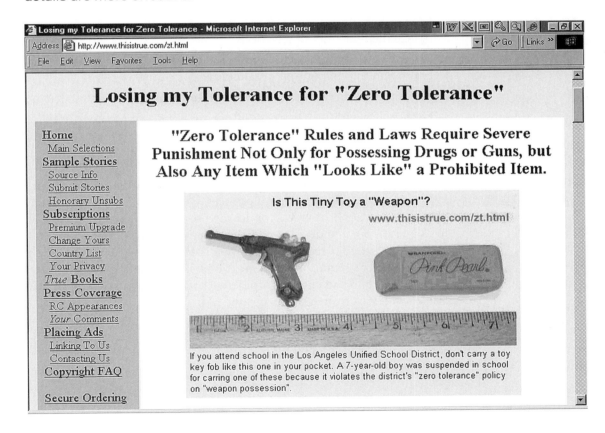

Losing my Tolerance for Zero Tolerance - Microsoft Internet Explorer

Address http://www.thisistrue.com/zt.html

File   Edit   View   Favorites   Tools   Help

Losing my Tolerance for "Zero Tolerance"

Home
Main Selections
Sample Stories
Source Info
Submit Stories
Honorary Unsubs
Subscriptions
Premium Upgrade
Change Yours
Country List
Your Privacy
True Books
Press Coverage
RC Appearances
Your Comments
Placing Ads
Linking To Us
Contacting Us
Copyright FAQ

Secure Ordering

"Zero Tolerance" Rules and Laws Require Severe Punishment Not Only for Possessing Drugs or Guns, but Also Any Item Which "Looks Like" a Prohibited Item.

Is This Tiny Toy a "Weapon"?

www.thisistrue.com/zt.html

If you attend school in the Los Angeles Unified School District, don't carry a toy key fob like this one in your pocket. A 7-year-old boy was suspended in school for carring one of these because it violates the district's "zero tolerance" policy on "weapon possession".

Thinking about the Web Page

1. What is "zero tolerance"?

2. Do you think the author approves or disapproves of "zero-tolerance" policies for drugs and guns? Why do you think so?

3. What major and minor supporting details does this Web page use to support the writer's position?

Reviewing

Recall / Remember

1. Explain what supporting details are and why it is important to recognize them in reading selections.
2. What is the relationship between the supporting details of a paragraph and that paragraph's main idea?
3. Explain the difference between major and minor supporting details.
4. Explain how you can understand the main idea of a paragraph or a passage when it is implied or not stated directly.

Chapter Summary

In this chapter you learned how to identify supporting details—the specific examples, illustrations, instances, and reasons that support a writer's idea or point of view. You learned to distinguish between major and minor supporting details and had opportunities to practice identifying them in different reading selections. And you also learned how to identify a writer's main idea when it is implied or not stated directly. In addition, you had the chance to practice each of these skills on longer reading selections from a magazine and a textbook.

The next chapter, "Examining Sentences in Context," will show you how supporting details work together and will give you more opportunities to practice identifying them.

Examining Sentences in Context

Getting Ready

Now that you've learned to identify the sentences that express and support a writer's main idea, you're ready to look more closely at how those sentences function. Sentences are the fundamental unit of thought used by all writers. The sentence you just read, for example, expresses a simple thought with a simple sentence. Some sentences, though, put forward more complex thoughts—largely by expressing relationships *within* their parts. Writers also provide relationships *between* sentences. Together, these different kinds of sentence relationships work to express and support a writer's ideas.

This chapter provides an overview of how ideas are related to one another within sentences and how sentences link with one another in paragraphs. It shows you how to identify coordinated and subordinated ideas and how to recognize sentence relationships whether they're explicit or implicit. You will also learn how to use your understanding of sentence relationships to better understand the relationships between paragraphs.

Chapter Overview

Focusing
Questions

When you look at the parts of a sentence, how do you figure out how they relate to one another?

How do you know which part of a sentence is most important?

What key words can help you understand the relationship between parts of a sentence? How can you determine the relationship if there aren't key words to provide clues?

When you read a paragraph, how do you know how its sentences relate to one another?

How do you determine the role or function of each sentence in a paragraph?

How are the paragraphs in a piece of writing related to one another?

Everyday
Reading

If you sometimes prepare your own meals and snacks, you've learned how to read recipes or cooking instructions. Some are very simple, like "microwave on high for 4 minutes," "heat five quarts of water to a boil," or "simmer and serve." Other instructions, especially if you're preparing something from scratch, are more complex. For example: "Mash the paste in a bowl of warm water, then push it through a strainer into a bowl, keeping the paste that sticks to the outside of the strainer." It's important to understand how the parts of the directions relate—especially if you want the dish to come out right! For the next couple of days, pay close attention to any cooking directions you follow. Notice how all of the steps work together toward an end result. How do you determine how the parts of the recipes or instructions relate to each other? Is every step equally important? Are the relationships always stated directly, or are they implied?

Learning the Skills

■ Coordination and Subordination

It's important to understand how the parts of a sentence relate to one another. There are six primary kinds of relationships found within sentences:

- Addition: One part of the sentence adds something to the other part.
- Clarification: One part of the sentence explains another part.
- Contrast: One part shows a difference from another part.
- Comparison: One part shows a similarity to another part.
- Example: One part illustrates another part.
- Cause and/or effect: One part shows how another part made something happen or how one part of a sentence was the result of another part.

The information in two clauses might be equally important, or one part of the sentence might be provided only to help readers know more about another part. Writers use coordination and subordination to indicate the relative importance of the parts of a sentence.

COORDINATION

To coordinate means to connect, or to put together. Writers use **coordination** to join equally important ideas or details.

The following sentences each contain two coordinated ideas:

> The Civil War began in 1861 and it ended in 1865.
>
> Law school applications decreased last year, but they increased this year.

Both parts of the sentence about the beginning and end of the Civil War are equally important. The information about the increase and decrease of law school applications are also given equal weight. Notice the word that joins the equally important ideas: *and* in the Civil War sentence, *but* in the law school sentence. Both words are examples of **coordinating conjunctions.** These key words tell readers how the parts of the sentences relate to one another.

COMMON COORDINATING CONJUNCTIONS

Conjunction	Sentence Relationship
and	addition
but	contrast
for	explanation
nor	negation
or	alternative
so	consequence or conclusion
yet	qualification or contrast

Exercise 5-1

In each sentence, underline the coordinating conjunction that makes the sentence compound and identify its function.

Example:

His first three attempts failed, <u>yet</u> he didn't give up.

FUNCTION: *contrast*

1. There were seven talented applicants for the available position, <u>so</u> six were bound to be disappointed.

    FUNCTION: *consequence*

2. Do you enjoy cooking, <u>or</u> would you prefer to have meals appear in front of you as if by magic?

    FUNCTION: *alternative*

3. Some people have an overwhelming urge to gamble their money away, <u>but</u> the urge may be a symptom of a deeper problem.

    FUNCTION: *contrast*

4. During the 2002 Winter Olympics, Derek Parra turned the tables by winning the gold and the silver in speed skating, <u>and</u> Sarah Hughes surprised everyone by winning the gold in women's figure skating.

    FUNCTION: *addition*

5. The news media should be allowed to operate freely, <u>for</u> a democracy
   needs to be able to learn the truth and to evaluate policies and politicians.

   FUNCTION: *explanation* _____

· ·

SUBORDINATION

The parts of a sentence are not always equally important. To combine an
idea or thought with a related but less important bit of information,
a writer can subordinate the less important part. To subordinate means
to put one thing under or below another. Writers use **subordination** to
stress the primary importance of one idea in relation to another, less
important one.

The following sentences each subordinate one part to the other:

> Although he was a fast skater, Bill was not a good hockey player.
>
> The students became restless because the introductory lecture was
> unusually long.

The information in the parts of each sentence are not of equal importance. In the first sentence, the emphasis—the main idea—is that Bill
was not a good hockey player. The point that he was a fast skater is subordinated to that main idea. In the second example, the idea emphasized
is that the students became restless. The less important point describes
why they became restless: The introductory lecture was too long. Notice
the words that begin the less important clauses: *although* in the hockey
sentence and *because* in the sentence about the students. Both words are
examples of **subordinating conjunctions.** Like coordinating conjunctions,
these key words tell readers how the parts of a sentence fit together.

COMMON SUBORDINATING CONJUNCTIONS

Conjunction	Sentence Relationship
because, since	reason or explanation
although, if, even though, except that, in order that, so that	contrast
unless	purpose
whether, rather than	condition
	choice

Exercise 5-2

· ·

In each sentence, underline the subordinating conjunction and identify its function.

Example:

Although Yogi Berra was a Hall of Fame major league baseball player, he is remembered today mostly for his hilarious remarks, such as "When you come to a fork in the road, take it," and "The future ain't what it used to be."

FUNCTION: *contrast* _____

1. Because teenagers spend a lot of money, advertisers pitch many products to teens.

   FUNCTION: *explanation* _____

2. We will miss the beginning of the movie unless we get in the car right now.

   FUNCTION: *condition* _____

3. Women are urged to consume enough calcium so that they do not get the bone disease known as osteoporosis.

   FUNCTION: *purpose* _____

4. Since he wants a more exciting life, let's give him a snowboard for his birthday.

   FUNCTION: *reason* _____

5. Cable channels do not really provide ordinary folk the promised "voice through television," even though access channels promote citizen participation.

   FUNCTION: *contrast* _____

· ·

■ Recognizing Implicit Sentence Relationships

As you have seen, conjunctions and key words often provide an explicit connection between one part of a sentence and another part. Sometimes, however, parts of a sentence may be related even without the use of a conjunction or key word. Such relationships are **implicit**—implied or suggested.

> The managers were unsure what to do; they needed more information before making a decision.
>
> It was not the best game the team played this season; it was not the worst either.

Look again at the list of primary sentence relationships on page 143. Those same relationships can be implied. The punctuation in the preceding examples helps you see that the parts are related. Semicolons and colons often link independent clauses, so even without key words you can infer what the relationships between the parts of a sentence are. In the first example, the second part of the sentence *clarifies* or explains why the managers weren't sure what to do. In the second example, the second part of the sentence provides a *contrast* with the first part.

Exercise 5-3

Each of the following sentences includes an implicit relationship between its parts. Using the list of primary sentence relationships on page 143 (addition, clarification, contrast, comparison, example, and cause/effect), infer what the relationship is and write it in the space provided.

Example:

> The fruiting bodies of some species are simple globes more than 1 mm in diameter; those of other species are more complex, branched structures. (William K. Purves et al., *Life: The Science of Biology*)

RELATIONSHIP: *comparison*

1. In December 1949, Mao established the People's Republic of China; the Nationalists fled to the island of Taiwan two months later. (James L. Roark et al., *The American Promise: A History of the United States*)

   RELATIONSHIP: *cause and effect*

2. Even service marketers can benefit from joint ventures: A Washington, D.C., law firm that specializes in transportation law has a joint-venture law practice with a Belgian firm. (James William G. Nickels and Marian Burk Wood, *Marketing: Relationships, Quality, Value*)

   RELATIONSHIP: *example*

3. Percentage-wise, *The Blair Witch Project* is one of the most profitable films of all time; it was produced for $40,000 and earned over $140 million at the box office. (Richard Campbell, *Media and Culture: An Introduction to Mass Communication*)

   RELATIONSHIP: *clarification*

4. With muscles tense, the rabbit is poised to leap away at the first sign that it has been detected; its heart races, and its adrenal glands secrete hormones that help prepare the body for extended flight if necessary. (Peter Gray, *Psychology*)

   RELATIONSHIP: *addition*

5. Moral pragmatists do not maintain a stable, consistently applied set of moral principles; the decision regarding what is ethical varies from situation to situation. (Daniel J. Canary, Michael J. Cody, and Valerie L. Manusov, *Interpersonal Communication: A Goals-Based Approach*)

   RELATIONSHIP: *clarification*

■ Recognizing Relationships between Sentences: The Paragraph

Sentences exist in relation to other sentences. Rarely will you read single sentences in isolation, except in advertisements and bumper stickers—and textbook exercises. Sentences usually appear in the context of longer chunks of writing, in paragraphs that make up essays, stories, articles, and books.

Writers express and develop their ideas through paragraphs—series of related sentences that are unified around a single topic. The sentences may develop a single idea or serve as a bridge between different ideas. The central challenge for you as a reader is to understand writers' ideas by interpreting the relationships among the sentences.

The following paragraph is developed through the use of examples:

> (1) The Vietnam War has inspired many artists to produce outstanding works of art. (2) For instance, the modern films *Apocalypse Now,* directed by Francis Ford Coppola, and *Full Metal Jacket,* directed by Stanley Kubrick, were influenced by the experience of American troops in Vietnam. (3) Another example is *In Country* by Bobbie Ann Mason, a novel that examines the consequences of a veteran's experiences in the war after he returns home. (4) Other books of note include Robert Olen Butler's collection of stories *A Good Scent from a Strange Mountain* and Phil Caputo's *A Rumor of War,* a memoir by a soldier who fought in the war. (5) In addition, the popular films *Coming Home,* starring Jane Fonda and Jon Voight, and *Born on the Fourth of July,* starring Tom Cruise, examine this theme. (6) Perhaps the best-known work of art that resulted from the Vietnam War is Maya Lin's monument in Washington, D.C.—the Vietnam Veterans Memorial Wall, more commonly known as the Vietnam Wall.

The opening sentence of the paragraph states the main idea, and the second sentence links with it through the words "For instance." Sentence 3 begins "Another example," which also identifies a relationship with the paragraph's topic sentence. Sentence 4 adds to sentence 3 by providing other examples of books about the Vietnam War. Sentence 5 begins with "In addition," a clue that it continues the pattern of providing examples. Finally, the last sentence identifies the most famous example of a work of art that grew out of the Vietnam War.

Exercise 5-4

Answer the questions about the relationships among the sentences in the following paragraph.

(1) The institution of the foreign migrant worker appears around the world when a relatively rich country is near a relatively poor one and there is access between them. (2) Mexican farm workers in the United States, Algerian farm workers in France, Turkish laborers in Germany, and Ethiopian domestic servants in Kuwait are all examples. (3) Each example shows the combined effects of overpopulation and unequal distribution of employment opportunity and wealth. (4) In all cases, there are dangers that migrant workers will be exploited by local employers who recognize their vulnerability and that they will be resented by local workers who see them as competitors. (5) Cesar Chavez (1927–1994) organized the United Farm Workers union in California in response to such problems in 1962 and after a multiyear strike was able to obtain better wages and working conditions for grape pickers. (6) Similar unions have developed in many places around the world. (Adapted from Lanny B. Fields, Russell J. Barber, and Cheryl A. Riggs, *The Global Past*)

Example:

What is the importance of sentence 1?

Sentence 1 states the main idea of the paragraph, which is that any

place in the world where people can move from a poorer country to a

nearby richer country, the richer country will get foreign migrant

workers.

1. How does sentence 2 relate to sentence 1? In other words, how does sentence 2 make the general statement in sentence 1 specific?

    Sentence 2 gives examples of richer countries that have access to

    workers from poorer countries.

2. How does sentence 3 relate to sentence 2? What new point is introduced in sentence 3?

   Sentence 3 refers back to the examples discussed in sentence 2.

   It explains what all the examples illustrate.

3. How does sentence 4 relate to sentence 3 (and sentence 2)? What new point does sentence 4 make?

   Sentence 4 refers back to the examples discussed in sentences 2 and 3.

   The new point is that migrant workers may be exploited and resented.

4. Which two specific words in sentence 5 relate back to sentence 4? How does sentence 5 expand on sentence 4?

   The two specific words in sentence 5 are "such problems." Sentence 5

   gives a specific example of a response to the problems raised in

   sentence 4.

5. How does sentence 6 relate to sentence 5? In other words, does sentence 6 give a specific example of sentence 5, or does it make a general statement based on sentence 5?

   Sentence 6 makes a general statement based on sentence 5.

   It expands the specific example given in sentence 5.

. . . .

▌ From Sentence Relationships to Paragraph Relationships

In the same way that you consider the relationship between sentences in a paragraph, to read with understanding you need to consider how one paragraph relates to the other paragraphs in a piece of writing. Here are two successive paragraphs from a recent best-selling book, *The Tipping Point* (2000), by Malcolm Gladwell:

> *The Tipping Point* is the biography of an idea, and the idea is very simple. It is that the best way to understand the emergence of fashion trends, the ebb and flow of crime waves, or, for that matter, the transformation of unknown books into bestsellers, or the rise of teenage smoking, or the phenomenon of word of mouth, or any number of the other mysterious changes that mark everyday life is to think of them as epidemics. Ideas and products and messages and behaviors spread just like viruses do.
>
> The rise of Hush Puppies and the fall of New York's crime rate are textbook examples of epidemics in action. Although they may sound as if they don't have very much in common, they share a basic, underlying pattern. First of all, they are clear examples of contagious behavior. No one took out an advertisement and told people that the traditional Hush Puppies were cool and they should start wearing them. Those kids simply wore the shoes when they went to clubs or cafes or walked the streets of downtown New York, and in so doing exposed other people to their fashion sense. They infected them with the Hush Puppies "virus."

Look first at the sentence relationships in the first paragraph. The first sentence makes a point quickly and directly—that the idea of the book *The Tipping Point* is a simple one. The second sentence identifies what this idea is. Notice how this sentence begins: "It is that. . . ." The "It" refers to the "simple" idea of the book, which is explained in the long sentence that ends "to think of them as epidemics." The author's idea is that fashion trends are like epidemics. He reinforces this idea in the last sentence of the paragraph. Notice the words "just like" in this sentence, which compare ideas, products, messages, and behaviors with "viruses" that "spread."

The second paragraph provides specific examples of how fashion trends and behaviors can be understood from the standpoint of epidemics. Notice how this entire paragraph is an example that illustrates the main idea of the first paragraph. Notice, too, how the second paragraph uses words that suggest comparisons: "share a basic, underlying pattern." And notice too how, to describe the behavior of people who wore Hush Puppies, the last two sentences of the paragraph use language that suggests an epidemic: "exposed," "infected," and "virus."

Exercise 5-5

Answer the questions about the following paragraph, the third in the sequence of successive paragraphs you just read from *The Tipping Point*.

> (1) The crime decline in New York surely happened the same way. (2) It wasn't that some huge percentage of would-be murderers suddenly sat up in 1993 and decided not to commit any more crimes. (3) Nor was it that the police managed magically to intervene in a huge percentage of situations that would otherwise have turned deadly. (4) What happened is that the small number of people in the small number of situations in which the police or the new social forces had some impact started behaving very differently, and that behavior somehow spread to other would-be criminals in similar situations. (5) Somehow a large number of people in New York got "infected" with an anti-crime virus in a short time.

Example:

What relationship does sentence 1 have to paragraphs 1 and 2?

The phrase in sentence 1 "happened the same way" refers back to the

rise of Hush Puppies in paragraph 2 and even further back to the idea

of "mysterious changes" that spread like viruses during an epidemic,

the main point of paragraph 1. The first sentence of paragraph 3

suggests that "the fall of New York's crime rate" mentioned in

sentence 1 of paragraph 2 is going to be discussed in detail.

1. To what in sentence 1 does the first word ("It") of sentence 2 refer?

   the decline of crime in New York

2. Which words in sentence 3 more or less repeat the words "It wasn't" in sentence 2, with the effect of connecting the two sentences?

   "Nor was it"

3. What negative phrase in paragraph 2 is roughly equivalent to "It wasn't" in sentence 2 (and its counterpart in sentence 3), which results in tying paragraph 2 and paragraph 3 together in "negative language"?

    "No one"

4. Which two specific words in sentence 5 refer back to the epidemic mentioned in paragraphs 1 and 2?

    " 'infected' "; "virus"

5. In what way is paragraph 3 like paragraph 2, and how do they both connect to paragraph 1?

    Paragraph 3 is like paragraph 2 because it presents a specific example.

    Both paragraphs are detailed examples of the general point in para-

    graph 1 that "ideas and products and messages and behaviors spread"

    in the same way as viruses do.

. . . .

Applying the Skills

Reading the Parts

One of the best-selling books of 2002 was Eric Schlosser's *Fast Food Nation: The Dark Side of the All-American Meal,* a shocking exposé that explores the rise of the fast-food industry and the effect it has had on the production of beef in America. This chapter from the book describes the cattle slaughtering process and working conditions in one of the country's biggest meat processing plants. As you read, pay close attention to how Schlosser coordinates and subordinates the parts of his sentences and how each sentence relates to the ones around it. Notice also how the paragraphs relate to one another to support the author's main idea, much of which is implied rather than stated outright. After reading each section and the questions that follow, move on to the next section. You will have a chance to read the entire chapter when you finish.

ERIC SCHLOSSER
The Most Dangerous Job

One night I visit a slaughterhouse somewhere in the High Plains. The slaughterhouse is one of the nation's largest. About five thousand head of cattle enter it every day, single file, and leave in a different form. Someone who has access to the plant, who's upset by its working conditions, offers to give me a tour. The slaughterhouse is an immense building, gray and square, about three stories high, with no windows on the front and no architectural clues to what's happening inside. My friend gives me a chain-mail apron and gloves, suggesting I try them on. Workers on the line wear about eight pounds of chain mail beneath their white coats, shiny steel armor that covers their hands, wrists, stomach, and back. The chain mail's designed to protect workers from cutting themselves and from being cut by other workers. But knives somehow manage to get past it. My host hands me some Wellingtons, the kind of knee-high rubber boots that English gentlemen wear in the countryside. "Tuck your pants into the boots," he says. "We'll be walking through some blood."

1

I put on a hardhat and climb a stairway. The sounds get louder, factory sounds, the noise of power tools and machinery, bursts of compressed air. We start at the end of the line, the fabricating room. Workers call it "fab." When we step inside, fab seems familiar: steel catwalks, pipes along the walls, a vast room, a maze of conveyer belts. This could be the Lamb Weston plant in Idaho, except hunks of red meat ride the belts instead of french fries. Some machines assemble cardboard boxes, others vacuum-seal subprimals of beef in clear plastic. The workers look extremely busy, but there's nothing unsettling about this part of the plant. You see meat like this all the time in the back of your local supermarket.   2

The fab room is cooled to about 40 degrees, and as you head up the line, the feel of the place starts to change. The pieces of meat get bigger. Workers—about half of them women, almost all of them young and Latino—slice meat with long slender knives. They stand at a table that's chest high, grab meat off a conveyer belt, trim away fat, throw meat back on the belt, toss the scraps onto a conveyer belt above them, and then grab more meat, all in a matter of seconds. I'm now struck by how many workers there are, hundreds of them, pressed close together, constantly moving, slicing. You see hardhats, white coats, flashes of steel. Nobody is smiling or chatting, they're too busy, anxiously trying not to fall behind. An old man walks past me, pushing a blue plastic barrel filled with scraps. A few workers carve the meat with Whizzards, small electric knives that have spinning round blades. The Whizzards look like the Norelco razors that Santa rides in the TV ads. I notice that a few of the women near me are sweating, even though the place is freezing cold.   3

Sides of beef suspended from an overhead trolley swing toward a group of men. Each worker has a large knife in one hand and a steel hook in the other. They grab the meat with their hooks and attack it fiercely with their knives. As they hack away, using all their strength, grunting, the place suddenly feels different, primordial. The machinery seems beside the point, and what's going on before me has been going on for thousands of years—the meat, the hook, the knife, men straining to cut more meat.   4

1. What is the relationship between sentences 2 and 3 of paragraph 1: "The slaughterhouse is one of the nation's largest. About five thousand head of cattle enter it every day, single file, and leave in a different form"?

   a. Sentence 3 clarifies why the slaughterhouse is one of the nation's largest.

   b. Sentence 3 offers an example of how cows go to slaughter.

   c. Sentence 3 clarifies where the slaughterhouse is located.

   d. Sentence 3 offers an example of how many slaughterhouses exist in the United States.

2. Which of the following sentences contains a subordinating conjunction indicating contrast?

   a. One night I visit a slaughterhouse somewhere in the High Plains.

   b. This could be the Lamb Weston plant in Idaho, except hunks of red meat ride the belts instead of french fries.

   c. The slaughterhouse is one of the nation's largest.

   d. Someone who has access to the plant, who's upset by its working conditions, offers to give me a tour.

3. Which of the following sentences contains a subordinating conjunction indicating contrast?

   a. But knives somehow manage to get past it.

   b. I put on a hardhat and climb a stairway.

   c. The fab room is cooled to about 40 degrees, and as you head up the line, the feel of the place starts to change.

   d. I notice that a few of the women near me are sweating, even though the place is freezing cold.

4. What is the relationship between the two parts of this sentence from paragraph 2: "The workers look extremely busy, but there's nothing unsettling about this part of the plant"?

   a. contrast

   b. comparison

   c. cause and effect

   d. example

5. What is the implicit relationship between the two parts of this sentence from paragraph 3: "A few workers carve the meat with Whizzards, small electric knives that have spinning round blades"?

a. The first part is a contrast to the second part.

b. The second part clarifies what a Whizzard is.

c. The second part of the sentence illustrates.

d. The second part is an example of what a Whizzard is.

On the kill floor, what I see no longer unfolds in a logical manner. It's one strange image after another. A worker with a power saw slices cattle into halves as though they were two-by-fours, and then the halves swing by me into the cooler. It feels like a slaughterhouse now. Dozens of cattle, stripped of their skins, dangle on chains from their hind legs. My host stops and asks how I feel, if I want to go any further. This is where some people get sick. I feel fine, determined to see the whole process, the world that's been deliberately hidden. The kill floor is hot and humid. It stinks of manure. Cattle have a body temperature of about 101 degrees, and there are a lot of them in the room. Carcasses swing so fast along the rail that you have to keep an eye on them constantly, dodge them, watch your step, or one will slam you and throw you onto the bloody concrete floor. It happens to workers all the time.

I see: a man reach inside cattle and pull out their kidneys with his bare hands, then drop the kidneys down a metal chute, over and over again, as each animal passes by him; a stainless steel rack of tongues; Whizzards peeling meat off decapitated heads, picking them almost as clean as the white skulls painted by Georgia O'Keeffe. We wade through blood that's ankle deep and that pours down drains into huge vats below us. As we approach the start of the line, for the first time I hear the steady *pop, pop, pop* of live animals being stunned.

Now the cattle suspended above me look just like the cattle I've seen on ranches for years, but these ones are upside down swinging on hooks. For a moment, the sight seems unreal; there are so many of them, a herd of them, lifeless. And then I see a few hind legs still kicking, a final reflex action, and the reality comes hard and clear.

For eight and a half hours, a worker called a "sticker" does nothing but stand in a river of blood, being drenched in blood, slitting the neck of a steer every ten seconds or so, severing its carotid artery. He uses a long knife and must hit exactly the right spot to kill the animal humanely. He hits the spot again and again. We walk up a slippery metal stairway and reach a small platform, where the production line begins. A man turns and smiles at me. He wears safety goggles and a hardhat. His face is splattered with gray matter and blood. He is the "knocker," the man who welcomes cattle to the building. Cattle walk down a narrow chute and pause in front of him, blocked by a gate, and then he shoots them in the head with a captive bolt stunner—a compressed-air gun attached to the ceiling by a long hose—which fires a steel bolt that knocks the cattle unconscious. The animals keep strolling up, oblivious to what comes next, and he stands over them and shoots. For eight and a half hours, he just shoots. As I stand there, he misses a few times and shoots the same animal twice. As soon as the steer falls, a workers grabs one of its hinds legs, shackles it to a chain, and the chain lifts the huge animal into the air.

6. How does paragraph 6 relate to paragraph 5?

   (a.) Paragraph 6 provides examples and descriptions of what the author sees on the kill floor.

   b. Paragraph 5 provides a comparison of different images the author sees on the kill floor.

   c. Paragraph 5 provides a contrast of different images the author sees on the kill floor.

   d. Paragraph 5 explains why the author passes out on the kill floor.

7. Which of the following sentences from paragraphs 5–8 includes a coordinating conjunction indicating contrast?

   a. On the kill floor, what I see no longer unfolds in a logical manner.

   b. It's one strange image after another.

   (c.) Now the cattle suspended above me look just like the cattle I've seen on ranches for years, but these ones are upside down swinging on hooks.

   d. For a moment, the sight seems unreal; there are so many of them, a herd of them, lifeless.

8. What is the implicit relationship between the two parts of the second sentence (separated by a semicolon) in paragraph 7: "For a moment, the sight seems unreal; there are so many of them, a herd of them, lifeless"?

   (a.) The second part of the sentence explains the first.

   b. The first part of the sentence is the cause, the second the effect.

   c. The two parts of the sentences compare the carcasses.

   d. The second part of the sentence provides an example of the first.

9. What is the relationship between the two parts of this section of paragraph 6, sentence 2: "Whizzards peeling meat off decapitated heads, picking them almost as clean as the white skulls painted by Georgia O'Keeffe."

   a. clarification

   (b.) comparison

   c. contrast

   d. example

10. What is the relationship of paragraph 8 to paragraphs 5, 6, and 7?

   a. Paragraph 8 offers additional examples of what happens on the kill floor.

   b. Paragraph 8 is an independent paragraph, with no relationship to the other paragraphs.

   (c.) Paragraph 8 explains what happened to the animals before they got to the kill floor.

   d. Paragraph 8 further defines the term *Whizzard,* from a mechanical standpoint.

> I watch the knocker knock cattle for a couple of minutes. The animals are powerful and imposing one moment and then gone in an instant, suspended from a rail, ready for carving. A steer slips from its chain, falls to the ground, and gets its head caught in one end of a conveyer belt. The production line stops as workers struggle to free the steer, stunned but alive, from the machinery. I've seen enough. 9

I step out of the building into the cool night air and follow the 10
path that leads cattle into the slaughterhouse. They pass me, driven
toward the building by workers with long white sticks that seem to
glow in the dark. One steer, perhaps sensing instinctively what the
others don't, turns and tries to run. But workers drive him back to
join the rest. The cattle lazily walk single file toward the muffled
sounds, *pop, pop, pop,* coming from the open door.

The path has hairpin turns that prevent cattle from seeing what's 11
in store and keep them relaxed. As the ramp gently slopes upward,
the animals may think they're headed for another truck, another
road trip—and they are, in unexpected ways. The ramp widens as
it reaches ground level and then leads to a large cattle pen with
wooden fences, a corral that belongs in a meadow, not here. As I
walk along the fence, a group of cattle approach me, looking me
straight in the eye, like dogs hoping for a treat, and follow me out
of some mysterious impulse. I stop and try to absorb the whole
scene: the cool breeze, the cattle and their gentle lowing, a cloudless
sky, steam rising from the plant in the moonlight. And then I notice
that the building does have one window, a small square of light on
the second floor. It offers a glimpse of what's hidden behind this
huge blank facade. Through the little window you can see bright
red carcasses on hooks, going round and round.

11. To what does the author compare the cattle in paragraph 11?

   a. animals from Georgia O'Keeffe paintings

   (b.) dogs hoping for treats

   c. cows in a meadow

   d. ghosts

12. What is the relationship of sentences 3 and 4 in paragraph 9:
"A steer slips from its chain, falls to the ground, and gets its
head caught in one end of a conveyer belt. The production line
stops as workers struggle to free the steer, stunned but alive,
from the machinery"?

   a. contrast

   b. comparison

   (c.) cause and effect

   d. clarification

13. What is the relationship between paragraphs 9 and 10?

    a. comparison

    (b.) contrast

    c. cause and effect

    d. example

14. What is the relationship of the final sentence in paragraph 11 (sentence 8) and sentence 5: (8) "Through the little window you can see bright red carcasses on hooks, going round and round"; (5) "I stop and try to absorb the whole scene: the cool breeze, the cattle and their gentle lowing, a cloudless sky, steam rising from the plant in the moonlight"?

    a. The last sentence compares the peaceful outside world to the peaceful carcass room.

    b. The last sentence offers an example of what happens to the cattle when they go inside.

    (c.) The last sentence describes the world inside the slaughter-house and contrasts it with the description in sentence 5 of the world outside the slaughterhouse.

    d. The last sentence clarifies where the cattle end up.

15. Which of the following sentences contains a coordinating conjunction?

    a. They pass me, driven toward the building by workers with long white sticks that seem to glow in the dark.

    b. But workers drive him back to join the rest.

    c. The cattle lazily walk single file toward the muffled sounds, *pop, pop, pop,* coming from the open door.

    (d.) The path has hairpin turns that prevent cattle from seeing what's in store and keep them relaxed.

Reading the Whole

Now that you have had a chance to read Eric Schlosser's chapter in its parts and to practice examining its sentences in context, you are ready to read the chapter in its entirety. As you read, remain aware of how the clauses, sentences, and paragraphs relate to one another, but also pay attention to the chapter as a whole and to how Schlosser develops his point.

ERIC SCHLOSSER
The Most Dangerous Job

One night I visit a slaughterhouse somewhere in the High Plains. The slaughterhouse is one of the nation's largest. About five thousand head of cattle enter it every day, single file, and leave in a different form. Someone who has access to the plant, who's upset by its working conditions, offers to give me a tour. The slaughterhouse is an immense building, gray and square, about three stories high, with no windows on the front and no architectural clues to what's happening inside. My friend gives me a chain-mail apron and gloves, suggesting I try them on. Workers on the line wear about eight pounds of chain mail beneath their white coats, shiny steel armor that covers their hands, wrists, stomach, and back. The chain mail's designed to protect workers from cutting themselves and from being cut by other workers. But knives somehow manage to get past it. My host hands me some Wellingtons, the kind of knee-high rubber boots that English gentlemen wear in the countryside. "Tuck your pants into the boots," he says. "We'll be walking through some blood." 1

I put on a hardhat and climb a stairway. The sounds get louder, factory sounds, the noise of power tools and machinery, bursts of compressed air. We start at the end of the line, the fabricating room. Workers call it "fab." When we step inside, fab seems familiar: steel catwalks, pipes along the walls, a vast room, a maze of conveyer belts. This could be the Lamb Weston plant in Idaho, except hunks of red meat ride the belts instead of french fries. Some machines assemble cardboard boxes, others vacuum-seal subprimals of beef in clear plastic. The workers look extremely busy, but there's nothing unsettling about this part of the plant. You see meat like this all the time in the back of your local supermarket. 2

The fab room is cooled to about 40 degrees, and as you head up the line, the feel of the place starts to change. The pieces of meat get bigger. Workers—about half of them women, almost all of them young and Latino—slice meat with long slender knives. They stand at a table that's chest high, grab meat off a conveyer belt, trim away fat, throw meat back on the belt, toss the scraps onto a conveyer belt above them, and then grab more meat, all in a matter of seconds. I'm now struck by how many workers there are, hundreds of them, pressed close together, constantly moving, slicing. You see hardhats, white coats, flashes of steel. Nobody is smiling or chatting, they're too busy, anxiously trying not to fall behind. An old man walks past me, pushing a blue plastic barrel filled with scraps. A few workers carve the meat with Whizzards, small electric knives that have spinning round blades. The Whizzards look like the Norelco razors that Santa rides in the TV ads. I notice that a few of the women near me are sweating, even though the place is freezing cold.

Sides of beef suspended from an overhead trolley swing toward a group of men. Each worker has a large knife in one hand and a steel hook in the other. They grab the meat with their hooks and attack it fiercely with their knives. As they hack away, using all their strength, grunting, the place suddenly feels different, primordial. The machinery seems beside the point, and what's going on before me has been going on for thousands of years—the meat, the hook, the knife, men straining to cut more meat.

On the kill floor, what I see no longer unfolds in a logical manner. It's one strange image after another. A worker with a power saw slices cattle into halves as though they were two-by-fours, and then the halves swing by me into the cooler. It feels like a slaughterhouse now. Dozens of cattle, stripped of their skins, dangle on chains from their hind legs. My host stops and asks how I feel, if I want to go any further. This is where some people get sick. I feel fine, determined to see the whole process, the world that's been deliberately hidden. The kill floor is hot and humid. It stinks of manure. Cattle have a body temperature of about 101 degrees, and there are a lot of them in the room. Carcasses swing so fast along the rail that you have to keep an eye on them constantly, dodge them, watch your step, or one will slam you and throw you onto the bloody concrete floor. It happens to workers all the time.

I see: a man reach inside cattle and pull out their kidneys with his bare hands, then drop the kidneys down a metal chute, over and over again, as each animal passes by him; a stainless steel rack of tongues; Whizzards peeling meat off decapitated heads, picking them almost as clean as the white skulls painted by Georgia O'Keeffe. We wade through blood that's ankle deep and that pours down drains into huge vats below us. As we approach the start of the line, for the first time I hear the steady *pop, pop, pop* of live animals being stunned.

Now the cattle suspended above me look just like the cattle I've seen on ranches for years, but these ones are upside down swinging on hooks. For a moment, the sight seems unreal; there are so many of them, a herd of them, lifeless. And then I see a few hind legs still kicking, a final reflex action, and the reality comes hard and clear.

For eight and a half hours, a worker called a "sticker" does nothing but stand in a river of blood, being drenched in blood, slitting the neck of a steer every ten seconds or so, severing its carotid artery. He uses a long knife and must hit exactly the right spot to kill the animal humanely. He hits the spot again and again. We walk up a slippery metal stairway and reach a small platform, where the production line begins. A man turns and smiles at me. He wears safety goggles and a hardhat. His face is splattered with gray matter and blood. He is the "knocker," the man who welcomes cattle to the building. Cattle walk down a narrow chute and pause in front of him, blocked by a gate, and then he shoots them in the head with a captive bolt stunner—a compressed-air gun attached to the ceiling by a long hose—which fires a steel bolt that knocks the cattle unconscious. The animals keep strolling up, oblivious to what comes next, and he stands over them and shoots. For eight and a half hours, he just shoots. As I stand there, he misses a few times and shoots the same animal twice. As soon as the steer falls, a workers grabs one of its hinds legs, shackles it to a chain, and the chain lifts the huge animal into the air.

I watch the knocker knock cattle for a couple of minutes. The animals are powerful and imposing one moment and then gone in an instant, suspended from a rail, ready for carving. A steer slips from its chain, falls to the ground, and gets its head caught in one end of a conveyer belt. The production line stops as workers struggle to free the steer, stunned but alive, from the machinery. I've seen enough.

I step out of the building into the cool night air and follow the path that leads cattle into the slaughterhouse. They pass me, driven toward the building by workers with long white sticks that seem to

7

8

9

10

glow in the dark. One steer, perhaps sensing instinctively what the others don't, turns and tries to run. But workers drive him back to join the rest. The cattle lazily walk single file toward the muffled sounds, *pop, pop, pop,* coming from the open door.

The path has hairpin turns that prevent cattle from seeing what's in store and keep them relaxed. As the ramp gently slopes upward, the animals may think they're headed for another truck, another road trip—and they are, in unexpected ways. The ramp widens as it reaches ground level and then leads to a large cattle pen with wooden fences, a corral that belongs in a meadow, not here. As I walk along the fence, a group of cattle approach me, looking me straight in the eye, like dogs hoping for a treat, and follow me out of some mysterious impulse. I stop and try to absorb the whole scene: the cool breeze, the cattle and their gentle lowing, a cloudless sky, steam rising from the plant in the moonlight. And then I notice that the building does have one window, a small square of light on the second floor. It offers a glimpse of what's hidden behind this huge blank facade. Through the little window you can see bright red carcasses on hooks, going round and round.

11

Integrated Skills

1. How did you respond to this reading selection? Would you recommend it to others? Why or why not? Are you interested in reading more of the book from which this chapter has been excerpted? Why or why not?

2. What do you think is the author's purpose in this chapter? Why do you think so?

3. Which details best convey the author's main point? What is the author's main point?

4. Why is the selection entitled "The Most Dangerous Job"? Do you agree with that title? Why or why not?

5. Did you find this piece interesting? Engaging? Upsetting? Something else? Why?

Reading/Writing Connection
. . . .

"The Most Dangerous Job" presents a not so pleasant picture of what happens to a cow or steer in a slaughterhouse as it is killed and butchered. Write a paragraph explaining why you do or do not eat meat, fish, or poultry. You may wish to make reference to Eric Schlosser's article, or you may wish simply to write about your food preferences without such a reference. What do you think is the author's purpose in writing his article? Where does that purpose appear most clearly?

Reading Textbooks

Thematic Connections. In his description of what goes on inside a slaughterhouse, Eric Schlosser reveals how dangerous it is to work there; he even goes so far as to title his description "The Most Dangerous Job." The following passage from the business textbook *Exploring the World of Business,* by Kenneth Blanchard, Charles Schewe, Robert Nelson, and Alexander Hiam, briefly outlines the history of labor safety laws and discusses the role of OSHA, or the Occupational Safety and Health Administration. As you read through it, think about how the dangerous conditions at the meatpacking plant compare to the conditions that prompted tougher labor laws. Why do you think Schlosser doesn't talk about labor safety law in his description of the slaughterhouse? How would an OSHA inspector react to what Schlosser describes?

Vocabulary Preview

impetus (para. 1): starter, inspiration (n.)

industrialization (para. 1): the process by which a society and its economy become centered on industry, manufacturing, and the production of goods (n.)

wages (para. 1): money paid for services (n.)

impoverish (para. 1): make poor (v.)

originated (para. 1): started (v.)

mandatory (para. 1): required (adj.)

premiums (para. 2): fees (n.)

incentive (para. 2): motivation, reason (n.)

ravages (para. 3): severe damages (n.)

regulation (para. 3): a system of rules (n.)

simultaneously (para. 3): at the same time (adv.)

occupational (para. 3): work-related (adj.)

compliance (para. 4): obedience (n.)

chronic (para. 4): happening on a regular basis with no sign of improvement (adj.)

prevailed (para. 5): were common (v.)

Employee Health and Safety

A . . . group of employer-related laws address the health and safety of workers. The initial impetus for their creation was actually the cost of injuries to businesses and to society. During the nineteenth century, the rapid industrialization of the American economy, coupled with the introduction of heavy machinery in production operations, greatly increased the number of significant injuries on the job. With more people working for wages, serious injuries

1

accompanied by lengthy recovery periods could impoverish entire families. Workers' Compensation laws, which provide a continuing, though decreased, income for an injured or disabled worker, originated in Wisconsin in 1911 as a response by the state's government to companies that simply fired workers injured on the job with no compensation. Such compensation is now mandatory in 47 states and voluntary in New Jersey, South Carolina, and Texas.

Workers' Compensation laws made businesses responsible for such compensation as a normal cost of doing business. Insurance companies began to provide insurance coverage for business to meet the expense of compensating injured or disabled workers. As the hazards of the industrialization and mechanization of work increased, and as insurance premiums rose, business finally had an economic incentive to try to reduce the risk of injury to workers. But this incentive left it to the individual business owner to decide if the costs of reducing the risk of injury were worth the possible savings in compensation costs and insurance premiums.

2

Although labor groups had a long history of campaigning for better workplace safety, the seriousness of unsafe work sites drew national attention in 1968 when a coal mine explosion killed 78 workers in Farmington, West Virginia. This tragedy helped to reveal the extent of preventable danger some workers faced; at the same time, it focused public attention on the ravages of black lung disease among mine workers. In 1969 the federal government entered the arena of workplace safety with the Coal Mine Health and Safety Act. In response to mounting public pressure for an effective national system of regulation to cover all industries, Congress passed the Occupational Health and Safety Act in 1970. The act's stated goal was to ensure, as far as possible, that working conditions for all Americans were healthful and safe. Congress simultaneously created the Occupational Safety and Health Administration (OSHA) to enforce this act. OSHA's duties are to:

3

- Develop and enforce mandatory job safety and health standards.
- Maintain a reporting and recordkeeping system to monitor job-related illness and injury.
- Establish training programs for occupational safety personnel.
- Develop, analyze, evaluate, and improve state occupational safety and health programs.

- Provide for research in workplace safety and health and develop responses to health and safety problems.
- Establish rights and responsibilities for both employers and employees for workplace safety and health.
- Encourage the reduction of workplace hazards with improved or new health and safety programs.

OSHA inspectors conduct "walkaround" surveys of a work site to examine practices visually. Workplaces found to be out of compliance are given a chance to correct the problem and are later reinspected. Businesses that commit serious violations of safety and health requirements may be cited, fined, or both, depending on the seriousness of the violation and whether it is chronic.   4

Many of the terrible conditions that prevailed in factories and sweatshops have been eliminated in the United States, though some employers do still break the law and expose workers to hazardous work conditions. But many factory jobs have been exported to other countries, where some U.S. firms are recreating a harmful work environment. In Mexico's enterprise zones, young women labor long hours for low pay in hazardous conditions, only a few miles beyond the reach of the Mexican labor laws. And companies that design and market goods produced abroad face questions that were resolved generations ago in the United States.   5

Nike's annual revenue from the sale of sports shoes alone is $2 billion. Nike handles the design and marketing of the shoes but does not produce them directly. It contracts abroad, mostly in Asia, for their actual production. Many of Nike's contractors are in Indonesia. The factories employ mostly girls and young women, who get an entry-level salary of $1.80 a day for sewing the shoes. Basic workers' rights and protections are nearly nonexistent for these employees, who are often forced to do mandatory overtime work. It costs Nike about $17.50 to produce the shoes, which usually sell for between $45 and $80. Nike claims that it does not know much about either the production processes or conditions under which its shoes are made. But as a *New York Times* article asks, "If Nike, which profits from these shoes, does not take responsibility for the people who make the shoes, who does?" . . . Nike's competitor, Reebok, emphasizes human rights as a business value. It, too, does business in Indonesia. Do you think its business ethics lead it to treat foreign workers better than Nike does?   6

Thinking about the Textbook Selection

1. What are "workers' compensation" laws? When were they initiated? Why are they important?

2. Why do you think it took so long for Congress to enact health and safety laws to protect workers?

3. How do businesses sometimes get around or avoid being subject to health and safety laws for workers? What do you think of these evasive tactics?

4. Why does the author mention Nike? What is your response to Nike's labor practices?

5. What is your answer to the last sentence of "Employee Health and Safety"? Why?

Reading the Web

In *Fast Food Nation,* Eric Schlosser pays a lot of attention to ConAgra Foods, the largest food processor in the United States. Although he doesn't explicitly name the company in the chapter "The Most Dangerous Job," he does imply that he holds it at least partly responsible for the dangers imposed on meatpacking workers. Not surprisingly, ConAgra has a different point of view. Take a look at this section of ConAgra's corporate Web site, which talks about the company's commitment to food safety.

Thinking about the Web Page

1. What is the purpose of the words in large type that come before each of the two paragraphs included on this Web page?

2. What is the topic sentence of each paragraph? How do the other sentences of each paragraph relate to the topic sentence of that paragraph?

3. What is the overall point of this Web page? What does the Web page suggest about ConAgra?

Reviewing

1. Why is it important to relate one part of a sentence to another?
2. What are coordination and subordination, and how do they join ideas in sentences?
3. How do key words help readers relate parts of sentences?
4. What do readers do when there are no key words to relate parts of a sentence explicitly?
5. What are paragraphs, and how should you read the series of sentences that make them up?
6. Why is it important to relate paragraphs to one another?

In this chapter you learned why it is important to understand the relationships among the parts of sentences. You learned how coordination signals that parts of sentences emphasize ideas or details equally. You also learned that subordination emphasizes the importance of one idea in a sentence over others that are less important in relation to the main idea. You learned too that sentences exist in the context of other sentences and that sentences must be related to one another so you can understand the main idea of a paragraph. You saw how paragraphs relate to one another to help readers understand the development of an idea. And you had the opportunity to practice looking at the relationships among parts of sentences, among sentences, and between paragraphs.

Analyzing a Writer's Structures

Getting Ready

To read with comprehension, you need to understand how a piece of writing is organized. By identifying the structure of what you read, you will better understand the relationship of its parts—whether it's an article, an essay, or a chapter in a textbook. If you can identify a selection's **introduction, body,** and **conclusion,** you can usually find an author's main idea and understand how supporting details contribute to the point of the selection.

Very commonly, writers organize their ideas according to predictable patterns. This chapter explains these organizational structures and helps you identify them. Recognizing these patterns will help you follow the ideas in what you read. Among the typical patterns of organization writers use are **definition; example; lists** and **sequences; comparison, contrast,** and **analogy; classification;** and **cause and effect.** Writers often use more than one of these patterns in their work. Mixing the patterns provides more ways for readers to understand a subject. By carefully observing these organizational patterns—whether they are used separately or are mixed—you can make connections among the details the author includes to increase your comprehension of what you read.

Chapter Overview

Focusing
Questions

What do you expect to find in the first paragraph or so of an essay, article, or book chapter? In the last paragraphs?

Where do you usually find the body of a writer's argument? In the beginning, the middle, or the end of a reading?

How do you use lists in everyday life? How are they helpful?

When is the order of a list important in everyday life?

How can examples help you understand ideas when you read?

When do you compare two items or ideas — while shopping, while driving? What other personal decisions require comparison?

When is it important to you to understand the causes of things? Where do you encounter cause-and-effect analysis?

How might organizational patterns in general help you as a reader?

Everyday
Reading

When you recognize the organizing pattern of something, you are able to follow it more easily. Think of your favorite half-hour television comedy. You know that the writers of the show have about twenty-two minutes (if you take out the commercials) to introduce the story, create a conflict or situation, and resolve it. So you as the viewer know that before the first commercial you will learn who the key players will be and what situation will occur. After the first commercial break, you will learn the consequences of the conflict or situation and how the characters will resolve it. And how do you know this? Because you've watched the show or shows like it before, and you know how the action will be presented.

Think about other kinds of television programs whose typical organization you know well. Pick a genre — such as crime or hospital dramas, evening news, documentaries, game shows, or mystery programs — and identify how shows in that genre tend to be organized. What would happen to your ability to follow the show if the writers and producers were to stray from what you've come to expect? Share your findings with your classmates and compare what you observe. How can you apply your understanding of television structure to your reading? Do you think writers of articles, essays, and books also use predictable patterns?

Learning the Skills

■ Identifying the Parts of an Essay

An essay, article, or chapter typically has three parts: an introduction, a body, and a conclusion. The introduction gets the piece going, the body includes the substance of the work and presents the details and the evidence, and the conclusion wraps things up.

THE INTRODUCTION: HOW A PIECE OF WRITING BEGINS

The introduction sets the stage for what comes after. Almost always found in the first paragraph or paragraphs, the introduction identifies the subject or topic of the piece. It often states an idea or makes a point (sometimes called a **thesis**) as well. You will find this pattern in much of the nonfiction you will read in your textbooks and in other assigned works, but be aware that it is not always the case in literature. Although the introduction to an article or essay does not *explain* the writer's idea, it does often *identify* it. When an article or essay is long, a dozen pages or more, its introduction tends to be more than a simple paragraph. With practice, you will be able to sense when a writer has reached the end of an introduction and begins to move into the body of the essay, article, or chapter.

Here is the introduction to "King or Queen of the Road: A Girl's View," an essay written in 1999 by Rachael Cowley when she was a student at Park University in Missouri. As you read it, try to get a sense of what her topic and her main idea are.

> Women make better drivers than men for so many reasons, yet we take all the flack about being horrible drivers. Why is that, do you suppose? Wouldn't you think that competing at who has better driving abilities is juvenile and pointless? If you ask me, men crack their obnoxious jokes because they have some sort of inferiority complex. They know that women are superior drivers but have too much testosterone running through their veins to admit the truth—women are queens of the road.

1

As you can see, Cowley's introduction is one paragraph; this is appropriate because her essay itself is very short—only six paragraphs. She begins with some general observations and examples, waiting until the end of her introduction to announce her topic: "women are queens of the road."

THE BODY: HOW A PIECE OF WRITING DEVELOPS

The middle, or body, of a piece of writing expands and elaborates on its introduction. In working your way through the body, ask yourself how the details—the information, arguments, examples, and evidence—develop the main idea suggested in the introduction. The body can be a paragraph or two in a short essay or article or many pages in longer pieces of writing. In reading the body of a selection, look for the supporting details the writer includes and try to link them together to see how they develop and support the writer's main idea. You learned how to do this in Chapter 4.

A helpful tactic for reading the body of a selection is to mentally break it into smaller chunks. Often college textbooks contain headings that break the body of a chapter into smaller pieces so the content is easier to digest. Sometimes, however, they do not. When an article, essay, or chapter is not arranged with headings, you might want to supply your own, using marginal annotations. You can also try to identify the focus of each paragraph or group of related paragraphs by adding notes in the margin.

Here is the body of Rachael Cowley's essay:

> Unlike men, women stop for directions when they have no clue as to where they are going. We don't drive around for hours pointlessly wasting a tank of gas only to find ourselves stranded and heading in the wrong direction. Have you ever been in the car with a man who is lost? He tells you to shut up when you even begin to open your mouth because he is a "human compass" and knows exactly what he's doing. And every five minutes or so he takes a turn going forty-five miles per hour, smashing your face against the window, or recklessly cuts across four lanes of traffic only to find out he's made another wrong turn. If he would have simply stopped and asked directions in the first place, he wouldn't have found himself kissing someone else's bumper at a stoplight.
>
> 2
>
> Why is it that men continually think they're driving in a competitive race? If they are stopped at a red light, they rev their engines the entire time, and the instant the light changes to green they take off squealing their tires. This is annoying and dangerous. What if there was a car or pedestrian that missed its own red light and
>
> 3

snuck out into the road? Guys, if you're doing this because you think it's cool or attracts women, you're wrong. It makes us more nervous than anything and it's very uncool and unsafe.

Speeding is what men do best on the road. Traffic is not a race. It   4
isn't a competition as to who reaches their destination first, or who can turn corners the fastest, or who gets the most speeding and reckless driving tickets. There is a reason why men get more speeding tickets than women. Not because we flirt to get out of tickets but only because we don't get pulled over as frequently. We don't speed. We have more intelligence than senselessly to put our own lives as well as the lives of others in danger.

My largest issue with male drivers is how a majority of them   5
drive with one hand on the wheel and the other hand doing only God knows what. The seat is reclined as far back as possible, and they're banging their heads to loud obnoxious music cranked way beyond a necessary audible level. How can anyone possibly be able to maneuver a vehicle safely while driving in this manner? How did they even get their licenses in the first place? You don't ever see women driving like that. In my opinion, any man seen driving in this manner should be reported to the proper authorities, have his license revoked, and serve jail time not only for driving dangerously but also for looking utterly ridiculous.

The middle, or body, of Cowley's essay consists of four paragraphs. In each one she takes up an example of why she believes women are better drivers than men, and then she elaborates. You can see that the topic of paragraph 2 is stopping for directions; paragraph 3 is squealing tires; paragraph 4 is driving too fast; and paragraph 5 is driving with only one hand.

THE CONCLUSION: HOW A PIECE OF WRITING ENDS

A concluding paragraph (or paragraphs) closes an article or essay. It pulls together the elements discussed in the body and provides a final perspective on the writer's main idea. Authors often use their concluding paragraphs to drive home or restate their idea. It's their last chance to make their point. Sometimes, however, a conclusion will introduce a new idea suggested by the details in the body paragraphs.

Here is the conclusion to Rachael Cowley's essay about men's driving habits.

> I feel that the above evidence more than proves my point that   6
> women are not only better drivers but also safer drivers than men.
> We definitely rule the road. Oh, and men, if you want to continue
> bashing women for being bad drivers, bring it on. We know you're
> insecure, or else you wouldn't be wasting your valuable time crack-
> ing jokes about the ones you may choose to spend the rest of your
> days with.

Cowley uses her conclusion to restate her main idea — that women are
better drivers than men are. Notice how she also uses the opportunity to
raise a new idea, that men should think twice before making fun of
women's driving.

Exercise 6-1
. . . .

The following passage is a brief essay from the textbook *Psychology* by Don H. Hockenbury and Sandra E. Hockenbury. Read the
paragraphs carefully and answer the questions that follow them.

The Power of Touch

Touch is an important source of information about the world. It   1
can also be the source of great pleasure or great pain. Psychologist
Tiffany Field and pediatrician Saul Schanberg discovered that touch can
have a positive impact on the growth and development of premature
babies.

Schanberg and Field studied 40 premature infants with very low   2
birth weights. Their medical condition had stabilized, but the infants
still had to be kept in incubators in a special hospital nursery. According
to the prevailing medical wisdom at that time, infants who were that
premature were rarely handled. Field and Schanberg wanted to see if
sensory stimulation — specifically, touch — would affect the infants'
growth and development.

For a period of 10 days, half of the preterm infants were gently   3
massaged for 15 minutes three times a day. That is, the infants' head,
neck, shoulders, arms, legs, and back were gently but firmly stroked.
The results were impressive. Compared to the control infants, who did
not receive the massage, the massaged infants averaged 47 percent more
weight gain. This weight gain did not occur because the massaged
babies ate more. Both the massaged and the control infants ate the same

amount of food. The weight gain appeared to be due to the effect of touch on their metabolism.

Additional benefits were equally impressive. The massaged infants were more active and spent longer periods awake than the control infants. They were more responsive to people and objects, such as a rattle, and had higher scores on tests that measured mental and motor development. Finally, they were hospitalized an average of six days fewer than the control infants.   4

Remarkably, these benefits seemed to be long-term. At eight months of age, the massaged infants continued to weigh more and to show better performance on tests that assessed mental and motor development than did the babies who had not been massaged.   5

Infant massage is common to many cultures, and need not be limited to premature babies. In India, for example, infant massage is a common practice. In her research, Field found that infants respond best to gentle, firm, and slow strokes, much like a Swedish massage. When touch is too light, it tends to be overstimulating and may even be irritating.   6

Not surprisingly, different areas of the infant's body respond differently to touch. Stroking the face, stomach, or feet tends to stimulate babies; stroking the back or legs tends to soothe and relax them. Touch may be especially important in early infancy because it is the most mature sensory system for the first few months of life.   7

Example:

What does the essay's introductory paragraph (paragraph 1) tell you about the topic and the main idea of the essay?

TOPIC: *touch* _____

MAIN IDEA OF THE ESSAY: *Touch can have a positive impact on the growth and development of premature babies.*

1. Is paragraph 2 a continuation of the introduction or the beginning of the body of the essay? How can you tell?

   It's a continuation of the introduction. You can tell because the general

   topic of the paragraph is touch, but it doesn't provide any supporting

   details for the main idea of the essay, stated in paragraph 1.

2. What are the topic and main idea of paragraph 3?

    TOPIC: _weight gain_

    MAIN IDEA: _Massaged infants gained 47 percent more weight._

3. What details provided in paragraphs 4 and 5 support the main idea of the essay?

    Massaged infants are more active and more responsive, scored higher

    on tests, and were hospitalized for fewer days than nonmassaged

    babies; those benefits were long-term.

4. Does paragraph 6 sound like a middle paragraph or a concluding paragraph? Explain your answer.

    This sounds like a concluding paragraph, not a middle paragraph. It no

    longer focuses on the narrow scope of the research study but instead

    discusses infant massage in general and gives the findings of another

    study by Field.

5. Does paragraph 7, the concluding paragraph, restate the main idea of the selection or develop a new idea? Explain your answer.

    It develops a new idea. Rather than restate the benefits of touch for

    babies, it suggests that the importance of touch could be due to how

    developed that sensory system is in early life.

· ·

■ Recognizing Patterns of Organization

Writers use the same organizational patterns in their writing that you use to think about things in your everyday life. In deciding, for example, what kind of stereo equipment or car to buy, you compare and contrast one brand and one model with another. When you select courses for an upcoming term, you categorize or classify them by type—according to their academic discipline or department, their content, their instructors, their level of difficulty, the degree of interest they hold for you, and so on. If you are considering joining a fraternity or sorority, living on or off campus, or changing your major, you analyze the effects such an action would have and think about the reasons (the causes) that prompted you to consider the issue in the first place.

These thinking patterns—comparison and contrast, classification, cause and effect—are just a few of the approaches to thinking you use every day. At the same time, these are common patterns writers use to organize and develop their ideas. As a result, you will encounter them—and other patterns of organization and thinking—when you read.

■ Definitions

Writers use **definitions** to provide the meanings of key terms or concepts. Sometimes they give a formal dictionary definition of a key term in a sentence. A definition may also include examples, comparisons, and other kinds of explanation discussed later in this chapter.

Textbooks are often designed to make spotting definitions easy. The key term is often in **boldface** or *italics* and the entire definition might be as well. For example, look at the following passage from the textbook *The Bedford Introduction to Literature* by Michael Meyer:

> Some flat characters are immediately recognizable as ***stock characters***. These stereotypes are particularly popular in formula fiction, television programs, and action movies. Stock characters are types rather than individuals. The poor but dedicated writer falls in love with a hard-working understudy, who gets nowhere because the corrupt producer favors his boozy, pampered mistress for the leading role. Characters such as these—the loyal servant, the mean stepfather, the henpecked husband, the dumb blonde, the sadistic army officer, the dotty grandmother—are prepackaged; they lack individuality because their authors have, in a sense, not imaginatively created them but simply summoned them from a warehouse of clichés and social prejudices. Stock characters can become fresh if a good writer makes them vivid, interesting, or memorable, but too often a writer's use of these stereotypes is simply weak characterization.

In this case the key term, or word being defined, appears in italicized boldface. The paragraph proceeds to define the term in a few different ways: stock characters are "stereotypes," "prepackaged," "clichés," and "social prejudices."

Another way to spot a definition is to look for key words that may indicate that a definition is contained in a sentence. For instance, if a word or term is followed by *is, is defined as, refers to,* or *means,* you know that a definition will follow. Here is another example from the literature textbook:

> *Theme* is the central idea or meaning of a story. It provides a unifying point around which the plot, characters, setting, point of view, symbols, and other elements of a story are organized.

One last way to spot a definition is to see if the author uses a dash or parentheses to define terms. Here is an example of a definition from the 2001 annual report for TJX Companies, Inc., which owns Marshalls, T.J. Maxx, HomeGoods, and A.J. Wright:

> For our customers, these brands are synonymous with *value* — which is represented by the wide selection and rapidly changing assortments of brand name merchandise offering the combination of fashion, quality, and price.

Often writers need to define concepts that are larger or more complicated than single words. Such definitions are usually longer than a sentence or even a paragraph. They can span several paragraphs or even take up a whole essay. Defining the complicated feelings a brother and sister have for each other, for example, may take many pages, since the definition cannot be summed up in a single word, phrase, or paragraph.

Exercise 6-2

Underline the definitions for the terms highlighted in boldface in each of the following paragraphs.

Example:

A more precise measure of body fat is provided by **hydrostatic weighing.** In this procedure, a person is weighed twice: once in the normal way and then submerged in water. Body fat is lighter than water; muscle and bone are heavier. The body's weight under water largely reflects the density of body mass. The more people weigh submerged, relative to dry weight, the less body fat they carry. This method is not flawless. It requires expensive equipment and a skilled technician. Measurements may also be thrown off by fluid retention and other factors. (Jeffrey S. Nevid, Spencer A. Rathus, and Hannah R. Rubenstein, *Health in the New Millennium*)

1. All scientific thought involves simplifications of reality. The real world is far too complex for the human mind—or the most powerful computer—to consider. Scientists use models instead. A **model** is a set of simplifying assumptions about some aspect of the real world. Models are always based on assumed conditions that are simpler than those of the real world, assumptions that are necessarily false. A model of the real world cannot *be* the real world. (Timothy Tregarthen and Libby Rittenberg, *Economics*)

2. Assume that a certain number of identical processors (machines, humans, or robots) work on a series of tasks that make up a job. Associated with each task is a specified amount of time required to complete the task. For simplicity, we assume that any of the processors can work on any of the tasks. Our problem, known as the **machine-scheduling problem,** is to decide how the tasks should be scheduled so that the completion time for the tasks collectively is as early as possible. (COMAP, *For All Practical Purposes*)

3. **Plutons** are large igneous bodies that formed at depth in the earth's crust; they range in size from 1 km^3 to hundreds of cubic kilometers. These large bodies become accessible to study when uplift and erosion uncover them or when mines and drill holes cut into them. Plutons are highly variable, not only in size but also in shape and in their relation to the surrounding country rock. (Frank Press and Raymond Siever, *Understanding Earth*)

4. A **storyboard** is a series of drawings (or occasionally photographs) of each shot (or sometimes part of a shot) of a planned film or video story, usually accompanied by brief descriptions or notes. Storyboards are the visual equivalent of a rough draft of a written story. They allow filmmakers to see how the finished film might look before the laborious

and costly processes of filming and editing begin. Storyboards are useful for deciding how to divide the script into shots, determining how to arrange the shots (a sort of preediting), and deciding camera placement. (William H. Phillips, *Film: An Introduction*)

5.   There are several disadvantages, however, to the decentralized nature of the Internet. One drawback has been the increased circulation of data and "news," sometimes called **cyberspace litter**—the Internet equivalent of unwanted junk mail or newspaper advertising supplements. Unlike traditional news media, which routinely employ editors as information gatekeepers, many individuals and newsgroups on the Internet send out data that are not checked by anyone. (Richard Campbell, *Media and Culture: An Introduction to Mass Communication*)

. . . . , ...

■ Examples

Writers often use **examples** to illustrate and explain an idea. Sometimes they explain an idea by describing one example in detail. Sometimes they provide a series of examples but give each example brief treatment. Well-chosen examples add interest to a writer's idea and make it easier to understand.

In the following paragraph, from *Sociology* by Ian Robertson, the author explains the idea of *population transfer* by providing a number of examples of it:

In some situations of intense hostility between groups, the problem is "solved" by removing the minority from the scene altogether. In 1972, for example, the entire Asian population was ordered to leave the African country of Uganda, in which they had lived for generations. In a few cases, population transfer may involve outright partition of a territory. Hostility between Hindus and Muslims in India was so intense that in 1947 the entire subcontinent was divided between them, creating a new Muslim state, Pakistan. Today, Cyprus is becoming divided into Greek and Turkish territories, and Lebanon into Muslim and Christian territories. Voluntary and forced population transfers have been taking place in both countries.

Throughout the passage the author clues the reader with signal words, such as "for example," "In a few cases," and "Today," that introduce his examples. These examples help readers understand the author's point that removing minorities from a culture or location happens with some frequency.

Exercise 6-3

. . . .

This passage from a psychology textbook uses example as its organizational pattern. Read it and answer the questions that follow.

By definition, experience is key to learning. More than 200 years ago, philosophers such as John Locke and David Hume echoed Aristotle's conclusion from 2000 years earlier: We learn by association. Our minds naturally connect events that occur in sequence: We *associate* them. If, after seeing and smelling freshly baked bread, you eat some and find it satisfying, then the next time you see and smell fresh bread, your experience will lead you to expect that eating some will be satisfying again. And if you associate a sound with a frightening consequence, then your fear may be aroused by the sound itself. As one 4-year-old exclaimed after watching a TV character get mugged, "If I had heard that music, I wouldn't have gone around the corner!"

Simpler animals can learn simple associations. When disturbed by a squirt of water, the sea snail *Aplysia* will protectively withdraw its gill. If the squirts continue, as happens naturally in choppy water, the withdrawal response diminishes. (The snail's response "habituates.") But if the sea snail repeatedly receives an electric shock just after being squirted, its withdrawal response to the squirt alone becomes stronger. The animal associates the squirt with the impending shock. More complex animals can learn more complex associations, especially those that bring favorable consequences. Seals in an aquarium will repeat behaviors, such as slapping and barking, that prompt people to toss them a herring.

By linking two events that occur close together, both the sea snail and the seal exhibit *associative learning*. The sea snail associates the squirt with impending shock; the seal associates slapping and barking with receiving a herring. In both cases, the animals learned something important to their survival: to associate the past with the immediate future. (David G. Myers, *Psychology*)

Example:

Does the author provide signal words to indicate examples?
_No_

1. What main idea are the examples in this excerpt meant to illus-
    trate?

    "Our minds naturally connect events that occur in sequence: We

    associate them."

2. What examples does the author provide to support his point?

    the smell of bread, TV soundtracks, sea snails, and seals

3. How do the examples in the first paragraph and the second
    paragraph differ?

    In the first paragraph, the examples are personal, human experiences

    that draw in the reader. In the second paragraph, the examples illustrate

    the same principle (occurring both naturally and experimentally) with

    two animals, the sea snail and the seal.

4. What connection does the author make between the examples
    of the behavior of the sea snail and that of the seal?

    "In both cases, the animals learned something important to their

    survival: to associate the past with the immediate future."

5. The examples in this passage help the author define "associa-
    tive learning." What is the definition?

    "Linking two events that occur close together . . . to associate the

    past with the immediate future."

. . . .

■ Lists and Sequences

A **list** is a collection of details arranged one beneath the other or one after another. A list is usually presented in no special order; instead, it simply enumerates a collection of details to support the writer's point. These details, which may include reasons, examples, or facts, are often but not always numbered.

The following paragraph, from the American government textbook *The Politics of American Government* by Stephen J. Wayne et al., contains two terms, *newsworthiness* and *public,* that are defined by lists:

> The key to news media coverage of political events (as well as other kinds of events) is their **newsworthiness.** This complex concept includes timeliness, importance, conflict, drama, and surprise. To be considered news, an event must have the potential to capture the attention of the public: readers, listeners, and viewers. From the news media's perspective, their job is to emphasize events that have this potential.

Sequences are similar to lists, in that both patterns present a series of supporting details that are often but not always numbered. Unlike lists, however, sequences follow a particular order of steps or stages—chronological order, for example, or the order of importance. Sequence refers to the order in which things happen, as when a history book describes the series of events leading up to a war. Sequences are used to describe the development of the planet Earth in geology, the emergence of evolutionary life forms in biology, and the influence of factors causing a disease, such as cancer.

Read the following excerpt from "Dirty Work," an article by Mark Cloud from the magazine *Parents* (June 2002), and see if you can identify the sequence as well as the words the author uses to signal the order of the sequence:

> Obviously, this is not a preferred strategy and should be used only as a last resort. First, prepare the following items: a fresh diaper, baby wipes, protective eye goggles, a nose clip, a plastic baby pool, rubber gloves, a sturdy two-ply grocery bag, and a stapler. Assemble everything, along with your child, in the front yard. Put on the goggles, the nose clip, and the rubber gloves. Settle your
>
> *(continued)*

child in the empty baby pool, and then join him there. Remove all of the baby's clothing, especially the diaper. Holding the toxic items between your thumb and forefinger, place them in the paper bag. Then ease the baby onto his back. While cradling his ankles in one hand, softly clean the baby's bottom with one wipe—or several. Afterward, place soiled wipes in the paper bag.

Once you've completely cleansed the baby, put on the fresh diaper. But wait—you're not done. Because of your recent proximity to the dirty diaper, the safest thing to do at that moment is to remove all of your own clothing (except boxer shorts) and place them in the paper bag too. Immediately staple shut this bag of contaminants. If a neighbor's garbage can is accessible, put the sealed bag there. If you can't find a can, go to the edge of your property and fling the bag as far away from your yard as possible.

Finally, pick up your freshly diapered darling, kiss him on the cheek, and carry him inside. Before you put any clothes on either of you, roll around on the floor with your little bundle of joy. And while you're rolling around, try to recall how good old Sparky used to wag his tail and lick your face. You'll realize immediately that this is even better!

If you identified "First," "then," "While," "Afterward," "Once," "Immediately," and "Finally" as the signal words, you are correct. These words indicate that the author was developing an idea that has steps or stages.

It is relatively easy to identify a sequence when the author uses signal words. But how do you identify a sequence when such words are not provided? Take another look at the passage about diaper changing. Not every step is preceded by a signal word. You can also tell, by reading closely, that the author is providing a (humorous) series of the steps he recommends fathers take when they have to change a diaper: That is also a sequence.

Exercise 6-4

. . . .

The following passages contain lists. Read each passage, and answer the questions that follow it.

Infants' expression of emotion also seemed to change in conjunction with locomotion. The parents of babies who had begun to crawl reported that their babies now became angry more frequently and more intensely when their efforts to achieve a goal were frustrated. The babies who crawled also seemed to become more upset when their parents left their sides. One mother reported:

> If I leave [the room] she gets upset unless she's busy and doesn't see it. But as soon as she notices, she starts hollering. I don't think it mattered the first four months. When she started doing more, sitting up, crawling, that's when she'd get upset when I would leave.

Many developmental psychologists believe that these new forms of emotional expression signal a new, emotionally charged bond, which they call **attachment**. Eleanor Maccoby lists four signs of attachment in babies and young children:

1. They seek to be near their primary caregivers. Before the age of 7 to 8 months, few babies plan and make organized attempts to achieve contact with their caregivers; after this age, babies often follow their caregiver closely, for example.

2. They show distress if separated from their caregivers. Before attachment begins, infants show little disturbance when their caregivers walk out of the room.

3. They are happy when they are reunited with the person they are attached to.

4. They orient their actions to the caregiver, even when he or she is absent. Babies listen for the caregiver's voice and watch the caregiver while they play.

(Michael Cole and Sheila R. Cole, *The Development of Children*)

Example:

What is described in the numbered list?

Eleanor Maccoby's four signs of attachment in babies and young children

1. To what other function does infants' expressions of emotion seem to be linked?

   locomotion (that is, crawling)

2. According to Maccoby, at what age would babies start showing attachment behaviors?

   at about 7 to 8 months

The Problem-Solving Process

If you go to work at a quality-conscious company like Xerox, you will become expert in using the problem-solving process. You will also find it invaluable in many other situations. In fact, formal problem solving can even help you study better. Here is the process.

STEP 1. *Identify the problem.* The individual or group considers various ways of looking at the problem and chooses the one that is most helpful in solving it. This requires opening your mind (and your team's agenda) to lots of ideas, then focusing in on the most useful problem definition.

STEP 2. *Analyze the problem.* Look for causes, issues, and questions. Gather the information you need to understand the problem. Again, start by opening up to lots of potential causes. Then close in on one or a few key causes for action.

STEP 3. *List possible solutions.* Be creative. Think of lots of ideas. At Xerox, employees ask, "How could we make a change?" Then think about each option to make it as clear as possible.

STEP 4. *Select and plan one solution.* Which is the best way? Compare the options in as many ways as possible. Then focus on *how* to implement the one you chose.

STEP 5. *Implement the solution.* Follow through on your plan to solve the problem or make the change.

STEP 6. *Check the solution.* How well does it work? Identify any continuing problems and start the process again.

(Kenneth Blanchard et al., *Exploring the World of Business*)

3. What does the word *process* in the title suggest?

    The word "process" suggests a sequence of actions designed to produce a certain result.

4. Why is a problem-solving process useful?

    By really understanding a problem and thinking through possible solutions, people can avoid going off in scattered directions. The process should save time and wasted effort.

5. Does this problem-solving process always lead to "the right answer"? According to Step 6, what should people do if problems continue?

No, the process doesn't always lead to the right answer. People should

identify any continuing problems and begin the process again.

· ·

■ Comparison, Contrast, and Analogy

COMPARISON AND CONTRAST

To illustrate or explain features of ideas or things, writers often compare them to, or contrast them with, other things. By setting one thing off against another, writers can provide a clearer picture of both. **Comparing** two things is looking at their similarities. **Contrasting** two things is noting the differences between similar aspects.

Certain signal or cue words help identify when a writer is comparing or contrasting two or more different topics or concepts. If you see the following types of words in a reading, they usually signal that the writer is comparing two or more things. Signal words used to indicate comparison include the following:

in comparison	parallels	similar
in the same way	resembles	similarly
like		

Similarly, certain words signal that a writer is contrasting rather than comparing things. The following are examples:

although	in contrast	on the other hand
but	instead	whereas
different	nevertheless	yet
however		

Signal words are not necessary for making comparisons and contrasts. Sometimes the comparison and contrast organizational pattern omits signal words. In this case, it will be up to you to figure out if the writer is either comparing how two or more things are alike or contrasting two or more things to show how they are different.

Sometimes writers organize their comparison-contrast discussion in a "block" structure by discussing first one part fully and then the other. The following example, from the world history textbook *The Global Past* by Lanny B. Fields, Russell J. Barber, and Cheryl A. Riggs, illustrates the block format:

> The idea that spoken language could be converted into a written form and preserved is such a revolutionary idea that it took true genius to conceive of it. Some forms of writing are **alphabetic,** using a limited number of symbols to represent the component sounds of a language. English is alphabetic and uses just twenty-six letters (and a few punctuation marks) to produce all of its messages. In contrast, some forms of writing are **ideographic,** wherein each symbol represents an idea, irrespective of the pronunciation of the spoken word. (Chinese and Mayan writing systems are largely ideographic, although each also incorporates some phonetic [pronunciation-based] elements.) Ideographic writing has many more symbols than alphabetic writing, often thousands of characters.

Writers may also use an alternating structure, in which they move back and forth between the things being compared by taking up one aspect at a time for each of the compared items. The following is an example of alternating structure from "Celebrity Sauces," a 2002 *Consumer Reports* article on fancy spaghetti sauces:

> In the beginning, there was Paul Newman. The tomato sauce featuring the actor's name and recipe was so successful that it became a supermarket staple. Now, *Newman's Own* shares the shelves with a bevy of sauces sponsored by chefs who have won celebrity of sorts by cooking on television, or by restaurants that have created a buzz. There's even a sauce named for Francis Coppola—perhaps the sauce that The Godfather's colleagues cooked on their nights off.
>
> These newer products are touted as haute cuisine with all the complexity of fine wine, and they carry haute prices—as much as $10 per jar, before shipping. We set out to see how nine tomato-based celebrity sauces compared with a couple of $2 national brands—*Prego* and *Ragu.* The sauces we chose carry the names of Lidia Matticchio Bastianich (chef, cookbook author, and creator of

the public-television series *Lidia's Italian-American Kitchen*); Coppola (unlike the legion of Hollywood types who say, "I really want to direct," this director wants to cook); Bobby Flay (restaurateur and host of *Hot Off the Grill* and *FoodNation* on The Food Network); Emeril Lagasse (restaurateur and host of *Emeril Live!* on The Food Network); Newman (he gives all profits, after taxes, to charity); Bove's of Vermont (lines snake out the door of this Burlington restaurant); Patsy's restaurant in New York City (said to have been a favorite of Frank Sinatra's); Rao's restaurant in New York City (so exclusive it's all but restricted to family members and friends); and The Silver Palate (a former fancy-foods shop in New York City that spawned a series of cookbooks).

All of the celebrity sauces except *Bobby Flay's Spicy Tomato* are sold in stores, although distribution may be spotty and limited to specialty stores, some supermarket chains, and a few nationwide stores (we've found *Emeril's* in Costco and *Rao's* in Bed, Bath & Beyond). All but *Newman's Own, Prego,* and *Ragu* are sold online, but shipping charges can nearly double the cost. Buy a 21-ounce jar of *Bobby Flay's* and you'll fork over a total of $15.50 (about $3 per typical half-cup serving). When ordering products online, you may also have to buy a minimum number of bottles.

And yet, you may want to splurge. When our panel of tasters assessed the flavor and texture of each sauce in blind taste tests, they found that the celebrity sauces were quite tasty, and all were better than the mass-market brands.

Five—from Emeril Lagasse, Bobby Flay, Rao's, Francis Coppola, and Lidia Bastianich—tasted freshly prepared, like a good homemade sauce. And if you go to a store to buy the best of that bunch, *Emeril's Kicked Up Tomato,* its price is fairly reasonable: 66 cents per serving.

Three other pedigree products, from Bove's, Patsy's, and The Silver Palate, were very good. And what about the marinara from Paul Newman? If the best sauces are like fine wine, you might think of *Newman's Own* as a decent jug wine—hardly better than the notably cheaper *Prego* and *Ragu,* which landed at the end of the Ratings.

Notice how the magazine article begins with an overview of the new trend in celebrity pasta sauces and then compares and contrasts them point-by-point: price, celebrity, distribution, and taste.

Exercise 6-5

The following passages contain comparisons and contrasts. Read each passage, and answer the questions that follow it.

Unlike most Westerners, who now raise their children to be independent, many Asians and Africans live in communal cultures, cultures that focus on cultivating emotional closeness. Rather than being given their own bedrooms and entrusted to day care, infants and toddlers typically sleep with their mothers and spend their days close to a family member. Children of communal cultures grow up with a stronger sense of "family self" — a feeling that what shames the child shames the family. Compared with Westerners, people in Japanese and Chinese cultures, for example, exhibit greater shyness toward strangers and greater concern for social harmony and loyalty. "My parents will be disappointed in me" is a concern of 7 percent of American and Italian teenagers and 14 percent of Australian teens, but nearly 25 percent of teens in Taiwan and Japan. . . .

Because we are so mindful of how others differ from us, we often fail to notice the similarities predisposed by our shared biology. Cross-cultural research can help us by leading us to appreciate both our cultural diversity *and* our human kinship. Compared with person-to-person differences within groups, the differences between groups are small. Regardless of our culture, we humans share the same life cycle. We all speak to our infants in similar ways and respond similarly to their coos and cries. All over the world, the children of parents who are warm and supportive feel better about themselves and are less hostile than the children of parents who are punitive and rejecting. (David G. Myers, *Psychology*)

Example:

Does the passage use block structure or alternating structure to organize the compare-and-contrast pattern?

block structure

1. Does the preceding passage emphasize similarities or differences?

The passage emphasizes similarities. Although more space is given to

differences, the main point of the passage is that humans share the

same life cycle and that differences between groups are really small.

2. In the preceding passage, underline the signal words that indicate both contrast (differences) and comparison (similarities).

> Animals have two types of glands. Some, such as sweat glands and salivary glands, release secretions that are not hormones through ducts that lead outside the body. Sweat gland ducts open onto the surface of the skin, salivary gland ducts open into the mouth, and the duct from the pancreas carries digestive enzymes into the digestive tract. Such glands are called **exocrine glands** because they secrete their products to the outside of the body (the Greek *exo-* means "outside of").
>
> Glands that secrete hormones do not have ducts; they are called **endocrine glands** because they secrete their products into extracellular fluid, from which the hormones enter the blood, which is inside the body. Cells of most endocrine glands synthesize hormones and store them until they are stimulated to secrete their signals. Collectively, endocrine glands make up the endocrine system. (William K. Purves et al., *Life: The Science of Biology*)

3. What is compared and contrasted in this passage?

    exocrine glands and endocrine glands

4. What do exocrine glands have that endocrine glands do not have? Define the word that you write.

    ducts: tube-shaped channels or passages

5. Does the passage use block structure or alternating structure to discuss the comparison and contrast?

    block structure

ANALOGY

Analogy is a special type of extended comparison for the purpose of explanation. Writers use analogy to explain something unfamiliar to their readers by comparing it with something more familiar. For example, you might explain the game of football to someone who didn't understand it by making an analogy with war—the offense attacks the defense by attempting to invade its territory.

Appreciating how writers use analogy to clarify and explain their ideas can help you understand complex ideas. This example comes from the book *The Disuniting of America: Reflections on a Multicultural Society* by Arthur Schlesinger Jr.:

> History is to the nation rather as memory is to the individual. As an individual deprived of memory becomes disoriented and lost, not knowing where he has been or where he is going, so a nation denied a conception of its past will be disabled in dealing with its present and its future.

In this analogy the author explains his idea about the need for a knowledge of history by comparing the loss of that knowledge to someone who has lost his way. Schlesinger uses his analogy to support his idea that historical memory is as important to the nation as individual memory is to each individual person.

The following example, from the textbook *Health in the New Millennium* by Jeffrey S. Nevid, Spencer A. Rathus, and Hannah R. Rubenstein, uses a fruit analogy to explain body fat distribution:

> **Body Fat Distribution and Health** Body shape, like body composition, is an index of health. Two people may weigh the same amount and even have the same amount of body fat. Yet different distributions of fat may affect their relative health risks. Some people are "pears"; they carry excess fat in their hips, buttocks, and thighs. Others are "apples"; they carry excess fat around their midsections (waists). (See the figure opposite.) Though both kinds of obesity are associated with poor health, excess fat around the midsection appears to be a greater risk factor. Pears stand less of a risk of chronic diseases such as coronary heart disease, hypertension,

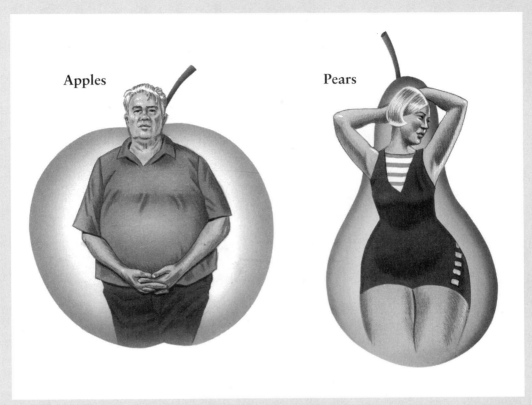

Apples

Pears

Apples vs. Pears
Apple-shaped people carry much of their excess weight around their middles, while pear-shaped people carry excess weight on their buttocks, thighs, and hips. Though both patterns of obesity are unhealthy, carrying fat around the waist is linked to a greater risk of serious chronic diseases, including heart disease, hypertension, and diabetes.

and diabetes than apples. For example, a five-year-study of 41,000 women aged 50 to 69 found that the higher the waist-to-hip ratio (the more "apple-shaped"), the greater the risk of death.

Why are apples at greater risk than pears? A possible reason is that abdominal fat, which accumulates around the pelvis, is connected with higher blood levels of HDL. (HDL is the so-called good cholesterol that sweeps away artery-clogging deposits.) Fat in the waist is linked to lower levels of HDL. Men are more likely to be apples than women, so it is not surprising that they stand a greater risk of coronary heart disease (at least until about age 65, when the rates between men and women even out).

Exercise 6-6

The following passages contain analogies. Read each passage, and answer the questions that follow it.

> Apparently, establishing a long-term memory is like creating a cement wall—it needs time to "set" before it becomes permanent. This process of "setting" a new memory permanently in the brain is called memory consolidation. (Don H. Hockenbury and Sandra E. Hockenbury, *Psychology*)

Example:

To what is establishing a long-term memory compared?

to creating a cement wall

1. What is the crucial factor that makes the analogy work?

   the process of setting

2. What is the technical term for setting a new memory permanently in the brain?

   memory consolidation

> No animal acquires its macromolecules directly from its food. Instead, it uses the subcomponents of its food to construct new macromolecules suited to its unique needs. For example, we eat proteins constructed by other animals and plants, but we break these proteins down into their amino acids and then reassemble the amino acids into the chemically different proteins of our own bodies. This process is like picking up Lego toys that somebody else has made, taking them apart, and putting the parts together again to make the toys *we* want. (William K. Purves et al., *Life: The Science of Biology*)

3. What familiar objects are used in the analogy in this passage?

   Lego toys

4. What are Lego toys compared to in this passage?

   macromolecules

5. The analogy explains how the human body breaks down pro-
   teins into amino acids and then reassembles them. How does
   the analogy explain that?

   It "is like picking up Lego toys that somebody else has made, taking

   them apart, and putting the parts together again to make the toys

   we want."

. . . .

■ Classification

To **classify** things is to categorize them—to put them into groups or
classes. Classified ads in the newspaper organize goods for sale or services for hire. You can find listings for houses and apartments for rent or
sale; cars both new and used for sale or lease; job opportunities; and
merchandise or services. Each section of the classifieds is subdivided into
smaller categories based on things such as location (for houses); size (for
apartments); type of merchandise (domestic/imported for cars).

Textbooks use classification extensively. A psychology textbook, for
example, might devote chapters to personality development, perception,
consciousness, learning, memory, motivation, emotions, disorders, statistics, and other topics related to the study of human behavior. Textbooks use classification to organize information within chapters and
parts of chapters as well. A discussion in a literature textbook may classify poems into the types narrative, lyric, and dramatic; or fiction into
novels, novellas, and short stories. Biology textbooks often present the
various classifications of animal and plant species. A music textbook
may classify popular music as folk, country, rock, disco, reggae, blues,
jazz, and other contemporary styles.

Sometimes it is helpful to look at a classification in an outline format
to see what the author intended. For instance, classifying the different
types of literature may look something like this:

I. Literature
   A. Poetry
      1. Narrative
      2. Lyric
      3. Dramatic
   B. Fiction
      1. Novels
      2. Novellas
      3. Short stories

This outline format helps you visualize the main topic (literature), the two subtopics (poetry and fiction), and the categories within each (narrative, lyric, dramatic; novels, novellas, short stories).

Writers use classification to organize information, to order data and information so readers can see connections between different concepts and different topics more readily. Classification enables writers to clarify their ideas; it enables readers to better understand the writers' points.

In the following passage from the textbook *Psychology* by David G. Myers, the author describes psychological disorders called anxiety disorders. He classifies these into three types: generalized anxiety disorder, phobic (fear) disorders, and obsessive-compulsive disorder.

Anxiety Disorders

Anxiety becomes disabling when people are unexplainably and uncontrollably tense (general anxiety disorder), irrationally fearful of something (a phobia), or troubled by repetitive thoughts and actions (obsessive-compulsive disorder). What do these disorders look like in real people? What causes them?

Anxiety is part of life. When speaking in front of a class, when peering down from a ledge, when waiting to play in a big game, any one of us might feel anxious. At one time or another, most of us feel enough anxiety that we fail to make eye contact or we avoid talking to someone — "shyness" we call it. Fortunately for most of us, our occasional uneasiness is not intense and persistent. If it becomes so, we may have one of the *anxiety disorders,* marked by distressing, persistent anxiety or maladaptive behaviors that reduce anxiety. In this section we focus on *generalized anxiety disorder,* in which a person feels unexplainably tense and uneasy; *phobias,* in which a person has a disruptive, irrational fear of a specific object or situation; and *obsessive-compulsive disorder,* in which a person is troubled by repetitive thoughts and/or actions.

GENERALIZED ANXIETY DISORDER

Tom, a 27-year-old electrician, seeks help, complaining of dizziness, sweating palms, heart palpitations, and ringing in his ears. He feels edgy and sometimes finds himself shaking. With reasonable success he hides his symptoms from his family and co-workers. Nevertheless, he has had few social contacts since the symptoms began two years ago. Worse, he occasionally has to leave work. His family doctor and neurologist can find no physical problem.

Tom's unfocused, out-of-control, negative feelings suggest a generalized anxiety disorder. The symptoms of this disorder are commonplace; their persistence is not. The sufferers are continually tense and jittery, worried about bad things that might happen, and experience all the symptoms of autonomic nervous system arousal (racing heart, clammy hands, stomach butterflies, sleeplessness). The tension and apprehension may leak out through furrowed brows, twitching eyelids, or fidgeting. One of the worst characteristics of a generalized anxiety disorder is that the person cannot identify, and therefore cannot avoid, the cause of these persistent, unpleasant symptoms. To use Freud's term, the anxiety is "free-floating."

As some 1 in 75 people with *panic disorder* know, anxiety may at times suddenly escalate into a terrifying *panic attack*—a minutes-long episode of intense fear that something horrible is about to happen to them. Heart palpitations, shortness of breath, choking sensations, trembling, or dizziness typically accompany the panic. The experience is unpredictable and so frightening that the sufferer often comes to fear the fear itself and to avoid situations where panic has struck. *Agoraphobia* is fear or avoidance of situations in which escape or help might not be available when panic strikes. Given such fear, people may avoid being outside the home, being in a crowd, or traveling in a plane or train or on an elevator.

PHOBIAS

Phobias *focus* anxiety on some specific object, activity, or situation. Phobias—irrational fears that disrupt behavior—are a common psychological disorder that people often accept and live with. Some *specific phobias* are incapacitating, however. Marilyn, a 28-year-old homemaker, so fears thunderstorms that she feels anxious as soon as a weather forecaster mentions possible storms later in the week. If her husband is away and a storm is forecast, she sometimes stays with a close relative. During a storm, she hides from windows and buries her head to avoid seeing the lightning. She is otherwise healthy and happy.

Other people suffer from irrational fears of specific animals or insects, or of such things as heights, blood, or tunnels. Sometimes it is possible to avoid the fear-arousing stimulus: One can hide during thunderstorms or avoid high places. With a *social phobia*, an intense fear of being scrutinized by others, the anxious person will avoid potentially embarrassing social situations. The person may

(continued)

avoid speaking up, eating out, or going to parties—or will sweat, tremble, or have diarrhea when doing so. Compared with the other disorders discussed in this chapter, phobias appear at a younger age—often by the early teens.

OBSESSIVE-COMPULSIVE DISORDER

As with generalized anxiety and phobias, we can see aspects of our own behavior in the obsessive-compulsive disorder. We may at times be obsessed with senseless or offensive thoughts that will not go away. Or we may engage in compulsive, rigid behavior— rechecking a locked door, stepping over cracks in the sidewalk, or lining up our books and pencils "just so" before studying.

Obsessive thoughts and compulsive behaviors cross the fine line between normality and disorder when they become so persistent that they interfere with the way we live or when they cause distress. Checking to see that the door is locked is normal; checking the door 10 times is not. Hand washing is normal; hand washing so often that one's skin becomes raw is not. At some time during their lives, often during their late teens or twenties, 2 or 3 percent of people cross that line from normal preoccupations and fussiness to debilitating disorder. The obsessive thoughts become so haunting, the compulsive rituals so senselessly time-consuming, that effective functioning becomes impossible.

One such person was billionaire Howard Hughes. Hughes would compulsively dictate the same phrases over and over again. Under stress, he developed an obsessive fear of germs. He became reclusive and insisted that his assistants carry out elaborate hand-washing rituals and wear white gloves when handling documents he would later touch. He ordered tape around doors and windows and forbade his staff to touch or even look at him. "Everybody carries germs around with them," he explained. "I want to live longer than my parents, so I avoid germs."

Exercise 6-7

Reread the preceding passage from *Psychology* and answer the following questions.

Example:

What is another term for "generalized anxiety disorder"?

"free-floating" anxiety

1. Prepare an outline of the textbook passage. Refer back to page 201 of this textbook for an example.

   I. Anxiety Disorders

      A. Introduction

      B. Generalized Anxiety Disorder

         1. Free-floating anxiety

         2. Panic disorder

      C. Phobias

         1. Specific phobias

         2. Irrational fears of objects or situations

      D. Obsessive-Compulsive Behavior

2. What are the symptoms of generalized anxiety disorder?

   "Sufferers are continually tense and jittery, worried about bad things

   that might happen, and experience all the symptoms of autonomic

   nervous system arousal (racing heart, clammy hands, stomach

   butterflies, sleeplessness)."

3. What are the symptoms of phobic disorders?

   They include anxiety, avoidance, and fear, as well the physical symptoms

   of sweating, trembling, or diarrhea; they often disrupt a person's life.

4. How do people compensate for phobic disorders?

   Some people accept and learn to live with their fears; others avoid or

   hide from the thing or situation that frightens them.

5. What examples of obsessive-compulsive behavior does the author provide?

Rechecking a locked door, stepping over cracks in a sidewalk, lining up

books and pencils "just so" before studying, hand washing, and Howard

Hughes's fear of germs.

■ Cause and Effect

One of the most common organizational patterns writers use is that of **cause and effect.** Sometimes referred to as *causal analysis,* the cause and effect organizational pattern explains why something happened or developed as it did. If you were to list, for example, your reasons for attending college, including why you chose the school and program you did, you would be thinking about causes. In listing the reasons for going to college — intellectual, social, financial — you complete a causal analysis of your decision to continue your education. In a historical account of the American Civil War, the writer would explain both the causes of the war and the effects it had socially, politically, and economically.

Writers often use cause and effect as an organizing pattern when making an argument about why or how something happened and what might result from it. The causes of the event or situation are the reasons it occurred; the effects are its results or consequences. The following are typical words that signal causes: *because, cause, due to, for this reason, on account of,* and *since.* These words typically signal effects: *as a result, consequently, in effect, outcomes, result,* and *therefore.*

In the following selection from the mass communication textbook *Media and Culture* by Richard Campbell, the author examines the question of whether advertising and consumer culture are to blame for some acts of violence among inner-city youth.

Fighting over Sneakers

During the 1950s and 1960s, most serious basketball players wore simple canvas sneakers — usually Converse or Keds. Encouraged by increasing TV coverage, interest in sports exploded in the late 1960s and 1970s, as did a wildly competitive international sneaker industry. First Adidas dominated the industry, then Nike and Reebok. The Great Sneaker Wars have since continued unabated, although they may have peaked at the 1992 Olympics when pro-basketball stars Michael Jordan and Charles Barkley—Nike endorsers—refused to display the Reebok logo on their team jackets at the awards ceremony. Reebok had paid dearly to sponsor the Olympics and wanted the athletes to fall in line. A compromise was eventually worked out in which the two players wore the jackets but hid the Reebok name.

Although the Olympic incident seems petty, battles over brand-name sneakers and jackets in the 1980s were a more dangerous "game." Advertisers found themselves embroiled in a controversy that, for a time, threw a bright and uncomfortable spotlight on the advertising industry. In many poor and urban areas throughout the United States, kids and rival gangs were fighting over and stealing brand-name sportswear from one another. Particularly coveted and targeted were $100-plus top-of-the-line basketball shoes, especially the Nike and Reebok brands heavily advertised on television. A few incidents resulted in shootings and killings. Articles in major newspapers and magazines, including *Sports Illustrated* ("Your Sneakers or Your Life") took advertisers to task. Especially hard hit was Nike, which by the early 1990s controlled nearly 30 percent of the $5.5 billion world sneaker market. Nike's slogan—"Just do it"—became a rallying cry for critics who argued that while for most middle-class people, the command simply meant get in shape, work hard, and perform, for kids from poorer neighborhoods, "Just do it" was a call to arms: "Do what you have to do to survive."

The problem was exacerbated during the 1980s by underlying economic conditions. As the gap between rich and poor grew, advertisements suggested that our identities came from the products that we own. It is not surprising, then, that the possession of a particular brand-name product became increasingly significant for kids who felt they did not own much. Having the "right" sneaker or jacket came to represent a large part of their identities. For some groups and gangs, such possession became a requirement for membership.

The controversy over brand-name products has raised serious concerns about the moral responsibilities of agencies and advertisers. On one hand, Nike and other advertisers have become a lightning rod for the problems of a consumer culture that promises the good life to everyone who "just does it." On the other hand, criticisms of advertising have often stopped with the ads and have not examined whether they *cause* the violence or are simply *symptoms*

(continued)

of the inequities in contemporary America. Although many critics vilified Nike at the time, few were willing to discuss the drawbacks of capitalism and consumerism in general.

Fights over sneakers and jackets generate significant questions at the heart of our consumer culture. Does brand-name advertising unrealistically raise hopes about attaining the consumer "dreams" that some ads promise? Who should share the ultimate responsibility for violence that takes place in the name of a coveted shoe or jacket? As a society, should we mandate noncommercial messages and public-service announcements that offer alternative visions? While we need to debate these issues vigorously as individuals and as a society, in some communities kids and adults have already acted. Although brand-name products continue to sell well, an alternative attitude rejects such labeling and opts for cheaper generic product and used rummage-sale clothing. Posing a challenge to the advertising industry, this attitude undermines the view that brand-name identification is a requirement of our times.

Exercise 6-8

Refer back to the selection "Fighting over Sneakers" and answer the following questions.

Example:

Why did Michael Jordan and Charles Barkley refuse to show the Reebok logo on their 1992 Olympic jackets?

They were paid endorsers for Nike, a rival brand.

1. What were the causes of the sneaker war in the late 1960s and the 1970s?

    the "exploding" interest in sports produced by increased TV coverage

    and a "wildly competitive international sneaker industry"

2. What added to the causes in the 1980s?

    the growing gap between rich and poor; the connection between owning

    particular sneakers and identity and self-esteem

3. What was the effect of the sneaker war on kids and rival gangs?

    fights, shootings, killings

4. What was the effect of the sneaker war on advertisers?

    They were blamed for suggesting that our identities come from the

    products we own; they became "embroiled in controversy."

5. Does the author agree with critics that sneaker advertisements
    cause violence?

    Not necessarily. He notes that critics "have not examined whether

    [ads] cause the violence or are simply symptoms of the inequities in

    contemporary America."

- -

■ Mixing the Patterns

Most often, writers employ more than one pattern of organization in a
paragraph or a section of an article, an essay, or a chapter. You might
find, for instance, that a paragraph or longer piece of writing classifies
things while simultaneously analyzing their causes or effects. An essay
may use examples to help define a word or concept. Or an essay or paragraph may present all of the patterns that you have learned.

In the following passage, from the mass communication textbook
Media and Culture by Richard Campbell, the author uses at least four
different organizational patterns. See if you can identify them as you
read.

Barter vs. Cash

Most financing of television syndication is based on either cash
or barter. In a *cash deal*, the distributor of a program offers a series
for syndication to the highest bidder in a market—typically a station trying to fill a particular time slot. Due to exclusive contractual
arrangements, programs air on only one broadcast outlet per market.

(continued)

For example, Viacom, which distributes the *Cosby Show*, offers it in hundreds of television markets around the country. Whichever local station bids the most in a particular market gets the rights to that program, usually for a contract period of two or three years. A small-market station in Fargo, North Dakota, might pay a few thousand dollars to air a week's worth of episodes; in contrast, some Top 10 markets paid well over $150,000 a week for *Cosby* in the late 1980s.

One common variation of a cash deal is called *cash-plus*. For shows that are successful in syndication, distributors may retain some time to sell national commercial spots. When *Cosby* went into syndication, for example, Viacom, in addition to receiving cash for the show from various local outlets, also sold a minute of ad time to national advertisers. When the two-hundred-plus local stations received the programs, they already contained a minute's worth of national ads. Some syndicators use cash-plus deals to keep down the cost per episode; in other words, stations pay less per episode in exchange for giving up ad slots to a syndicator's national advertisers.

Although syndicators prefer cash deals, *barter deals* are usually arranged for new or untested programs. In a straight barter deal, no money changes hands between the local station and the syndicator. Instead, a syndicator offers a new program to a local TV station in exchange for a split of the advertising revenue. The program's syndicator will try to make an arrangement with the station that attracts the largest number of local viewers, though this is not always possible. The syndicator then sells some ads at the national level, charging advertisers more money if the program has been sold into a large number of markets. This guarantees the wide national distribution that the networks receive for prime-time shows.

As an example, in the early 1990s, *Star Trek: The Next Generation* (before it became a part of the new UPN network) was offered by its producer-distributor, Paramount, in a 7/5 barter deal. Paramount did not charge cash per episode. Instead, during each airing it retained seven minutes of ad time to sell national spots and left stations with five minutes of ad time to sell local spots. The *Jenny Jones Show* also started out as a barter show. As it became a proven product, its syndicator, Time Warner, repackaged the show as a cash-plus deal.

Exercise 6-9

Answer the questions based on your reading of the selection "Barter vs. Cash."

Example:

   Identify the paragraph or paragraphs where the author uses classification.

   Paragraphs 1, 2, and 3

1. List three examples the author uses to support his main point.

    "The Cosby Show"; "Star Trek: The Next Generation"; and the "Jenny

    Jones Show"

2. This passage uses classification. What is divided into categories, and what are the categories the author identifies?

    The passage classifies systems of television financing and identifies

    two categories: barter and cash.

3. What additional type of television financing is described in this passage?

    the cash-plus model

4. What other organizational pattern can you find in "Barter vs. Cash"?

    Comparison and contrast, definition

5. What is the definition of a "barter deal"?

    "No money changes hands between the local station and the syndicator.

    Instead, a syndicator offers a new program to a local TV station in

    exchange for a split of advertising revenue."

As a collaborative exercise, work with two or three of your classmates to find a piece of writing that exhibits a mixed pattern of organization. Once you have found such a piece, collaborate to identify the types of organizational patterns used. Label each pattern of organization in the margin next to where it is used in the reading selection.

Applying the Skills

Reading the Parts

Ellen Goodman's Pulitzer Prize–winning column "At Large" is syndicated in more than 440 newspapers across the United States. "What Matters," her "At Large" column for April 7, 2002, provides many examples of most of the patterns of organization you've learned in this chapter. As you read it, pay close attention to how Goodman organizes each paragraph. After you read each section and answer the questions that follow, move on to the next section. You will have a chance to read the whole column when you finish.

ELLEN GOODMAN
What Matters

1   We are adding another relic to the huge pile that looms outside our door when a neighbor walks by and asks approvingly, "Spring cleaning?"

2   "Sort of," I answer and turn my eyes to the sidewalk that looks like a giant yard sale of cardboard boxes, plastic bags, and broken furniture.

3   At one end of the pile is a decaying red cardboard table that my daughter once used for her preschool Play-Doh. Spring cleaning, 1975. Not far away there is an ancient and honorable and defunct box of tax returns. Spring cleaning, 1987. Nearby are my father's law school notes. Spring cleaning, 1932.

4   We are finally excavating the archaeological layers of our past, digging artifacts out of corners of the house that have been untouched nearly as long as Tutankhamen's tomb. The pharaoh's tomb-diggers, however, didn't uncover a macrame plant holder or a dozen plastic planters.

5   It has taken us five weekends to get this far. That's if you don't count the boxes that originated in our old house. Or if you don't count the cartons inherited from our families.

6   From time to time, from spring to spring, we would talk about retrieving whole rooms from their musty existence as museum hall and storage company. But like an annual resolution to lose weight and shape up, our good intentions would disappear behind closed doors.

1. Paragraphs 1 and 2 of Goodman's selection are organized primarily by

    a. example.

    b. narration.

    c. cause and effect.

    d. definition.

2. By discussing ancient Egypt in paragraph 4, Goodman is

    a. making an analogy between archaeology and her spring cleaning.

    b. discussing archaeology.

    c. giving an example of how hard spring cleaning is.

    d. giving a description of ancient Egypt.

3. Paragraph 3 of Goodman's selection is included to

    a. provide a list of things that she is discarding.

    b. make an analogy between old things and spring cleaning.

    c. give examples of the types of things she is discarding and the years they came into existence.

    d. classify unnecessary items discarded during spring cleaning.

4. "But like an annual resolution to lose weight and shape up, our good intentions would disappear behind closed doors" (paragraph 6) is an example of

    a. cause and effect.

    b. definition.

    c. analogy.

    d. classification.

5. Which of the following paragraphs uses a list?

    a. Paragraph 1

    b. Paragraph 2

    c. Paragraph 3

    d. Paragraph 4

I suppose the fault was largely mine. I belong to a family of pack-rats. I grew up in a home where rubber bands were saved on door-knobs for a rainy day, although what we would do with those bands when it rained was unclear. My aunt next door has a collection of plastic ice cream containers that date back to the invention of plastic.   7

My husband, on the other hand, has been nicknamed the human Zamboni. He would weed a garden with a backhoe if you gave him half a chance. His idea of cleaning out the house was to hire a dump-ster and slowly tip the attic into it.   8

When we talked of cleaning, he would begin with the assump-tion that everything was junk. I would begin with the idea that everything was an heirloom. He saw the aging, peeling Playskool giraffe as kindling wood. I saw it as something to be resurrected for grandchildren. He looked at the old school supplies as Goodwill, I saw them as *Antiques Roadshow.*   9

"*Why, Ms. Goodman, do you have any idea how much this 1954 cardboard stencil is worth today?*"   10

"*Why, no, my mother bought it for 39 cents at Woolworth's.*"   11

"*Well, she got quite a bargain. Today at the right auction you could get $1,300 for this!*" *Tears, followed by applause.*   12

If I was intimidated by the quantity of the stuff, I was more in-timidated by the quantity of decisions: Treasure or trash? Who sez?   13

6. In paragraph 7, the author refers to her family as a "family of packrats." The rest of the paragraph then goes on to

   a. provide examples of packrat behavior in her family.

   b. provide an analogy between a packrat and a person who saves junk.

   c. provide a narration of the author on *Antiques Roadshow.*

   d. provide a detailed description of a packrat.

7. Paragraphs 7 and 8 are organized primarily around

   a. narration.

   b. description.

   c. comparison and contrast.

   d. cause and effect.

8. The author's inclusion of sentence 3 in paragraph 9 ("He saw the aging, peeling Playskool giraffe as kindling wood") and the language that she uses in that paragraph are an example of

    a. narration.

    (b.) description.

    c. classification.

    d. analogy.

9. Paragraph 9 also provides

    a. an example of a cause and effect structure.

    (b.) a comparison and contrast between the author and her husband.

    c. a comparison between *Antiques Roadshow* and the author's packrat behavior.

    d. a cause and effect relationship between packrats and crowded attics.

10. What is the primary organizational pattern of paragraphs 10–13?

    a. description

    b. classification

    c. analogy

    (d.) cause and effect

The hardest part was imagining what lay in the boxes we had inherited, boxes that had acquired a kind of sacred, untouchable quality. How could we dare to triage our elders' leftovers? How do you pick and choose what matters? To them. To us.   14

Was it Sept. 11 that made us want to get down to basics? Get unstuffed. Divide history from clutter. Was it simply to figure out what of my own collecting and consuming will matter to our kids?   15

Gradually, corner by corner, box by box, we have been separating the "antiques" from the candidates for Goodwill from the junk unceremoniously deposited on the sidewalk. One by one, I have figured out what matters to us. Not the carton of china, but my mother's wedding dress. Not the crystal vases but the photographs. Not my grandmother's watch but her soup pot. And above all, the unexpected treasure trove of World War II letters my father wrote.   16

Our spring cleaning is by no means complete. My daughter, heiress to my DNA, retrieved half the stuffed animals—"just the ones with names, mom"—from the junk heap. I salvaged the soap collection of my childhood. (*"Why, do you know how much that Waldorf-Astoria 1956 soap is worth?"*) Stuff will accumulate again the way dust settles in the corners of every life.   17

But having cleaned so many springs from our lives, I recognize that most of what we acquire will inevitably end up on some sidewalk.   18

What will remain for our own antiques *home* show? Letters, photographs, the occasional family soup pot.   19

This packrat has learned that what the next generation will value most is not what we owned but the evidence of who we were and the tales of how we loved. In the end, it's the family stories that are worth the storage.   20

11. In paragraph 15, the author asks the question "Was it Sept. 11 that made us want to get down to basics?" In asking the question the author is

 a. looking for a cause to explain her need to clean out her junk.

 b. creating an opportunity to give examples.

 c. describing her feelings about September 11.

 d. narrating.

12. The primary organizational pattern used in paragraph 16 is

 a. analogy.

 b. classification.

 c. definition.

 d. narration.

13. By saying that her daughter is "heiress to my DNA" in paragraph 17, the author is

 a. making a contrast between her packrat behavior and her daughter's ability to throw things out.

 b. making a comparison between the two of them.

 c. saying that the cause of her daughter's behavior is that she shares DNA with her mother.

 d. saying that DNA is a strong indicator of packrat behavior.

14. In paragraph 20, the effect that the spring cleaning has had on the author is

    a.   that she has learned to throw things away rather than keep them.

    b.   that she now knows what matters most—family stories.

    c.   that she will remain a packrat.

    d.   that she and her husband, who throws everything away, will "agree to disagree."

15. The primary purpose of paragraphs 18–20 is

    a.   to define "what matters."

    b.   to offer examples of what will appear on the author's "antiques home show."

    c.   to function as a conclusion for the essay.

    d.   to show what the author has learned along the way.

Reading the Whole

Now that you have had a chance to read Ellen Goodman's column in its parts, identifying its patterns of organization, you will find that you have a deeper understanding of her main point when you read her column straight through. As you read, continue to pay attention to the patterns of organization, but think also about what Goodman is trying to convey to her audience. The way she combines patterns will shed new light on her perspective.

ELLEN GOODMAN
What Matters

We are adding another relic to the huge pile that looms outside our door when a neighbor walks by and asks approvingly, "Spring cleaning?" 1

"Sort of," I answer and turn my eyes to the sidewalk that looks like a giant yard sale of cardboard boxes, plastic bags, and broken furniture. 2

At one end of the pile is a decaying red cardboard table that my daughter once used for her preschool Play-Doh. Spring cleaning, 1975. Not far away there is an ancient and honorable and defunct box of tax returns. Spring cleaning, 1987. Nearby are my father's law school notes. Spring cleaning, 1932. 3

We are finally excavating the archaeological layers of our past, digging artifacts out of corners of the house that have been untouched nearly as long as Tutankhamen's tomb. The pharaoh's tomb-diggers, however, didn't uncover a macrame plant holder or a dozen plastic planters. 4

It has taken us five weekends to get this far. That's if you don't count the boxes that originated in our old house. Or if you don't count the cartons inherited from our families. 5

From time to time, from spring to spring, we would talk about retrieving whole rooms from their musty existence as museum hall and storage company. But like an annual resolution to lose weight and shape up, our good intentions would disappear behind closed doors. 6

I suppose the fault was largely mine. I belong to a family of pack-rats. I grew up in a home where rubber bands were saved on door- 7 knobs for a rainy day, although what we would do with those bands when it rained was unclear. My aunt next door has a collection of plastic ice cream containers that date back to the invention of plastic.

My husband, on the other hand, has been nicknamed the human Zamboni. He would weed a garden with a backhoe if you gave him half a chance. His idea of cleaning out the house was to hire a dumpster and slowly tip the attic into it. 8

When we talked of cleaning, he would begin with the assumption that everything was junk. I would begin with the idea that everything was an heirloom. He saw the aging, peeling Playskool giraffe as kindling wood. I saw it as something to be resurrected for grandchildren. He looked at the old school supplies as Goodwill, I saw them as *Antiques Roadshow.* 9

"Why, Ms. Goodman, do you have any idea how much this 1954 cardboard stencil is worth today?" 10

"Why, no, my mother bought it for 39 cents at Woolworth's." 11

"Well, she got quite a bargain. Today at the right auction you could get $1,300 for this!" Tears, followed by applause. 12

If I was intimidated by the quantity of the stuff, I was more intimidated by the quantity of decisions: Treasure or trash? Who sez? 13

The hardest part was imagining what lay in the boxes we had inherited, boxes that had acquired a kind of sacred, untouchable quality. How could we dare to triage our elders' leftovers? How do you pick and choose what matters? To them. To us. 14

Was it Sept. 11 that made us want to get down to basics? Get unstuffed. Divide history from clutter. Was it simply to figure out what of my own collecting and consuming will matter to our kids? 15

Gradually, corner by corner, box by box, we have been separating the "antiques" from the candidates for Goodwill from the junk unceremoniously deposited on the sidewalk. One by one, I have figured out what matters to us. Not the carton of china, but my mother's wedding dress. Not the crystal vases but the photographs. Not my grandmother's watch but her soup pot. And above all, the unexpected treasure trove of World War II letters my father wrote. 16

Our spring cleaning is by no means complete. My daughter, heiress to my DNA, retrieved half the stuffed animals—"just the ones with names, mom"—from the junk heap. I salvaged the soap collection of my childhood. (*"Why, do you know how much that Waldorf-Astoria 1956 soap is worth?"*) Stuff will accumulate again the way dust settles in the corners of every life. 17

But having cleaned so many springs from our lives, I recognize   18
that most of what we acquire will inevitably end up on some sidewalk.

What will remain for our own antiques *home* show? Letters,   19
photographs, the occasional family soup pot.

This packrat has learned that what the next generation will value   20
most is not what we owned but the evidence of who we were and
the tales of how we loved. In the end, it's the family stories that are
worth the storage.

Integrated Skills

1. Why does Goodman call her essay "What Matters"? What does matter most to the author?

2. How does Goodman organize her essay? Where does her introduction end, and where does her conclusion begin?

3. How does Goodman use contrast as an organizing strategy? Do you think that her use of contrast is effective? Why or why not?

4. What examples does Goodman use to classify the kinds of things her family has saved over the years?

5. What distinction does Goodman make between the items that can be discarded and those that must be saved? Do you agree with her about this distinction? Why or why not?

Reading/Writing Connection

One thing Ellen Goodman highlights in "What Matters" is family pictures. She mentions that these are among the things that are most important to her. What are some of the things that you hold dearly? Write a paragraph in which you describe and explain at least one thing that matters a lot to you.

Reading Textbooks

Thematic Connections. In "What Matters," Ellen Goodman examines her family's choices of what material objects are worth keeping and what aren't, concluding that none of them are particularly important. In the following passage from the economics textbook *Macroeconomics* by Timothy Tregarthen and Libby Rittenberg, the authors examine the process of decision making from the perspective of social science, noting that every choice involves looking at "opportunity costs," which they define earlier as "the value of the best alternative forgone in making any choice." This approach to decision making sheds an interesting light on Goodman's experience. As you read the textbook passage, pay attention to the authors' uses of patterns of organization, especially definition, comparison and contrast, lists, and examples.

Vocabulary Preview

scarcity (para. 1): rarity, lack (n.)

objective (para. 3): goal (n.)

constitute (para. 4): form, make up, serve as (v.)

pursuing (para. 8): seeking, looking for, trying to achieve (v.)

constraints (para. 9): restrictions, limits (n.)

curtailing (para. 14): restricting, limiting, cutting back (v.)

induce (para. 14): encourage, force, cause (v.)

assert (para. 14): argue, claim (v.)

plausible (para. 15): believable, likely (adj.)

The Field of Economics

We've examined the basic concepts of scarcity, choice, and opportunity cost in economics. In this section, we'll look at economics as a field of study. We begin with the characteristics that distinguish economics from other social sciences.

THE ECONOMIC WAY OF THINKING

Economists study choices that scarcity requires us to make. This fact is not what distinguishes economics from other social sciences; all social scientists are interested in choices. An anthropologist might study the choices of ancient peoples; a political scientist might study the choices of legislatures; a psychologist might study how people choose a mate; a sociologist might study the factors that

1

2

have led to a rise in single-parent households. Economists study such questions as well. What is it about the study of choices by economists that makes economics different from these other social sciences?

Three features distinguish the economic approach to choice from the approaches taken in other social sciences: 3

1. Economists give special emphasis to the role of opportunity costs in their analysis of choices.
2. Economists assume that individuals make choices that seek to maximize the value of some objective, and that they define their objectives in terms of their own self-interest.
3. Individuals maximize by deciding whether to do a little more or a little less of something. Economists argue that individuals pay attention to the consequences of small changes in the levels of the activities they pursue.

The emphasis economists place on opportunity cost, the idea that people make choices that maximize the value of objectives that serve their self-interest, and a focus on the effects of small changes are ideas of great power. They constitute the core of economic thinking. The next three sections examine these ideas in greater detail.   4

Opportunity Costs Are Important. If doing one thing requires giving up another, then the expected benefits of the alternatives we face will affect the ones we choose. Economists argue that an understanding of opportunity cost is crucial to the examination of choices.   5

As the set of available alternatives changes, we expect that the choices individuals make will change. A rainy day could change the opportunity cost of reading a good book; we might expect more reading to get done in bad than in good weather. A high income can make it very costly to take a day off; we might expect highly paid individuals to work more hours than those who aren't paid as well. If individuals are maximizing their level of satisfaction and firms are maximizing profits, then a change in the set of alternatives they face may affect their choices in a predictable way.   6

The emphasis on opportunity costs is an emphasis on the examination of alternatives. One benefit of the economic way of thinking is that it pushes us to think about the value of alternatives in each problem involving choice.   7

Individuals Maximize in Pursuing Self-Interest. What motivates people as they make choices? Perhaps more than anything else, it is the economist's answer to this question that distinguishes economics from other fields.   8

Economists assume that individuals make choices that they expect will create the maximum value of some objective, given the constraints they face. Furthermore, economists assume that people's objectives will be those that serve their own self-interest.   9

Economists assume, for example, that the owners of business firms seek to maximize profit. Given the assumed goal of profit maximization, economists can predict how firms in an industry will respond to changes in the markets in which they operate. As labor costs in the United States rise, for example, economists aren't surprised to see firms such as Nike move some of their manufacturing operations overseas.   10

Similarly, economists assume that maximizing behavior is at work when they examine the behavior of consumers. In studying consumers, economists assume that individual consumers make choices aimed at maximizing their level of satisfaction. In the next chapter, we'll look at the results of the shift from skiing to snowboarding; that's a shift that reflects the pursuit of self-interest by consumers.   11

In assuming that people pursue their self-interest, economists are not assuming people are selfish. People clearly gain satisfaction by helping others, as suggested by the charitable contributions of Bill and Melinda Gates. Pursuing one's own self-interest means pursuing the things that give one satisfaction. It need not imply greed or selfishness.   12

Choices Are Made at the Margin. Economists argue that most choices are made "at the margin." The **margin** is the current level of an activity. Think of it as the edge from which a choice is to be made. A **choice at the margin** is a decision to do a little more or a little less of something.   13

Assessing choices at the margin can lead to extremely useful insights. Consider, for example, the problem of curtailing water consumption when the amount of water available falls short of the amount people now use. Economists argue that one way to induce people to conserve water is to raise its price. A common response to this recommendation is that a higher price would have no effect on water consumption, because water is a necessity. Many people   14 assert that prices don't affect water consumption because people "need" water.

But choices in water consumption, like virtually all choices, are made at the margin. Individuals don't make choices about whether they should or should not consume water. Rather, they decide whether to consume a little more or a little less water. Household water consumption in the United States totals about 175 gallons per person per day. Think of that starting point as the edge from which a choice at the margin in water consumption is made. Could a higher price cause you to use less water brushing your teeth, take shorter showers, or water your lawn less? Could a higher price cause people to reduce their use, say, to 174 gallons per person per day? To 173? When we examine the choice to consume water at the margin, the notion that a higher price would reduce consumption seems much more plausible. Prices affect our consumption of water because choices in water consumption, like other choices, are made at the margin.

15

Thinking about the Textbook Selection

1. To what extent can Tregarthen and Rittenberg's ideas about economic value be used to explain Goodman's point about what is valuable?

2. According to the authors, what does economics have in common with other social sciences, such as political science and anthropology?

3. What three kinds of choices are at the center of economic thinking?

4. Why are "opportunity costs" important? Do the authors' examples clarify this concept?

5. What does it mean to pursue economic self-interest? How do the authors' examples illustrate the concept of economic self-interest?

6. How is this reading selection organized? What different patterns can you identify?

Reading the Web

The many patterns of organization show up in all sorts of writing, even on Web pages. Depending on a Web site's purpose, it might use comparison and contrast to help viewers decide between products, classification to help visitors navigate the contents, definition to advance an argument (as you saw on the Web site in Chapter 2), or cause and effect to examine a political issue, among other possibilities. Goodwill's "About" page includes a number of different organizational patterns.

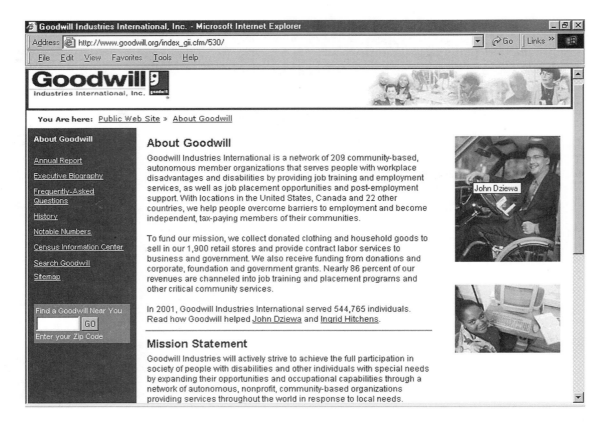

Thinking about the Web Page

1. What patterns of organization can you find in this page?

2. In her column "What Matters," Ellen Goodman says her family chose to throw out belongings that were unimportant to them.

Might another family's definition of "what matters" have induced the Goodmans to do something else with what they didn't want?

3. What is the main point of this Web page? What kinds of details support it?

Reviewing

1. What are the three major parts of every reading selection?
2. What can you expect to find in the beginning, the middle, and the end of a reading selection?
3. What are patterns of organization, and why do writers use them?
4. Explain how recognizing patterns of organization can help you understand what you read.
5. Identify the common patterns of organization writers frequently use.
6. Why is it important to recognize mixed patterns of organization?
7. Which is your favorite pattern of organization? Why?

**Recall /
Remember**

In this chapter you learned how to analyze the structure or organization of a reading selection. You saw how introductions serve to identify an author's topic and main idea, how the middle or body portion of an article, an essay, or a chapter provides details and evidence for the author's idea, and how authors conclude by reemphasizing their main idea or by leaving readers with something to think about.

You learned to identify the common patterns of organization writers use to develop their ideas. You can now recognize the following organizational patterns when you read: definitions, examples, lists and sequences, comparison and contrast, analogy, classification, and cause and effect. You have learned to use these patterns to understand reading selections. And you have seen how the patterns of organization can be combined.

In the chapters that follow, you will continue to practice your reading comprehension skills. Chapter 7 focuses on how understanding the subtleties of a writer's style can help you be a more critical, active reader.

**Chapter
Summary**

Examining a Writer's Language

Getting Ready

Chapter Overview

You've probably heard the expression "read between the lines." But what does that mean? To "read between the lines" is to go beyond the obvious, to look past what a writer says explicitly and to understand less directly expressed meanings in a piece of writing. In other words, it is a form of active reading.

Writers use **specialized meanings, connotation,** and the **context** of words to go beyond their "everyday" meanings. In addition, writers use **figures of speech** to express complex ideas and meanings in a way that is easy to follow and to enliven their writing. In particular, they might communicate an idea through **simile** and **metaphor, hyperbole, understatement, personification,** or **irony.** All of these uses of language contribute to the meanings of what you read. This chapter will show you how they work and help you become more confident in your ability to understand what you read through a careful look at language in context.

What besides dictionary meaning is important in understanding how words convey a writer's idea, feeling, or attitude?

How do you determine the meaning of a familiar word that is used in an unfamiliar way?

Focusing Questions

What is the difference between literal language and a figure of speech?

Why do writers sometimes use words in a nonliteral, or figurative, way?

Everyday Reading

In many of the things you might read or hear on an average day, you will find different kinds of language. Product manuals often use technical language (special terms) for the components of a computer or stereo system, for example. A friend giving you directions to a meeting spot might tell you to "bear" right at a "fork" or to "bang" a left. In the next day or two, pay close attention to what you see and hear. Write down any words or phrases you encounter that aren't used literally or that are used to mean something different from their dictionary definitions. Why do you think people use words in these special ways?

Learning the Skills

■ Specialized Meanings of Words

Some words have **specialized meanings** when they are used in different academic disciplines or contexts. The word *drug,* for example, means one thing to a pharmacist and something very different to a law enforcement agent. The word *depression* has different meanings in economics ("a period of reduced earnings and spending"), geology ("a dent in a physical part of the earth such as a boulder or a sea floor"), and psychology ("a mental illness characterized by an extended period of sadness along with physical symptoms such as fatigue, headache, and unexplained weight gain or loss"). These academic meanings of *depression* differ from its everyday meaning as well. To speak of being *depressed*—or "sad"—in an average conversation does not carry with it the same degree of seriousness as its more clinical meaning in psychology. Nor does its everyday meaning have anything to do with an economic downturn in production or a geological description of land.

In the following paragraph from *The Fire Inside: Firefighters Talk about Their Lives* by Steve Delsohn (1995), words that you run across often in your daily life are used with specialized meanings:

Most new firefighters are sent to engines. There are more engine companies, for one thing, than truck and rescue companies combined. San Diego, for instance, has one rescue, fifteen trucks, and forty-two engines. This is because you need water to extinguish fire—often a lot of water—and this is the primary role of the engine company. The fire engine itself carries the hose lines. Then its personnel stretches those lines inside burning buildings.

Note the words that don't mean what you would normally expect: *engine, company, truck, line.* Usually these refer to, in order, a machine that powers something, a business, a type of vehicle, and a connection between two points. But for firefighters, these words have very different meanings: An *engine* is the vehicle that carries hoses for extinguishing fires; a *company* is a fire department or one of its teams (engine, truck, or rescue); a *truck* is the vehicle equipped with a ladder and other heavy-duty equipment; and a *line* is a fire hose. You need to understand these specialized meanings in order to understand the passage.

Exercise 7-1

. . . .

Define the ordinary, everyday meaning of each word. Then define the more specialized meaning(s). Use a dictionary when necessary.

Example:

depression   ORDINARY MEANING: *feelings of sadness*

SPECIALIZED MEANING FOR *meteorology*: *an area of low barometric pressure*

SPECIALIZED MEANING FOR *economics*: *a period of great decline in the*

economy

1. *stern*   ORDINARY MEANING: *harsh; mean*

   SPECIALIZED MEANING FOR *sailing*: *the back part of a boat*

2. *defend*   ORDINARY MEANING: *to keep or make something safe from danger*

   SPECIALIZED MEANING FOR *sports*: *to play defense*

   SPECIALIZED MEANING FOR *law*: *to represent someone in a criminal or civil*

   action

3. *magnitude*   ORDINARY MEANING: _greatness in size, extent, position, etc._

   SPECIALIZED MEANING FOR *geology*: _a measure of the amount of energy_
   released by an earthquake, as indicated on the Richter scale

   SPECIALIZED MEANING FOR *mathematics*: _a number assigned to a quantity_
   so that it can be compared with other quantities

4. *point*   ORDINARY MEANING: _a sharp tip_

   SPECIALIZED MEANING FOR *printing*: _a unit of type size (approximately_
   1/72 of an inch)

   SPECIALIZED MEANING FOR *games* OR *sports*: _a scoring unit_

   SPECIALIZED MEANING FOR *jewelry*: _a unit of weight (.01 carat)_

5. *subject*   ORDINARY MEANING: _something about which something is said_
   or done; someone under the rule of another

   SPECIALIZED MEANING FOR *grammar*: _a noun or pronoun that names who_
   or what a sentence is about

   SPECIALIZED MEANING FOR *music*: _the theme of a piece of music_

. . . .

■ Distinguishing Denotation and Connotation

A word's **denotation** is its dictionary definition, or its literal meaning. A word's **connotation** refers to the suggested meanings a word may possess beyond its denotation. The word *mother,* for example, means, literally, "a female parent." One dictionary defines *mother* as "a female that has borne an offspring." The connotations of *mother,* however, suggest much more than this. Most of us associate the word *mother* with a specific woman—our own "female parent"—and have personal feelings, attitudes, and experiences about her. Furthermore, a given culture makes assumptions about the meaning of *mother.* In the United States, it is usually assumed that a mother is the primary caregiver of a child; it is furthermore assumed that she will protect that child fiercely. In the movie *Aliens,* Ripley is an adoptive mother to the little girl she finds; the monster she battles is the mother of thousands of monsters waiting to hatch from their pods. Ripley and the Alien mother are very different creatures, but both embody the behaviors Americans expect of mothers.

The connotations of a word can vary significantly in intensity. They can also change in a number of ways. For example, at different periods of your life, or on a given day, the word *school* will mean different things. To young children, it may be a building, the place where they spend the bulk of their day with a group of other children. School is associated with activities and friends. Education, of course, is the reason for attending, but most children don't necessarily think of school in terms of learning. For adults, *school* might refer to the college they attend; but it could also refer to the place where their children are educated. A person's attitude toward school will also affect the connotation of the word: For someone who fought hard to save for tuition and takes education seriously, *school* can mean opportunity. But for students whose families pressed them to go to college whether they wanted to or not, *school* might carry unpleasant connotations of obligation and resentment.

Exercise 7-2

Fill in the denotation or the connotation, as indicated, of each of the following words. Use a dictionary if you need help.

Example:

childish   DENOTATION: like a child

CONNOTATION: *immature; silly*

1. *childlike*   DENOTATION: like a child

   CONNOTATION: *innocent; trusting*

2. *Hollywood*   DENOTATION: a section of Los Angeles, California

   CONNOTATION: *flashy; sensational; romantic; wealthy; successful;*

   related to the film industry

3. *Washington*   DENOTATION: the capital of the United States

   CONNOTATION: *political; powerful*

4. *thrifty*   DENOTATION: saving money

CONNOTATION: _skillfully and intelligently saving money_

5. *penny-pinching*   DENOTATION: saving money

CONNOTATION: _stingy; selfish; miserly_

. . . .

■ Connotation and Context

The connotations of words are important for another reason: They may carry built-in judgments. Consider, for example, how different are the connotations of the following sentences, in which only a single word has been changed:

> I soon found out that the cat I adopted is *weird:* Mocha jumps on my shoulders when I'm not looking.
>
> I soon found out that the cat I adopted is *funny:* Mocha jumps on my shoulders when I'm not looking.

In these sentences, *weird* and *funny* mean more or less the same thing—"odd." But these two sentences have two very different meanings. Part of the meaning of each sentence derives from its **context**—from what you imagine would come before and after. In the first sentence, for example, you infer that the writer was unhappy to discover the cat's strange behavior and that she doesn't want Mocha jumping on her shoulders unexpectedly. In the second sentence, however, you infer that the writer enjoys the cat's eccentricities and is amused by them.

But why is that? Part of the meaning of these sentences resides in the different connotations evoked by the words *weird* and *funny.* The word *weird* connotes oddness, of course, but it suggests something unacceptable or inappropriate. The word *funny* also connotes oddness, but it suggests humor and implies approval of the oddness. In another context, either of these words could mean something entirely different: *Weird,* for example, can also connote something supernatural; *funny* can suggest deception, as in *funny money.*

The following passage, from the self-help book *Don't Sweat the Small Stuff at Work* by Richard Carlson (1998), examines the connotation of a single word in a sentence you've heard—and probably said—hundreds of times: "I have to go to work."

> Other than your thoughts, your words are your primary entry point into your experience. They paint a picture of your expectation and pave the way toward your experience. When you "have" to do something, it implies that it's not a choice—that you'd rather be somewhere else, doing something different. This, in turn, implies that your heart isn't fully into what you are doing, which makes living up to your potential extremely difficult and enjoying your experience near impossible. So, when you say, "I have to go to work," you are in a subtle way setting yourself up for a bad day. This doesn't mean you'll always have a bad day—but it certainly increases the likelihood.
>
> Beyond that, however, there is a more subtle negative message you send to yourself and to others. It seems that deep down, what you're really saying is, "I don't like my work. I'm not capable of choosing work that I enjoy." What a horrible message to say to yourself (or to someone else) about something you spend most of your time doing! Think about it. If you really loved your work, why would you be saying, "I have to go to work"? Do you say, "I have to start my weekend now"? Wouldn't it make more sense to be saying, "I get to go to work," or "I'm off to earn my livelihood," or "I'm off to another day," or something even simpler like, "I'm off to work" without the attached negativity?

Exercise 7-3

. . . .

Write *positive* or *negative* to indicate which word in each pair carries the positive connotation and which one carries the negative connotation.

Example:

gang ____negative____   group ____positive____

1. *reckless* ____negative____   *adventurous* ____positive____

2. *individualist* ____positive____   *kook* ____negative____

3. *average* ____positive____   *mediocre* ____negative____

4. *stubborn* ___negative___   *principled* ___positive___

5. *firm* ___positive___   *pigheaded* ___negative___

6. *thrifty* ___positive___   *miserly* ___negative___

7. *concise* ___positive___   *curt* ___negative___

8. *shack* ___negative___   *cottage* ___positive___

9. *nitpicking* ___negative___   *precise* ___positive___

10. *trusting* ___positive___   *gullible* ___negative___

. . . .

■ Understanding Figures of Speech

Another feature of language that is important for understanding what you read is figurative language, especially figures of speech. **Figures of speech** are expressions that differ from words' literal meanings. For example, when you've had enough to eat and you say, "I'm stuffed," you are using a figure of speech. You are not literally "stuffed"; you simply feel full. *Stuffed,* in this case, indicates that you have had enough to eat.

SIMILE AND METAPHOR

Two of the most frequently appearing figures of speech are simile and metaphor. Both are types of comparisons between dissimilar things in which one of those things is used to explain the other. It's important to understand that these figures of speech are different from the organizational pattern of comparison-contrast, which you learned about in Chapter 6. Whereas a writer using comparison and contrast might note the similarities and differences between football and baseball, for example, a writer using simile might compare politics to a game of football to describe a government's aggressive behavior or to baseball to explain how politicians use strategy and patience to achieve their goals. Simile and metaphor are especially helpful for a writer who wants to explain a complex idea in different terms.

A **simile** explicitly makes a comparison by using key words such as *like, as,* variations on the word *similar,* or *as though.* Some examples: "He works like a horse," "The baby's skin is as smooth as silk," or

Robert Burns's famous "My love is like a red, red rose." Textbook authors frequently use simile to clarify a difficult concept. Consider this paragraph from the geology textbook *Understanding Earth* by Frank Press and Raymond Siever, in which the authors use something very familiar to most readers to explain a more difficult geological process:

> We are all familiar with the ways in which heat can transform material. Frying raw ground meat changes it into a hamburger composed of chemical compounds very different from those in the raw meat. Cooking batter in a waffle iron not only heats up the batter but also puts pressure on it, transforming it into a rigid solid. In similar ways, rocks change as they encounter high temperatures and pressures. Deep in Earth's crust, tens of kilometers below the surface, the temperatures and pressures are high enough to metamorphose rock without being high enough to melt it. Increases in heat and pressure and changes in the chemical environment can alter the mineral compositions and crystalline textures of sedimentary and igneous rocks, even though they remain solid all the while. The result is the third large class of rocks, the metamorphic or "changed form" rocks, which have undergone changes in mineralogy, texture, composition, or all three.

A **metaphor** serves the same purpose as a simile does (to compare unlike things in order to describe one of them), but it expresses the comparison without using explicit comparative words. If you call a friend and she says your voice is "music to my ears," you have been complimented with a metaphor. Or an admirer might say, "All the De Beer daughters are jewels, but Francie is the diamond among them." The daughters are described favorably, flatteringly, with Francie receiving the highest compliment in being compared to the most precious jewel, the diamond. Metaphors are especially common in literature, but you can find them just about anywhere, as in this passage from Burton G. Malkiels's *A Random Walk down Wall Street:*

> A random walk is one in which future steps or directions cannot be predicted on the basis of past actions. When the term is applied to the stock market, it means that short-run changes in stock prices cannot be predicted. Investment advisory services, earnings
>
> *(continued)*

predictions, and complicated chart patterns are useless. On Wall Street, the term "random walk" is an obscenity. It is an epithet coined by the academic world and hurled insultingly at the professional soothsayers. Taken to its logical extreme, it means that a blindfolded monkey throwing darts at a newspaper's pages could select a portfolio that would do just as well as one carefully selected by the experts.

Now, financial analysts in pin-striped suits do not like being compared with bare-assed apes. They retort that academics are so immersed in equations and Greek symbols (to say nothing of stuffy prose) that they couldn't tell a bull from a bear.

Notice that the author uses a couple of metaphors in this passage. First is the statement that a random walk "means that a blindfolded monkey throwing darts at a newspaper's pages could select a portfolio that would do just as well as one carefully selected by the experts." When he wrote the first edition of his book in 1973, Malkiel didn't literally mean that monkeys were throwing darts at newspapers (although about ten years later, a journalist set up an experiment in which real monkeys were given real darts, and they did do better than the experts!). The stock market symbols of a bull and a bear are also metaphors used to describe the condition of the stock market: A bear market is one in which values are plummeting; a bull market is a market in which stock prices are rising.

Exercise 7-4

Underline the figures of speech in each passage. Then identify each figure of speech as a metaphor or simile, and explain it.

Example:

Sugar Boy turned the car off on the gravel and we sprayed along with the rocks crunching and popping up against the underside of the fender like grease in a skillet. (Robert Penn Warren, *All the King's Men*)

FIGURE OF SPEECH: *simile*

EXPLANATION: *The popping, crunching rocks are likened to hot grease*

bubbling up and sputtering in a frying pan.

1. Absence in love is like water upon a fire; a little quickens, but much extinguishes it. (Hannah More, *The Last Word*)

    FIGURE OF SPEECH: *simile*

    EXPLANATION: *Just as a little water makes the fire flare up more, a little absence stimulates love. However, just as too much water puts out a fire, too much absence extinguishes love.*

2. I started with a jam session . . . trying to lift them out of their seats if only by sheer strength, digging down deeper than ever before to entertain them, to get them involved, to get a response — but it was as though I were playing hardball with an orange. (Sammy Davis Jr., *Yes I Can*)

    FIGURE OF SPEECH: *simile*

    EXPLANATION: *The singer is comparing his attempts to involve the audience to trying to play hardball with an orange. There's only a flat, squishy, dead response.*

3. All the world's a stage,
    And all the men and women merely players,
    They have their exits and their entrances;
    And one man in his time plays many parts.

    (William Shakespeare, *As You Like It*)

    FIGURE(S) OF SPEECH: *metaphors*

    EXPLANATION: *The world is compared to a stage, and people are compared to actors — whose birth and death are compared to going on and off stage — all of them playing different, multiple roles in their lifetimes.*

4. My moods are constantly shifting like the weather. I am definitely not in control of what thoughts or emotions are going to arise, nor can I halt their flow. Stillness is followed by movement, movement flows back into stillness. Even the most persistent physical pain, when I pay attention to

it, changes like the tides. (Pema Chödrön, *The Places That Scare You: A Guide to Fearlessness in Difficult Times*)

FIGURE(S) OF SPEECH: _similes_ _____

EXPLANATION: _The writer compares her moods to the weather because of_ _their variability. She compares physical pain to the tides because her_ _pain, too, is always changing (something she is aware of only when she_ _pays attention)._

5. Do not go gentle into that good night,
   Old age should burn and rage at close of day;
   Rage, rage against the dying of the light.
         (Dylan Thomas, "Do Not Go Gentle into That Good Night")

FIGURE(S) OF SPEECH: _metaphors_ _____

EXPLANATION: _Death is compared to a (final) night's sleep._ _____

· ·

HYPERBOLE, UNDERSTATEMENT, PERSONIFICATION, AND IRONY

In addition to simile and metaphor there are many other figures of speech. **Hyperbole,** or exaggeration, occurs when a person says more than he or she means. For example, you might say, "I'm going to die if I don't get an A in this course." You're not really going to die, but you use the expression to indicate the intensity of your feelings. The opposite of hyperbole is **understatement**—saying less than you mean, as when you say you are "just a tad tired" even though it's clear to you and everybody else that you are exhausted.

Although you will sometimes find exaggeration and understatement in your reading, more often you will find another, more common figure of speech: personification. In **personification,** human characteristics are given to inanimate, or nonliving, things. If you were to describe the only tomato in your salad as "lonely," you would be using personification. Or if you read that the wind "whispered" through the trees or that flowers "danced" and the skies "wept" you would be encountering personification.

Perhaps the most often used figure of speech is **irony,** in which the idea of opposition, contrast, or surprise is central. There are different kinds of irony. In **verbal irony** (sometimes accompanied by a tone of sarcasm), you say the opposite of what you mean. For example, if in hearing about something foolish done by one of your friends you teasingly say, "That was a smart thing to do," you are being ironic.

In **dramatic irony,** which you will find in works of literature such as plays, poems, novels, and stories, the reader or audience knows things that some of the characters do not know. Dramatic irony can create suspense, as when a character in a horror movie is about to enter a dangerous environment unaware of the threat that the audience plainly sees.

In **situational irony,** we expect something to happen only to have the opposite of what we expected actually occur. For example, if you plan to avoid driving on a certain road because you fear a traffic jam and you take an alternate route only to find—what else, a traffic jam—you experience situational irony. In literary and other creative works, authors describe events that may surprise not only the characters in those works but the readers as well. The surprises in such cases often take the form of an ironic twist or an ironic reversal, in which the opposite of what is expected, happens. One of the best-known literary examples of both dramatic and situational irony is Kate Chopin's 1894 story "The Story of an Hour." Here is the first third of the short story:

The Story of an Hour

Knowing that Mrs. Mallard was afflicted with a heart trouble, great care was taken to break to her as gently as possible the news of her husband's death.   1

It was her sister Josephine who told her, in broken sentences; veiled hints that revealed in half concealing. Her husband's friend Richards was there, too, near her. It was he who had been in the newspaper office when intelligence of the railroad disaster was received, with Brently Mallard's name leading the list of "killed." He had only taken the time to assure himself of its truth by a second   2

(continued)

telegram, and had hastened to forestall any less careful, less tender friend in bearing the sad message.

She did not hear the story as many women have heard the same, with a paralyzed inability to accept its significance. She wept at once, with sudden, wild abandonment, in her sister's arms. When the storm of grief had spent itself she went away to her room alone. She would have no one follow her.

There stood, facing the open window, a comfortable, roomy armchair. Into this she sank, pressed down by a physical exhaustion that haunted her body and seemed to reach into her soul.

She could see in the open square before her house the tops of trees that were all aquiver with the new spring life. The delicious breath of rain was in the air. In the street below a peddler was crying his wares. The notes of a distant song which some one was singing reached her faintly, and countless sparrows were twittering in the eaves.

There were patches of blue sky showing here and there through the clouds that had met and piled one above the other in the west facing her window.

Paragraphs 5 and 6 are the story's first instance of situational irony. Although Mrs. Mallard is reacting to the news of her husband's unexpected death, she is surrounded by, and recognizes, trees "that were all aquiver with the new spring life," a "peddler crying his wares," songbirds, and "patches of blue sky." The reader expects the grieving Mrs. Mallard to notice or dwell upon sad things, but instead she is aware of the pleasant indications of spring.

Now read the next part of the story:

She sat with her head thrown back upon the cushion of the chair, quite motionless, except when a sob came up into her throat and shook her, as a child who has cried itself to sleep continues to sob in its dreams. She was young, with a fair, calm face, whose lines bespoke repression and even a certain strength. But now there was a dull stare in her eyes, whose gaze was fixed away off yonder on one of those patches of blue sky. It was not a glance of reflection, but rather indicated a suspension of intelligent thought.

There was something coming to her and she was waiting for it, fearfully. What was it? She did not know; it was too subtle and elusive to name. But she felt it, creeping out of the sky, reaching toward her through the sounds, the scents, the color that filled the air. 8

Now her bosom rose and fell tumultuously. She was beginning to recognize this thing that was approaching to possess her, and she was striving to beat it back with her will—as powerless as her two white slender hands would have been. 9

When she abandoned herself a little whispered word escaped her slightly parted lips. She said it over and over under her breath: "free, free, free!" The vacant stare and the look of terror that had followed it went from her eyes. They stayed keen and bright. Her pulses beat fast, and the coursing blood warmed and relaxed every inch of her body. 10

She did not stop to ask if it were or were not a monstrous joy that held her. A clear and exalted perception enabled her to dismiss the suggestion as trivial. 11

She knew that she would weep again when she saw the kind, tender hands folded in death; the face that had never looked save with love upon her, fixed and gray and dead. But she saw beyond that bitter moment a long procession of years to come that would belong to her absolutely. And she opened and spread her arms out to them in welcome. 12

There would be no one to live for her during those coming years; she would live for herself. There would be no powerful will bending hers in that blind persistence with which men and women believe they have a right to impose a private will upon a fellow-creature. A kind intention or a cruel intention made the act seem no less a crime as she looked upon it in that brief moment of illumination. 13

And yet she had loved him—sometimes. Often she had not. What did it matter! What could love, the unsolved mystery, count for in face of this possession of self-assertion which she suddenly recognized as the strongest impulse of her being! 14

"Free! Body and soul free!" she kept whispering. 15

These paragraphs build on the irony of Mrs. Mallard's focus on the living things she heard and saw from her room. There's a new dramatic irony here. Although readers expect that Mrs. Mallard would be saddened and upset by her husband's death, we—and she—learn that in fact it fills her with joy. Now read the rest of the story:

> Josephine was kneeling before the closed door with her lips to the keyhole, imploring for admission. "Louise, open the door! I beg; open the door—you will make yourself ill. What are you doing, Louise? For heaven's sake open the door."   16
>
> "Go away. I am not making myself ill." No; she was drinking in a very elixir of life through that open window.   17
>
> Her fancy was running riot along those days ahead of her. Spring days, and summer days, and all sorts of days that would be her own. She breathed a quick prayer that life might be long. It was only yesterday she had thought with a shudder that life might be long.   18
>
> She arose at length and opened the door to her sister's importunities. There was a feverish triumph in her eyes, and she carried herself unwittingly like a goddess of Victory. She clasped her sister's waist, and together they descended the stairs. Richards stood waiting for them at the bottom.   19
>
> Some one was opening the front door with a latchkey. It was Brently Mallard who entered, a little travel-stained, composedly carrying his grip-sack and umbrella. He had been far from the scene of accident, and did not even know there had been one. He stood amazed at Josephine's piercing cry; at Richards' quick motion to screen him from the view of his wife.   20
>
> But Richards was too late.   21
>
> When the doctors came they said she had died of heart disease—of joy that kills.   22

The ending of the story contains three instances of irony. In the first situational irony, the characters learn that Brently Mallard is not dead at all, that he wasn't even aware there had been an accident. His entrance to the house is an example of dramatic irony. The readers know what Brently Mallard does not: Everybody in the house is reacting to the news of his death. There is situational irony in the fact that her husband's return kills Mrs. Mallard: Under normal circumstances one would expect her to be overjoyed. The final—and most powerful—instance of dramatic irony is Mrs. Mallard's sudden death. The doctor and the other characters attribute it to a "joy that kills," but the readers know that Louise Mallard died of grief over the loss of the freedom she thought had been given to her.

Exercise 7-5

Reread "The Story of an Hour" and answer the following questions about it.

Example:

> There is an example of personification in paragraph 4. What is personified?
>
> *"Physical exhaustion" is personified. It "haunts" Mrs. Mallard and*
>
> *seems "to reach into her soul."*

1. What is the simile in paragraph 7? Explain the comparison.

   The simile is "as a child who has cried itself to sleep continues to sob in

   its dreams." Mrs. Mallard is motionless, but sobs come up and shake

   her just as sobs come up to shake a sleeping child.

2. What is the simile in paragraph 9? Explain the comparison.

   The simile is "as powerless as her two white slender hands would have

   been." Mrs. Mallard's "will" to fight whatever is approaching to possess

   her is as weak as her hands would be to fight.

3. There is something personified that runs through paragraphs 8 through 15. At first, Mrs. Mallard doesn't know what it is. She just feels it as a personified "thing." It "creeps" out of the sky; it "reaches" toward her; she tries unsuccessfully to battle it. What is personified? Why does Mrs. Mallard feel it?

   Joy is what is personified (paragraph 11: "She did not stop to ask if it

   were or were not a monstrous joy that held her"). Mrs. Mallard feels joy

   because she realizes she is about to become free.

4. What is the simile in paragraph 19? Explain the comparison.

The simile is "like a goddess of Victory." Although Mrs. Mallard is

expected to be heartbroken, without meaning to she stands like a

goddess of Victory. She believes that she has won the freedom of her

body and soul.

5. In paragraph 22, the phrase "joy that kills" is used ironically, but it also serves as an example of another figure of speech. What is that figure of speech?

hyperbole

· ·

Applying the Skills

Reading the Parts

Sheila Patek's 2001 discovery of how lobsters make the noise that scares off their predators was very important news to the scientific community. (You can listen to this sound at amnh.org/naturalhistory/0601/0601_media.html.) Patek, now a biologist at the University of California at Berkeley, learned when researching at Duke University that lobsters create sound by using parts of their bodies in much the same way musicians play violins. The following article from the popular-science magazine *Discover* reports Patek's finding. In Greene's article you will find many of the special uses of language you learned in this chapter, including specialized meanings of words, metaphor, and personification. As you read it, pay close attention to Greene's uses of words and figures of speech. After you read each section and answer the questions that follow, move on to the next section. You will have a chance to read the whole article when you finish.

SARAH GREENE
Musical Lobsters

They might not be up to playing Beethoven, but spiny lobsters share a talent with virtuoso musicians like Itzhak Perlman. Research at Duke University has revealed that the creatures produce sound much like a violinist does by pulling a bow across the instrument's strings. 1

While violinists play for pleasure, spiny lobsters "play" under more stressful conditions, explains Sheila Patek, a biologist now at the University of California at Berkeley who did this research while at Duke. Using underwater microphones, she listened in on the loud sounds the lobsters make to scare off potential predators. The creatures' music is more of an unpleasant rasp than a sweet vibrato, she says, but that is exactly the point. 2

Unlike the North Atlantic lobsters commonly consumed in American seafood restaurants, spiny lobsters from sub-tropical to tropical oceans do not have claws (see image at photo1.dukenews.duke.edu/pages/Duke_News_Service/lobster/lobster2.jpg). Instead they protect 3 themselves with their hard exterior skeleton and spiny antennae, fending off predators such as sharks, grouper, triggerfish, and sometimes even other lobsters.

1. The "music" of spiny lobsters is compared to that of
   a. underwater sounds.
   b. virtuoso violinists like Itzhak Perlman.
   c. other sea creatures.
   d. the unpleasant rasps of North Atlantic lobsters.

2. From the following list, choose the ordinary and specialized meaning of the word *antennae* as used in paragraph 3.
   a. Ordinary: devices for sending or receiving electromagnetic waves
      Specialized: a pair of flexible sensory attachments on the head of a lobster
   b. Ordinary: rabbit ears on top of a television set
      Specialized: eyes on a crustacean
   c. Ordinary: a music-making device
      Specialized: a lobster's claws
   d. The ordinary and specialized meanings of *antennae* are the same.

3. Using your knowledge of context clues, what is the meaning of *vibrato* as used in paragraph 2?
   a. dull monotone
   b. an unpleasant sound
   c. tremulous or vibrating sound
   d. high-pitched wail

4. Which of the following context clues from paragraph 3 would help you determine the meaning of the phrase *fending off* as used in the same paragraph?
   a. "protect themselves"
   b. "hard exterior skeleton"

c.   "spiny antennae"

d.   "even other lobsters"

5. The word *music* has a specialized meaning in this essay. From the description of lobsters and their musical "ability," what does *music* mean?

a.   the underwater sounds of the ocean

b.   the sounds that lobsters hear around them

c.   the "unpleasant rasp" that lobsters create to protect themselves against predators

d.   There is no specialized meaning used in these paragraphs.

But like all arthropods, the spiny lobster goes through molting periods during which it sheds its outer shell. After molting, the new exoskeleton can take a couple of days to a week to harden, says Patek. During this soft state, the lobster is vulnerable, so it has evolved a sound-based defense mechanism that doesn't rely on hard structures, unlike the sound-making organs of other arthropods. For example, a cricket requires two hard surfaces to rub together, much like a prick running over a washboard, explains Patek.   4

The spiny lobster has two structures, called files, which sit just below its eyes. Resting directly underneath each of them is a soft, leathery piece of tissue called a plectrum, jutting back from the base of its antennae, that acts like a violinist's bow. With one muscle contraction, the lobster pulls the plectra over the files, producing several pulses of sound that are quite audible to the human ear. "I had to learn not to be startled and drop them when they made noise," Patek says.   5

The files are covered with microscopic structures that Patek likens to shingles on a roof. These shingles contribute to what she calls a "stick and slip" mechanism: When the plectrum is pulled across the file against the direction in which the shingles lie, the plectrum briefly sticks due to friction. Once that friction is overcome, the plectrum slips, causing both it and the file's shingles to vibrate and generate a sound pulse. Since there are hundreds of shingles on the file, one motion of the plectrum sticks and slips numerous times and generates several pulses. This method of generating sound is much the same as that caused by the friction between a bow and the strings of a violin.   6

6. Which of the following sentences from paragraph 4 contains a simile?

   a. "But like all arthropods, the spiny lobster goes through molting periods during which it sheds its outer shell."

   b. "After molting, the new exoskeleton can take a couple of days to a week to harden, says Patek."

   c. "During this soft state, the lobster is vulnerable, so it has evolved a sound-based defense mechanism that doesn't rely on hard structures, unlike the sound-making organs of other arthropods."

   d. "For example, a cricket requires two hard surfaces to rub together, much like a pick running over a washboard, explains Patek."

7. Which of the following context clues from paragraph 4 would help you determine the meaning of the word *molting* as used in the same paragraph?

   a. "during which it sheds its outer shell"

   b. "a couple of days to a week to harden"

   c. "sound-based defense mechanism"

   d. "hard structures"

8. According to Greene, the spiny lobsters' method of generating sound is similar to the

   a. sounds made by sharks.

   b. friction between a bow and the strings of a violin.

   c. "stick and slip" mechanism.

   d. sound made by the plectrum.

9. In this context, the word *vulnerable*, as used in paragraph 4, means

   a. safe.

   b. careful.

   c. unprotected.

   d. dead.

10. From the following list, choose the ordinary and specialized meaning of the word *files* as used in paragraph 5.

   a. Ordinary: places to keep documents
      Specialized: structures that sit below a spiny lobster's eyes

    b.   Ordinary: computer documents

         Specialized: a soft, leathery piece of tissue on a spiny lobster

    c.   Ordinary: computer documents

         Specialized: the pulsing sounds made by a spiny lobster

    d.   Ordinary: ready reference lists

         Specialized: a spiny lobster's claws

    Being able to scare away predators even when their bodies are soft is a vital adaptation for the spiny lobster. "They can make powerful sound throughout the molt," says Patek. The most effective noises for deterring predators are loud, pulsing sounds that can startle an attacker, possibly opening an escape route. "If you're reaching to pick up a food item and it makes a noise, you might drop it," says Patek.   7

    While scientists have known of the spiny lobster noise for years, Patek is the first to discover such a novel mechanism, directly comparable to a musical instrument, says Jelle Atema, director of the Boston University Marine Program. The lobsters, however, probably don't hear their handiwork. Unlike humans, lobsters communicate mainly through chemical signals they release into the water, but they seem to detect sound by detecting the motion of the water created by sound waves. There is still much to learn, Atema says. Patek concurs: "Lobsters are fascinating because we know so much about how to catch them but relatively little about their behavior."   8

11. What is the specialized meaning of the word *novel* in paragraph 8?

    a.   a long book

    b.   uninspired

    (c.) new and different; unique

    d.   similar; ordinary

12. What is the specialized meaning in marine biology of the word *waves* as used in "sound waves" in paragraph 8?

    (a.) vibrations

    b.   antennae

    c.   reflectors

    d.   the motion of ocean water

13. From context clues, what does *concur* mean as used in paragraph 8?
    a. doesn't understand
    b. understands
    c. says the same thing
    d. agrees

14. An extended comparison or metaphor made throughout this selection is between
    a. violin music and sound waves.
    b. sound waves and crashing waves.
    c. violin music and the sounds produced by spiny lobsters.
    d. picks on a washboard and the sounds produced by spiny lobsters.

15. In the context of paragraph 7, what is the connotation of the word *powerful*?
    a. very effective
    b. strong
    c. lackluster
    d. weak

Reading the Whole

Now that you have had a chance to read Sarah Greene's article in its parts and to examine the author's use of language, you will find that you are better able to "read between the lines" when you read her article as a whole. As you read, continue to pay attention to Greene's use of language, but think also about how her use of an extended metaphor helps you understand Sheila Patek's discovery in a way that more literal language could not.

SARAH GREENE
Musical Lobsters

They might not be up to playing Beethoven, but spiny lobsters share a talent with virtuoso musicians like Itzhak Perlman. Research at Duke University has revealed that the creatures produce sound much like a violinist does by pulling a bow across the instrument's strings.

While violinists play for pleasure, spiny lobsters "play" under more stressful conditions, explains Sheila Patek, a biologist now at the University of California at Berkeley who did this research while at Duke. Using underwater microphones, she listened in on the loud sounds the lobsters make to scare off potential predators. The creatures' music is more of an unpleasant rasp than a sweet vibrato, she says, but that is exactly the point.

Unlike the North Atlantic lobsters commonly consumed in American seafood restaurants, spiny lobsters from sub-tropical to tropical oceans do not have claws (see image at photo1.dukenews.duke.edu/pages/Duke_News_Service/lobster/lobster2.jpg). Instead they protect themselves with their hard exterior skeleton and spiny antennae, fending off predators such as sharks, grouper, triggerfish, and sometimes even other lobsters.

But like all arthropods, the spiny lobster goes through molting periods during which it sheds its outer shell. After molting, the new exoskeleton can take a couple of days to a week to harden, says Patek. During this soft state, the lobster is vulnerable, so it has evolved a sound-based defense mechanism that doesn't rely on hard structures, unlike the sound-making organs of other arthropods. For example, a cricket requires two hard surfaces to rub together, much like a prick running over a washboard, explains Patek.

The spiny lobster has two structures, called files, which sit just below its eyes. Resting directly underneath each of them is a soft, leathery piece of tissue called a plectrum, jutting back from the base of its antennae, that acts like a violinist's bow. With one muscle contraction, the lobster pulls the plectra over the files, producing several pulses of sound that are quite audible to the human ear. "I had to learn not to be startled and drop them when they made noise," Patek says.

The files are covered with microscopic structures that Patek likens to shingles on a roof. These shingles contribute to what she calls a "stick and slip" mechanism: When the plectrum is pulled across the file against the direction in which the shingles lie, the plectrum briefly sticks due to friction. Once that friction is overcome, the plectrum slips, causing both it and the file's shingles to vibrate and generate a sound pulse. Since there are hundreds of shingles on the file, one motion of the plectrum sticks and slips numerous times and generates several pulses. This method of generating sound is much the same as that caused by the friction between a bow and the strings of a violin.

Being able to scare away predators even when their bodies are soft is a vital adaptation for the spiny lobster. "They can make powerful sound throughout the molt," says Patek. The most effective noises for deterring predators are loud, pulsing sounds that can startle an attacker, possibly opening an escape route. "If you're reaching to pick up a food item and it makes a noise, you might drop it," says Patek.

While scientists have known of the spiny lobster noise for years, Patek is the first to discover such a novel mechanism, directly comparable to a musical instrument, says Jelle Atema, director of the Boston University Marine Program. The lobsters, however, probably don't hear their handiwork. Unlike humans, lobsters communicate mainly through chemical signals they release into the water, but they seem to detect sound by detecting the motion of the water created by sound waves. There is still much to learn, Atema says. Patek concurs: "Lobsters are fascinating because we know so much about how to catch them but relatively little about their behavior."

Integrated Skills

1. What connection does the author describe between spiny lobsters and virtuoso violinists?

2. What is different about the "music" spiny lobsters make compared with the music made by violinists?

3. In what paragraphs does the author describe how the spiny lobster makes its distinctive musical sounds? Do you find the author's explanation clear and understandable? Why or why not?

4. Why do spiny lobsters make loud pulsing sounds if it is unlikely that other lobsters can hear the sounds they make?

5. In what ways did you find this article interesting, engaging, or informative?

Reading/Writing Connection

In "Musical Lobsters," Sarah Greene describes the unusual sounds the spiny lobster makes and how it makes those sounds, which she compares to violin music. Think of another kind of sound that is not normally considered "music," and explain in a paragraph why you think it can be considered a kind of music. You might write about the sound an animal makes, a sound that people make, or a type of sound that you hear as you go to work or school.

Reading Textbooks

Thematic Connections. Sheila Patek caused a lot of excitement in the scientific community when she discovered how lobsters make their distinctive noise. In her article, Sarah Greene uses a metaphor of the bow and strings of a violin to describe the lobster's body and to help nonbiologist readers understand Patek's discovery. But how does a violin work? The following passage from the music textbook *Listen* by Joseph Kerman and Gary Tomlinson explains. As you read the passage, look for specialized meanings of words, positive and negative connotations, and figures of speech.

Vocabulary Preview

rapid (para. 1): fast (adj.)

vibrations (para. 1): the quick back-and-forth, up-and-down, or in-and-out movement of an object, such as on a cellular phone set to "vibrate" (n.)

distinct (para. 1): unique, separate (adj.)

taut (para. 2): pulled tightly (adj.)

amplify (para. 2): make louder (v.)

registers (para. 5): vocal or musical ranges (n.)

pitches (para. 5): the "highness" or "lowness" of sounds (n.)

ensemble (para. 6): group (n.)

composite (para. 6): made up of different parts (adj.)

indispensable (para. 7): necessary, irreplaceable (adj.)

Instruments of the Orchestra

Musical instruments can be categorized into four groups: *stringed instruments* or *strings*, *woodwinds*, *brass*, and *percussion*. Musical sound, as we know, is caused by rapid vibrations. Each of the four groups of instruments produces sound vibrations in its own distinct way. 1

STRINGED INSTRUMENTS

These are instruments that have their sound produced by taut strings. The strings are always attached to a "sound box," a hollow box containing a body of air that resonates (that is, vibrates along with the strings) to amplify the string sound. 2

The strings themselves can be played with a bow, as with the violin and other orchestral strings; the *bow* is strung tightly with horsehair, which is coated with a substance called rosin, so that the bow grips the strings. Or else the strings can be plucked or strummed, as on the guitar or the banjo, using the fingers or a small pick. 3

Strings can be plucked on bowed instruments, too, for special effects. This is called **pizzicato**.   4

The Violin and Its Family The **violin** is often called the most beau-   5
tiful instrument used in Western music. Also one of the most versatile of instruments, its large range covers alto and soprano registers and many much higher pitches. As a solo instrument, it can play forcefully or delicately, and it excels in both brilliant and songlike music. Violinists also play chords by bowing two or more of the four strings at once, or nearly so.

The violin is an excellent ensemble instrument; and it blends   6
especially well with other violins. An orchestra violin section, made up of ten or more instruments playing together, can produce a strong, yet sensitive, flexible tone. Hence the orchestra has traditionally relied on strings as a solid foundation for its composite sound.

Like most instruments, violins come in *families*, that is, in several   7
sizes with different pitch ranges. Three members of the violin family are basic to the orchestra.

- The **viola** is the tenor-range instrument, larger than a violin by several inches. It has a throaty quality in its lowest range, from middle C down an octave, yet it fits especially smoothly into accompaniment texture. The viola's highest register is powerful and intense.

- The **cello**, short for *violoncello*, is the bass of the violin family. This large instrument is played between the legs. Unlike the viola, the cello has a rich, gorgeous sound in its low register. It is a favorite solo instrument, as well as an indispensable member of the orchestra.

Bass Viol Also called **string bass, double bass**, or just **bass**, this   8
deep instrument is used to back up the violin family in the orchestra. (However, in various details of construction the bass viol differs from members of the violin family; the bass viol actually belongs to another, older stringed instrument family, the *viol* family.)

Played with a bow, the bass viol provides a splendid deep sup-   9
port for orchestral sound. The bass viol is often (in jazz, nearly always) plucked to give an especially vibrant kind of accent and to emphasize the meter.

Harp Harps are plucked stringed instruments with one string for   10
each pitch available. The modern orchestral harp is a large instrument with forty-seven strings covering a range of six and a half

octaves. A pedal mechanism allows the playing of chromatic (black-key) as well as diatonic (white-key) pitches.

In most orchestral music, the swishing, watery quality of the   11
harp is treated as a striking occasional effect rather than as a regular texture.

Thinking about the Textbook Selection

1. What connection can you make between this reading selection from a music textbook and the magazine article "Musical Lobsters"?

2. Why do you think the authors begin this selection by mentioning the woodwinds, brass, and percussion?

3. What do the members of the musical string family have in common?

4. How do the various stringed instruments differ?

5. What is meant by the use of the term "violin family"?

6. Which is your favorite stringed instrument? What do you like about this instrument?

Reading the Web

The Dave Matthews Band is known for, among other things, its unique sound, driven largely by the use of string music—unusual for a rock band. Here is the biography for violinist Boyd Tinsley from the official Dave Matthews Band Web site. Your new skills for interpreting a writer's language will help you get more information from the biography than if you were to read its surface only. Read closely and you'll find connotations, metaphors, figures of speech, and even irony.

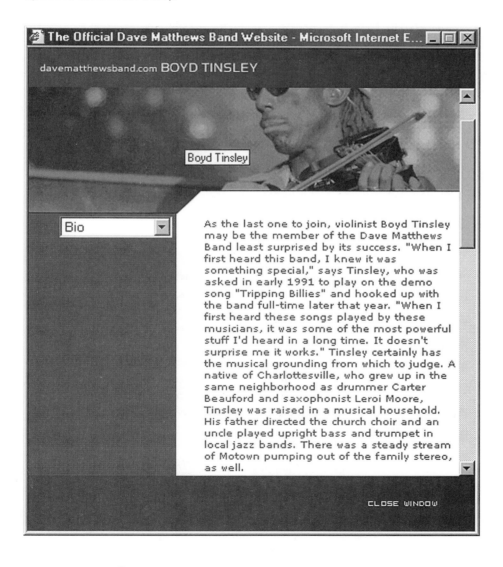

The Official Dave Matthews Band Website - Microsoft Internet E...

davematthewsband.com BOYD TINSLEY

Boyd Tinsley

Bio

As the last one to join, violinist Boyd Tinsley may be the member of the Dave Matthews Band least surprised by its success. "When I first heard this band, I knew it was something special," says Tinsley, who was asked in early 1991 to play on the demo song "Tripping Billies" and hooked up with the band full-time later that year. "When I first heard these songs played by these musicians, it was some of the most powerful stuff I'd heard in a long time. It doesn't surprise me it works." Tinsley certainly has the musical grounding from which to judge. A native of Charlottesville, who grew up in the same neighborhood as drummer Carter Beauford and saxophonist Leroi Moore, Tinsley was raised in a musical household. His father directed the church choir and an uncle played upright bass and trumpet in local jazz bands. There was a steady stream of Motown pumping out of the family stereo, as well.

CLOSE WINDOW

Thinking about the Web Page

1. What kind of language does the writer of this Web page use in writing about Boyd Tinsley, the violinist for the Dave Matthews Band?

2. What metaphors, or comparisons, are used in the last sentence? What do these metaphors suggest about Tinsley's attitude toward Motown music?

Reviewing

Recall / Remember

1. What are specialized meanings of words?
2. What is the difference between denotation and connotation?
3. How can you figure out a word's connotation? How do you determine whether it is negative or positive?
4. What is the difference between literal language and figures of speech in language?
5. What are simile and metaphor? How are they alike, and what are the differences between them?
6. What is irony, and why do you think writers use it?

Chapter Summary

In this chapter, you have focused on how a writer's language conveys the idea of a reading selection. You have examined words in context, determining their meaning from the words, sentences, and paragraphs that come before and after them. You have explored the difference between the denotations, or dictionary definitions, of words and their connotations, or additional personal, emotional, and contextual meanings. Finally, you have learned about figures of speech—nonliteral forms of language that convey meanings in different ways, such as through comparison (simile and metaphor), exaggeration (hyperbole), personification, and irony.

In the following chapter, you will use this new knowledge as you continue to learn how to read critically, or between the lines.

Chapter 8

Becoming an Interpretive Reader

Getting Ready

You know from experience that your mind tries to make sense of what you are reading. What you may not realize is that you perform very specific intellectual acts in the process of making sense as you read. Together, those acts of making sense are called interpretive reading. This chapter will show you how to read interpretively and become a more confident reader.

Reading interpretively involves four primary skills:

- Making **observations** about what you read.
- Establishing **connections** among the details you observe.
- Formulating **inferences,** or educated guesses, about those connections.
- Drawing **conclusions** about the reading's meaning or idea.

This chapter shows you how to combine these skills to make sense of and interpret what you read. It builds on what you have learned in Chapters 6 and 7 about how writers structure their writing to organize their ideas and how they use language to convey them.

Chapter Overview

Focusing Questions

When you read, how often do key words, phrases, and sentences seem to attract your attention?

How do you decide which details are important in a reading selection?

What connections do you look for among different details? Do you look for patterns or repeated examples?

How carefully do you think about what you read? Do you try to figure out what an author might be implying or suggesting?

Everyday Reading

Many of the places you go to on a regular basis — a bus or subway stop, the post office, the entryway to a grocery store, the student lounge — are plastered with posters, notices, and advertisements. These may contain straightforward information ("Open auditions this Friday!" or "Baby-sitter wanted," for example); or they might contain some language that you have to interpret by making inferences about what the suggested message is. (An **inference** is an educated guess based on limited knowledge from what you have observed.) The next time you stop to read a message in a public place, see what inferences you can make based on the details the message includes.

Learning the Skills

■ The Interpretive Impulse

You are not a stranger to the act of interpretation. Your daily life offers you many opportunities to think interpretively. For example, if you succeed or fail in performing a task, in taking a test, or in getting through a difficult day, you seek to understand why. You might try to analyze what went wrong on the one hand or, on the other, what enabled you to accomplish what you did successfully.

To take another example, when you move to an unfamiliar place, make a new acquaintance, or undertake a new responsibility, you adjust to the unfamiliar situation by trying to relate your new experience to what you already know. In the process you build up your storehouse of knowledge and experience. This need to understand the unfamiliar is equally true of what you read. The act of making sense of what you see, hear, read, and otherwise experience is an act of interpretation.

Making sense of what you read is something like doing detective work. Like a detective studying clues and formulating a hypothesis, a reader studies textual details to arrive at an understanding of a writer's meaning. Good detectives and good readers use similar critical skills to develop their interpretations of the evidence: They make careful observations, they develop strong impressions, and they revise their thinking in light of discovering new information or evidence.

■ Making Observations

Your first step toward interpretive reading is to make observations about what you are reading. Interpretive readers observe how a writer uses details and language to identify a topic and explain his or her thinking about it. The details might be words or phrases; they might be facts or examples; they might be references to past history or the contemporary world—among other kinds of things.

Many of the strategies described in the first seven chapters of this book support the specific kinds of observation necessary for interpreting what you read. In Chapters 3 and 4, when you practiced the skill of identifying the main idea of a reading passage, for example, you made observations about a main idea and its supporting details, which helped you comprehend the meaning of what you read. And the skill of making connections, which you learned in Chapter 5, is very helpful in interpreting what a writer has to say. In Chapter 6 you learned about some of the ways writers organize their material; understanding these relationships helps you to follow an author's thinking.

Observing an author's examples, in particular, will enable you to understand what the author is saying, especially when you analyze those examples in the context of the reading overall. After reading more than one example of a concept, ask yourself the question "What do these examples have in common?" Thinking about the examples together and considering the traits they share will help you understand the concept they illustrate.

Other details—the elements, the bits and pieces of something—provide the specifics of a reading passage. One strategy you can use to observe details is to underline them or list them as you read. Careful observation of the details a writer uses is essential for comprehending what a writer is saying. Like examples, all the details a writer includes will help you understand the main point more fully.

Finally, writers often repeat themselves for emphasis. They may state an idea at the beginning of a passage and restate it later, in the middle or at the end. They may express an idea in the same words each time, or they may vary the words used to convey their ideas. Focusing on repetition while reading helps you focus on the author's most important points. Observing repeated examples, statements, and ideas in a passage helps you interpret the writer's meaning, even if it is unstated.

To practice making observations, read the following passage from the textbook *Health in the New Millennium* by Jeffrey S. Nevid, Spencer A. Rathus, and Hannah R. Rubenstein:

Viva Mexican Food!

First the good news. The foundations of Mexican food, beans, rice, and tortillas, together with grilled fish or skinless chicken, can be quite healthy. So what's the bad news? Mexican dishes, at least those typically served in Mexican restaurants in the U.S. (as opposed to the food that Mexicans themselves consume) are so laden with fatty additions, like cheese, sour cream, and guacamole, that they are the food equivalent of a heart attack waiting to happen.   1

The CSPI [Center for Science in the Public Interest] sampled the fare in some popular Mexican restaurants like Chi Chi's, El Torito, and Chevy's. They found that many menu selections contained more total fat, more saturated fat, and more sodium than one should eat during an entire day. For instance, one beef burrito with beans, rice, sour cream, and guacamole registered 1,639 calories and exceeded the total daily values for fat, saturated fat, and sodium. The worst offender, a main dish consisting of two chiles with beans and rice, contained 1,578 calories and tipped the scale at about 150% of the daily totals for fat, saturated fat, and sodium. And don't forget those tasty but oh-so-fatty appetizers, like nachos. A serving of 50 tortilla chips without cheese and guacamole contains 645 calories and accounts for about three-fourths of the daily fat value. But nachos (tortilla chips smothered in cheese and guacamole) logged in at 136% of the daily fat value and contained 1,362 calories. As the CSPI reviewers put it, if they're out of nachos, you might as well ask the waiter for a stick of butter and some salt.   2

Are there healthier alternatives for those who savor the taste of Mexican food? Fortunately, yes, but you have to be careful about the add-ons. Chicken fajitas, for instance, consisting of strips of chicken breast with sauteed peppers and onions, wrapped in flour   3 tortillas, was the least fatty entree sampled by the CSPI staffers. But make sure to have it plain—no sour cream or guacamole, please. Or spread a tablespoon of salsa over it. Salsa adds flavor but little fat and sodium. A chicken or beef burrito is also a good alternative, but skip the cheese or sour cream. Sticking to rice and beans will save you calories and fat, but CSPI found that the typical restaurant serving of Mexican rice (¾ cup) contained more than 800 milligrams of sodium, about a third of the daily maximum. The beans had almost as much. Then too, many restaurants offer refried beans that are cooked with fat, such as lard, bacon, or cheese. Order plain beans instead.

What can you observe about this reading selection? First, identify its main idea: Mexican fast food is generally full of fat, but there are ways to eat a healthy meal in Mexican restaurants. If you read carefully, you'll see that the authors use a comparison-contrast organization: First unhealthy choices, then healthy ones. Consider the kinds of examples and details the authors provide. Examples of unhealthy Mexican food include cheese, sour cream, guacamole, the calories and fat in a single beef burrito and in a chile dish, and nachos. Healthy alternatives suggested by the authors include chicken fajitas (plain), salsa, burritos without sour cream or cheese, and plain beans. For details, they offer specific calorie, fat, and sodium counts of various menu options. Many things are repeated as well—the words *fat, calories,* and *sodium* in particular, so you know that these concerns are very important to the reading selection's main idea.

Exercise 8-1

Answer the questions about the selection by making observations about organization, structure, examples, details, and repetition.

(1) Scholars, of course, vary somewhat in their ideas of which elements are essential to a definition of civilization. (2) Nonetheless, there is consensus that some elements are crucial to the definition and always must be present, while others are sometimes important but more variable. (3) This section discusses what we consider the six essential elements of civilization, and the section that follows discusses the variable ones.

(4) The following are the core, invariable elements of civilization:

- dependence on agriculture;
- occupation specialization;
- class stratification;
- state government;
- long-distance trade; and
- urbanism.

(Lanny B. Fields, Russell J. Barber, and Cheryl A. Riggs, *The Global Past*)

1. What is the structure of this passage?

   It is a paragraph that ends in a list.

2. What is the topic of the paragraph?

   the elements that are essential to a definition of civilization

3. The authors ensure that readers understand the topic by using repetition. The words "elements are essential to a definition of civilization" in the first sentence are repeated in some form in every sentence that follows. List each form of the repetition.

   a. SENTENCE 2: *"elements are crucial to the definition"*

   b. SENTENCE 3: *"essential elements of civilization"*

   c. SENTENCE 4: *"core, invariable elements of civilization"*

4. The authors say that this section of the chapter will discuss only the essential elements of civilization. What will the next section discuss?

   The next section will discuss elements that are important but more

   changeable ("more variable") — elements that are not essential.

5. Is the list in this passage in any kind of order (time, space, importance)? If so, why? If not, why not?

The list is not in any kind of order. All the elements have to exist at the

same time; all are equally important.

. . . .

■ Establishing Connections

Now that you have practiced observation strategies for reading, the next step is to make connections among your observations. When you make connections, you identify relationships among details that you observe. You look for what your observations might have in common, and you ask how your observations relate to one another. Perhaps a writer uses similar kinds of examples. Perhaps he or she includes repeated references to science or to popular television shows. Or perhaps there is a pattern of figurative language or connotation.

As you make connections among observations, you discover how one example is related to another. You also discover how one paragraph is related to another, and you realize how one part of a passage is related to the other parts. You've already had some practice doing this in Chapter 5. In making these kinds of connections, you will more fully understand what the author says, and you will be better able to interpret his or her use of information.

As you read and make observations, ask yourself just how the details you observe can be connected. These observations and connections help you see how the author organizes material. Understanding a writer's organization helps you understand his or her ideas. For practice, reread the passage about Mexican food on pages 264–65. Then consider some connections among the observations mentioned on page 265.

The authors open the passage with "good news" and "bad news." The connection between them is Mexican food: The foundations are healthy (the good news), but the way in which Mexican dishes are typically served in restaurants is unhealthy (the bad news). Furthermore, there is an important connection between the Mexican dishes—beef burritos, chiles-beans-and-rice, and nachos—given as examples: They are all tremendously high in fat, sodium, and calories, with the chiles-

and-beans dish targeted as "the worst offender." The CSPI reviewers also make a connection when they say that if the restaurant is out of nachos, "you might as well ask the waiter for a stick of butter and some salt": They're saying that eating nachos is equivalent — in terms of fat, calories, and sodium — to eating a stick of butter with salt. Finally, consider the connection between the title and the passage itself: *Viva* often means "long live. . . ," and the word is sometimes used as a toast or applause. By saying, in effect, "Long live Mexican food!" the authors are connecting the title with their third paragraph: They are telling readers that despite all its problems, Mexican food can still be enjoyed in a healthy way that enables you to live long.

Exercise 8-2

Answer the questions about the following passage by making connections.

Forgetting: You *Forgot* the Plane Tickets?!

In the everyday sense, forgetting is simply not being able to remember some piece of information. Often, this involves information we intended to remember, such as removing the brownies from the oven before they're burned to a crisp (again). More formally, **forgetting** is the inability to recall information that was previously available. 1

Forgetting is so common that our lives are filled with automatic reminders to safeguard against forgetting important information. Cars are equipped with buzzers so you don't forget to put on your seatbelt or turn off your lights. News announcements remind you to reset your clocks as Daylight Savings Time begins or ends. Dentists thoughtfully send brightly colored postcards so that your root canal appointment doesn't slip your mind. 2

Sometimes, of course, we *want* to forget. From the standpoint of a person's psychological well-being, it's probably just as well that we tend to forget the details of unpleasant memories, such as past failures, social embarrassments, and unhappy relationships. Even more generally, it's easy to argue that our minds would be cluttered with mountains of useless information if we remembered every television program, magazine article, billboard, or conversation we've ever experienced. So forgetting *does* have some adaptive value. (Don H. Hockenbury and Sandra E. Hockenbury, *Psychology*) 3

Example:

The first sentence of this passage begins with the words "In the everyday sense." The third sentence begins with the words "More formally." These phrases are connected because they are both referring to what?

forgetting (or the definition of "forgetting")

1. In paragraph 1, the example of the burning brownies connects to which definition of *forgetting*—the everyday definition or the more formal definition?

   the everyday definition

2. Three examples are given in paragraph 2: cars with buzzers, news announcements about Daylight Savings Time, and post-cards from dentists. What is the connection among these examples? In other words, what common purpose do the examples have?

   They are all reminders to keep people from forgetting important

   information.

3. In paragraph 3, what do the examples "past failures, social embarrassments, and unhappy relationships" have in common? How are they connected?

   They are examples of unpleasant memories people want to forget.

4. In paragraph 3, what do the examples "every television program, magazine article, billboard, or conversation we've ever experienced" have in common? How are they connected?

   They are examples of useless information that would clutter our minds

   if we remembered them all.

5. What does paragraph 3 discuss about forgetting that the first two paragraphs do not discuss?

   The paragraph discusses why forgetting is sometimes a good thing

   instead of a bad thing.

■ Formulating Inferences

You have now performed two very important steps toward making an interpretation. The next step in analytical reading, formulating **inferences**, is key. *Inference* comes from the verb "to infer." When you infer, you make an educated guess about meaning and the significance of details and connections, based on what you observe and what you know. These inferences represent a reader's thinking about a reading selection. They are essential for being able to arrive at a critical understanding of a writer's idea.

What exactly do you do when you make an inference? Essentially, you make a little mental leap—an intellectual jump. You jump mentally or intellectually from what you know to what you don't know. This mental leap is based on the observations you make and the connections you discover among your observations. If you see a man entering an apartment with a key, you infer that he lives there. If you see a couple entering a house through a window, you infer perhaps that they don't live there—or that they locked themselves out.

Inferences can be right or wrong. That is, an inference is not necessarily true. In the example about the man entering an apartment with a key, you inferred that he lived there. But that inference would be incorrect if he had borrowed the key from a relative or friend or if he was hired to walk the dog.

Making inferences also requires you to make sense of a text by building on your observations of particular details in the passage. For example, in reading about a psychological experiment, you may be given information such as the following:

a. For forty-eight hours volunteers were put in a room where the lights were always on.

b. The volunteers were given no food during those forty-eight hours.

c. Experimenters placed sensory devices on the volunteers' heads during the experiment.

d. Experimenters did not allow the volunteers to talk with each other during the time of the experiment.

e. Volunteers were not allowed to read, listen to a radio, or watch television during the experiment.

As you were reading these facts about the experiment, you were probably developing inferences based on them. For example, you might have inferred that the experimenters were testing how well people can cope with silence or how well they adjust to the presence of others when they can't communicate with them. These inferences would be based on your prior experience, drawing not on your own participation in such an experiment but on your knowledge of how psychological experiments are conducted and your understanding of how people react when they cannot change their environment or when they must obey a strict set of rules.

What other inferences might you make about the experiment and about the people who volunteered for it? Ask yourself, for example, how the volunteers may have responded to the experiment. In making such inferences, consider how you and some people you know might have responded.

Exercise 8-3

Read the following passages and answer the questions that follow them by making inferences.

Psychologist Martin Seligman noticed that phobias seem to be quite   1
selective. Extreme, irrational fears of snakes, spiders, heights, and small enclosed places . . . are relatively common. But very few people are phobic of stairs, ladders, electrical outlets or appliances, or sharp objects, even though these things are far more likely to be associated with traumatic experiences or accidents.

Seligman has proposed that humans are biologically prepared to de-   2
velop fears of objects or situations—like snakes, spiders, and heights— that may have once posed a threat to humans' evolutionary ancestors. As Seligman puts it, "The great majority of phobias are about objects of natural importance to the survival of the species." According to Seligman, people don't commonly develop phobias of knives, stoves, or cars because they're not biologically prepared to do so.

Support for this view is provided by early studies that tried to repli-   3
cate Watson's Little Albert research. Elsie Bregman was unable to produce a conditioned fear response to wooden blocks and curtains, although she followed Watson's procedure carefully. And Horace English was unable to produce a conditioned fear of a wood duck. Perhaps we're more biologically prepared to learn a fear of furry animals than wooden ducks, blocks, or curtains. (Don H. Hockenbury and Sandra E. Hockenbury, *Psychology*)

Example:

Using the second sentence to help explain the first sentence, infer the meaning of the term *phobia*.

The term "phobia" means "an extreme, irrational fear."

1. What is the connection among snakes, spiders, heights, and small enclosed spaces?

   People often develop phobias of them.

2. What is the connection between the examples "stairs, ladders, electrical outlets or appliances, or sharp objects" and "knives, stoves, or cars"?

   They're relatively dangerous to people.

3. After identifying what things people do develop phobias of, Seligman notes that "very few people are phobic of stairs, ladders, electrical outlets or appliances, or sharp objects, even though these things are far more likely to be associated with traumatic experiences or accidents." From this statement, what can you infer about "snakes, spiders, heights, and small enclosed places"?

   We can infer that snakes, spiders, heights, and small enclosed spaces

   are unlikely to cause people harm.

4. "According to Seligman, people don't commonly develop phobias of knives, stoves, or cars because they're not biologically prepared to do so." What can you infer from this statement?

   We can infer that knives, stoves, and cars were not threats to our

   earliest ancestors.

5. Using the complete passage, but especially the last line, infer what Watson's Little Albert research must have involved.

   Watson's Little Albert research most likely involved a furry animal that

   was used to produce fear or a phobic response in subjects.

Boston has Heartbreak at mile 21. Bloomsday has Cemetery and 1 Doomsday. The San Blas Half-Marathon has The Strangler. Apparently, just plain running isn't tough enough. So race directors, in their infinite wisdom, have decided we need hills. Big ones. And if they have sadistic-sounding names, so much the better.

Many upcoming spring races will be run on hilly courses. The ques- 2 tion is: How should you prepare? According to the principle of training specificity, in order to improve a certain aspect of physical fitness, you must train specifically for it. This means one thing: If you want to turn those looming hills into nothing more than speed bumps, you need to do some hill workouts.

Think of a hill workout as a running-specific weight workout. The 3 exaggerated knee lift, driving arms, and pronounced toe-off necessary to run up hills strengthens you every bit as much as hitting the weight room. Hill running also works the cardiovascular system as your heart tries to keep pace with the increased energy required to fight gravity. Consequently, hill workouts are very taxing and should be done only once or twice a week. (Ed Eyestone, "Head for the Hills," *Runner's World*, February 2002)

6. The first paragraph begins with examples, but the writer does not say what the examples are. What can you infer that Heart-break, Cemetery, Doomsday, and The Strangler are?

   From the rest of the paragraph, we can infer that the examples are hills

   on marathon-running courses.

7. What can you infer about race directors from the last sentence of paragraph 1?

   Race directors want the hills to seem tough and punishing rather than

   easy. Race directors want to make the course seem hard rather than

   downplay the difficulties.

8. Considering the language in paragraph 1, how would you say the writer feels about race directors? Which words or phrases influenced your answer?

The writer seems to be making fun of race directors; the writer is

sarcastic about them: "race directors, in their infinite wisdom, have

decided"; "we need hills. Big ones"; "if they have sadistic-sounding

names, so much the better."

9. Roughly half of one sentence in paragraph 2 allows the reader to infer that all the tough-sounding hills can be conquered very easily. Which words permit the reader to make that inference?

"If you want to turn those looming hills into nothing more than speed

bumps"

10. What can you infer about the audience for this article? By the way this passage is written, would you infer that this is an informational piece for nonrunners, an entertaining piece for casual runners, a how-to piece for serious runners? Explain your answer by quoting specific words from the passage.

The piece is written for marathon runners. "How should you prepare?"

addresses those who want to run tough hills. "The exaggerated knee lift,

driving arms, and pronounced toe-off" is somewhat technical language

that the author expects the reader to understand. Hill workouts "should

be done only once or twice a week" is advice to serious marathon runners.

· ·

■ Drawing Conclusions

A reader's conclusions make up an overall sense of what a reading selection means. Readers draw conclusions from their inferences as they read. After making some inferences, readers look for connections among them. The connections among inferences lead to conclusions.

This experience of building toward a conclusion while you read is part of the process of reading interpretively. As an active, engaged reader, you seek connections not only among your observations but also among your inferences. Active readers continue making observations and connections even after they have begun making inferences. After they have made a few inferences, active readers will make connections among their inferences in a process that leads to conclusions about the writer's purpose and ideas.

Interpretive readers modify their conclusions as they read, adjusting them as they make additional observations, establish new connections, and develop more or different inferences. Even the conclusions you reach at the end of a reading selection, however, do not have to be final. You can change your mind about your understanding of what you have read. Drawing conclusions about reading selections is a continuing process that occurs both while you read and later, when you think back over what you have read.

The conclusions you draw, therefore, might be tentative or uncertain, rather than final or absolute. You can always think more about what a text or passage says or implies. You can change your mind about its meaning, just as you do with the inferences you make during reading. Your freedom to change the way you understand a reading selection and your responsibility as a reader to base your conclusions on connected inferences are part of what is meant by critical reading, which is the focus of the next chapter.

Exercise 8-4

Answer the questions about the following passages by connecting inferences and drawing conclusions.

Example:

Contrary to popular belief, people in the European Middle Ages did not believe that the earth was flat. Christopher Columbus's voyage is often touted as the triumph of science over the ignorant view of medieval Christianity that the world was flat and any voyage into the unknown waters of the Atlantic Ocean would result in ships' falling off the edge into oblivion. This perception, however, was held by only a few medieval church leaders and some educated people in Europe prior to the transoceanic voyages of the fifteenth century.

How did such an error originate? The history of this little tale falls at the feet of two nineteenth-century men: Washington Irving (1783–1859), who wrote a semifictitious biography of Christopher Columbus, and Antoine-Jean Letronne (1787–1848), who wrote several works, including the four-volume geographical *Histoire de géographie moderne*

(Paris, 1806). Unfortunately for later history, the sources these men used to weave their interpretations of medieval and Christian thinkers were not carefully checked by other scholars until recently, and, therefore, their imaginative embellishments were accepted as fact. (Lanny B. Fields, Russell J. Barber, and Cheryl A. Riggs, *The Global Past*)

A. Infer the current "popular belief" mentioned in the first sentence of the passage.

The current popular belief is that people during the European Middle

Ages thought the earth was flat.

B. Why did future generations believe that those who lived in the European Middle Ages thought the earth was flat?

People were influenced by the semifictitious biography of Christopher

Columbus written by Washington Irving and by the works of Antoine-Jean

Letronne.

C. Did anybody in medieval Europe believe that the earth was flat?

Yes. A few church leaders and some educated people did, but they were

in the minority.

D. According to the passage, why did later people accept the writings of Washington Irving and Antoine-Jean Letronne as fact?

People accepted Irving's and Letronne's work as fact because scholars

did not carefully check those writers' sources.

E. Since the current popular belief is still held, what can you conclude about the research that was done on this matter?

It never replaced the older, untrue belief in the public mind. Either it

was never publicized well enough and remained an academic matter, or

somehow the earlier belief was so strong that it couldn't be uprooted.

As a result, "popular belief" is still wrong.

(1) Every society trades goods with its neighbors, often as symbols of their mutual good will. (2) Civilizations, however, typically conduct large-scale trading operations at great distances. (3) In part, this is in response to their greater ability to devote labor and resources to the activities necessary for this kind of trade. (4) The mounting of a trading expedition begins with the amassing of goods to trade (and possibly the securing of loans to purchase the goods), an operation that requires up-front investment. (5) Next, a team of skilled specialists must be assembled. (6) They must be able to navigate to the intended distant place, to translate from one language to another, to defend the trading party from raiders and robbers along the way, to make judgments about values of goods, and to organize the entire operation. (7) Finally, the organizers of the trade must accept the possibility that they will have to absorb big losses, because the risks in long-distance trade are usually great; but so are the profits. (Lanny B. Fields, Russell J. Barber, and Cheryl A. Riggs, *The Global Past*)

1. From sentences 1 and 2, is it reasonable to conclude that the authors use the terms *society* and *civilizations* to mean the same thing? Explain why or why not.

   No. Since "every" society trades goods, but ("however") civilizations

   conduct trade at great distances, we can infer that there is a difference

   in the definitions of the two terms.

2. Which group—societies or civilizations—can you conclude is wealthier in goods, has more skilled and available labor, and is willing to take more risks?

   civilizations

3. What connections and inferences can you make from *begins* in sentence 4, *Next* in sentence 5, and *Finally* in sentence 7?

   A sequence is going to explain what a trading expedition requires.

4. Can you reasonably infer from sentence 7 that organizers of long-distance trade sometimes do, in fact, absorb big losses?

   Yes, that is a reasonable inference.

5. Since there are both great risks and great profits in long-distance trading, what conclusion can you draw about which of the two outweighs the other?

The profits must outweigh the risks (or at least trade organizers must

believe that the profits outweigh the risks); otherwise, no one would

bother with long-distance trading.

Applying the Skills

Reading the Parts

The following essay was written by science fiction writer Kim Stanley Robinson and originally appeared in the September 23, 1996, issue of *Newsweek*. A Hugo and Nebula Award–winning author best known for the novels in his Mars Trilogy (*Red Mars, Green Mars,* and *Blue Mars*), Robinson has done extensive research on the planet. As *Space.com* puts it, he is "the man who can tell you everything about what it takes to terraform Mars." His most recent novel is *The Years of Rice and Salt* (2002). As you read, be aware of observations you can make and connections among them. Continue to make inferences, and begin to draw conclusions about Robinson's points. After reading each section and answering the questions that follow, move on to the next section. You will have a chance to read the entire essay when you finish.

KIM STANLEY ROBINSON
A Colony in the Sky

One day early in the next century, several people will land on Mars. They will put on spacesuits and leave their vehicle, bounding over red rocks under a pink sky. After this exhilarating day, seen on Earth by billions, they will move into a cluster of habitats already on site. They will spend a year living there making scientific studies, and then they will return to Earth. Another team will cycle in. Back at home we will start to take the base for granted. Nevertheless, something very big will have begun.

The initial crossing to Mars will be made for a great number of reasons, some of them solid (to see if there really are fossil bacteria there), some of them not (to look for Elvis). Most of the reasons will be scientific and practical: the more we know about the solar system's other planets, the better we will understand Earth, and the safer we will be. It's not heroic but it makes sense, and it is important. Even if these were the only reasons, they would be good enough to send us.

But Mars will never remain just a research site to sharpen Earth management skills. We've been fascinated by the red wanderer ever since our days on the savannah, and even if life at the research

1

2

3

station proves to be quite ordinary, the videos they send back will show us a magnificent world of volcanoes and canyons, icecaps and sand dunes, wind and weather. These wild new landscapes will also look somewhat familiar, especially in comparison to the bone-white moon. This familiar quality is not just superficial, for Mars does resemble Earth in several important ways—general size, presence of water, length of day, range of temperatures—so many similarities, in fact, that some people are beginning to ask if it might be possible to make Mars even more like Earth than it is now. And that's the question that will shift us to the next level of our fascination with the place: the idea that we could live there, that Mars could be "terraformed."

1. Kim Stanley Robinson uses figurative language in paragraph 1 of this selection to convey a feeling about an event that will happen in the twenty-first century. "They will put on space-suits and leave their vehicle, bounding over red rocks under a pink sky. After this exhilarating day, seen on Earth by billions, they will move into a cluster of habitats already on site. . . . something very big will have begun." What can you infer about how Robinson feels about this event from his writing and use of language? Pay particular attention to his use of the verb *bounding* and the adjectives to describe rocks, the sky, and the day on which this will take place.

   a.   He is neutral.

   (b.) He is extremely excited by the coming of this event.

   c.   He thinks the event is a bad idea.

   d.   He is worried that something will go wrong.

2. Robinson states that "Mars does resemble Earth in several important ways." What can you infer about Robinson's stance on the settlement of Mars in considering this and his earlier statement that future trips to Mars make "sense" and are "important"?

   a.   Robinson is not in favor of space travel.

   b.   Robinson is a spokesperson for NASA.

   (c.) Robinson believes that Mars may be a viable habitat for future generations.

   d.   Robinson has no interest in Mars as a future settlement.

3. Which of the following is *not* one of the details that Robinson includes in paragraph 3 to support his assertion that "Mars does resemble Earth in several important ways"?

   (a.) the amount of time the sun is seen on Mars

   b. the length of the day on Mars, in comparison to that on Earth

   c. the range of temperatures on Mars and how this would affect human beings

   d. the general size of Mars as a planet

4. What conclusion can you draw from Robinson's statement that "most of the reasons [we visit Mars] will be scientific and practical" in paragraph 2 and his statement "But Mars will never remain just a research site to sharpen Earth management skills" in paragraph 3? Connecting the two observations, which is the most reasonable inference?

   (a.) Our visits to Mars will serve a number of purposes, some scientific and some to satisfy our curiosity with this far-away planet.

   b. Robinson thinks Mars should remain just a research site.

   c. Robinson doesn't think we should go to Mars.

   d. Robinson has never seen a picture of Mars.

5. Knowing that *terra* means "earth" and based on your reading of paragraphs 1–3, what prediction can you make about the definition of the word *terraformed* as used in Robinson's description of a future Mars?

   a. It probably means "uninhabitable."

   (b.) *Terraformed* probably means "making Mars habitable to Earth dwellers."

   c. It probably means "bringing water" to Mars.

   d. It probably means "rough earth."

> To terraform means to alter a planet's surface until Earth's life forms can survive there. It's a hypothetical discipline at this point, born in science-fiction stories. But in the last 30 years a number of scientists have taken up the concept. Their studies make it clear that the process would be somewhat slower than the cork-popping   4

transformations seen in some recent sci-fi movies; in reality, it would take centuries. But it is an idea that operates within physical reality as we know it. It's possible to do it.

The recipe is simple. Add nitrogen and oxygen to the atmosphere; pump water to the surface; cook for decades, spicing first with cyanobacteria, then with all the rest of Earth's plants and animals, adding them in the order they evolved here. Mars is blessed with all the ingredients called for in the recipe; indeed, Mars turns out to be perfect for terraforming. So, because we have all the life forms here at hand, we can try replaying evolution at extreme fast forward.

Of course it will be more complex than the recipe — it always is. And the process will certainly spiral out of our control. Eventually, however, if all goes well, we will have helped to start a new biosphere. Think of that! It's hard to know how even to characterize such an activity. It would be something like growing a garden, or creating a wilderness, or building a cathedral, or flying seeds over an ocean to drop them on a new island. It would be unlike anything else, a new thing in history.

6. What conclusion can you draw from the author's statement in paragraph 5 that "Mars is blessed with all the ingredients called for in the recipe; indeed, Mars turns out to be perfect for terraforming"?

a. Life on Mars is a definite possibility.

b. Life on Mars will never happen.

c. Life on Mars is only a few years away.

d. Life on Mars will be difficult.

7. What can you infer about science fiction movies from Robinson's statement in paragraph 4 that "the process would be somewhat slower than the cork-popping transformations seen in some recent sci-fi movies"?

a. Science fiction movies are extremely realistic.

b. Science fiction is a new type of movie genre.

c. Science fiction movies are unrealistic in their portrayal of scientific advancements.

d. Many foreign countries make science fiction movies.

8. What observation can you make about what would have to happen in order for Mars to become terraformed? Reread paragraph 5.

    a. Scientists would have to re-create the "Big Bang" in order to make Mars habitable.

    (b.) Scientists would have to re-create the process of evolution but in a compressed time frame in order to make Mars habitable.

    c. Scientists will never be able to make Mars habitable.

    d. Humans would never be able to survive on Mars.

9. What connection can you make from the first and last sentences of paragraph 6?

    (a.) Although there will be problems in trying to make Mars habitable for humans, it will eventually become a reality.

    b. Robinson thinks this plan is silly.

    c. This plan will never happen.

    d. We will need really strong rocket ships to get to Mars.

10. What can you conclude about the substance cyanobacteria, mentioned in paragraph 5, as part of the "recipe" that Robinson thinks is necessary to terraform Mars?

    a. It is a dangerous substance when used for terraforming.

    b. It is an unnecessary substance in this recipe.

    (c.) It is a necessary "ingredient" in the terraforming recipe and not harmful to human beings.

    d. There is nothing to conclude about the substance cyanobacteria.

Some people may believe that such a project is too large or slow or presumptuous for humanity to undertake. But consider our current situation on Earth. There are nearly 6 billion of us now, and the number may double, though we have no good idea how many of us the Earth can support. Many larger species are in danger of extinction unless we protect them from us. We have rearranged much of the land, and we have altered the atmosphere to the point where the global climate in the future will be a matter of legislation

7

and industrial practice. In other words, we are already starting to terraform Earth by necessity to keep it livable. Given this situation, the attempt to terraform Mars does not look so outlandish. Doing it could be regarded as a valuable experiment, with Mars as a giant lab or university, in which we learn how to steward a planet's biosphere for long-term sustainability.

Long term indeed! Terraforming Mars would take 300 years at least. It's not a time scale we often think about, and it does seem unlikely that any society could persist in anything for so long. Luckily, the process will not depend on our consistent backing, but on the people who settle there and pursue it as their own closest interest.

8

As for us, here on Earth in the age of the quarterly statement, it is probably a good thing occasionally to contemplate a really long-term project. Humanity's existence on this Earth is a long-term project, after all, and it's important to remember what that means. People will be living here 500 years from now, and they will all be our relatives. These distant children of ours deserve to be given a livable planet to care for in their turn. For their sake we need to work out a sustainable way of life on Earth. Going to Mars will be part of that larger environmental project, and terraforming it will be an education that we will apply at home as we learn it — pausing, from time to time, to look up at our wilderness garden in the sky.

9

11. What connection can you make between these two sentences: "Many larger species are in danger of extinction unless we protect them from us" (paragraph 7) and "For their [children's] sake we need to work out a sustainable way of life on Earth" (paragraph 9)?

   a. The way we live now is a threat to both human beings and animals.

   b. Animals are in graver danger than children of becoming extinct.

   c. Robinson thinks that we should kill larger species to make more room for human beings.

   d. Human beings don't know what they are doing when it comes to animals.

12. Which of the following sentences does Robinson use to support his statement "In other words, we are already starting to terraform Earth by necessity to keep it livable" in paragraph 7?

a. "Some people may believe that such a project is too large or slow or presumptuous for humanity to undertake."

b. "But consider our current situation on Earth."

c. "We have rearranged much of the land, and we have altered the atmosphere to the point where the global climate in the future will be a matter of legislation and industrial practice."

d. "There are nearly 6 billion of us now, and the number may double, though we have no good idea how many of us the Earth can support."

13. What can you infer about what Robinson thinks the Earth will be like five hundred years from now from the statement "These distant children of ours deserve to be given a livable planet to care for in their turn"?

a. He thinks that the Earth will be a wonderful place to live.

b. He thinks that the "distant children" will be crowded together.

c. He thinks that there will be fewer children on Earth.

d. He thinks that Earth will not be as habitable as it is today.

14. "As for us, here on Earth in the age of the quarterly statement, it is probably a good thing occasionally to contemplate a really long-term project" (paragraph 9). Considering the terms "quarterly statement" and "long-term project" you might conclude that Robinson is contrasting the terraforming of Mars with

a. a business project.

b. an ambitious project.

c. a project that will last another year or two.

d. a lab experiment.

15. Reread paragraph 8. What observation can you make about current human beings from this paragraph?

a. We have taken on a lot of long-term projects.

b. We have not undertaken projects of this length or magnitude before.

c. We will enjoy doing terraforming Mars.

d. We don't have enough money to terraform Mars yet.

Reading the Whole

Now that you have had a chance to read Kim Stanley Robinson's article in its parts, have made observations, connections, inferences, and conclusions about each, and have answered questions, you are prepared to read the article as a whole, practicing your skills on the entire essay. As you read, continue to make observations, connections, inferences, and conclusions, and pay attention to the ways in which all the parts fit together to help Robinson make his main point.

KIM STANLEY ROBINSON
A Colony in the Sky

One day early in the next century, several people will land on Mars. They will put on spacesuits and leave their vehicle, bounding over red rocks under a pink sky. After this exhilarating day, seen on Earth by billions, they will move into a cluster of habitats already on site. They will spend a year living there making scientific studies, and then they will return to Earth. Another team will cycle in. Back at home we will start to take the base for granted. Nevertheless, something very big will have begun.

The initial crossing to Mars will be made for a great number of reasons, some of them solid (to see if there really are fossil bacteria there), some of them not (to look for Elvis). Most of the reasons will be scientific and practical: the more we know about the solar system's other planets, the better we will understand Earth, and the safer we will be. It's not heroic but it makes sense, and it is important. Even if these were the only reasons, they would be good enough to send us.

But Mars will never remain just a research site to sharpen Earth management skills. We've been fascinated by the red wanderer ever since our days on the savannah, and even if life at the research station proves to be quite ordinary, the videos they send back will show us a magnificent world of volcanoes and canyons, icecaps and sand dunes, wind and weather. These wild new landscapes will also look somewhat familiar, especially in comparison to the bone-white moon. This familiar quality is not just superficial, for Mars does resemble Earth in several important ways—general size, presence of water, length of day, range of temperatures—so many similarities, in fact, that some people are beginning to ask if it might be possible to make Mars even more like Earth than it is now. And that's the question that will shift us to the next level of our fascination with the place: the idea that we could live there, that Mars could be "terraformed."

To terraform means to alter a planet's surface until Earth's life forms can survive there. It's a hypothetical discipline at this point, born in science-fiction stories. But in the last 30 years a number of scientists have taken up the concept. Their studies make it clear that the process would be somewhat slower than the cork-popping transformations seen in some recent sci-fi movies; in reality, it would take centuries. But it is an idea that operates within physical reality as we know it. It's possible to do it.

The recipe is simple. Add nitrogen and oxygen to the atmosphere; pump water to the surface; cook for decades, spicing first with cyanobacteria, then with all the rest of Earth's plants and animals, adding them in the order they evolved here. Mars is blessed with all the ingredients called for in the recipe; indeed, Mars turns out to be perfect for terraforming. So, because we have all the life forms here at hand, we can try replaying evolution at extreme fast forward.

Of course it will be more complex than the recipe — it always is. And the process will certainly spiral out of our control. Eventually, however, if all goes well, we will have helped to start a new biosphere. Think of that! It's hard to know how even to characterize such an activity. It would be something like growing a garden, or creating a wilderness, or building a cathedral, or flying seeds over an ocean to drop them on a new island. It would be unlike anything else, a new thing in history.

Some people may believe that such a project is too large or slow or presumptuous for humanity to undertake. But consider our current situation on Earth. There are nearly 6 billion of us now, and the number may double, though we have no good idea how many of us the Earth can support. Many larger species are in danger of extinction unless we protect them from us. We have rearranged much of the land, and we have altered the atmosphere to the point where the global climate in the future will be a matter of legislation and industrial practice. In other words, we are already starting to terraform Earth by necessity to keep it livable. Given this situation, the attempt to terraform Mars does not look so outlandish. Doing it could be regarded as a valuable experiment, with Mars as a giant lab or university, in which we learn how to steward a planet's biosphere for long-term sustainability.

Long term indeed! Terraforming Mars would take 300 years at least. It's not a time scale we often think about, and it does seem unlikely that any society could persist in anything for so long. Luckily, the process will not depend on our consistent backing, but on the people who settle there and pursue it as their own closest interest.

As for us, here on Earth in the age of the quarterly statement, it is probably a good thing occasionally to contemplate a really long-term project. Humanity's existence on this Earth is a long-term project, after all, and it's important to remember what that means. People will be living here 500 years from now, and they will all be our relatives. These distant children of ours deserve to be given a livable planet to care for in their turn. For their sake we need to work out a sustainable way of life on Earth. Going to Mars will be part of that larger environmental project, and terraforming it will be an education that we will apply at home as we learn it—pausing, from time to time, to look up at our wilderness garden in the sky.

9

Integrated Skills

1. What assumptions or predictions does Kim Stanley Robinson make at the beginning of this article?

2. What reasons does the author propose for why people will one day go to Mars? What other possible reasons can you think of?

3. What is "terraforming"? Why does Robinson think that "terraforming" is possible on Mars?

4. Why does the author say that terraforming Mars is a "long-term project"? How long term, and why?

5. What do you think of Robinson's idea about terraforming Mars? Why?

Reading/Writing Connection

In "A Colony in the Sky," science fiction novelist Kim Stanley Robinson projects us into the future to describe people inhabiting the planet Mars. Write a paragraph in which you respond to Robinson's argument that it would be good to colonize Mars. You may wish to write about the likelihood of such an event occurring. Or you may wish to accept his fantasy as a reality and then discuss its implications and value.

Reading Textbooks

Thematic Connections. You have just read Kim Stanley Robinson's vision of the future human colonization of the Earth's closest planetary neighbor, Mars. His idea may sound fantastic, especially because he is a writer of science fiction and, although he is clearly knowledgeable, he is not a scientist. But is his idea so far-fetched? In the following selection from the textbook *Universe* by William J. Kaufmann III and Roger A. Freedman, two respected astronomers describe what is known about the planet Mars and what people have imagined about it. As you read the selection, zero in on the differences between facts and beliefs—between truths and fictions about Mars.

Vocabulary Preview

speculated (para. 1): guessed (v.)

linear (para. 1): resembling lines (adj.)

arid (para. 1): dry, as in a desert (adj.)

microorganisms (para. 1): forms of life so small they can be seen only under a microscope (n.)

orbit (para. 1): the path of a planet, moon, satellite, or spaceship around a planet (n.)

opposition (para. 2): a period when Mars can be easily seen from the Earth because of the two planets' aligned position in orbit (n.)

refracting telescope (para. 2): a telescope that views objects through lenses alone (n.)

superficial (para. 3): on the surface (adj.)

inclination (para. 4): tilt (n.)

axis (para. 4): center point (n.)

pronouncements (para. 7): statements, claims (n.)

irrigation (para. 8): system of bringing water from a source to a destination (n.)

Mars Attacks! Invaders from Mars! Martians, Go Home! Mars, 1
the fourth planet from the Sun, has been the inspiration for many
science-fiction films and novels about alien invasion. But why Mars?
People have long speculated that life might exist there, because the
red planet has many Earthlike characteristics. Around 1900 some
astronomers claimed to have seen networks of linear features on the
Martian surface, perhaps "canals" built by an advanced civilization. Seven decades later, spacecraft made many surprising discoveries about Mars—including an enormous volcano and a huge
canyon—but found no canals and no signs of life. But life may
have existed on Mars in the distant past. Spacecraft that landed on
Mars, including the hugely successful Mars *Pathfinder*, found that

water once flowed on this now-arid planet. And some scientists claim to have found fossil microorganisms within an unusual meteorite that came to the Earth from Mars. Is there now, or was there ever, life on Mars? How much liquid water once existed on Mars? How active were the planet's volcanoes? We may have the answers to these questions soon, because we are now in a golden age of Martian exploration, during which a series of spacecraft will observe Mars from orbit while others land on the planet's surface.

The first reliable record of surface features on Mars was made by the Dutch scientist Christian Huygens, who observed the planet during the opposition of November 1659. Using a refracting telescope of his own design, Huygens identified a prominent dark feature that we now call Syrtis Major. . . . After observing this feature for several weeks, Huygens concluded that the rotation period of Mars is approximately 24 hours, the same as the Earth's.   2

In 1666, the Italian astronomer Giovanni Cassini made the first accurate measurements of Mars's rotation period. He found that a Martian day is about 37½ minutes longer than an Earth solar day. Cassini was also the first to see the Martian polar caps, which bear a striking superficial resemblance to the Arctic and Antarctic polar caps on Earth. . . . More than a century later, the German-born English astronomer William Herschel suggested that the Martian polar caps might be made of ice or snow.   3

Herschel also determined the inclination of Mars's axis of rotation. Just as the Earth's equatorial plane is tilted 23½° from the plane of its orbit, Mars's equator makes an angle of about 25° with its orbit. This striking coincidence means that Mars experiences Earthlike seasons. However, the Martian seasons last nearly twice as long as the Earth's, because Mars takes nearly two (Earth) years to orbit the sun.   4

The Martian surface exhibits striking seasonal variations. During spring and summer in a Martian hemisphere, the polar cap shrinks and the dark markings (which often look greenish) become very distinct. Half a Martian year later, with the approach of fall and winter, the dark markings fade and the polar cap grows. These observations were widely held to mean that there is vegetation on Mars that changes seasonally, just like on the Earth. And if there was plant life, might there not also be intelligent beings? So strong was this suspicion that in 1802 the German mathematician Karl Friedrich Gauss proposed that we signal the Martian inhabitants by   5 drawing huge geometric patterns in the snows of Siberia. His plan was never carried out.

Observations by Giovanni Schiaparelli in 1877 fueled further speculations about life on Mars. During a favorable opposition, the Italian astronomer reported seeing 40 straight-line features criss-crossing the Martian surface. He called these dark linear features *canali,* an Italian word for "channels," which was soon mistranslated into English as "canals." The alleged discovery of canals seemed to imply that there were intelligent creatures on Mars capable of substantial engineering feats. This speculation caught the public's ear and fired its imagination. It also helped motivate Percival Lowell, an American millionaire, to finance a major new observatory near Flagstaff, Arizona, primarily to study Mars. By the end of the nineteenth century, Lowell had reported observations of 160 Martian canals.

6

Not all astronomers saw the canals. In 1894, the American astronomer Edward Barnard, working at Lick Observatory in California, complained that "to save my soul I can't believe in the canals as Schiaparelli draws them." However, the skepticism of cautious observers was drowned out, and Lowell's pronouncements soon became fashionable. When Barnard first saw craters on Mars, evidence of a more barren planet, he did not publish his observations for fear of ridicule.

7

Speculation about mars grew more and more fanciful at the end of the nineteenth century. Perhaps the red color of the planet meant that Mars was a desert world, and perhaps the Martian canals were an enormous planetwide irrigation network. From these ideas, it was a small leap to envision Mars as a dying planet and the canals as carrying water from melting polar caps to farmlands near the equator. The terrible plight of the Martian race formed the basis of inventive science fiction by Edgar Rice Burroughs, Ray Bradbury, and many others. It also led to the less comforting notion that the Martians might be a warlike race who schemed to invade the Earth for its abundant resources. (The planet, after all, was named for the Roman god of war.) Stories of alien invasion, from H. G. Wells's 1898 novel *The War of the Worlds* down to the present day, all owe their existence to the *canali* of Schiaparelli.

8

Thinking about the Textbook Selection

1. How does this textbook selection relate to the magazine article "A Colony in the Sky"? Besides being about the planet Mars, what other connections do the two pieces share?

2. Why do the authors say people think there has been life on Mars? What do you think about this notion? Why?

3. What did the scientists Giovanni Cassini and William Herschel discover about Mars? Why were their discoveries considered important?

4. How did the mistaken notion that there were canals on Mars originate? What was one consequence of people believing that Mars had canals?

5. Why does the author mention science fiction writers and science fiction novels?

Reading the Web

The Mars Project is described by its creators, graphic artist Rob Martin and game writer Gary Rosenzweig, as an "educational simulation of the colonization of the red planet." The project's elaborate Web site includes tours of a colonized Mars, links to other sites about the "red planet," and animated views of many parts of the planet as it may look when it becomes inhabited by humans. This page, part of the tour, provides an image of a futuristic highway and a description of how it works.

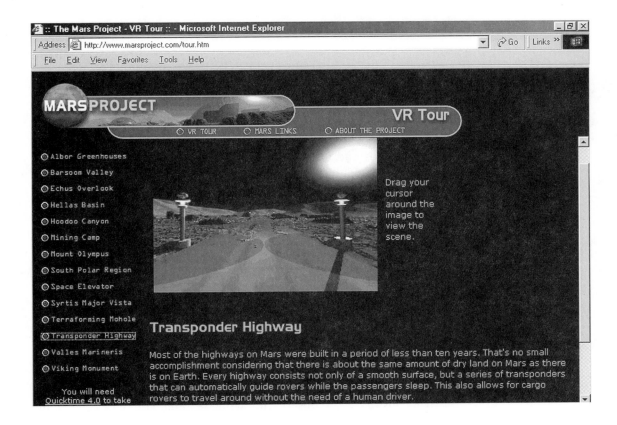

Thinking about the Web Page

1. How would you characterize this Web page and site for the Mars Project? To what extent is it based on fact or fantasy? Why do you think so?

2. How does this site's vision of Mars compare with Kim Stanley Robinson's ideas? To the textbook description of the planet?

3. What inferences can you make about the purpose of this site, based on your observations and connections?

4. What conclusion might you draw about the purpose and value of this Web site? Is it a site that you would like to explore in more detail? Why or why not?

Reviewing

Recall / Remember

1. Explain how making observations helps you comprehend what you read.
2. Why is it important to make connections among the details you notice when you read?
3. How does the use of repetition in a reading selection help you to observe details and make connections among them? Why is it important to notice and connect repeated details?
4. What are inferences, and why are they important for reading?
5. What do you do with inferences once you have made them?
6. Explain why the conclusions you draw about reading selections can be tentative—why, that is, you can change your mind about how you understand them.
7. What are some things that might influence a change in how you understand a reading selection?

Chapter Summary

Throughout this chapter you have been practicing four essential steps of the reading process: making observations, establishing connections, making inferences, and drawing conclusions.

By means of careful observation while reading, you have been laying the foundation for better reading comprehension. You have been observing different kinds of information writers include. You also have become more observant about how authors organize their writing. Being able to identify the structure of a piece of writing is an important key to comprehending an author's meaning.

Making observations leads to asking questions about them. The key question concerns how those observations can be connected or related.

You have been introduced to the way interpretive reading requires you to make adjustments and reconsider your observations, connections, and inferences in the process of reading. You have also been introduced to the pleasures and powers that derive from comprehending a reading selection and coming to your own conclusions about what it says and means.

You can apply this interpretive approach to everything you read — newspaper and magazine articles, textbooks, works of literature, even bumper stickers and graffiti. You can also use this four-stage approach to interpret things you listen to and watch, such as songs, television commercials, and movies.

The next chapter will further the work of interpretive reading by showing you how to apply your new skills as a critical, engaged reader.

Practicing Critical Reading

Getting Ready

Critical reading describes an active and thoughtful approach to what you read. The word *critical* indicates thinking carefully and evaluating what a writer says. Reading critically means thinking about and analyzing what you read. It involves identifying an author's purpose, distinguishing between facts and opinions, recognizing and making judgments, and understanding the writer's perspective, or point of view, about a topic. Critical readers are able to detect an author's bias, if there is one. They are also able to understand an author's tone or attitude toward a subject.

Everything you have learned so far about reading comprehension is useful for critical reading. Identifying an author's topic and main idea, recognizing implied main ideas, and understanding supporting details are all necessary as a foundation for critical reading. So too are recognizing a writer's patterns of organization, examining a writer's language and selection of details, and understanding how sentences relate to one another and to the paragraphs in which they appear.

Chapter Overview

What does critical reading mean to you? Why?

What are some different purposes authors have for writing? How can you tell an author's purpose from reading his or her work?

Focusing Questions

How do facts and opinions differ? Are all opinions equally valid and equally persuasive?

How can you tell what an author's attitude is toward the subject he or she is writing about?

How does a writer's tone change the way he or she comes across? Think of an example.

Why is making judgments about what you read important?

Everyday Reading

Articles in newspapers are supposed to be factual and not serve to express the writer's opinion about the news being reported. However, news stories are not always as factual as they may appear to be. By carefully attending to their language, you can determine whether writers express a bias in favor of or against a subject or topic. When you read editorials and op-ed pieces in a newspaper, you expect the writers to express personal points of view. Read your local newspaper to find the point of view expressed in an op-ed piece or an editorial. And read a news article to see if you can detect a hidden bias.

Learning the Skills

■ Identifying a Writer's Purpose

Determining an author's purpose is essential for critical reading. An author may write to inform or explain, as the author of this book is doing now. An author may write to persuade readers to think a certain way or to follow a particular course of action. Sometimes, authors write to amuse and entertain readers.

Historians, for example, write to inform readers about the past. Scientists write to explain their experiments and research findings. Advertising copywriters attempt to persuade readers to buy the products they advertise. Authors of novels, plays, and poems write to convince readers of their view of the world through imaginative literature. In everyday experience people write to express sympathy, to argue a point of view, to explain their actions, and to ask and answer questions people have about all sorts of things.

Among the most common purposes authors have for writing is simply to provide information. Authors write to *inform* their readers about historical events, political realities, scientific discoveries, sports, travel, and so on. The following paragraph is from "The Mystery of AIDS in South Africa," a 2000 essay by biologist Helen Epstein. As you read the passage, think about why Epstein might have written it.

> I went to South Africa for three weeks in May 2000 to write about the AIDS epidemic there. AIDS is caused by the HIV virus, which is passed from person to person through sexual fluids, blood, or blood products, or from mother to unborn child in the womb or through breast-feeding. The virus destroys the immune system that protects the body from infectious diseases. A person may live for ten years or more with HIV and have no symptoms, but eventually his immune system begins to disintegrate, and other viruses, bacteria, and fungi, which a healthy immune system would normally fight off, take hold. AIDS is the name given to the syndrome in which the patient slowly rots alive from these opportunistic infections.

In this passage, Helen Epstein *informs* her audience about the nature of Acquired Immune Deficiency Syndrome (AIDS).

Authors also write to *explain* things to readers. Explanation is closely linked with providing information. Authors of how-to books explain how to use information to achieve a desired result. A writer might explain why something happened. The author of the book you're reading right now provides many explanations to help you understand how to become a more confident and competent reader.

In the following paragraph from the textbook *Health in the New Millennium* by Jeffrey S. Nevid, Spencer A. Rathus, and Hannah R. Rubenstein, the authors explain why Janet Reed decided to make a workout video for people confined to wheelchairs.

> Reed was thrown from a horse and suffered spinal cord injuries that paralyzed her from the waist down. She had difficulty accepting these new limitations for many years. One year, however, a friend asked her to dance during a fund-raiser, and her outlook began to change. The friend manipulated her wheelchair while she moved her upper body in time with the music. It was the most fun she had had since her accident and eventually led to the idea that she could help other physically challenged people profit from physical activity.
>
> *(continued)*

> She put together her "Wheelchair Workout" with the assistance of a physical therapist and found that creating the program helped her take charge of her life. Working out regularly "strengthens the body, relaxes the mind, and toughens the spirit," she says. "It can prove to you that you have what it takes to do what is necessary."

As you can see, passages that *explain* often include information as well. When you read informative or explanatory pieces, try to keep in mind that explanation is a kind of in-depth way to inform. Try to pay attention to which parts consist more of explanation and which are meant simply to inform.

Another common reason for writing is to *persuade*. Sometimes writers may wish to convince their readers to adopt a course of action—to send money to support a fund drive, for example. Writers may write to criticize an idea or to support it. Advertising is a form of persuasion that you're very familiar with. Here is an example:

> GlobalCall provides the lowest rates of virtually any calling card—just 5 cents a minute within the U.S. It also offers some of the lowest international rates you can find—as low as 10 cents a minute. In fact, compared to other calling cards, you could save up to $500 a year on phone charges using GlobalCall. And GlobalCall delivers crystal clear connections to anywhere you call.

This advertisement, which appeared in the January/February 2002 issue of *Arrive,* a magazine for riders of the Amtrak Acela train, attempts to persuade readers to purchase the GlobalCall telephone service.

A writer may provide information as part of an attempt to persuade readers of a particular point of view. In the following example from a 2002 article called "The Counter Man," author Gary Gately offers information partly to inform readers and partly to persuade them about the importance of the Internet for the National Basketball Association (NBA).

> NBA.com averages more than 20 million visitors a month and consistently ranks among the top five sports sites on the Internet. Leading the sports pack once more, the NBA became, in April, the first major professional league to webcast a live game in streaming video, enabling fans worldwide to catch the game free.

Finally, many writers write simply to entertain or amuse their audiences. Here is an example by humorist Ezra Dyer in "Ennui Weekend," a 2002 column about attending his brother's graduation from Ithaca College:

> Our hotel was located in the charmingly named town of Horseheads, a good 30 miles beyond Ithaca. Apparently, what with graduation, all the local hotels named after equine anatomy were booked solid.
>
> However, "Where do you think you are, the Horseheads Holiday Inn?" is a phrase I derisively asked myself many times the next day, when a hair dryer, comforter, or hot bath would have been welcome indeed. I'd forgotten to bring a jacket, and upstate New York rewarded my lack of respect with late-May weather as cold as any day in Boston last winter. It snowed. James Earl Jones was the commencement speaker, and in one part of his speech, he bellowed, "The reason that we are all here today is . . . (trying futilely to turn the page with his frozen hands) . . . my hands are very cold." I don't remember any other nuggets of wisdom, but I think that other colleges considering his services should stipulate in his contract that he has to say "Simba," "Luke, I am your father," and "Welcome to 411" at least once.

Exercise 9-1

Identify the author's purpose(s) in each of the following passages. Check the appropriate blank(s) after each passage, and then explain the writer's purpose more fully.

Example:

> I am pedaling home at sunset, a cold wind aching in my throat, pangs in my unaccustomed legs. Already the purples of November are becoming prominent in some of the far-turned oaks, the sumac, the cranberry leaves. As I ride the bike across the marsh, things begin whispering to me: the soft rustle-whispers of the tawny marsh grass and cattails; the feather-whispers of the tall, dust-grey phragmites seed heads; the clatter-whispers of the drooping clusters of bleached canoe-paddle seeds as I pedal beneath the ash trees; and the dry whispers of the crumpled grape leaves in the viburnum, faded and closed for the season. Even the silent cranberry bog beside the road seems to whisper. (Robert Finch, *Death of a Hornet and Other Cape Cod Essays*)

PURPOSE: _____ to persuade   __✔__ to inform/explain
          __✔__ to entertain

EXPLANATION: _The writer's purpose is to explain to readers how he feels,_

what he sees, and what he hears. He probably also wants to entertain

readers with his essay.

1. Stunning sets, gorgeous costumes, intoxicating action, dancing to make
   you tap your feet, and music to stir your senses: *42nd Street* is the musical every New Yorker should see. Award-winning *42nd Street* is back,
   and it's a blockbuster of a show.

   PURPOSE: __✔__ to persuade   _____ to inform/explain
             _____ to entertain

   EXPLANATION: _The writer's purpose is to persuade New Yorkers to see the_

   show 42nd Street. This seems to be an ad for the show.

2. Newspapers, radio, and television are essential for a democracy. They
   are a vital link between the people and their public officials. They provide information and analysis about policy issues; they also sensitize
   those in government to public opinion, enabling policy makers to
   respond to the needs and desires of the population. Moreover, the news
   media play an important role in reporting and evaluating the decisions
   of government, a role that is critical for holding those in power account-
   able for their decisions and actions. (Stephen J. Wayne et al., *The Politics of American Government*)

   PURPOSE: __✔__ to persuade   _____ to inform/explain
             _____ to entertain

   EXPLANATION: _The writer's purpose is to persuade readers that the news_

   media are essential for a democracy.

3. I pull up the line that had tied me to my friend, my hope for food and
   water and clothing. The rope is in one piece. Perhaps the loop I had tied
   in the mainsheet broke during the last shock. Or the knot; perhaps it

was the knot. The vibration and surging might have shaken it loose. Or I may have made a mistake in tying it. I have tied thousands of bowlines; it is a process as familiar as turning a key. Still . . . No matter now. No regrets. I simply wonder if this has saved me. Did my tiny rubber home escape just before it was torn to pieces? Will being set adrift kill me in the end? (Steven Callahan, *Adrift: Seventy-Six Days Lost at Sea*)

PURPOSE: _____ to persuade   ✔ to inform/explain
✔ to entertain

EXPLANATION: *The writer's purpose is to explain to readers what happened to him and probably also to entertain readers with his story.*

4. Like clinical psychologists, psychiatrists also study the causes, treatment, and prevention of psychological disorders. How are clinical psychologists and psychiatrists different? A *clinical psychologist* typically has a doctorate in psychology, which includes intensive training in treating people with psychological disorders. In contrast, a *psychiatrist* has a medical degree plus years of specialized training in the treatment of psychological disorders. While both clinical psychologists and psychiatrists can treat patients with psychological disorders, only psychiatrists can prescribe medications and order medical procedures, such as electroshock treatments. Finally, a *psychoanalyst* is a clinical psychologist, psychiatrist, or other mental health professional with extensive training in Freud's psychoanalytic method of psychotherapy. (Don H. Hockenbury and Sandra E. Hockenbury, *Psychology*)

PURPOSE: _____ to persuade   ✔ to inform/explain
_____ to entertain

EXPLANATION: *The writer's purpose is to inform readers about the similarities and differences among clinical psychologists, psychiatrists, and psychoanalysts.*

5. For years, researchers have pointed to America's fast food diet and our love affair with television to explain why we're becoming an obese nation. But a new study by the U.S. Centers for Disease Control and Prevention may finger a new culprit: the suburbs.

As James Langton reports in the *London Telegraph*, researchers at the agency suspect Americans don't walk enough. To prove their thesis, they plan to equip 800 people in the Atlanta area with satellite tracking devices to see how much they walk each day. While most adults consume only about 100 calories a day more (and less fat) than they did 20 years ago, Langton writes, they're less and less likely to get out of their cars. "The problem now seems to be a way of life so sedentary that it involves little more than a few steps between the home, driveway, and office," Langton observes. ("Livin' Large in America," *Utne Reader*, November–December 2001)

PURPOSE: __✔__ to persuade   __✔__ to inform/explain
_____ to entertain

EXPLAIN: *The writer's purpose is to persuade readers that the United States is becoming an obese nation because Americans don't walk enough. The passage also explains some recent research.*

■ Distinguishing between Facts and Opinions

Writers often present facts as evidence to support their ideas. Those facts may appear as examples to illustrate ideas or to refer to events, collections of data, or information in written sources. Factual statements are based on observations that can be demonstrated to be true. As a critical reader, you will have to check each observation against other available experience and evidence to make sure it is true and is indeed a fact.

Facts and opinions are very different. Unlike facts, opinions express an attitude or a point of view *about* a fact or a set of facts. People have opinions about how welfare should be reformed, about whether citizens should be permitted to carry guns, about who is the best team in baseball. Opinions by themselves may be interesting to state, to hear, and to debate. But they are of little value unless they are supported with evidence in the form of facts, details, examples, reasons, and information.

It is a fact, for example, that Robert Frost is a well-known American poet. To say that he is one of the greatest of modern poets would be to express an opinion. The opinion is arguable—that is, different people might have different opinions about Frost's greatness.

A statement of opinion cannot be completely proved or disproved the way a statement of fact can. Statements of opinion reflect the point of view of a speaker or a writer. For example, you may think college athletes should spend more time on their studies and less on their sports — or vice versa. Your opinion on this issue may reflect your point of view about the value of college sports in general. The evidence you use as support for your opinion might include such things as the money and/or the prestige athletic teams bring to the university. It might also include statistics about the graduation rates of NCAA athletes or about the ratio of college to professional athletes.

Critical readers distinguish between facts and opinions. They evaluate an author's opinions by considering how well they are supported by evidence in the form of facts, details, statistics, and other kinds of information. As a thoughtful critical reader, you are obliged to consider how well a writer's opinion is supported by facts.

One way to identify opinions is to be alert for words that indicate that an opinion is being expressed. Words and phrases such as the following often introduce an author's expression of an opinion:

INTRODUCTORY OPINION WORDS

apparently	it might be	one possibility is
in my view	it seems	perhaps
it appears	maybe	

Notice how these words also seem to qualify what a writer says. That is, the writer who introduces an idea or an opinion by saying "it appears" or "perhaps" is not insisting that he or she is right or that this idea or opinion is either the best or the only one that might be held. Instead, such opinion words indicate that a writer recognizes that his or her opinion is one among others and that the ideas and opinions of other people (including readers) also have merit, even when they differ from those of the writer.

Exercise 9-2

· ·

Identify each of the following statements as fact or opinion by writing **F** for fact and **O** for opinion.

Example:

The sun rose over Atlanta at 6:05 A.M. ___*F*___

The sunrise was especially beautiful this morning. ___*O*___

1. Amateur marathon runners risk damaging their knees. ___F___

2. The Boston Marathon draws thousands of competitors from all over the world. ___F___

3. The grandest of all marathons is the New York City marathon. ___O___

4. My brother has run in the NYC marathon for the last five years. ___F___

. . . .

Statements of opinion come in various forms and thus can be tricky to recognize. Sometimes an opinion is expressed as an indication that something is possible or even probable. You've probably heard and read recently that terrorism will continue to be a threat to Western countries in the next decade. While this may indeed be highly likely, it is, nonetheless, a prediction about the future and thus an opinion rather than a verifiable statement of fact. Finally, opinions can appear as suggestions for what should be done (or not be done). For example, a magazine edi-

Figure 9.1

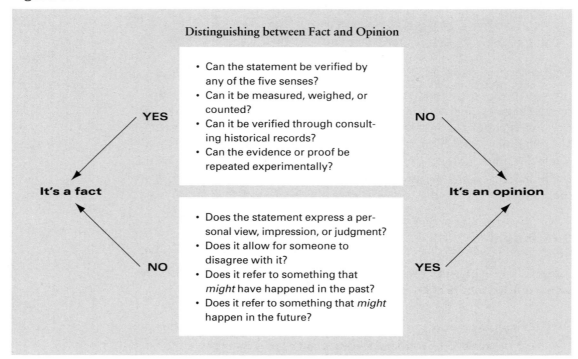

Distinguishing between Fact and Opinion

- Can the statement be verified by any of the five senses?
- Can it be measured, weighed, or counted?
- Can it be verified through consulting historical records?
- Can the evidence or proof be repeated experimentally?

YES → It's a fact

NO → It's an opinion

- Does the statement express a personal view, impression, or judgment?
- Does it allow for someone to disagree with it?
- Does it refer to something that *might* have happened in the past?
- Does it refer to something that *might* happen in the future?

NO → It's a fact

YES → It's an opinion

tor who writes that readers should recycle more to help the environment is making a good suggestion—but it's still an opinion.

If facts can be labeled true or false, accurate or inaccurate, right or wrong, how can we characterize opinions? Opinions can be well founded or ill founded, sound or unsound, reasonable or unreasonable. But be careful: What appears sound or reasonable to one person may seem unsound or unreasonable to another.

Facts and opinions are both important. Facts provide information and evidence on which to form opinions. Opinions put a personal stamp on a topic or offer an individual perspective on an issue. It is important for critical reading that, first, you are able to distinguish between fact and opinion and, second, you are able to evaluate how well supported, how carefully thought through opinions may be.

Exercise 9-3

Each of the following statements contains both fact and opinion. Underline the fact(s). Double underline the opinion(s).

Example:

The Boston Marathon, which was held for the first time in 1897, is most runners' favorite race.

1. The Cinderella story exists in many versions, but the Walt Disney version is the most important by far.

2. The New York Yankees, probably the greatest team in the history of sports, have won more World Series titles than any other team.

3. Although aspirin is the most commonly prescribed medication for headaches, colds, and the flu, I believe it should not be taken by pregnant women or by people who are at risk for heart attacks.

4. The Bush-Gore presidential election of 2000, the most exciting election in political history, was one of only three in which the winner did not receive a majority of the popular vote.

5. Abraham Lincoln was wrong when he said in his Gettysburg Address that "the world will little note nor long remember what we say here, but

it can never forget what they did here"; most people know the words that end the address — "government of the people, by the people, for the people, shall not perish from the earth" — and have completely forgotten what was done at Gettysburg.

. . . .

■ Determining an Author's Point of View

An author's point of view is his or her position or stance on a topic. Authors express their points of view through the kinds of words they use and by the kinds of details they include in their writing.

It is important to recognize an author's point of view when you read. Identifying an author's point of view helps you understand the author's position on a topic, it helps you compare it with your own position, and it may help you understand differences of opinion among authors on a topic.

As a critical reader, your recognition of an author's point of view enables you to actively engage the author. For example, you may agree with, disagree with, or wish to qualify what the author says. By identifying an author's point of view, you become not merely a passive accepter of another's ideas and opinions, but someone with ideas and opinions of your own.

In the readings for your college courses, you will be exposed to many different topics with multiple points of view. Part of your responsibility as a student in those courses will be to understand the value of competing points of view and to make reasoned judgments about their strengths and weaknesses.

A writer's point of view may be approving or disapproving, positive or negative, offensive or defensive. Or it may simply be the perspective an author is writing from. Take, for example, Bob Karwin's description of mechanical difficulties with his car, taken from his Web column "Just a Thought" (2002):

My car is possessed by the devil. By all outside appearances, my 1996 Honda Accord is a bright, shiny, well-maintained automobile with no suspicious motives. But inside lies the very soul of evil.

One of my car's favorite ways to chip away at the balance of power in our relationship is to make me look like a complete idiot in front of skilled repair people. This minion of the netherworld is

> fully aware that my knowledge of cars falls somewhere just below that of an Amish hermit. There are some guys who bring their car to the shop and can explain the defect with such confidence that it is clear to everyone in earshot that the only reason they don't perform the repairs themselves is because they don't have access to a hydraulic lift and the correct size torque wrench. I, on the other hand, must resort to using silly noises to describe the problem so that it sounds like I need the tune-up instead of the car.

Bob Karwin is a musician and a lawyer. But that's not his point of view in these paragraphs. His point of view, his perspective, is that of a frustrated car owner trying to keep a sense of humor about his situation.

INTERPRETING A WRITER'S TONE

You can gauge a writer's attitude toward a subject by his or her tone. Tone is the way the writer's voice sounds in your mind as you read. Writers convey their attitude toward a subject with the kinds of words they choose to describe or explain it. A writer's tone may be enthusiastic, as in the ad for GlobalCalling. It may be supportive, as in the article about the NBA and the Internet. It may be matter-of-fact, as in Helen Epstein's description of AIDS. It may be humorous, like Bob Karwin's assessment of the extent of his automotive know-how. And, of course, a writer's tone can be angry or joyful, serious or playful, admiring or sarcastic or mocking. The key to understanding tone is to look closely at and listen closely to a writer's sentences and language, which you learned to do in Chapters 5 and 7.

Exercise 9-4

Identify the tone of each paragraph.

Example:

> I'm fascinated and thrilled that there has been such a surge in new immigration from across the Pacific these past few years, that, as a country, we are again in the process of being renewed and reformed by the new Americans from Asia and elsewhere. These newly arrived peoples, I know, come not so much from Japan and Okinawa and Guangdong as did the ancestors of we third- and fourth-generation Asian Americans, but rather they are now coming, in increasing numbers,

from Taiwan, Hong Kong, Southeast Asia, Tonga, Fiji, Samoa, the Caribbean, Central America, and the Philippines. Their presence has charged our society with energy and change. (Garrett Hongo, "America Singing")

What is the tone of the paragraph?

The tone is enthusiastic and positive.

Which words or phrases help convey the author's attitude?

"fascinated"; "thrilled"; "surge"; "process of being renewed and

reformed"; "charged our society with energy and change"

1. Some people do not understand the dangers of a credit card. They mistakenly believe that charging a purchase means paying for that purchase. However, a credit card simply gives them some time before they have to pay up. When the bill comes, an even worse alternative presents itself. Buyers are offered the possibility of making a small partial payment instead of paying in full for what they have already charged. This so-called privilege costs money, though. People have to pay high interest on the amount they postpone paying.

    What is the tone of the paragraph?

    pessimistic, cautionary, somewhat sarcastic ("so-called privilege")

    List four words or phrases that help convey the author's attitude.

    "dangers"; "mistakenly"; "an even worse alternative"; "so-called privilege"

2. Don't be afraid. Just sit down next to a person you want to date and engage him or her in small talk. If you are in a classroom, talk about an assignment, the seating arrangement, or the instructor (be kind). If you are at work, talk about the building or some recent interesting event in the neighborhood. Ask your intended date how he or she feels about the situation. If you are at a group function and you have never been there before, tell the other person that you are there for the first time and ask for advice on how to relate to the group. Most people like to be spoken

to. You'll do just fine. (Adapted from Jeffrey S. Nevid, Spencer A. Rathus, and Hannah R. Rubenstein, *Health in the New Millennium*)

What is the tone of the paragraph?

encouraging, patient, sensible

Which two sentences are the most emotionally supportive?

"Don't be afraid." "You'll do just fine."

3. In the United States, one of four children is born into poverty. The United States is the world's wealthiest nation, but much of that wealth is concentrated in the hands of a few. The combined wealth of the top 1 percent of American families is nearly equal to that of the entire bottom 95 percent. Such obscene inequality is totally inappropriate for a democratic country. (Adapted from Holly Sklar, *Chaos or Community*)

What is the tone of the paragraph? *angry*

Which sentence is strongest in tone? *the last sentence*

4. Certainly one of the most important values of literature is that it nourishes our emotional lives. An effective literary work may seem to speak to us, especially if we are ripe for it. The inner life that good writers reveal in their characters often gives us glimpses of some portion of ourselves. We can be moved to laugh, cry, tremble, dream, ponder, shriek, or rage with a character by simply turning a page instead of turning our lives upside down. Although the experience itself is imagined, the emotion is real. . . . Human emotions speak a universal language regardless of when or where a work was written. (Michael Meyer, *The Bedford Introduction to Literature*)

What is the tone of the paragraph? *heartfelt, appreciative*

Which sentence is strongest in tone? *Answers will vary.*

5. Hundreds of thousands of years ago, America was very different. There was no civilization: no roads, no cities, no shopping malls, no Honda dealerships. There were, of course, obnoxious shouting radio

commercials for car dealerships; these have been broadcast toward Earth for billions of years by the evil Planet of Men Wearing Polyester Sport Coats, and there is nothing anybody can do to stop them. But back then, you see, there was no way to *receive* them, so things were pretty peaceful. (Dave Barry, *Dave Barry Slept Here*)

What is the tone of the paragraph?   *humorous, sarcastic*

List three words or phrases that help convey the author's attitude.

"no Honda dealerships"; "obnoxious shouting radio commercials";

"evil Planet of Men Wearing Polyester Sport Coats"

. . . .

DETECTING BIAS

Bias refers to a person's disposition or inclination to favor one side of an issue or topic. Advertisers, for example, are biased toward the products they promote. Music lovers might be biased toward a particular genre: opera, country, hip-hop, or folk, perhaps. A person can be biased *in favor* of something or biased *against* it. A Boston Red Sox fan may hate the New York Yankees. Or a newspaper whose political bias is *for* the Democratic Party will very likely be biased *against* the Republicans. Although bias does suggest preference, it isn't necessarily a matter of unfairness. Sometimes bias is simply a person's point of view.

Recognizing bias will help you determine how objectively, or evenly, an author treats his or her subject. Writers who hold strongly biased views might ignore or dismiss opposing points of view. Consider, for example, this paragraph from a 2001 Cal Thomas article, "New Study: Gays Can Go Straight," about a controversial psychological study that found that homosexuals can change their sexual orientation:

> Many homosexuals with whom I have spoken are not aware of the availability of nonjudgmental counseling to help them escape the "gay life." Many feel trapped in their "orientation," not because of dwindling cultural disapproval but because of pressure to conform to gay society. They are told that a desire to change indicates they hate themselves and that it is impossible for them to reject their "true identity."

To detect bias when you read, look closely at the language used to describe someone or something. You should also look closely at the way writers attempt to persuade their readers. Consider the language Cal Thomas uses. His quotation marks around *gay life, orientation,* and *true identity* suggest that he dismisses these terms, but he doesn't offer any explanation for his dismissal. He speaks of escaping, feeling trapped, and pressure to conform; his choice of these words suggests his point of view—that being homosexual is necessarily unpleasant. Notice also the details—or lack of them—that he uses to support his argument: He says *many* are not aware of counseling, that *many* feel trapped. How many is many? He doesn't say. Maybe he spoke to hundreds of gay men and women. Maybe he spoke to four. Maybe "many" is the majority of the people he spoke to; maybe it's a minority. The reader has no way of knowing. With these clues, you can determine that Cal Thomas is biased against homosexuality; knowing that will affect how you respond to his argument.

Exercise 9-5

Identify which statement in each pair illustrates positive or negative bias. Explain your choice by pointing out at least one biased word or phrase in each statement.

Example:

    a. The figure skaters glided through their program with ease and grace.

    b. The figure skaters slogged through their program with flagging energy.

Which statement has a positive bias? ___*a*___

Which words support your answer? *"glided"; "ease"; "grace"*

_____

Which statement has a negative bias? ___*b*___

Which words support your answer? *"slogged"; "flagging energy"*

_____

1. a. There was no good reason for such a disgustingly emotional outburst.

    b. There was good cause for such a passionate, committed plea.

Which statement has a positive bias? ___b___

Which words support your answer? _"good cause"; "passionate,_

committed plea"

Which statement has a negative bias? ___a___

Which words support your answer? _"no good reason";_

"disgustingly emotional outburst"

2. a. Cat fanciers see no faults in those most spoiled and selfish of pets.

   b. Cat owners delight in the independence and liveliness of their pets.

   Which statement has a positive bias? ___b___

   Which words support your answer? _"delight in"; "independence";_

   "liveliness"

   Which statement has a negative bias? ___a___

   Which words support your answer? _"cat fanciers"; "see no faults";_

   "most spoiled and selfish of pets"

3. a. The mayor's strong personal convictions roused admiration in everyone in the audience.

   b. The mayor's irrational stubbornness annoyed everyone in the audience.

   Which statement has a positive bias? ___a___

   Which words support your answer? _"strong personal convictions";_

   "roused admiration"

   Which statement has a negative bias? ___b___

   Which words support your answer? _"irrational stubbornness";_

   "annoyed"

4. a. James is such a tightwad that he refuses to waste money by going to the movies.

b.   James is so thrifty that he saves money by borrowing videotapes and CDs from the library.

Which statement has a positive bias?   _b_

Which words support your answer?   _"so thrifty"; "saves money"_

Which statement has a negative bias?   _a_

Which words support your answer?   _"such a tightwad";_

"refuses to waste money"

5.   a.   Carol's loyal defense of her friend's compassionate reaction was praiseworthy.

b.   Carol's ridiculous defense of her friend's bad manners was totally inappropriate.

Which statement has a positive bias?   _a_

Which words support your answer?   _"loyal defense";_

"compassionate reaction"; "praiseworthy"

Which statement has a negative bias?   _b_

Which words support your answer?   _"ridiculous defense";_

"bad manners"; "totally inappropriate"

. . . .

RECOGNIZING SLANTING

Slanting is a technique some writers use to persuade their readers to adopt a particular belief or point of view. In slanting, a writer uses language that conveys a strongly positive image toward a favorable topic or a strongly negative image toward an unfavorable topic. Look again at the Cal Thomas paragraph on page 313. As you've seen, his words and details portray a negative slant on homosexuality. What would a positive slant look like? Here is a passage on the same study Thomas discusses. This one, from the 2000 article "Why Not Turn Them All Gay?" by John McCalla takes a different point of view, suggesting that perhaps society should encourage straight men and women to convert to homosexuality.

> Gays and lesbians are—all false humility aside—not only good enough and smart enough, they're smarter, better-looking, more stylish, better-mannered, more artistic, sexier, funnier, and, in general, preferable at cocktail parties and cook-outs. This is not a secret. Why else are city governments encouraging more gay and lesbian home ownership? Gays are better for urban-renewal, aesthetically improving neighborhoods while at the same time contributing much and taking little from the tax base. More gays and lesbians on the planet would be, in corporate America cliché-speak, a "win-win" across the board.

Like Thomas, McCalla uses language and slanting that reveal his bias: "smarter, better-looking, more stylish, better-mannered, more artistic, sexier, funnier, and, in general, preferable at cocktail parties and cook-outs." He also makes his argument without substantial supporting detail.

Another aspect of slanting involves omitting details in a description or an argument that convey an opposite impression, position, or point of view. This is a more difficult aspect to detect. One way to decide whether a writer is using slanting in presenting information, evidence, or a point of view is to ask yourself what someone with an opposite point of view might say. Ask yourself what the writer is omitting. Consider what could be said from the other side of the issue.

Exercise 9-6

The following paragraph is negatively slanted. Your answers to the questions will reveal how the writer gets that effect.

(1) One sad rainy morning last winter, I talked to a woman who was addicted to crack cocaine. (2) She was twenty-two, stiletto thin, with eyes as old as tombs. (3) She was living in two rooms in a welfare hotel with her children, who were two, three, and five years of age. (4) Her story was the usual tangle of human woe: early pregnancy, dropping out of school, vanished men, smack and then crack, tricks with johns in parked cars to pay for the dope. (5) I asked her why she did drugs. (6) She shrugged in an empty way and couldn't really answer beyond "makes me feel good." (7) While we talked and she told her tale of squalor, the children ignored us. (8) They were watching television. (Pete Hamill, "Crack and the Box")

Example:

What is the first negatively slanted phrase in the paragraph?

"one sad rainy morning"

1. Which two phrases in sentence 2 have a negative slant?

   "stiletto thin"; "eyes as old as tombs"

2. Which sentence is more negatively slanted, sentence 3 or sentence 4?

   sentence 4

3. What phrase is most negatively slanted in sentence 5?

   "shrugged in an empty way"

4. Which two words are most negatively slanted in sentence 7?

   "squalor"; "ignored"

5. What is the overall impression conveyed by the paragraph?

   The impression is one of hopelessness and loss of control. The young woman is addicted to drugs, lives a tragically self-destructive life, may be neglecting her children, has little (if any) support, and seems to have little (if any) hope of escaping from her miserable circumstances.

. . . .

■ The Internet and Critical Reading

Learning to read Web sites and Web sources critically is a major challenge, and a necessary one. The Web is becoming increasingly important as an information provider. But be careful: The information you find on the Web is only as good as the organizations and individuals who put it there. There are two critical issues involved in reading Web content: The first is simply learning how to read and navigate around a Web site to see just how much or how little is actually there; the second is to evaluate Internet sources for their value, currency, and reliability.

READING WEB PAGES

All Web pages and all Web sites are not of equal value. You will find some that provide you with information you can trust, while others are virtually useless. With an increasing number of people publishing their own Web pages, you will find a wide range of content, organization, graphics, and degrees of functionality and scannability.

In reading a Web page, the first thing to check is whether you are actually on the site you were looking for, if you were looking to find a particular site. If you are simply seeing what's out there, you will first try to scan a home page to see what resources it includes. The tabs or other clickable elements on the home page will take you to linked pages with specific and more detailed information about the subjects listed. In going to your own university's site, for example, you would expect to see links to information about the school's mission, its academic programs, its sports teams, its library, its social events, alumni, and so on. Clicking on any of those buttons from the home page would get you to specific information about each topic.

In reading a Web page or a series of Web pages on a Web site, look to see if the content provided is worth your time. Look at the graphics to see whether they add information, help you understand how to navigate the site, or are simply a distraction. You should be able to move around the Web site easily and naturally, even intuitively. If you can't do that, you may decide that the site is not worth the trouble.

Being a critical reader of the Web involves all of the skills for critical reading you learned in this chapter and throughout this book. Pay attention to vocabulary, main points, and supporting details. Consider the site's context and the writer's language and structures. Point of view, tone, bias, and slanting are particularly relevant on the Web. Later in this book you'll learn how to assess persuasive writing, another skill that will help you read Web pages with a critical eye.

EVALUATING INTERNET SOURCES

Evaluating an Internet source when you need information for a paper, project, or report is an important academic skill. What do you look for when deciding which Internet sources to use for your academic assignments?

The first thing to consider is reliability. How reliable is the source? How much do you trust that the information and perspective it offers are valid and reasonable? To answer this fundamental question, you need to ask yourself a few others:

- Who is responsible for the Internet site—the Web source you are reading? Is it a recognizable institution, organization, or other known quantity?

- How current is the information on the site? When was it last updated?
- How thorough is the site? How much information is provided?
- How professional does it look and feel?
- How does the Web site compare with others on the same subject?
- How does the Web site compare with print sources of information you have consulted?

You will have a chance to apply these questions and others as you view sample Web pages from different Web sites in each chapter of this book.

Exercise 9-7

. . . .

The following Web page was the first result of a Google search on a common writing assignment topic: the death penalty. If you have access to a computer with an Internet connection, go to the site at deathpenaltyinfo.org/ and look around. Look at the site carefully and answer the following questions.

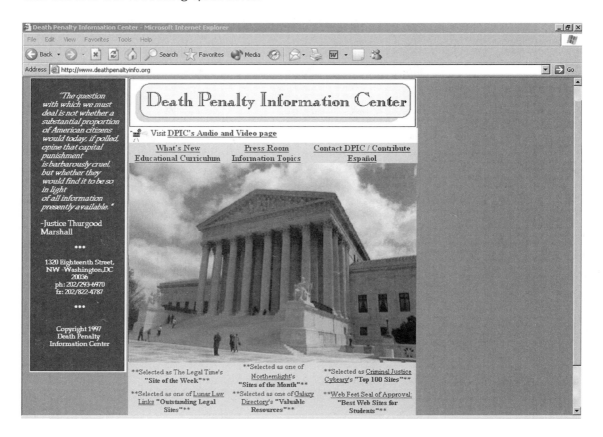

Example:

Who is responsible for this Web site? Is it a recognizable institution, organization, or other known quantity?

This Web site was prepared by the Death Penalty Information Center,

operating out of Washington, D.C. It is not an immediately recognizable

institution, but it cites other organizations (The Legal Times,

NorthernLight, the Criminal Cybrary) that have praised it, suggesting

that it is a legitimate source.

1. How current is the information on the site? When was it last updated?

    By clicking on the What's New link, students can see when it was last

    updated. It appears that it is updated daily.

2. How thorough is the site? How much information is provided?

    The site is very thorough, with hundreds of links and related news articles,

    information resources, and educational and Spanish-language resources.

3. How professional does it look and feel?

    It is moderately professional but not glossy or overproduced.

4. How does the Web site compare with others on the same subject?

    It is less biased than most. Others tend to argue strongly for or against

    the death penalty, but this site seems more objective and even-handed.

5. How does the Web site compare with print sources of information you have consulted?

    Like many Web sites, printed resources tend to argue for or against the

    death penalty.

Applying the Skills

Reading the Parts

The following essay by Eric Alterman originally appeared as an online article for MSNBC.com, the Web presence of the financial news cable channel. Alterman is a contributing editor and media columnist for MSNBC.com and the *Nation;* he has also written for a number of magazines including *Worth, Rolling Stone, Elle,* and *Mother Jones* and teaches media history at New York University and Hofstra University. As you read, pay particular attention to the author's purpose and point of view. Make observations about Alterman's use of facts, opinions, and strong judgment words. After you read each part of his essay, answer the questions that follow and move on to the next section. You will have a chance to read the entire article when you finish.

ERIC ALTERMAN
A Trip to Cell Hell

1   I am considering a random act of violence. Before you condemn me, consider the situation. I have a cell phone, but no cell phone company. They say I owe them $506.05 including $246.20 for charges in New York City, where I live and where my calls are supposed to be free. But they won't tell me who they are. And they won't take my calls. I'm not even certain if "they" exist. The situation calls for drastic measures, but I don't know where to direct them. I believe this is what revolutions are for.

2   I hate my DSL service, but at least I know whom to hate. I hate my regular phone service, my fax service, the people who are supposed to fix my ZIP drive, and the people who are supposed to make all my peripherals connect with my two new Windows XP computers. (Did I mention that already?) As an independent contractor dependent on all kinds of information and new economy products for my livelihood, I am constantly losing extremely expensive amounts of precious time trying to get things fixed that were never supposed to be that complicated in the first place.

3   Whatever these people were spending their ill-gotten gains on during the orgiastic days of NASDAQ 5000, it sure wasn't the hiring and training of qualified people to help you when their products don't work.

1. Which of the following sentences from paragraphs 1–3 is a fact?

   a. "I believe this is what revolutions are for."

   b. "Whatever these people were spending their ill-gotten gains on during the orgiastic days of NASDAQ 5000, it sure wasn't the hiring and training of qualified people to help you when their products don't work."

   c. "I hate my DSL service, but at least I know whom to hate."

   d. none of the above

2. Which of the following words best characterizes the author's opinion in the one sentence that makes up paragraph 3?

   a. sound

   b. unsound

   c. founded

   d. reasonable

3. Which of the following words from paragraph 3 indicates the author's negative bias toward cell phone companies?

   a. "ill-gotten"

   b. "people"

   c. "NASDAQ"

   d. "qualified"

4. Of the following statements, which one best characterizes the author's feelings toward his cell phone company, as expressed in paragraphs 1–3?

   a. The author is happy with his service.

   b. The author doesn't have a strong opinion of his company.

   c. The author thinks that the service he has is one of the best.

   d. The author is annoyed with his cell phone company.

5. Which of the following sentences from paragraphs 1–3 blends fact with opinion?

   a. "I am considering a random act of violence."

   b. "The situation calls for drastic measures, but I don't know where to direct them."

   c. "I believe this is what revolutions are for."

   d. "I hate my DSL service, but at least I know whom to hate."

The Sound and Fury

The added ingredient of fury regarding my cell phone is that I can't even find a provider who will take responsibility for screwing up my bill. A few years ago, I signed up with Verizon. Then I started getting bills from WorldCom Wireless. I reached them on the phone once, about a year ago, and the person there said they were not really my company. They had merely subcontracted for the billing. They did not know who my real company was. Neither do the guys around the corner who sold me the phone. Yesterday, when I called information, I got a Sprint/PCS operator. Are they my company? It used to be that when I dialed 611 I got customer service. That doesn't work anymore. I don't know whether my contract was transferred, my company was bought out, or these guys are just playing poker and trading their customers instead of chips.

4

Customer Disservice?

When I got my latest insanely inflated bill from WorldCom Wireless, it advised me, "Should you have any questions please refer to the Customer Service number on the back of this invoice." "Customer Service" was capitalized, I think, because it is a proper name and has nothing whatever to do with actual customer service. If you call the number, as I have done, say, 50 or so times, you will hear a lengthy and annoyingly peppy pitch from a robot for even more products from these evil people that I am certain cannot possibly work, before being advised to punch zero to speak to an actual human being. Ha ha, as they are probably saying at WorldCom Wireless headquarters right now. The only words this alleged human being seems to know are "We are currently experiencing an unusually large number of calls. Please try your call again later. Your call cannot be completed."

5

Don't believe me? Be my guest. 1-800-254-8991. If you reach a real person, ask them to give me a call before anyone else is made to suffer for their sins. I value my credit rating more than I value the continued existence of WorldCom Wireless as a global conglomerate. As old Joe Stalin used to say in another context "No person, no problem."

6

6. What is the author's point of view toward WorldCom?

   (a.) WorldCom is evil.

   b. WorldCom has a peppy staff.

   c. WorldCom cares about its customers.

   d. WorldCom isn't to blame for the author's problems.

7. Which of the following words best characterizes the author's opinion in the third sentence of paragraph 5?

   a. reasonable

   b. sound

   c. well founded

   d. unreasonable

8. Which of the following is Eric Alterman's opinion?

   a. "'Customer Service' was capitalized, I think, because it is a proper name and has nothing whatever to do with actual customer service."

   b. "As old Joe Stalin used to say in another context 'No person, no problem.'"

   c. "A few years ago, I signed up with Verizon."

   d. "Yesterday, when I called information, I got a Sprint/PCS operator."

9. In paragraphs 5 and 6 in particular, the author's tone is

   a. happy.

   b. amused.

   c. sarcastic.

   d. serious.

10. The purpose of paragraphs 5 and 6 is

    a. to persuade.

    b. to entertain.

    c. to explain.

    d. none of the above.

The Info-Age Plague

Why, you politely ask, is this rant worth a column in the highly esteemed and desirable space of MSNBC.com's Opinions page? Two reasons. First off, this problem is endemic to information-age technologies. Once they get you to invest in their hardware, the cost of switching is so high that you're stuck with their crappy service. Startacs are not cheap, you know. If I decide to switch companies, I have to get rid of the phone I've purchased (and continue to pay insurance on, though I've tried to cancel that numerous times as well) and pony up another couple of hundred bucks for whatever the latest equivalent is. The same goes for computers, DSL lines, cable modems, etc. It's a real problem beyond the confines of my little world.

Second, since these people are obviously not working anywhere   8
near the "Customer Service" phones at WorldCom Wireless, maybe they're reading MSNBC. It's not too late to save yourselves, folks.

11. What is the purpose of paragraphs 7 and 8 of "A Trip to Cell Hell"?

    a. to persuade

    b. to entertain

    c. to explain

    d. none of the above

12. Which of the following words from paragraphs 7 and 8 indicates the author's negative bias concerning his cell phone service and provider?

    a. "politely"

    b. "crappy"

    c. "numerous"

    d. "hundred"

13. Based on his choice of words (such as *esteemed* and *desirable*) in paragraph 7, what do you think the author's slant is toward the MSNBC.com Opinions page?

    a. He has no respect for this page.

    b. He likes the editors of this page.

    c. He has great respect for this page.

    d. He has no opinion of this page.

14. The author's tone in paragraphs 7 and 8 is mostly

    a. happy.

    b. playful.

    c. angry.

    d. serious.

15. Based on the first sentence of paragraph 8, what do you think the author's opinion of WorldCom Wireless "Customer Service" is?

 a. He thinks they provide poor or no service.

 b. He likes their service.

 c. He thinks the customer service representatives are well read.

 d. He has no opinion.

Reading the Whole

Now that you have had a chance to read Eric Alterman's article in its parts and identified the author's purpose and point of view as well as his use of facts, opinions, and judgment words, you'll be better prepared to read the essay in its entirety. As you read the whole essay, continue to apply the skills of critical reading, paying attention to the main point Alterman makes about his experience with WorldCom and customer service in general and identifying any detectable bias or slanting.

ERIC ALTERMAN
A Trip to Cell Hell

I am considering a random act of violence. Before you condemn me, consider the situation. I have a cell phone, but no cell phone company. They say I owe them $506.05 including $246.20 for charges in New York City, where I live and where my calls are supposed to be free. But they won't tell me who they are. And they won't take my calls. I'm not even certain if "they" exist. The situation calls for drastic measures, but I don't know where to direct them. I believe this is what revolutions are for. 1

I hate my DSL service, but at least I know whom to hate. I hate my regular phone service, my fax service, the people who are supposed to fix my ZIP drive, and the people who are supposed to make all my peripherals connect with my two new Windows XP computers. (Did I mention that already?) As an independent contractor dependent on all kinds of information and new economy products for my livelihood, I am constantly losing extremely expensive amounts of precious time trying to get things fixed that were never supposed to be that complicated in the first place. 2

Whatever these people were spending their ill-gotten gains on during the orgiastic days of NASDAQ 5000, it sure wasn't the hiring and training of qualified people to help you when their products don't work. 3

The Sound and Fury

The added ingredient of fury regarding my cell phone is that I can't even find a provider who will take responsibility for screwing 4 up my bill. A few years ago, I signed up with Verizon. Then I started getting bills from WorldCom Wireless. I reached them on the phone once, about a year ago, and the person there said they were not really my company. They had merely subcontracted for the billing. They did not know who my real company was. Neither do the guys around the corner who sold me the phone. Yesterday, when I called information, I got a Sprint/PCS operator. Are they my company? It used to be that when I dialed 611 I got customer service. That doesn't work anymore. I don't know whether my contract was transferred, my company was bought out, or these guys are just playing poker and trading their customers instead of chips.

Customer Disservice?

When I got my latest insanely inflated bill from WorldCom Wireless, it advised me, "Should you have any questions please refer to the Customer Service number on the back of this invoice." "Customer Service" was capitalized, I think, because it is a proper name and has nothing whatever to do with actual customer service. If you call the number, as I have done, say, 50 or so times, you will hear a lengthy and annoyingly peppy pitch from a robot for even more products from these evil people that I am certain cannot possibly work, before being advised to punch zero to speak to an actual human being. Ha ha, as they are probably saying at WorldCom Wireless headquarters right now. The only words this alleged human being seems to know are "We are currently experiencing an unusually large number of calls. Please try your call again later. Your call cannot be completed." 5

Don't believe me? Be my guest. 1-800-254-8991. If you reach a real person, ask them to give me a call before anyone else is made to suffer for their sins. I value my credit rating more than I value the continued existence of WorldCom Wireless as a global conglomerate. As old Joe Stalin used to say in another context "No person, no problem." 6

The Info-Age Plague

Why, you politely ask, is this rant worth a column in the highly esteemed and desirable space of MSNBC.com's Opinions page? Two reasons. First off, this problem is endemic to information-age technologies. Once they get you to invest in their hardware, the cost of switching is so high that you're stuck with their crappy service. 7

Startacs are not cheap, you know. If I decide to switch companies, I have to get rid of the phone I've purchased (and continue to pay insurance on, though I've tried to cancel that numerous times as well) and pony up another couple of hundred bucks for whatever the latest equivalent is. The same goes for computers, DSL lines, cable modems, etc. It's a real problem beyond the confines of my little world.

Second, since these people are obviously not working any- 8 where near the "Customer Service" phones at WorldCom Wireless, maybe they're reading MSNBC. It's not too late to save yourselves, folks.

Integrated Skills

1. Why does the author say that he is "considering a random act of violence"? Do you think Alterman will actually commit such an act? Why or why not?

2. What is the author's complaint about his cell phone? How is this complaint related to his comments about his regular phone service, his DSL service, and other kinds of technical support for phones and computers?

3. Why does the author name three different cell phone providers?

4. What is the purpose of the headings Alterman provides — "The Sound and Fury"; "Customer Disservice?"; and "The Info-Age Plague"?

5. What is the author's tone in this article? What words and phrases help you understand Eric Alterman's attitude and his point of view?

6. Where does the author address his readers directly? Why does he do this? Is this an effective persuasive strategy? Why or why not?

Reading/Writing Connection
· ·

In "A Trip to Cell Hell," Eric Alterman describes the many kinds of repeated problems he has with cellular telephone service. Write a paragraph about a time when you had difficulty getting adequate or acceptable service for a product that you purchased. Describe what happened and why you took whatever action you might have taken—or why you did not do anything about the bad service.

Reading Textbooks

Thematic Connections. Eric Alterman writes very forcefully about his personal experiences with bad customer service and describes an almost unbelievable chain of difficulties he has had with his cellular phone company. The following excerpt from the textbook *Exploring the World of Business* by Kenneth Blanchard, Charles Schewe, Robert Nelson, and Alexander Hiam examines the topic of customer service from a business perspective. As you read it, try to apply the authors' explanations of the importance of customer service and their recommendations for it to Alterman's experience with WorldCom Wireless. What could the telecommunications giant have done differently to satisfy its customer?

Vocabulary Preview

essence (para. 1): core, main idea (n.)

intently (para. 2): carefully, closely (adj.)

intermediary (para. 2): person or business who serves as a contact between two or more others, as in the case of a wholesaler (n.)

frequency (para. 2): schedule, intervals (n.)

eliminating (para. 2): getting rid of (v.)

orientation (para. 3): introduction (n.)

Customer Service

Successful companies now realize that whatever their product, they must surround it with extraordinary **customer service** — paying attention to every detail in the process of delivering satisfaction. Customer service is a companywide commitment that means more than satisfying the customer. It means pleasing and delighting the customer, often with the unexpected. A business consultant captured the essence of customer service–driven companies: "They have to make heroes and heroines out of the people who use their products." Consider these examples:

- By joining Hertz's #1 Club Gold program, members can avoid airport lines. They reserve the vehicle by phone, jump on the shuttle, tell the driver their last name, and get dropped off at their car. They know it's theirs because their name is in glowing lights above it!

- Home Depot offers low, low prices for its hardware products, but service is the real difference. The company trains all salespeople in home repair techniques and encourages them to spend as much time with customers as necessary to help them solve their repair problems.

• Knowing that summer is vacation time for nearly everyone in France, Nestlé built rest stops along the main roads. At all times of day, trained hostesses offer free samples of Nestlé baby food, free diapers, and other forms of travel assistance. These areas have become social gathering spots.

To offer superior customer service, you have to analyze the entire process of buying and using a product. Customer service means treating customers with courtesy, listening intently to their desires, correctly supplying the requested product, delivering it on time, and following up to make sure the customer is satisfied. And when the customer is an intermediary or other business buyer, customer service entails knowledgeable salespeople calling with just the desired frequency, efficient and error-free handling of all orders, perfect product packaging, and always having the correct balance in the customer's account. In short, it means eliminating all problems and hassles throughout the entire process of buying and using the product.

In successful companies, every employee understands that full customer satisfaction is important, and every employee is intensely and personally interested in keeping the customer happy. All company personnel who come in contact with customers must have the authority and motivation to do anything it takes to improve customer satisfaction. The Ritz-Carlton hotel chain is one company that works hard to maintain its reputation for service and quality. This means that all employees begin their jobs by participating in a two-day orientation program followed by an additional 100 hours of customer training. They learn to warmly welcome each guest every day, saying "Good morning" or "Good afternoon," never "Hi" or "How's it going?" Expected to act as responsible professionals caring for other professionals, employees are permitted to spend up to $2,000 to resolve a guest's problem without asking for authorization! Said Ritz-Carlton's director of quality, "One of our biggest challenges is to prevent any difficulties from ever reaching the customer." Companies with such a focus design all their activities to ensure that the customer's experience exceeds in satisfaction any encounter he or she may have with the competition.

Thinking about the Textbook Selection

1. What relationship do you see between this textbook selection and the Internet article "A Trip to Cell Hell"?

2. What should companies try to do beyond simply satisfying their customers? Why?

3. Why is providing good service important from a business standpoint?

4. What do you think of the suggestions for quality service that are provided in the final paragraph? Why?

Reading the Web

Here are the main customer service pages for Verizon Wireless and WorldCom Wireless. Most wireless phone companies offer similar sites, which suggests that they expect their customers to go to the Web for customer service, rather than call on the phone. As you examine these pages, look for examples of fact and opinion and think about the sites' points of view. Be aware, also, of bias and slanting, if there is any.

Thinking about the Web Pages

1. Which of these two Web pages do you think Eric Alterman (author of "A Trip to Cell Hell") would find more useful? Why?

2. Which of the Web pages is easier to navigate? Which has the friendlier tone?

3. How do the pages for Verizon and WorldCom differ? What is the purpose of each page?

Reviewing

**Recall /
Remember**

1. What is critical reading? Why is it important to develop habits of a critical reader?

2. Identify two aspects of critical reading and explain why they are important for becoming a critical reader.

3. Explain the difference between a fact and an opinion.

4. What is bias and how can you detect it?

5. Explain why it is important to recognize a writer's purpose.

6. Identify the skills and questions that help you to read Web sites critically.

**Chapter
Summary**

In this chapter you learned that critical reading is not simply being "critical" of something that you read, that it is, instead, the practice of reading with care and attentiveness so you can think about and respond to an author's point of view toward a subject.

You learned how to distinguish among the purposes for which authors write—to inform, explain, persuade, or entertain. You also worked on distinguishing facts from opinions, by attending carefully to a writer's choice of language and details. In addition, you learned how to read a writer's tone, and you learned that an author's bias toward a subject can be determined by looking closely at the language the author uses to describe or explain it.

This chapter builds on the earlier ones in requiring you to read carefully in order to comprehend an author's meaning. It goes beyond the previous chapters in encouraging you to read critically, that is, to come to a judgment about how well writers present information or persuade you that their opinions are well supported. In the next two chapters you will continue to practice the critical reading skills you have been developing in this one. You will have a chance to continue to develop these and other reading skills on textbook materials and selections from popular reading.

Chapter 10

Understanding Persuasive Writing

Getting Ready

All communication is, to some extent, persuasive. Think, for example, of how you try to convince people to share your ideas, your values, or simply your plans for the evening. Writers do the same thing. Whether they write a news story, an article in a magazine, or a book, their goal is to get readers to believe something or to do something.

In the previous two chapters you learned important interpretive and critical-reading skills that will help you become a savvy reader of arguments. This chapter focuses on explicitly **persuasive writing,** in which a writer presents his or her main idea as a claim or assertion and supports that assertion with evidence. The chapter describes and illustrates the strategies persuasive writers use; it also introduces you to common errors of logic to help you detect faulty arguments when you read.

Chapter **Overview**

Where can you find examples of persuasive writing?

When are you convinced or persuaded by someone's argument? Why are those arguments effective?

When are you not convinced or persuaded by a person's argument? Why are those arguments ineffective?

How do you determine if you can trust a person who is making an argument?

Focusing Questions

Why do writers and speakers sometimes appeal to authorities and testimonials to support their claims?

How do you know when an argument is not logical?

Everyday
Reading

Persuasion is all around you. Radio and television ads attempt to persuade you to buy their products. Politicians try to get you to adopt their point of view on various issues. Friends and family members encourage you to make particular kinds of choices, such as what movies to see and what clothes to buy. During the next few days, look for ways that the print media — newspaper articles, magazine advertisements, billboards, fliers — attempt to persuade you about something. Cut out or copy down three examples and explain what they want you to do or think and why you are — or are not — convinced by them.

Learning the Skills

■ The Elements of Argumentative Writing

Persuasive writing has three central elements: claim, evidence, and assumptions. These elements are parallel to the parts of reading you learned in earlier chapters. The **claim** or assertion of an argument is its main idea or its topic sentence. It is the central point a writer wants to persuade you of. An argument's **evidence** is the supporting details a writer provides as proof for his or her claim. **Assumptions** — the unstated ideas related to the claim or central point of an argument — are a little trickier: You have to infer what they are by reading the argument closely and looking for missing connections.

The following one-paragraph argument contains a single claim and two kinds of evidence. There are also a couple of unstated assumptions.

Americans watch too much television. It is estimated that the average American viewer spends more than six hours a day staring at TV. This time could be spent doing a variety of other things, such as reading, studying, cooking, cleaning, exercising, and so on. A number of recent studies have shown American students to be less

> knowledgeable in many subjects than their counterparts from other countries. Other studies have suggested that Americans are less active than they should be. The time spent idly and passively watching TV could be put to far better use. If the average American viewer cut his or her television time in half, each viewer could put to use more than twenty hours per week.

The claim of this argument is stated in the first sentence: "Americans watch too much television." Statistics and information are provided as evidence to support the claim. A number of assumptions are implicit or unstated. One is that nothing much is learned from television and that time spent watching TV is wasted. Another assumption is that being active—doing things—is better than being passive. A third, related assumption is that American students compare unfavorably with foreign students because they watch TV instead of studying. Finally, the argument assumes that American viewers who watched less television would put their time into study or exercise rather than into sleeping or playing. If any of these assumptions is untrue, the argument loses some of its strength.

Exercise 10-1

Answer the questions about the following brief argument.

> For the United States the Vietnam War was the wrong war in the wrong place at the wrong time. War is, above all else, a political event. Wars are won only when political goals are achieved. Military firepower and troops are—like diplomacy and money—essentially tools to achieve political objectives. The United States went into Indochina after World War II with imprecise, muddled political objectives. It departed in 1975 after a thirty-year effort with a political focus just as blurred as it was in the beginning. The war was unwinnable because the United States never decided what it was trying to achieve politically. (James S. Olson and Randy Roberts, *Where the Domino Fell*)

1. What claim do the authors make?

    The Vietnam War was wrong for the United States.

2. According to the authors' argument, what is war, above all else?

a political event

3. What is the main reason the authors give for why the Vietnam War was "the wrong war" for the United States?

The United States had "imprecise, muddled political objectives."

It "never decided what it was trying to achieve politically."

4. According to the authors, what do firepower and troops have in common with diplomacy and money?

They are "tools to achieve political objectives."

5. What assumption do readers have to accept in order to accept the authors' argument?

that wars are won only when political aims are clear and are achieved

· ·

CLAIM

Every argument is based on a **claim**—an opinion, recommendation, or idea that a writer wants readers to accept as true. Like a main idea, a claim can be explicit or implied, but most claims in persuasive writing are stated directly.

You find the claim of an argument the same way you find the topic sentence or thesis statement in any kind of writing. Look for the sentence or idea that many or most of the other sentences and ideas in the work support or relate to. As is the case with topic sentences, the claim of an argument might appear at any point: The author might begin with a direct statement of the claim; he or she may build up to it and not state it directly until the conclusion; it might appear somewhere in the middle of a selection; or it might be composed of related statements found in two or three different parts of the reading.

Here is the beginning of a *Newsweek* magazine article by Debra Rosenberg published in 2002. As you read it, look for the author's claim.

Fighting G-Force

Do the Faster, Scarier Roller Coasters Literally Shake Up the Brain?

Zipora Jacob wasn't exactly a thrill-seeker. On a 1995 day trip to Disneyland, the 42-year-old didn't venture onto a ride until evening, when she hopped on the Indiana Jones Adventure. Though it was slower than most roller coasters, its high-tech hydraulics made it seem speedier and jerkier. "When the ride stopped, I felt my head was exploding," says Jacob. By the next morning, she was in a coma from a massive brain bleed. She endured surgeries and memory loss, and still has a permanent shunt draining fluid from her brain. Jacob settled a lawsuit with Disney in 1999; two other lawsuits have claimed injuries on the ride. Disney says independent testing has shown that the G-forces and motion of the ride aren't sufficient to cause injury. Jacob thinks otherwise: "A nice day at the amusement park can become a nightmare for the rest of your life."

Rosenberg's claim is partly stated and partly implied. It appears at the end of her introduction in the form of a quotation from a person who was injured on a ride: "A nice day at the amusement park can become a nightmare for the rest of your life." Her subtitle, furthermore, reinforces and implies Rosenberg's main point—her claim: The new thrill rides at amusement parks are dangerous.

EVIDENCE

In argumentative or persuasive writing, the details that support the writer's main idea are called **evidence.** These supporting details are critical to the success of an argument. Without them, a person is merely stating an opinion. With them, a writer's claim is backed up by examples, stories, statistics, and other forms of information and detail that help prove a claim or encourage readers to respond a certain way.

In Debra Rosenberg's article about thrill rides, the introductory paragraph (above) provides an example of a person injured by Disneyland's Indiana Jones Adventure ride. This is only one piece of Rosenberg's evidence. The body of her argument offers more:

In the past decade, new megacoasters have gone extreme, boasting speeds of more than 100 mph, back-to-back loops, and G-forces that rival the space shuttle's. "We've moved from an era of Model T roller coasters to one of supersonics," says Massachusetts Rep. Ed Markey, who has catalogued 58 brain injuries—including eight fatalities—on thrill rides, most since 1990. The roller coaster industry says 320 million people enjoyed rides last year mostly without incident. "It truly is one of the safest family activities you can engage in," says Bret Lovejoy of the International Association of Amusement Parks and Attractions.

That hasn't stopped a new drive to regulate the rides' gravitational or G-forces. The normal pull of gravity upon the body is one G, but acceleration increases that pull. Some scientists believe that high G-forces on coasters could distort the brain within the skull. The space shuttle maxes out at less than four Gs, but some parks used to brag that their coasters fleetingly topped six Gs—an unsafe level according to Markey, who's introduced a bill to create a national G-force standard. Last month, New Jersey became the first state to issue its own G-force limits. The coaster industry insists engineers have better control over G-forces than ever. Even so, the industry is announcing standards of its own later this month.

Despite the flurry of rulemaking, the link between G-forces and injuries hasn't been scientifically proven. Some researchers say rapid jerking of the head could be far more dangerous than G-forces, tearing blood vessels in the brain. But even that may be rare, limited mainly to pre-existing conditions like aneurysms. Jacob says she was perfectly healthy before she stepped aboard the Disney ride—a cautionary tale for the millions who'll line up at parks this summer, hoping for the thrill of their lives.

Note how Rosenberg uses different kinds of evidence to support her claim. She provides statistics, examples, scientific explanations of G-force, a space shuttle analogy, and quotations from authorities on both sides of the issue. Authors of effective arguments like this one provide more than one piece of evidence. Together, the pieces of evidence support the claim and give it credibility.

Exercise 10-2

. . . .

Identify the claim and the evidence provided to support it in each of the following passages. Some claims are stated directly; some are stated indirectly.

Example:

> Let me put Professor Bromell at ease regarding computerized courses. They don't make for very lucrative profit centers except when delivered at high cost to very, very select cohorts. They require heavy front-end research and development, they operate best with low teacher-student ratios, and, as the University of Phoenix has effectively demonstrated, they succeed not so much because of electronic gizmos as because of outstanding student services.
>
> If it is the "profit center" we want to root out, we need look no further than the oldest form of "distance learning." I refer to the ever popular "goon bin" introductory course, for which professors lecture often to more than 500 unengaged freshmen.
>
> —Robert Herold, Ph.D.
> Professor of Government, Emeritus, Spokane, Washington
> (From Letter to the Editor, *Harper's Magazine*, May 2002)

CLAIM: *Computerized college courses are not strong profit centers.*

EVIDENCE: *They require heavy research and development, low student-teacher ratios, and outstanding student services, all of which are (the author implies) expensive.*

1. Nobody became a *repeat* hit songwriter by being trite or by trying to get away with doing the least amount of work possible. Most artists establish themselves and their reputations by creating words and music that blow the tiles off the collective industry roof. Think of Bob Dylan's early songs. They were all originals. So were Elton John's. Bruce Springsteen's. Lionel Richie's. Tracy Chapman's. U2's. They didn't try to copy anybody and they weren't trying to make a fast buck and get out. They pulled all stops and went for it, with material nobody else was doing—no special-effect chartreuse smoke, snake makeup, or topless Eskimo

backup singers in lavender glass G-strings. Each of these writer/artists has created a unique niche for him- or herself. What made room for them initially on the radio and on their labels' artist roster? The most important ingredient was the high level of writing and originality in their songs. (Molly-Ann Leikin, *How to Make a Good Song a Hit Song: Rewriting and Marketing Your Lyrics and Music*)

CLAIM: *To be a repeat hit songwriter, you have to work hard and be original.*

EVIDENCE: *examples of Bob Dylan, Elton John, Bruce Springsteen, Lionel Richie, Tracy Chapman, and U2*

2. Probably the biggest financial disaster that can befall a family occurs when the principal breadwinner becomes disabled. This can be a bigger calamity than death. If the source of the largest part of the family income is disabled, the healthy spouse not only has the challenge of providing for the children but also for the disabled spouse. On the other hand, if the principal provider dies, the surviving spouse has fewer responsibilities, and he or she is also free to marry somebody else.

   The first insurance that a family should buy is disability insurance that will replace the income of one or both spouses if they should become disabled and unable to work. Yet, most people buy life insurance long before they think about disability insurance, which really is reversing priorities. (Robert A. Cooke, *Personal Finance for Busy People*)

CLAIM: *"The first insurance that a family should buy is disability insurance."*

EVIDENCE: *In the case of disability, the healthy spouse has to support the family as well as the injured person; but in the case of death, the surviving spouse has fewer people to support as well as the option to find a new mate.*

3. Resumes have a lousy track record. A study of employers done a number of years ago discovered that there was one job offer tendered for

every 1470 resumes that employees received from job-hunters. Would you take a plane flight if you knew that only one out of every 1470 planes ever made it to its destination? (Richard Nelson Bolles, *What Color Is Your Parachute?*)

CLAIM: *"Resumes have a lousy track record."*

EVIDENCE: *Only one in 1470 resumes results in a job offer.*

4. I have often been utterly astonished, since I came to the north, to find persons who could speak of the singing, among slaves, as evidence of their contentment and happiness. It is impossible to conceive of a greater mistake. Slaves sing most when they are most unhappy. The songs of the slave represent the sorrows of his heart; and he is relieved by them, only as an aching heart is relieved by its tears. At least, such is my experience. I have often sung to drown my sorrow, but seldom to express my happiness. Crying for joy, and singing for joy, were alike uncommon to me while in the jaws of slavery. The singing of a man cast away upon a desolate island might be as appropriately considered as evidence of contentment and happiness, as the singing of a slave; the songs of the one and of the other are prompted by the same emotion. (Frederick Douglass, *Narrative of the Life of Frederick Douglass, an American Slave, Written by Himself*)

CLAIM: *"Slaves sing most when they are most unhappy."*

EVIDENCE: *Douglass's personal experience*

5. What an amazing turnabout: Scientists working in the field of nutrition now know the reassuring facts regarding the vegetarian choice. So do physicians who keep up with the latest findings on consuming meat versus eating vegetarian meals. Even the conservative American Dietetic Association jumped on the bandwagon with its strongly worded 1988 and 1993 position papers in favor of the vegetarian style of eating. And when the U.S. Department of Agriculture devised the Food Guide Pyramid, meat was put in a small trapezoid while grains, vegetables, and fruits made up the most significant part of the pyramid. The case for choosing vegetarian foods is shut tight. (Editors of the *Vegetarian Times* and Lucy Moll, *Vegetarian Times Complete Cookbook*)

CLAIM: _A vegetarian diet is the healthy choice._

EVIDENCE: _Scientists, physicians, and the American Dietetic Association favor vegetarianism. The Food Guide Pyramid puts grains, vegetables, and fruits as the foundation (and largest portion) of a healthy diet._

. . . .

ASSUMPTIONS

When a writer presents an argument, he or she makes certain **assumptions** about what the audience believes and what a reader's values are likely to be. For the argument to work, those assumptions have to be true. Consider a form of argument you're already familiar with—political campaigning:

> Mr. Carls will bring a new perspective to the city council: As the outsider candidate, he's the better choice.
>
> Ms. Carnathan has served the city for more than a decade. She knows the system and has the experience to get things done. She's the better person for the job.

The assumption behind the first argument is that outsiders make better political representatives than people who have held office for a long time. If you don't share this assumption—if you believe that experience is more important than "a new perspective"—the argument for Mr. Carls won't convince you. The second argument assumes the opposite, that experience is more important than a new perspective. If you believe that the city council is in dire need of fresh ideas, you won't accept the claim that Ms. Carnathan is the right choice.

Exercise 10-3

. . . .

Identify the claims and assumptions in the following arguments. (There may be more than one assumption.)

Example:

> We often hear about "spontaneous" women who go out with men on twenty-four hours' notice. We wish them luck. When a man knows he can have you five minutes after his last girlfriend gave him the boot,

he'll call you because he's lonely or bored, not because he's crazy about you. In such cases, buyer beware: it won't last. Free spirits might object to what we are saying, but for long-lasting results we believe in treating dating like a job, with rules and regulations. Just like you have to work from nine to five, no matter how you *feel*, we believe you have to silently train men to make plans with you (elusive, busy, happy you!) ahead of time. When you do *The Rules*, what you're really doing is giving men the secret, silent code that they understand very well. If you make it too easy for them, they're certain to take advantage and then you can forget about getting a *Rules* marriage. (Ellen Fein and Sherrie Schneider, *The Rules: Time-tested Secrets for Capturing the Heart of Mr. Right*)

CLAIM: _Dating is "like a job, with rules and regulations."_

ASSUMPTION(S): _Women date in order to find a husband; men are naturally_

looking to take advantage of women; men avoid marriage; men don't

respect available women.

1. Suggest sales as a career to most college sophomores and you'll raise suspicious laughter. They'd rather pursue something more "professional," like medicine, law, accounting, or management. The truth is that many salespeople earn *more* than doctors or lawyers, and the majority of *Fortune 500* presidents started their careers in sales. It's the fast track to professional leadership, income, and prestige, because people who can generate business are the lifeblood of any organization. They're in constant demand. As it turns out, sales is one of the most secure careers you can pursue. (Jay Conrad Levinson, Bill Gallagher, and Orvell Ray Wilson, *Guerrilla Selling: Unconventional Weapons and Tactics for Increasing Your Sales*)

CLAIM: _"Sales is one of the most secure careers you can pursue."_

ASSUMPTION(S): _Students go to college in order to make money after they_

graduate.

2. You'd make all their wishes come true if you could. You give them *quality* chicken that's all natural because you can.

Every Tyson chicken product begins with all-natural chicken. That means there are no additives, and it's minimally processed. And that means a lot. (Advertisement for Tyson chicken in *Better Homes and Gardens*, May 2002)

CLAIM: *Tyson chicken is quality, all-natural chicken.*

ASSUMPTION(S): *Parents want the best for their children; additives and processing are bad.*

3. The majority of our society does not want to be subject to the present speed laws. In this country "We, the People" are supposed to be the government and "We, the People" choose to drive cars faster than our elected officials choose to permit. Is it not logical to assume then that our elected officials, who have the capability of modifying our cars so they can't speed, know we want to go faster than the limits they have set and expect us to violate the law? (James M. Eagan, *A Speeder's Guide to Avoiding Tickets*)

CLAIM: *Elected officials expect drivers to violate the speed limit.*

ASSUMPTION(S): *Speeding is acceptable driver behavior.*

4. If we don't receive your payment by return mail, we must suspend service of your issues.

We don't want to do that. I'm sure you don't want us to. Each week, we've been sending you a fresh, bright, new issue of *The New Yorker*, packed with stimulating articles, captivating stories, a special sophisticated humor you won't find anywhere else. Without it, chances are your life (and you) wouldn't be quite as interesting anymore. (Letter to subscriber from the *New Yorker* circulation department, August 17, 1999)

CLAIM: *You don't want us to cancel your subscription.*

ASSUMPTION(S): *The subscriber likes the magazine; the subscriber depends on the magazine to make herself interesting; the subscriber worries that people will find her dull.*

5. Environmentalists do not underestimate the difficulties the United States faces in trying to wean itself from fossil fuel. Pretty much our entire transportation grid is based on the gasoline engine. "Lay rail" is one thing we could do. Switch to cars with hybrid engines, increase fuel-efficiency standards, change as rapidly as possible to renewable energy sources — the menu of alternative behaviors is already long and it works. We can cut greenhouse gases; we can even do it dramatically. We are not helpless. (Molly Ivins, "A Warmed Over Policy," June 6, 2002)

CLAIM: *"We are not helpless" to save the environment.*

ASSUMPTION(S): *Readers are concerned about the environment; they are willing to make behavioral changes in order to reduce greenhouse gases.*

■ The Art of Persuasion

An argument consists of more than the sum of its parts (claim, evidence, and assumptions). Other, less obvious things also contribute to an argument's success or failure. These additional supports include a writer's credibility, analogies, and a writer's uses of authority and testimony to support a claim.

CREDIBILITY

An argument's **credibility** is the extent to which it can be believed and trusted. The credibility of an argument depends on the believability of the writer who makes it. Writers gain credibility in the eyes and minds of readers by demonstrating knowledge, by providing clear and cogent reasoning, and by being reasonable and fair.

When you assess a piece of writing for its persuasiveness, think about how knowledgeable the writer appears. How much information is presented? How clearly and commandingly is that information provided? Decide whether you can trust the information based on the writer's credentials, sources, and command of the topic. Four simple questions can help you assess whether a writer deserves your consideration:

1. *How knowledgeable is the writer?* Writers who know what they're talking about provide plenty of evidence, from a number of sources, and acknowledge evidence that might contradict or weaken their

argument. Writers who aren't very knowledgeable are more likely to skim over evidence or not provide any at all.

2. *What are the writer's sources, and are they helpful and reliable?* Look at the sources a writer cites and the way he or she presents information. Consider also the reliability of those sources. A credible writer uses evidence from different kinds of authorities, often from both sides of an argument. A less believable writer might rely on limited examples or on sources that are not relevant to the argument.

3. *How clear and detailed is the writer's presentation?* You should be able to follow a writer's presentation easily. Examples and other details should directly support his or her idea. If an argument is difficult to follow and light on detail, the writer may not be credible.

4. *Is the writer reasonable and fair?* Consider whether the writer acknowledges opposing viewpoints and how much time he or she gives to different points of view. Are other points of view presented carefully and without condemnation? Or are they mocked and scorned without adequate explanation?

We can apply these questions to the following argument:

> Americans are among the most ignorant people in the world when it comes to history. Opinion surveys have shown that large percentages of them do not know the difference between World War I and World War II. Many believe that Germany and the Soviet Union were allies in the latter conflict. As already noted, relatively few ever heard of the multinational invasion of Soviet Russia in which the United States was a participant. Many never heard of Hiroshima and have no idea the United States dropped an atomic bomb on that city. Many could not tell you what issues were involved in the Vietnam War or other armed conflicts in which the United States has participated. Nor could they say much about the history of aggression perpetrated against Native Americans and the slavery inflicted upon Africans in America. . . . Not many Americans could put together two intelligent sentences about the histories of Mexico, Canada, Puerto Rico, or Cuba—to name the United States' closest neighbors. Most would not have the foggiest idea about what was at stake in the French Revolution, the Russian Revolution, the Spanish Civil War, or the Chinese Revolution. (Michael Parenti, *Make-Believe Media*)

How knowledgeable is the writer? Michael Parenti seems knowledgeable; he refers to a wide range of historical examples. He appears to know the answers to the historical issues he accuses most or many Americans of knowing little or nothing about. You can assume that he understands the issues involved in the Vietnam War and that he knows the details of the history of aggression conducted against Native Americans. But he does not provide any details in this paragraph to demonstrate his implied claim to such knowledge.

What are the writer's sources, and are they helpful and reliable? Parenti does not acknowledge any sources.

How clear and detailed is the writer's presentation? The writing is clear and the examples are numerous. The examples make the writer's point, or thesis, which is stated in the first sentence, very clearly. They also strongly support his claim that Americans are ignorant of history.

Is the writer reasonable and fair? There is no attempt in this paragraph to explain why so many people know so little about history—although the writer does provide that explanation elsewhere in his essay. You can surmise or guess from his title, "Make-Believe Media," that he holds the media largely to blame for Americans' ignorance of history. Nor does the author make any attempt to provide an alternative point of view. In this paragraph he presents one side only—his view—strongly and without considering any others.

Exercise 10-4

Evaluate the credibility of the following argument from the 2000 book *Dr. Shapiro's Picture Perfect Weight Loss: The Visual Program for Permanent Weight Loss* by Howard M. Shapiro.

To lose weight successfully, you either have to decrease your caloric 1 intake or increase the number of calories expended through exercise—preferably both. To lose weight successfully and keep it off, you have to accomplish calorie reduction without feeling deprived. This is a key concept, and it is at the heart of my program. Feeling deprived comes around and kicks you in the rear end—right in the direction of the nearest hot-fudge sundae or the local bakery.

I have been working with dieters for many years, and I know that 2 they do not have a problem with willpower. Quite the contrary. People who can cling to a rigid diet, despite everything else that's going on in their lives, often have unusual discipline in many areas. Some have managed to stick with extremely rigorous programs for an amazingly long time to reach their goal weights.

I have had people who stayed on a liquid protein fast without a 3 morsel of real food for as long as four months. Don't tell me this demonstrates a lack of willpower!

I have also seen, however, many people who have worked unbeliev- 4 ably hard to reach a certain weight-loss goal, only to gain all the weight back again. The feelings of deprivation were just too much for them, and once they had reached the numbers on the scale that they longed for, they resumed their old eating patterns. Yet, all the time they were dieting, they were not aware of feeling deprived.

People who are attempting to lose weight typically do not report 5 feelings of deprivation; they bury them instead. They say that they had a bad week or that they ate because they weren't focused. They will say things like, "I had plenty. I didn't need to eat the brownie"; "I wasn't hungry"; or "I don't know why I did it."

If those phrases sound familiar, I can assure you that people who are 6 deprived of food do need to eat. If you eat, it's because you're hungry.

Example:

What is the writer's claim?

Deprivation diets don't work. If you eat, it's because you're hungry.

1. How knowledgeable is the writer? How do you know?

   The writer seems very knowledgeable. He is a doctor and gives many

   examples from his own practice.

2. What are the writer's sources, and are they helpful and reliable?

   The writer's only source is his own experience, which is anecdotal and

   may or may not be typical. Also, although he mentions patients who

   showed great willpower, he doesn't say whether or not their diets were

   successful in the long run.

Would more sources be helpful?

Yes. The argument would be more convincing if the writer brought in

evidence from scientific studies or even from other doctors' experiences.

3. Do the examples and other details support the writer's argument?

    Most of them do, although his examples of people with strong willpower

    might suggest that in some cases, deprivation diets are indeed

    effective. Other examples seem to contradict his claim that "if you eat,

    it's because you're hungry."

4. How clear and detailed is the writer's presentation? Can you follow what he is saying?

    Answers will vary. Some students may find Shapiro's argument very easy

    to follow; others may find his examples of successful dieters distracting

    or confusing. The second part of his claim, "if you eat, it's because you're

    hungry," comes somewhat unexpectedly and may throw some students.

5. Is the writer reasonable and fair? Are opposing views presented carefully and without scorn? Do the opposing views change the writer's argument?

    The writer suggests that others have a different opinion, but he

    dismissively brushes aside opposing views without giving them much

    attention. Opposing views could indeed change the argument.

. . . .

ANALOGY

As you learned in Chapter 6, an **analogy** makes a comparison. Writers often use analogy to explain something unfamiliar to their readers by comparing it with something more familiar. For example, to illustrate how joints work at the wrist and knee, a writer might make an analogy with a hinge. Analogies help readers understand what writers mean. They also help writers clarify their thinking for readers.

Be careful, however, when you find analogy used in an argument. Analogies do not prove a point. Instead, they provide alternative ways of seeing or saying things. You can take an analogy only so far before the similarities between the two things compared end and important differences emerge. A baseball double play, in some ways, is like a dance. But in other ways it is not. A heart is like a pump, but only to a degree.

Consider the following argument by analogy:

> It is clear that the decline of a language must ultimately have political and economic causes: it is not due simply to the bad influence of this or that individual writer. But an effect can become a cause, reinforcing the original cause and producing the same effect in an intensified form, and so on indefinitely. A man may take to drink because he feels himself to be a failure, and then fail all the more completely because he drinks. It is rather the same thing that is happening to the English language. It becomes ugly and inaccurate because our thoughts are foolish, but the slovenliness of our language makes it easier for us to have foolish thoughts. (George Orwell, "Politics and the English Language")

In arguing that the English language is in decline, Orwell proposes that an effect (the decline of English) can become a cause furthering that decline. He then introduces his analogy of drinking to support his argument that effects of a problem can become causes that further intensify it. As a reader, you need to be clear, first, about the idea expressed in the analogy and, second, about how well the analogy supports Orwell's claim.

Just what does Orwell's analogy say? It says, essentially, that drinking intensifies a person's decline so that the person, as a result, drinks even more — which leads to even greater failure. You can see how Orwell's analogy explains how the effect of a failure can become a cause of further failures.

In applying his analogy about drinking as cause and effect, Orwell argues that the English language has declined because some people are sloppy in their thinking and writing. Orwell's analogy, however, does not *prove* that users of English contributed to its decline this way. Instead, it simply clarifies his idea, enabling readers to better understand his point.

Exercise 10-5

· ·

What is the claim of each argument? How does the analogy work?

Example:

> Give yourself time to think about a plan before you act on it. Let it percolate while your mind is on other things. Let the plan steep in your unconscious while you sleep. Like a strong flavorful cup of coffee or tea, a good plan needs time to brew.

CLAIM: *We should think about a plan before we act on it.*

ANALOGY: *Just like a good cup of coffee or tea, a good plan needs preparation time.*

1. At the turn of the twenty-first century, many people made quick—and huge—fortunes by investing in the stock market. Technology stocks soared, turning many investors into millionaires. However, like huge fireworks displays that shoot brilliant colors sky-high and then fade without a trace, most of the stocks that reached unprecedented heights yesterday are gone today. Do yourself a favor. Invest in real estate.

    CLAIM: *It is better to invest in real estate than in the stock market.*

    ANALOGY: *Stocks that reached unprecedented heights are like fireworks displays. They rose very high and shone intensely for a few moments, but then they disappeared.*

2. Investing in the stock market is never a mistake. Investors just need to diversify their portfolios. That is, they need to have different types of investments: stocks, bonds, mutual funds, and so on. It's the old story of not putting all your eggs in one basket. If you drop the basket, all the eggs break. If people put all their money in only one type of get-rich-quick investment (remember the investors who bought only technology stocks in the 1990s), they lose everything if that type of investment turns bad. Over time, however, the stock market always goes up. Wise investment in the market always pays off.

CLAIM: _Investing in the stock market always pays off._

ANALOGY: _Investing in only one get-rich-quick type of investment is like putting all your eggs in one basket. If that type of investment fails — if the egg basket breaks — everything is lost._

3. Anyone who wants a pet will be much happier with a dog than with a cat. A dog is a true friend. Like the best of human companions, a dog will sense your moods, comfort you when you're feeling down, rejoice with you when you're feeling happy. You can communicate with a dog. You can teach a dog. Best of all, a dog never judges you. A cat, on the other hand, acts like royalty. A cat looks down on you, doing whatever it wishes whenever it wishes, ignoring your commands, your moods, and your feelings.

CLAIM: _A dog is a better pet than a cat._

ANALOGIES: _Dogs are like the best human companions. They are true friends, responsive to moods. Cats are like royalty, looking down on people and doing whatever they please._

4. Anyone who wants a pet will be much happier with a cat than with a dog. A cat is a majestic creature that does not need to be taught to do anything. As graceful as a ballet dancer, as flexible as an acrobat, as balanced as a gymnast, a cat will hold you spellbound as it executes its magnificent jumps and leaps. For sheer beauty and majesty, no pet is as splendid as the dignified, independent cat.

CLAIM: _A cat is a better pet than a dog._

ANALOGIES: _Cats are as graceful as ballet dancers, as flexible as acrobats, and as balanced as gymnasts._

5. Running has many advantages. It's cheap (no lift tickets, membership fees, admission costs). You don't need special equipment (no bike, racket, treadmill). You don't need special clothing (no helmets, knee guards,

uniforms). You don't need a special location (no gym, pool, ski slope). You can run whenever and wherever appeals to you. Best of all, though, is the way running makes you feel. Like a kid on the first day of summer vacation, you find yourself bubbling with a sense of joyous freedom. You forget your cares and responsibilities. You're filled with appreciation for the present moment. Like that kid, you're really alive once again.

CLAIM: *"Running has many advantages."*

ANALOGY: *A runner is like a kid on the first day of summer vacation,*

feeling free, appreciative, and alive.

- -

AUTHORITY

An individual or institution whose expertise, knowledge, rank, position, or accomplishments can lend credibility to an assertion or claim is an **authority.** A writer's use of authority often offers powerful support that can strengthen an argument. But appeals to authority in persuasive writing are not always effective. In media advertising and political campaigns, for example, authorities frequently provide unsubstantiated or inadequate support for products and candidates. As a reader you need to be aware of how authority is used and whether each authority convincingly supports the claims it accompanies.

Any authority may be wrong in a particular instance. Authorities often disagree. Equally reputable authorities can—and do—arrive at conflicting or incompatible conclusions about complex matters, such as the causes of the American Revolution or the future of the National Rifle Association. When you encounter authorities as evidence in support of the arguments of others, consider their biases as well as their expertise. Medical experts testifying to the safety of a new drug, for example, may be biased, especially if they have been paid by the pharmaceutical company that developed the drug. Analyze the validity and accuracy of each authority's argument by checking with other authorities and by considering what you have learned from your own experience.

A few questions can help you analyze a writer's use of authority:

1.   *What are the authority's credentials and qualifications?* To be credible, an authority must be knowledgeable about the argument he or she (or it) supports. Britney Spears may be able to speak to questions

of young girls' experiences in the music business, but her opinions on international trade treaties would lack authority.

2. *Is the authority known and respected?* Good argumentative writers support their arguments with authorities whom their readers will recognize and whose opinions they will respect. In attempting to persuade readers about the health risks of smoking, for example, the surgeon general or an emphysema patient would be effective authorities to draw on; an advertising executive at a tobacco company such as R. J. Reynolds or Philip Morris would not.

3. *Is the authority's information or knowledge up-to-date?* Somebody who was at the top of his or her field thirty years ago may no longer be the best person to speak about a particular subject. In any discipline, knowledge advances and opinions change. To be effective, a writer should cite recent research and refer to individuals who are currently active in their fields.

TESTIMONY

Similar to authority, **testimony**—a statement made in support of a fact or a claim—can be offered by experts or by individuals with specialized knowledge. It can also be provided by ordinary people. Law courts, for example, typically rely on the testimony of both experts and witnesses to ascertain the facts of a case.

Testimonials rely on nonlogical attempts to influence decisions. Because athletes and stars who appear in advertisements typically receive large sums of money for their endorsements, you should view their testimonials with skepticism. This does not mean, however, that the claims made in testimonials are necessarily false. In fact, testimonials are often valuable when used to support arguments—as long as the testimony is credible. To be credible, the person providing the testimony must be operating within his or her area of competence or expertise. The testimony must also be accurate, current, and representative. You should subject testimony to the same kinds of logical analysis and careful questioning you bring to other forms of evidence.

Exercise 10-6

Debra Rosenberg's argument about the danger of thrill rides, which you read earlier in this chapter, appeals to authority and provides testimony. Reread her argument (reprinted here) and answer the questions that follow it.

Fighting G-Force

Do the Faster, Scarier Roller Coasters Literally Shake Up the Brain?

Zipora Jacob wasn't exactly a thrill-seeker. On a 1995 day trip to Disneyland, the 42-year-old didn't venture onto a ride until evening, when she hopped on the Indiana Jones Adventure. Though it was slower than most roller coasters, its high-tech hydraulics made it seem speedier and jerkier. "When the ride stopped, I felt my head was exploding," says Jacob. By the next morning, she was in a coma from a massive brain bleed. She endured surgeries and memory loss, and still has a permanent shunt draining fluid from her brain. Jacob settled a lawsuit with Disney in 1999; two other lawsuits have claimed injuries on the ride. Disney says independent testing has shown that the G-forces and motion of the ride aren't sufficient to cause injury. Jacob thinks otherwise: "A nice day at the amusement park can become a nightmare for the rest of your life."

In the past decade, new megacoasters have gone extreme, boasting speeds of more than 100 mph, back-to-back loops, and G-forces that rival the space shuttle's. "We've moved from an era of Model T roller coasters to one of supersonics," says Massachusetts Rep. Ed Markey, who has catalogued 58 brain injuries—including eight fatalities—on thrill rides, most since 1990. The roller coaster industry says 320 million people enjoyed rides last year mostly without incident. "It truly is one of the safest family activities you can engage in," says Bret Lovejoy of the International Association of Amusement Parks and Attractions.

That hasn't stopped a new drive to regulate the rides' gravitational or G-forces. The normal pull of gravity upon the body is one G, but acceleration increases that pull. Some scientists believe that high G-forces on coasters could distort the brain within the skull. The space shuttle maxes out at less than four Gs, but some parks used to brag that their coasters fleetingly topped six Gs—an unsafe level according to Markey, who's introduced a bill to create a national G-force standard. Last month, New Jersey became the first state to issue its own G-force limits. The coaster industry insists engineers have better control over G-forces than ever. Even so, the industry is announcing standards of its own later this month.

Despite the flurry of rulemaking, the link between G-forces and injuries hasn't been scientifically proven. Some researchers say rapid jerking of the head could be far more dangerous than G-forces, tearing blood vessels in the brain. But even that may be rare, limited mainly to pre-existing conditions like aneurysms. Jacob says she was perfectly healthy before she stepped aboard the Disney ride—a cautionary tale for the millions who'll line up at parks this summer, hoping for the thrill of their lives.

Example:

What purpose is served by Zipora Jacob's story?

Her experience of being injured by a thrill ride is used both as a testimony from an ordinary person ("When the ride stopped, I felt my head was exploding") and as an appeal to the authority of a victim ("A nice day at the amusement park can become a nightmare for the rest of your life").

1. What authorities does Rosenberg cite to support her argument that rides are unsafe?

   Massachusetts Representative Ed Markey, the state of New Jersey, some unnamed researchers, Zipora Jacob

2. What authorities' opposing views does Rosenberg cite?

   Disney, the rollercoaster industry, Bret Lovejoy of the International Association of Amusement Parks and Attractions

3. What are the credentials and qualifications of the authorities Rosenberg uses in support of her argument?

   Ed Markey is a state representative who has conducted research to document incidents of thrill ride injuries. The state of New Jersey is a government institution whose region includes a large amusement park (Six Flags Great Adventure). We don't know the credentials and qualifications of the unnamed researchers. Zipora Jacob is an everyday person who was injured by a ride in California.

4. Are the authorities Rosenberg cites in favor of her claim known and respected?

    Ed Markey is known but can't really be considered an expert on ride

    safety. The state of New Jersey is known and respected. The unnamed

    researchers are not known. Zipora Jacob is not known; we can respect

    her experience, but we can't assume it is representative of most

    amusement park visitors.

5. Rosenberg is careful to acknowledge opposing viewpoints. What are the credentials of the authorities she cites? Are they credible?

    All of the opposing viewpoints belong to individuals and institutions

    that have a vested interest in convincing people that the rides are safe.

    Some, like Disney, are well known but not necessarily credible. Others, like

    the coaster industry and the International Association of Amusement

    Parks and Attractions, must be viewed with skepticism.

■ Recognizing Logical Fallacies

A **fallacy** is an error in reasoning. Writers and speakers often make mistakes in their arguments, violating logic without realizing it. As you read and listen to others, being aware of common logical fallacies will help you assess the validity of their arguments. It will also make you a more critical thinker and prepare you to make more effective arguments yourself.

DOES NOT FOLLOW (NON SEQUITUR)

The Latin for "it does not follow" is *non sequitur*. This error in reasoning makes a conclusion that does not follow logically from an argument's statements and assumptions.

> I worked hard during the entire course of the term. I deserve an A for my final grade.

Common Logical Fallacies

- **Does not follow (non sequitur).** A statement of cause and effect that doesn't make sense.

- **Hasty generalization.** A conclusion based on insufficient evidence.

- **Either/or thinking (false dilemma).** Reasoning that limits possible explanations to only two.

- **After this, because of this (post hoc).** The assumption that an event is caused by another simply because one event occurs after the other.

- **Circular reasoning.** Repetition of the same idea but in different words.

- **Begging the question.** Assuming as true what needs to be proven.

- **Special pleading.** Argument that ignores opposing viewpoints.

- **Red herring.** Introduction of an irrelevant or distracting consideration into an argument.

- **Appeal to ignorance.** Assumption that something is true because the contrary cannot be proven.

- **Attacking the person (ad hominem).** Attacking a person's character rather than addressing the issue at hand.

- **Doubtful authority.** An appeal to an authority whose expertise is questionable or irrelevant.

- **False analogy.** An illogical connection based on irrelevant similarities.

This argument sounds reasonable if we grant credibility to the missing assumption (that students who work hard should receive A's.) Typically, however, instructors use other factors to determine grades, such as students' performance on tests and quizzes and the quality of their class participation.

HASTY GENERALIZATION

A hasty generalization bases a conclusion on inadequate evidence. Writers who jump to conclusions before considering additional or alternative information are not being logical.

> For our novels course we read ten books, and the two by Russian writers were the longest by far. The Russians write the longest books of anybody.

Ten books is not a sufficiently large sampling to conclude that Russian writers compose the longest books. Numerous exceptions—such as the works of English novelist Charles Dickens or American writer Theodore Dreiser's *An American Tragedy*—undermine the generalization.

Stereotyping is a form of hasty generalization. For example, you might describe bats as ugly or Miami as crime-ridden, when some bats might actually be considered cute and many sections of Miami are quite safe. Stereotypical thinking often makes unwarranted assumptions about an entire group of people. Thinking stereotypically is not only logically invalid; it is prejudicial and sometimes malicious.

EITHER/OR THINKING (FALSE DILEMMA)

Sometimes called false dilemma, either/or thinking admits only two solutions to a problem: either A or B. Other alternatives are ignored. Either/or thinking is limiting. It oversimplifies complex issues, reducing them to extreme explanations that ignore viable alternatives.

> Either the Republicans band together now behind one of the declared candidates or they will kill each other off politically and ensure an easy Democratic victory in the next presidential election.

While it may be true that multiple presidential candidates may create havoc in the initial stages of a campaign, eventually the party will choose one candidate and thus allow time to unite behind him or her. Moreover, there may be additional solutions to the apparent problem of political infighting.

AFTER THIS, BECAUSE OF THIS (POST HOC)

Thinkers who fall into this fallacy assume that simply because one event happens after another, the first caused the second to occur.

> In 1991 under coach Bill Parcells, the New York Giants won their division, their league championship, and ultimately the Super Bowl. The following year, under Ray Handley, the Giants ended the season with an 8–8 won–lost record. They did not make it even to the first round of the playoffs. Handley is a poor coach and is responsible for the Giants' slide into mediocrity.

Just because the Giants' decline occurred after Handley took over as head coach, it is not reasonable to conclude that he caused their mediocre seasonal performance. Some of his coaching decisions may have affected the team's overall performance, but other explanations can also account for the team's demise, from injuries to key players to the difficulty of playing up to peak after excelling the year before. In short, it is unlikely that the new coach alone caused the team's fall from championship-caliber play.

CIRCULAR REASONING

To engage in circular reasoning is to assert the same thing in different words without introducing evidence or reasons in support.

> The growing popularity of kickboxing shows that people are becoming increasingly interested in kickboxing.

The sentence says the same thing twice: That kickboxing has become popular, which is the same thing as saying that people are interested in it.

BEGGING THE QUESTION

To beg the question is to present a claim as truth without providing evidence or arguments in its support. It is a form of circular reasoning that uses the argument's assertion or claim as its conclusion.

> Administrators should be barred from faculty council meetings because those meetings should be reserved exclusively for members of the faculty council.

The statement does not provide reasons administrators should be excluded. It simply asserts that they should. The writer has begged the question and taken for granted that what he or she is arguing for is a given.

SPECIAL PLEADING

In special pleading a speaker or writer presents a one-sided argument, completely ignoring contradictory information and opposing perspectives. Special pleaders present their case without indicating the existence of contrary evidence or the possibility of alternative views.

> You should buy a Hyundai. It's inexpensive, fuel-efficient, and easy to park. It also provides excellent value.

All of the claims made for the car may indeed be true. The problem is what is left out. The car may be too small; it may have a poor repair record. And so on.

RED HERRING

Introducing a red herring into an argument deliberately sidetracks the discussion by bringing in an irrelevant matter. The fallacy derives its name from seventeenth-century criminals' practice of dragging a fish across their path to confuse the bloodhounds used to track them by scent.

> Officer, you shouldn't be giving me a speeding ticket when dangerous criminals are roaming the streets at this very moment. You could be spending your time solving more important crimes.

The issue is not other crimes and criminals but whether the speaker violated the speed limit.

APPEAL TO IGNORANCE

A speaker or writer who appeals to ignorance argues that a claim is true merely because strong evidence to the contrary is lacking. An appeal to ignorance assumes that what is being asserted must be true simply because it cannot be disproved.

> For centuries, scientists have been searching for evidence of life in outer space and have come up with nothing conclusive. Earth is the only planet with intelligent life forms.

The fact that the scientists have been searching for but have not found conclusive evidence of intelligent life on other planets does not necessarily imply what the speaker asserts. In fact, one can neither prove nor disprove the speaker's claim. There may be other life forms in the universe; there may not be. Simply because we don't have proof of extraterrestrial life, we cannot logically conclude that humans are the only intelligent beings in the universe. Nor can we conclude that they are not.

ATTACKING THE PERSON (AD HOMINEM)

One of the most common fallacies is to question an individual's character in order to prove a point about his or her beliefs. It is an attempt to discredit an idea by attacking the person presenting it rather than by addressing the issue itself.

> Senator Grindel argues that we should attempt to control the budget deficit by cutting spending in the military and social services sectors. But the senator has had serious problems handling his personal credit. Why should we listen to his views on the nation's economic plan when he can't manage his own personal finances?

The issue is the senator's position on cutting the budget deficit, not his personal financial situation. The senator's ideas should be evaluated on their own merit.

DOUBTFUL AUTHORITY

As you have seen, authorities cited to support an argument are not always credible. Writers who use doubtful authority appeal to testimony of individuals or institutions whose expertise or knowledge are questionable or not relevant to the claim.

> My father thinks that my foot injury can be cured with aspirin and stretching. Now that I know what to do I don't have to make an appointment with the doctor.

The speaker's father is not an expert in foot health. His suggestion may work in some cases, but without knowing the cause of the speaker's foot pain, a reasonable diagnosis is impossible.

FALSE ANALOGY

A false analogy misleads by comparing situations that are more unlike than similar. False analogies are also sometimes based on similarities that are irrelevant.

> If we add proficiency in a foreign language to the graduation requirements, we will deter students from attending this university, just as we did when we added math and science requirements ten years ago.

A foreign language requirement differs from one for math or science. In addition, attitudes about learning foreign languages today may be very different from attitudes toward math and science requirements a decade ago.

Exercise 10-7

Identify the fallacies of reasoning in the following statements. Explain what, if anything, might be wrong with each.

Example:

The electric bill has doubled since Chris moved into the apartment in June. He should pay half the cost.

FALLACY: *after this, because of this (post hoc)*

EXPLANATION: *The increased use of electricity is not necessarily due to Chris moving in. The air conditioners may have started running; perhaps the refrigerator in the apartment is getting old and using more power.*

1. If we don't do something to slow the growth of human population, the planet simply will be unable to accommodate — with sufficient food or adequate living space — the spiraling increase in people.

FALLACY: _either/or thinking_

EXPLANATION: _Overpopulation may be a serious issue, but reducing the growth of population isn't necessarily the only solution. Alternatives may include changes to food distribution and rethinking housing arrangements._

2. The burglary suspect was arrested two years ago for selling drugs. Therefore, he must be guilty.

FALLACY: _red herring_

EXPLANATION: _The suspect's past drug convictions have no bearing on his guilt or innocence in the robbery case currently being tried._

3. He is the best presidential candidate: As a successful professional basketball player he gets along well with his colleagues and has learned the importance of teamwork.

FALLACY: _false analogy_

EXPLANATION: _A person's skill as a basketball player is irrelevant to his qualifications as a political leader._

4. Something horrible must have happened to Melissa. She would have called if she was going to be this late.

FALLACY: _hasty generalization_

EXPLANATION: _The speaker is jumping to conclusions. Any number of things could have caused Melissa to be late without calling._

5. New Tread sports shoes are the best on the market. All the varsity basketball players wear them.

FALLACY: _doubtful authority_

EXPLANATION: _The shoe manufacturer may have given the shoes to the varsity players as a promotion._

6. Doberman pinschers make the best pets. They are alert, highly trainable, and handsome.

   FALLACY: *special pleading*

   EXPLANATION: *The speaker doesn't consider any of the negative aspects of Doberman pinschers, such as their aggressiveness and their known tendency to turn on their owners unexpectedly.*

7. People are not really free. They only think they are. Their lives are actually determined by forces that control them without their being aware of it. You can't prove that you are unaffected by numerous influences that bombard us throughout our lives.

   FALLACY: *appeal to ignorance*

   EXPLANATION: *Being unable to prove that unknown forces affect us does not prove that they do.*

8. That marriage counselor has been divorced twice. She is not qualified to help other couples.

   FALLACY: *attack on the person (ad hominem)*

   EXPLANATION: *Counselors are trained to listen to people and offer advice about their clients' situations. One counselor's own marital history is beside the point.*

9. If you don't buy this home theater setup now, it won't be here tomorrow. Besides, prices are expected to go up next month.

   FALLACY: *does not follow (non sequitur)*

   EXPLANATION: *If the home theater setup will be gone tomorrow, how can it get more expensive a month from now?*

10. Students should give themselves grades in their courses. No one knows better than they how much they have learned and what grade they deserve.

FALLACY: *begging the question*

EXPLANATION: *The speaker presents the assertion as the conclusion,*

arguing that students should grade themselves because they know best

what grades they deserve.

Applying the Skills

Reading the Parts

In the wake of the September 11, 2001, terrorist attacks in New York, Washington, D.C., and Pennsylvania, Americans have been considering new ways to ensure their safety and security. One proposal is to require all U.S. citizens to carry identification. In the following online article from January 14, 2002, *Time* magazine's political columnist Margaret Carlson argues in favor of instituting a national ID system. As you read her argument, pay close attention to her claim and the evidence she provides, as well as the assumptions her argument depends on. In particular, be on the lookout for logical fallacies. Try to determine if Carlson's position is reasonable and whether as a writer she is credible. After reading each section and answering the questions that follow it, move on to the next section. You will have a chance to read the entire argument when you finish.

MARGARET CARLSON
The Case for a National ID Card

1   After representative John Dingell was asked to drop his pants at Washington's National Airport last week, some people felt safer. Others, like me, decided that we'd lost our collective minds. A near strip search of a 75-year-old Congressman whose artificial hip has set off a metal detector—while suspected al-Qaeda operative Richard Reid slips onto a Paris-to-Miami flight with a bomb in his shoe—isn't making us safer. It's making us ridiculous for entrusting our security to an unskilled police force that must make split-second decisions on the basis of incomplete data.

2   Incidents like this—and airport waits longer than the flight itself—have pushed me into the camp of the national ID card. Yes, a tamperproof ID smacks of Big Brother[1] and Nazis intoning "Your papers, please," but the Federal Government already holds a trove of data on each of us. And it's less likely to mess up or misuse it than the credit-card companies or the Internet fraudsters, who have

---

[1] In the novel *1984* by George Orwell, Big Brother is the name of the fictional intrusive government that spies on every aspect of its citizens' lives.

> just as much data if not more. (Two years ago, for a *Time* article, I ordered dinner for 30 entirely online, and I am still plagued by vendors who know I like my wine French and my ham honey-baked.)
>
> The idea of a national ID card leaped into the headlines just after Sept. 11. Oracle chairman Larry Ellison offered to donate the pertinent software. Ellison went to see Attorney General John Ashcroft, who was noncommittal despite his obvious enthusiasm for expanding government powers into other areas that trouble civil libertarians.

3

1. What claim does Margaret Carlson make in paragraphs 1–3 of this selection?

   a.   There should be better airport security.

   b.) Because of recent events in airports and airplanes, there should be a national ID card.

   c.   Larry Ellison should pay for the creation of software to develop a national ID card.

   d.   John Ashcroft was noncommittal about the idea of a national ID card.

2. Which of the following sentences from Carlson's essay provides evidence for the central point or thesis of her argument?

   a.) "A near strip search of a 75-year-old Congressman whose artificial hip has set off a metal detector—while suspected al-Qaeda operative Richard Reid slips onto a Paris-to-Miami flight with a bomb in his shoe—isn't making us safer."

   b.   "Incidents like this—and airport waits longer than the flight itself—have pushed me into the camp of the national ID card."

   c.   "The idea of a national ID card leaped into the headlines just after Sept. 11."

   d.   "Oracle chairman Larry Ellison offered to donate the pertinent software."

3. Which of the following assumptions must a reader share with Carlson for her argument to be successful?

   a.   Honey-baked hams are delicious.

   b.   Everybody has flown on an airplane.

    c. Privacy is more important than security.

   (d.) Security is more important than privacy.

4. Which of the following fallacies of thinking is employed in the author's inclusion of this sentence: "Two years ago, for a *Time* article, I ordered dinner for 30 entirely online, and I am still plagued by vendors who know I like my wine French and my ham honey-baked"?

    a. begging the question

    b. hasty generalization

   (c.) false analogy

    d. circular reasoning

5. In paragraph 2, the author writes, "Yes, a tamperproof ID smacks of Big Brother and Nazis intoning 'Your papers, please,' but the Federal Government already holds a trove of data on each of us." Which of the following fallacies is inherent in this statement?

    a. red herring

   (b.) does not follow

    c. appeal to ignorance

    d. appeal to authority

    Enter Richard Durbin. In concert with the American Association of Motor Vehicle Administrators (yes, the dreaded DMVs have their own trade group), the Illinois Senator is proposing legislation that would create a uniform standard for the country's 200 million state-administered driver's licenses. Durbin noticed that the driver's license has become "the most widely used personal ID in the country. If you can produce one, we assume you're legitimate," he says. At present, nearly anyone can get a license; 13 of the 19 hijackers did. Having those licenses "gave the terrorists cover to mingle in American society without being detected."

    Since we're using the driver's license as a de facto national ID, Durbin argues, let's make it more reliable. As it stands, the chief requirement is that one knows how to drive. This is fine if the only intent is to ensure that someone behind the wheel has mastered turn signals, but it shouldn't be sufficient to get someone into a federal

4

5

building, the Olympics or an airplane. All a terrorist needs to do is shop around for a lax state (Florida still doesn't require proof of permanent residency) or resort to a forger with a glue gun and laminator.

A high-tech, hard-to-forge driver's license could become a 6
national E-ZPass, a way for a law-abiding citizen to move faster through the roadblocks of post–9/11 life. It's no digitalized Super-card, but the states would have uniform standards, using bar codes and biometrics (a unique characteristic, like a palm print) and could cross-check and get information from other law-enforcement agen-cies. Polls show 70% of Americans support an even more stringent ID. But Japanese-American members of Congress and Transporta-tion Secretary Norman Mineta are keenly sensitive to anything that might single out one nationality.[2] Yet an ID card offers prospects of less profiling. By accurately identifying those who are in the U.S. legally and not on a terrorist watch list, the card would reduce the temptation to go after random members of specific groups.

---

[2]After the Japanese attack on Pearl Harbor in December 1941 brought the United States into World War II, the U.S. government sent more than 100,000 Japanese Americans to internment camps solely because of their ethnicity.

6. Which of the following analogies is made in paragraph 6?

   a. High-tech driver's licenses are like college IDs.

   b. High-tech driver's licenses are like E-ZPass tags.

   c. E-ZPass tags are similar to national terrorist watch lists.

   d. There is no use of analogy in paragraph 6.

7. How does Carlson use testimony as evidence for her point in paragraphs 4–6?

   a. She quotes Richard Durbin.

   b. She quotes Norman Mineta.

   c. She quotes the head of the DMV.

   d. She quotes John Dingell.

8. Which of the following is a stated assumption in paragraphs 4–6 of Carlson's essay?

   a. If you're Japanese, you'll be singled out for discrimination.

   b. If you drive, you have mastered turn signals.

   c. If you have a driver's license, you're considered "legitimate" in this country.

   d. Terrorists have driver's licenses.

9. In paragraph 4, the author writes that "Durbin noticed that the driver's license has become 'the most widely used personal ID in the country. If you can produce one, we assume you're legitimate.'" Which of the following fallacies is evident in Durbin's quote?

   a. hasty generalization

   b. either/or thinking

   c. appeal to ignorance

   d. attacking the person

10. Which of the following sentences is used to support the author's central point in paragraphs 4–6?

   a. "As it stands, the chief requirement is that one knows how to drive."

   b. "But Japanese-American members of Congress and Transportation Secretary Norman Mineta are keenly sensitive to anything that might single out one nationality."

   c. "Since we're using the driver's license as a de facto national ID, Durbin argues, let's make it more reliable."

   d. "It's no digitalized Supercard, but the states would have uniform standards, using bar codes and biometrics (a unique characteristic, like a palm print) and could cross-check and get information from other law-enforcement agencies."

It is not ideal to leave a national problem to the states, but because of the general squeamishness about federal "papers" in the Congress, Durbin's proposal—congressional oversight of state DMVs—may be the best way to go. And if the government doesn't act, corporations will. Delta and American Airlines already provide separate lines for premium passengers; Heathrow Airport in London has an iris scan for people who have registered their eyeballs. An airline-industry association is at work on a Trusted Traveler card. Do we really want frequent-flyer status to be the basis for security decisions, or more plastic cards joining the too many we already have?

7

> This ID would require one virtual strip search instead of many
> real ones. Durbin says the card would remove the anonymity of a
> Mohamed Atta but not the privacy of others. With a card, Dingell
> could have confirmed his identity (though he made a point of not
> pulling rank). With the presumption that he wasn't a terrorist, a
> once-over with a wand—with his pants on—would have lent cre-
> dence to his claim that he possessed an artificial hip, not a gun. The
> Durbin card would at least let us travel with our clothes on.
>
> 8

11. Why is the first sentence in paragraph 7 an example of an appeal to ignorance?

    a. because Carlson attacked Durbin's credibility earlier

    b. because Carlson has not outlined any other options for the reader to consider

    c. because Carlson obviously has no respect for Congress

    d. because Carlson assumes everyone thinks the same way.

12. What assumption does Carlson makes about her readers in paragraphs 7–8?

    a. Everyone has a number of plastic cards.

    b. Everyone knows his or her congressional representative.

    c. Everyone will want a Trusted Traveler card.

    d. Everyone agrees with her.

13. What overall claim does Carlson make in paragraphs 7–8?

    a. The national ID card would save the country money.

    b. The national ID card would cut down on the number of fre-quent flyers.

    c. The national ID card would cut down on the number of strip searches, while ensuring that terrorists would be thwarted.

    d. The national ID card idea has a lot of flaws.

14. In paragraph 7, the sentence "And if the government doesn't act, corporations will" is an example of

    a. a false analogy.

    b. either/or thinking.

    c. a hasty generalization.

    d. an appeal to ignorance.

15. Carlson's comment that "the Durbin card would at least let us travel with our clothes on" is an example of

    a. a red herring.

    b. begging the question.

    c. attacking the person.

    d. circular reasoning.

Reading the Whole

Now that you have read Margaret Carlson's essay in its parts and have had a chance to analyze her argument bit by bit, you are ready to read the entire essay and analyze the argument as a whole, focusing more on its credibility and on the author's uses of evidence. As you read, continue to be aware of logical fallacies and to pay attention to the author's appeals to authority and testimony. Most important, consider the argument Carlson makes, and ask yourself if you are convinced.

MARGARET CARLSON
The Case for a National ID Card

After representative John Dingell was asked to drop his pants at Washington's National Airport last week, some people felt safer. Others, like me, decided that we'd lost our collective minds. A near strip search of a 75-year-old Congressman whose artificial hip has set off a metal detector—while suspected al-Qaeda operative Richard Reid slips onto a Paris-to-Miami flight with a bomb in his shoe—isn't making us safer. It's making us ridiculous for entrusting our security to an unskilled police force that must make split-second decisions on the basis of incomplete data.

Incidents like this—and airport waits longer than the flight itself—have pushed me into the camp of the national ID card. Yes, a tamperproof ID smacks of Big Brother and Nazis intoning "Your papers, please," but the Federal Government already holds a trove of data on each of us. And it's less likely to mess up or misuse it than the credit-card companies or the Internet fraudsters, who have just as much data if not more. (Two years ago, for a *Time* article, I ordered dinner for 30 entirely online, and I am still plagued by vendors who know I like my wine French and my ham honey-baked.)

The idea of a national ID card leaped into the headlines just after Sept. 11. Oracle chairman Larry Ellison offered to donate the pertinent software. Ellison went to see Attorney General John Ashcroft, who was noncommittal despite his obvious enthusiasm for expanding government powers into other areas that trouble civil libertarians.

Enter Richard Durbin. In concert with the American Association of Motor Vehicle Administrators (yes, the dreaded DMVs have their own trade group), the Illinois Senator is proposing legislation that would create a uniform standard for the country's 200 million state-administered driver's licenses. Durbin noticed that the driver's license has become "the most widely used personal ID in the country. If you can produce one, we assume you're legitimate," he says. At present, nearly anyone can get a license; 13 of the 19 hijackers did. Having those licenses "gave the terrorists cover to mingle in American society without being detected."

Since we're using the driver's license as a de facto national ID, Durbin argues, let's make it more reliable. As it stands, the chief requirement is that one knows how to drive. This is fine if the only intent is to ensure that someone behind the wheel has mastered turn signals, but it shouldn't be sufficient to get someone into a federal building, the Olympics or an airplane. All a terrorist needs to do is shop around for a lax state (Florida still doesn't require proof of permanent residency) or resort to a forger with a glue gun and laminator.

5

A high-tech, hard-to-forge driver's license could become a national E-ZPass, a way for a law-abiding citizen to move faster through the roadblocks of post–9/11 life. It's no digitalized Supercard, but the states would have uniform standards, using bar codes and biometrics (a unique characteristic, like a palm print) and could cross-check and get information from other law-enforcement agencies. Polls show 70% of Americans support an even more stringent ID. But Japanese-American members of Congress and Transportation Secretary Norman Mineta are keenly sensitive to anything that might single out one nationality. Yet an ID card offers prospects of less profiling. By accurately identifying those who are in the U.S. legally and not on a terrorist watch list, the card would reduce the temptation to go after random members of specific groups.

6

It is not ideal to leave a national problem to the states, but because of the general squeamishness about federal "papers" in the Congress, Durbin's proposal—congressional oversight of state DMVs— may be the best way to go. And if the government doesn't act, corporations will. Delta and American Airlines already provide separate lines for premium passengers; Heathrow Airport in London has an iris scan for people who have registered their eyeballs. An airline-industry association is at work on a Trusted Traveler card. Do we really want frequent-flyer status to be the basis for security decisions, or more plastic cards joining the too many we already have?

7

This ID would require one virtual strip search instead of many real ones. Durbin says the card would remove the anonymity of a

8

Mohamed Atta but not the privacy of others. With a card, Dingell could have confirmed his identity (though he made a point of not pulling rank). With the presumption that he wasn't a terrorist, a once-over with a wand—with his pants on—would have lent credence to his claim that he possessed an artificial hip, not a gun. The Durbin card would at least let us travel with our clothes on.

Integrated Skills

1. What is the connection between the opening paragraph of this article and the second paragraph? What is the purpose of each paragraph?

2. What arguments for having a national ID card does Carlson include?

3. What arguments against a national ID card does the author acknowledge? Which arguments do you think are stronger? Why?

4. What is Carlson's view of state driver's licenses issued by each state's Motor Vehicle Department? What does she want to happen to these licenses? Why?

5. Why does Carlson think that a national ID card would reduce "profiling"—the targeting of members of one nationality for thorough security searches?

6. What connections does the author provide between her introductory paragraph and her concluding paragraph? Do you think her conclusion is successful? Why or why not?

Reading/Writing Connection

In "The Case for a National ID Card," Margaret Carlson argues that the benefits of giving up some anonymity are balanced by the extra protection a national identity card can provide. Write a paragraph in which you explain your view about the need for and the value of a national identity card. You may wish to refer specifically to one or more points or examples Carlson mentions in her article.

Reading Textbooks

Thematic Connections. Many people have called the September 11, 2001, terrorist attacks the worst homeland disaster since Japan's December 7, 1941, bombing of Pearl Harbor. Similarly, many have raised concerns that American behavior toward people of Middle Eastern descent—even toward people who just look Middle Eastern—will mirror the U.S. government's treatment of Japanese Americans during World War II. Margaret Carlson, in her essay, alludes to this concern when she notes that "Japanese-American members of Congress and Transportation Secretary Norman Mineta are keenly sensitive to anything that might single out one nationality." But what exactly did happen to Japanese Americans in the 1940s? The following selection, from the American history textbook *The American Promise* by James L. Roark, Michael P. Johnson, Patricia Cline Cohen, Sarah Stage, Alan Lawson, and Susan M. Hartmann, explains.

Vocabulary Preview

dissent (para. 1): difference of opinion (n.)

propaganda (para. 1): a form of argument in which a government or group distributes information designed to convince people of a position (n.)

suppress (para. 1): keep down, minimize (v.)

espionage (para. 1): spying (n.)

aliens (para. 3): people who belong to another country, foreigners, outsiders (n.)

Fourteenth Amendment (para. 3): the amendment to the U.S. Constitution that guarantees civil liberties to all "persons born or naturalized in the United States" (n.)

influx (para. 3): flow (n.)

abate (para. 4): lessen, decrease (v.)

hailed (para. 4): cheered, approved of (v.)

descent (para. 5): heritage (adj.)

World War II did not witness a repetition of the hysteria and viciousness that had characterized the home front during World War I. With almost no dissent against the war, Roosevelt felt no need to engage in a high-powered propaganda campaign such as Wilson had unleashed in 1917. This time, the government took control of the media not to stir passions against the enemy, but to suppress bad news from the war effort. Americans did worry about espionage, however. Walls were plastered with slogans such as "Loose lips sink ships" and "Enemy agents are always near; if you don't talk, they won't hear."

1

There was one major exception to the atmosphere of tolerance—the drastic violation of the rights of Japanese Americans, the only minority group to lose ground during the war. From the time of their first entry into the country in significant numbers in the 1890s, mainly to settle on the West Coast, the Japanese had encountered hostility as economic competitors and intruders in a "white man's country." Although they were law-abiding and successful in small businesses and farming, white prejudice prevailed. In 1907, the Japanese government was forced to accept a humiliating "gentlemen's agreement" that reduced the numbers of new Japanese immigrants in exchange for the right of Asians to attend public schools in California.

Restrictions climaxed in 1924 when federal law established that Japanese immigrants were "aliens ineligible to citizenship." In rejecting an appeal claiming that the law violated the constitutional right of all citizens to equal protection, the Supreme Court declared that the Fourteenth Amendment applied only to whites and ex-slaves. As intended, the ruling halted the influx of Japanese and left unnaturalized Japanese ("Issei") permanently in limbo as residents who could never become citizens. The absurdity of the situation was heightened by the fact that the Issei's children (called "Nisei") were automatically citizens by virtue of having been born in the United States.

Hostility did not abate with the end of Japanese immigration, however. In the 1930s, the *Los Angeles Times* led a new anti-Japanese campaign, arguing that Japanese Americans were still a threat because they would multiply endlessly and outcompete "real" Americans. Any recognition that the actual role of most Japanese was to provide cheap food—exactly what white workers, managers, and homemakers should have hailed—was swallowed up in the storm of hatred that followed the attack on Pearl Harbor.

Even though a military survey concluded that Japanese Americans posed no danger, General John DeWitt, army commander for the West Coast, and California law officials decided to take them into custody. "A Jap's a Jap," DeWitt explained. "It makes no difference whether he's an American or not." On February 19, 1942, President Roosevelt gave that racist premise the force of law in an executive order authorizing the roundup of all Americans of Japanese descent. Allowed little time to secure or sell their property, the victims (most of whom were American citizens) lost assets, jobs, and homes. Not a single case of subversion or sabotage was ever uncovered, yet Japanese Americans were sent to "relocation centers"—basically makeshift prison camps—in remote areas of the Southwest and Great Plains, where they were penned in by barbed wire and armed guards for more than three years. Not until 1988 did Congress award modest reparations to Japanese Americans for their wartime losses.

Thinking about the Textbook Selection

1. What connections do you see between this textbook selection and the online magazine article "The Case for a National ID Card"?

2. What historical touchstones regarding American treatment of the Japanese do the textbook authors mention? Why do the authors discuss the internment of Japanese citizens during World War II last?

3. Why did the U.S. government act against the Japanese in the United States in this way? What do you think of the government's action? Why?

4. Why do the textbook authors mention U.S. army general John DeWitt? What does DeWitt say about the Japanese, and what does the comment reveal about him and his attitude toward the Japanese?

5. What larger issues about race and prejudice are suggested by this textbook reading selection?

Reading the Web

The American Civil Liberties Union (ACLU) is a national organization devoted to "the individual rights and liberties guaranteed to all people in this country by the Constitution and laws of the United States." Both Margaret Carlson in her essay "The Case for a National ID Card" and the authors of the textbook *The American Promise* mention issues of national security. In the following page on national security and civil liberties from the ACLU's Web site, the organization raises its own concerns about the effects national security scares can have on people's civil liberties. As you read it, consider the credibility of the ACLU and the uses of evidence and authority. Analyze the argument on the Web page, and determine whether or not you are convinced by it.

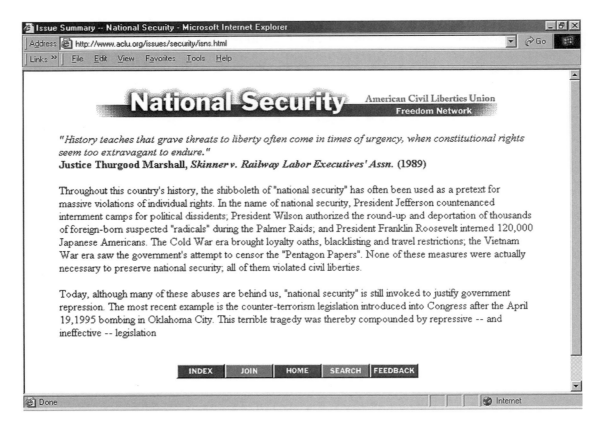

Issue Summary -- National Security - Microsoft Internet Explorer

Address: http://www.aclu.org/issues/security/isns.html

Links » File Edit View Favorites Tools Help

National Security
American Civil Liberties Union
Freedom Network

"History teaches that grave threats to liberty often come in times of urgency, when constitutional rights seem too extravagant to endure."
Justice Thurgood Marshall, *Skinner v. Railway Labor Executives' Assn.* (1989)

Throughout this country's history, the shibboleth of "national security" has often been used as a pretext for massive violations of individual rights. In the name of national security, President Jefferson countenanced internment camps for political dissidents; President Wilson authorized the round-up and deportation of thousands of foreign-born suspected "radicals" during the Palmer Raids; and President Franklin Roosevelt interned 120,000 Japanese Americans. The Cold War era brought loyalty oaths, blacklisting and travel restrictions; the Vietnam War era saw the government's attempt to censor the "Pentagon Papers". None of these measures were actually necessary to preserve national security; all of them violated civil liberties.

Today, although many of these abuses are behind us, "national security" is still invoked to justify government repression. The most recent example is the counter-terrorism legislation introduced into Congress after the April 19, 1995 bombing in Oklahoma City. This terrible tragedy was thereby compounded by repressive -- and ineffective -- legislation

INDEX | JOIN | HOME | SEARCH | FEEDBACK

Done

Internet

Thinking about the Web Page

1. What claim does the ACLU make about the behavior of American presidents? What evidence do they provide to support this claim?

2. Why do you think the quotation from Justice Thurgood Marshall is included? What point does Marshall make with his comment?

3. Do you find the Web site's main idea about national security persuasive? Why or why not?

4. To what extent can the actions taken by the U.S. government in the aftermath of the terrorist attacks of September 11 relate to the claim and the examples of this Web site?

Reviewing

**Recall /
Remember**

1. Explain the elements of argumentative writing.
2. Explain what credibility is and why it is important in persuasive writing.
3. What is analogy, and how do writers use it in their arguments? What are the limits of analogy for persuasive writing?
4. Why do writers sometimes appeal to authorities in their arguments? What questions should you ask about the authorities a writer uses in persuasive writing?
5. List and explain the fallacies of thinking outlined in this chapter. Why is it important to recognize them?

**Chapter
Summary**

In this chapter you have learned to apply your critical-thinking skills to a special kind of writing: argument. You have learned how writers develop arguments by using evidence in the form of examples and reasons to support their claims, and you have learned to identify and question the unstated assumptions that arguments rely on. You have also seen how writers use authority and testimony to argue for their ideas and beliefs. In addition, you have considered how to evaluate the credibility of writers by analyzing their knowledge, their use of sources, their consideration of multiple points of view, and their attempts to be fair and reasonable.

You have also learned about some types of fallacies, or errors in reasoning. Through practice with analyzing persuasive reading, you will improve your ability to read thoughtfully and critically. The focus of the next chapter is another special kind of reading: literature.

Enjoying and Interpreting Literature

Getting Ready

In many of your college courses you will be asked to read works of fiction, poetry, and drama. Literature is often assigned in psychology, sociology, history, philosophy, anthropology, political science, and many other courses. You may find this surprising, but many professors feel that literature expresses ideas in ways that nonfiction writing cannot. A story or novel can help you understand what life was like in another time or place or how other people experience the world—much more, perhaps, than if you were to read an academic explanation. A poem can help you understand a philosophical idea. A play can illustrate the effects of political and historical events. But most important, literature can bring pleasure to its readers.

You don't need to be intimidated by literature. The skills you've learned in this book—especially understanding a writer's main idea, reading interpretively and critically, making inferences, and examining a writer's language—can be applied to literature and help you understand it. This chapter introduces you to some ways to read literature with understanding and shows you how to apply your reading skills to poems and short stories.

Chapter Overview

Focusing
Questions

Do you read literature? Why or why not?

What has been your most positive experience in reading literature? What made it pleasurable?

What has been your most frustrating or unpleasant experience with literature? What do you think caused your frustration?

Why do you think teachers of subjects other than English assign short stories, novels, poetry, and drama in their courses?

What reading skills from previous chapters do you think will help you read literature? Why?

How can you gain confidence and competence when you read literature?

Everyday
Reading

Many people find poetry difficult to understand and argue that it's not relevant to their lives. But you hear poetry almost every day. Lyrics of popular songs share many of the characteristics of poems. For one thing, they usually rhyme. But there's more to song lyrics than just that. Popular songs have a very short time, usually about three minutes, to get an idea across. Because lyrics are rarely literal, different listeners will have different—often contradictory—interpretations of a song and often will argue over whose interpretation is correct. The same is true of poetry. Find the lyrics to your favorite song and think about them carefully. What do they mean? Why did the lyricist choose certain words and images? Compare your interpretation with a friend's. Chances are you'll have different ideas about the song's message.

Learning the Skills

■ Understanding Literary Writing

Because literary works have more than one meaning, you can interpret them according to your own way of reading. But be careful: Your understanding of a literary work must be based on its details. In reading a novel, for example, you might base your interpretation on how its characters act, what they say and how they say it, and what they say about each other. It's not very different from analyzing people in your own life. There's more, of course, to reading literature than understanding its characters. But if you concentrate on what happens in a work, and especially on its characters, you will be well on your way to understanding its meaning.

INTERPRETING A PARABLE

The following is an example of a very short work of literature—a parable—that we can use to see how literary interpretation works. A parable is a story with a moral or a main point that readers figure out from what happens. As with other forms of literature, different readers often understand a parable's moral in different ways.

This parable describes a group of young men who are studying to become Buddhist monks. They are preparing to devote their lives to prayer and religious observances. The first thing they are working on is learning how to keep silent.

Learning to Be Silent

The pupils of the Tendai school used to study meditation before Zen entered Japan. Four of them who were intimate friends promised one another to observe seven days of silence.

On the first day all were silent. Their meditation had begun auspiciously, but when night came and the oil lamps were growing dim one of the pupils could not help exclaiming to a servant: "Fix those lamps."

The second pupil was surprised to hear the first one talk. "We are not supposed to say a word," he remarked.

"You two are stupid. Why did you talk?" asked the third.

"I am the only one who has not talked," concluded the fourth pupil.

What is the situation in this little story? The four pupils have decided to be silent for a week. They are together at night on the first day when one of them speaks. Before long all four have spoken, thus breaking their promise to keep silent.

Each student speaks for a different reason. The first student's reason is given in the text of the story. He spoke because he wanted better light.

The second student, on the other hand, comments on the shared goal of the four pupils—to be silent. But in reminding the first speaker that he was not supposed to talk, the second pupil talks.

Why does the third pupil speak? Notice that he tells the two pupils who already spoke that they are "stupid." He may be right, but in saying so, he too talks. He then follows his comment by asking the other two pupils why they talked.

Now look at what the fourth pupil finally says. Isn't he boasting? Doesn't he try to act superior? Of course, he also talks, and thus he too breaks the promise to be silent.

How can we explain what happens to these pupils' intention to observe a week's silence—an intention they fail to observe on the very first night? We do that by making **inferences** about the purpose of the parable based on what we have observed in the action and dialogue of the story.

MAKING INFERENCES

You remember from Chapter 8 that inference is essential to all thoughtful reading. Making inferences is especially important when you read literature. By making inferences, you find something to say about a work—you interpret it.

Return to the parable for one more reading. Try to put together what you saw on your previous readings. What point do you think the storyteller might be attempting to convey? Once you have answered that, you have become involved in the act of interpreting literature. Your explanation of the parable's significance—what it shows—is one way to understand its meaning.

Exercise 11-1

Reread the parable on page 389 and make inferences about its meaning. Use the idea indicated in each question as the basis for your inference.

Example:

> Make an inference, based on the parable, about people and silence.
>
> *It is difficult for people to remain silent.*

1. Make an inference, based on the parable, about good friends and their promises to one another.

   Answers will vary.

2. Make an inference, based on the parable, about the importance of a promise versus the importance of physical comfort.

    _____

    _____

3. Make an inference, based on the parable, about people's need to feel superior to others as well as to fit in with the crowd.

    _____

    _____

4. Make an inference, based on the parable, about people and their judgments of others.

    _____

    _____

5. Make an inference, based on the parable, about feeling smart and acting foolishly.

    _____

    _____

. . . .

Working in a small group of four to six students, share your understanding of the parable with the others in your group. After discussing your ideas and hearing those of the others, write out a new possible moral for the parable.

Did you find in your discussion and from your own thinking that the parable shows something about how hard it is to keep silent? Does the parable also show how hard it is to be different from others, how easy it is to follow and do what others do? Maybe you focused on the motives the pupils had for speaking. Each pupil thinks he is better than the others. You might have suggested how the parable is partly about people's sense of superiority, or about their competitive nature, or about something else.

This little parable doesn't say a lot explicitly or directly. But when you start thinking about what it implies or suggests, there is much to consider. That's almost always the case with any kind of literary work.

■ Enjoying Literature

READING A POEM

When you read a poem you do many of the same things you do when you read an essay or a parable. First of all, you make observations about the work. In the case of a poem, your observations might concern the speaker—the voice you hear when you read the poem. Your initial observations about a poem might also concern the circumstances or the occasion behind what the speaker says. As with essays, when you read poems you connect your observations and make inferences based on what you see. Reading poetry requires the same kind of inferential reading and thinking you learned about in Chapters 8 and 9.

Even more than when you read a parable or a nonfiction work like an article or an essay, you need to attend very carefully to the words in a poem. This is particularly true for short lyric poems, which express a feeling or convey an attitude or idea with only a few lines.

Here is a short lyric poem by Robert Frost. Read it carefully three times.

The Span of Life

The old dog barks backward without getting up.
I can remember when he was a pup.

What observations can you make about these two lines? You probably noticed that both of them mention a dog. You might also notice that they end with the same sound—they rhyme.

Now read the poem aloud. What do you notice that you didn't see before? First, you might hear a difference between the lines: The sounds of the first line—the k and g, for example, and the repeated b sounds in "barks backward"—are difficult to articulate. In contrast, the second line is shorter and easier to pronounce. Try saying it again. Notice how the words of the second line just roll off your tongue.

You might imagine that the difficulty of pronouncing the poem's first line is similar to the difficulty an old dog would have in moving. What is he barking at? The poem doesn't say exactly. You have to make an inference. One possibility is that the dog barks at his master as the master comes home, or perhaps he hears a noise and barks in response. In either case the dog does not get up, probably because it isn't easy anymore for him to do so. He "barks backward," perhaps turning his head over his shoulder in the direction of the noise.

The second line of the poem invites you to consider the *relationship* between the old dog and a young pup. Imagine, for a moment, a puppy responding to a noise or to the return of his master. Most likely the puppy would not only get up but bound friskily to his master, to the door, or in the direction of the noise. From looking at the details of the lines and listening to their differing sounds, you see that the poem is built on contrast—the difference between an old dog and a young pup. This makes a good start toward understanding the poem's meaning—or at least one of its possible meanings.

There's no question that the dog is central to the poem. You might wonder, though, if the poem is not just about a dog but about a person as well. Since the speaker in the poem—the "I" who remembers—is a person, you have a possible reason to read the poem that way. The poem's title gives you another piece of evidence for this interpretation. Consider how, when the old dog barks, the speaker flashes back in memory to when the dog was young. The speaker remembers the "span" of years of the dog's life. Perhaps the poem suggests that the speaker is remembering the span of years that have flashed by in his own life as well. You cannot know this for sure; it is not directly stated in the poem. But you can infer it.

We have been asking quite a few questions about this little poem. It contains a lot of implications, or suggestions, in its details. But you can get at those implications only if you are willing to make inferences—to go out on a limb and think about possible meanings. Reading poems this way is similar to the kind of reading you learned and practiced in earlier chapters of this book. Both kinds of reading demand careful attention to the meanings of words and to the details of the text. But reading poetry differs in that you have to do more work in thinking about the implications of details. A poet does not explain things outright the way a writer of an essay or an article usually does.

Here is a poem by Margaret Walker. Read it carefully three times and then answer the questions in the exercise that follows.

Lineage

My grandmothers were strong.
They followed plows and bent to toil.
They moved through fields sowing seed.

They touched earth and grain grew.
They were full of sturdiness and singing.
My grandmothers were strong.

(continued)

> My grandmothers are full of memories.
> Smelling of soap and onion and wet clay
> With veins rolling roughly over quick hands
> They have many clean words to say.
> My grandmothers were strong.
> Why am I not as they?

Exercise 11-2

1. What words are repeated in the poem?

   "grandmothers," "they," "strong"

2. What line is repeated in the poem?

   "My grandmothers were strong."

3. What words and phrases are used to describe the speaker's grandmothers?

   "strong"; "full of sturdiness and singing"; "full of memories"; "smelling of

   soap and onion and wet clay"; "veins rolling roughly over quick hands"

4. What sense do you make of the last line? How is this last line different from the others in the poem?

   The speaker feels inadequate in comparison with her grandmothers.

   She does not feel as capable — as "strong" — as they were.

5. Is the poem's title appropriate? Why or why not? Look up *lineage* in your dictionary. Which meaning applies to the poem?

   The title is appropriate because the poem is about the speaker's

   connection to her grandmothers — her ancestors. "Lineage" means

   "ancestry."

READING A SHORT STORY

Everything you have been doing to interpret parables and poems you can do when you read and interpret other kinds of fiction. One of the most popular types of fiction—and one assigned often in college courses—is the short story.

When you read a short story, the first thing you will do is make observations about it. Your observations might include what happens, who the characters are (especially what they say and do), where the story takes place, who is telling the story, and what kinds of details the author provides. Just as when you read nonfiction works or poetry, you make connections among your observations and make inferences based on what you observe.

Other things to look for when reading fiction include the setting of the story; its plot, or sequence of events; its point of view, or the angle of vision from which it is told; its details, including objects described, the location of the action, and physical descriptions of characters; and its language, including dialogue.

As you read the following short story by Sandra Cisneros, pay close attention to the details.

Barbie-Q

Yours is the one with mean eyes and a ponytail. Striped swimsuit, stilettos, sunglasses, and gold hoop earrings. Mine is the one with bubble hair. Red swimsuit, stilettos, pearl earrings, and a wire stand. But that's all we can afford, besides one extra outfit apiece. Yours, "Red Flair," sophisticated A-line coatdress with a Jackie Kennedy pillbox hat, white gloves, handbag, and heels included. Mine, "Solo in the Spotlight," evening elegance in black glitter strapless gown with a puffy skirt at the bottom like a mermaid tail, formal-length gloves, pink chiffon scarf, and mike included. From so much dressing and undressing, the black glitter wears off where her titties stick out. This and a dress invented from an old sock when we cut holes here and here and here, the cuff rolled over for the glamorous, fancy-free, off-the-shoulder look.

Every time the same story. Your Barbie is roommates with my Barbie, and my Barbie's boyfriend comes over and your Barbie steals him, okay? Kiss kiss kiss. Then the two Barbies fight. You dumbbell! He's mine. On no he's not, you stinky! Only Ken's invisible, right? Because we don't have money for a stupid-looking boy doll when we'd rather both ask for a new Barbie outfit next Christmas. We

(continued)

have to make do with your mean-eyed Barbie and my bubblehead Barbie and our one outfit apiece not including the sock dress.

Until next Sunday when we are walking through the flea market on Maxwell Street and *there!* Lying on the street next to some tool bits, and platform shoes with the heels all squashed, and a fluorescent green wicker wastebasket, and aluminum foil, and hubcaps, and a pink shag rug, and windshield wiper blades, and dusty mason jars, and a coffee can full of rusty nails. *There!* Where? Two Mattel boxes. One with the "Career Gal" ensemble, snappy black-and-white business suit, three-quarter-length sleeve jacket with kick-pleat skirt, red sleeveless shell, gloves, pumps, and matching hat included. The other, "Sweet Dreams," dreamy pink-and-white plaid nightgown and matching robe, lace-trimmed slippers, hairbrush and hand mirror included. How much? Please, please, please, please, please, please, please, until they say okay.

On the outside you and me skipping and humming but inside we are doing loopity-loops and pirouetting. Until at the next vendor's stand, next to boxed pies, and bright orange toilet brushes, and rubber gloves, and wrench sets, and bouquets of feather flowers, and glass towel racks, and steel wool, and Alvin and the Chipmunks records, *there!* And *there!* And *there!* And *there!* and *there!* and *there!* and *there!* Bendable Legs Barbie with her new page-boy hairdo. Midge, Barbie's best friend. Ken, Barbie's boyfriend. Skipper, Barbie's little sister. Tutti and Todd, Barbie and Skipper's tiny twin sister and brother. Skipper's friends, Scooter and Ricky. Alan, Ken's buddy. And Francie, Barbie's MOD'ern cousin.

Everybody today selling toys, all of them damaged with water and smelling of smoke. Because a big toy warehouse on Halsted Street burned down yesterday—see there?—the smoke still rising and drifting across the Dan Ryan expressway. And now there is a big fire sale at Maxwell Street, today only.

So what if we don't get our new Bendable Legs Barbie and Midge and Ken and Skipper and Tutti and Todd and Scooter and Ricky and Alan and Francie in nice clean boxes and had to buy them on Maxwell Street, all water-soaked and sooty. So what if our Barbies smell like smoke when you hold them up to your nose even after you wash and wash and wash them. And if the prettiest doll, Barbie's MOD'ern cousin Francie with real eyelashes, eyelash brush included, has a left foot that's melted a little—so? If you dress her in her new "Prom Pinks" outfit, satin splendor with matching coat, gold belt, clutch, and hair bow included, so long as you don't lift her dress, right?—who's to know.

What happens in this story? Not much, really. Two girls buy damaged dolls at a flea market. But once you start noticing the details, you see that in only five paragraphs the story tells you much more than that.

Besides what happens, you might observe the details about the girls' dolls. They have one doll and one extra outfit apiece. They improvised a dress with a sock. Based on this observation and on the narrator's comment that they can't afford a boy doll or extra outfits, you can infer that the girls are poor.

Consider, also, how the girls play with their dolls. One has been dressed and undressed so many times that the doll's outfit is wearing thin. The girls make up the same story every time they play. From these details you might infer that the girls have learned to be happy with what they have.

Now consider the details of the flea market. Notice how the new dolls are mixed in jumbled piles of miscellaneous junk. From this, you might infer that the vendors see no value in the dolls. But you can see, from the girls' excitement over them, that they consider these dolls an unbelievable treasure. You know they are thrilled because the narrator says that "inside we are doing loopity-loops and pirouetting."

Finally, think carefully about how Cisneros uses the dolls to say something about the girls and their lives. If you read closely, you'll notice that there are important similarities between the dolls and the girls that play with them. The first Barbies in the story have limited accessories: Like the girls, they don't have much. The extra outfits are fantasy wardrobes that let the girls pretend the dolls are a glamorous singer and a wealthy sophisticate. You can imagine, based on how the narrator describes their play, that the girls fantasize about their own futures as well. But what about all of the new dolls? They smell bad; they're water-soaked; one is slightly melted. Because the girls identify with their dolls, you might conclude that the girls feel damaged and unvalued themselves.

Exercise 11-3

Reread "Barbie-Q" and answer the following questions about it.

Example:

> What are the names of the dolls' outfits? What do they have in common?
>
> *The outfits are called "Red Flair," "Solo in the Spotlight," "Career Gal,"*
>
> *"Sweet Dreams," and "Prom Pinks." The names suggest wealth,*
>
> *sophistication, fantasy, and being the center of attention.*

1. What story do the girls use every time they play with their old Barbies?

   The Barbies are roommates. One of them steals the other's boyfriend,

   and they fight over who gets to keep him.

2. Does the girls' play story have any similarity to their real lives? If so, what is it?

   Yes. Like the girls, the Barbies have one boy doll available to them, but

   he's imaginary. They have to share him or battle over his possession,

   just as the girls have to share their toys.

3. The girls play with real Barbies made by Mattel, not generic dolls, and they make a point of using the official names the toy company gives to the dolls and their outfits. What can you infer from this detail?

   The brand name is important to them. Although they're poor, the girls

   want the real thing, not an imitation. Readers can also infer that they

   have thoroughly accepted American consumerist values.

4. Take a close look at how the narrator describes the dolls as the story progresses. How do her descriptions change? What can you infer about the girls' attitude toward the dolls from this detail?

   The first two dolls are described in great detail. The first new dolls they

   find are also described thoroughly: what they look like, what accessories

   they come with. But as the girls find more and more dolls at the flea

   market, the detail dwindles down to just the names of the dolls. Readers

   can infer from this that the more dolls the girls have, the less important

   or precious they become to them.

5. Reread the final paragraph. Do you think the girls are proud or ashamed of their new dolls? Why? Be sure to use details from the story to back up your analysis.

Answers will vary.

_____

_____

_____

_____

· ·

■ The Elements of Literature

Reading literature is similar to reading any other kind of writing. You pay attention to its details, you look for the main idea, you make observations and draw conclusions. All of the reading skills you have learned in this book can be applied to reading poems and short stories.

You learned in Chapter 7 that academic disciplines often use specialized vocabularies. This is certainly true of literature. English teachers, literary critics, and people who read fiction and poetry for pleasure use special terms to describe what they read. In this section of the chapter you will learn what these terms are and how they can be compared to the elements of reading you have been learning.

PLOT

Plot is the sequence of action as it unfolds, the arrangement of events that make up a story. Plots often turn on a conflict that is resolved by the end of the work. Whether you are reading a novel, such as Jane Austen's *Pride and Prejudice,* an epic poem by Homer, or Shakespeare's play *Hamlet,* you typically expect a conflict that complicates the literary work, pushing it toward a climax and ultimately a resolution.

STRUCTURE

Related to plot, **structure** is the design or form of the completed action. In examining plot you look at how one action leads into or ties in with another. In examining structure, you look for patterns, the design the work possesses as a whole. Structure in literature is comparable to the organizational structures you studied in Chapter 6. A literary work's structure appears in its recurring details of action, gesture, dialogue, and description. It appears in shifts and changes of direction and character relationships. You could describe the structure of Sandra Cisneros's "Barbie-Q," for example, as a comparison and contrast or as an analogy.

You might notice, also, how the story is structured around descriptions of the dolls.

SETTING

Setting is the place or location—the context—of a story's, novel's, poem's, or play's action, along with the time(s) in which it occurs. The setting of the story "Barbie-Q," for example, is the Maxwell Street flea market. For some writers setting is essential to meaning. More than a simple backdrop for action, setting can provide a historical and cultural context that enhances readers' understanding of a writer's plots and characters.

CHARACTER

Character is the heart of fiction and drama. Often you read to find out what happens to the characters, how the plot works out for them, sometimes identifying with them. Characters become, for a time at least, intensely real and perhaps affecting enough to influence readers' lives after the characters have disappeared from the page or the stage.

In fiction and drama, characters' relationships with one another are among the reader's most important concerns. The relationships between characters contain essential clues to understanding a story's or play's significance. Fictional and dramatic characters also represent values that convey an author's attitude and ideas that embody the meaning of the work. Authors have a number of ways to convey attitudes, ideas, and values about their characters:

- What characters say—their speech
- What characters do—their actions
- What characters think and feel—their consciousness
- How characters look—their dress and physical appearance
- What others think about them—judgments

POINT OF VIEW

Point of view is the author's choice of who tells the story and how it is told. Just as you consider a writer's point of view when you read a nonfiction work, being aware of tone, bias, and slanting, paying attention to the point of view of a work of literature will help you read it critically.

Fiction writers use special kinds of point of view in telling a story. In *objective* point of view, the writer of a story or a novel shows what happens without directly stating more than what the action and dialogue of

the story imply. Stories with narrators who do not participate in the action are typically presented from a *third-person* point of view, in contrast to a *first-person* point of view, in which the narrator or narrators participate in the action directly, as in the case of the young girl who tells the story in "Barbie-Q." Whether they use a first- or a third-person narrator, writers of literature must decide how much to let the narrator know about the characters. Narrators who know everything about a work's characters are *omniscient* or all-knowing; narrators who know only some things about the characters possess *limited omniscience*.

A writer's choice of point of view will affect how you respond to the characters. Your response is affected especially by the degree of the narrator's knowledge, the narrator's objectivity, and the extent of the narrator's participation in the action. It is also affected by your sense of the narrator as a trustworthy guide to a work's characters and action. It is your responsibility as a reader to determine a narrator's reliability and to estimate the truth of what he or she discloses.

STYLE

Style refers to a writer's choice of words and to his or her arrangement of them in sentences and paragraphs. You can analyze style in literature much the same way you examine language (Chapter 7) and sentences (Chapter 5) in a nonfiction essay or article. Style is a writer's verbal identity. Aspects of style to consider when analyzing a fictional work include *diction* (the writer's choice of words), *syntax* (the order of words in sentences), *imagery, figurative language,* selection of *detail, pacing* of action, and the amount, kind, and purpose of *description*.

Diction.   **Diction** refers to a writer's choice of words and their connotations. In reading a poem, for example, it is necessary to know what the words mean, but it is equally important to understand what the words imply or suggest. Robert Frost in "The Span of Life," for example, uses "pup" rather than "young dog" to describe the old dog's youth; the word suggests playfulness and naiveté, which is important to your interpretation of the poem. Considering the connotations of the words used in a work of literature enables you to better understand its theme and the language resources the writer employs in expressing the theme.

Imagery.   Literary works are grounded in the concrete and the specific — in details that stimulate our senses. When specific details appear in poems, short stories, and novels, they are called images. An **image** is a concrete representation of a sense impression, feeling, or idea. Images may appeal to the senses of sight, hearing, touch, taste, or smell.

Poetry describes specific things: daffodils, fires, finches' wings. Typically poets describe such things in specific terms: the color of the daffodils, the glare of the fire, the beating of the finches' wings. From these and other specific details readers derive an understanding of the meaning of poems and the feelings they convey. The images in "Barbie-Q"—the jumble of the flea market, the smoke of the burning warehouse, the dolls' clothing, the smell of the damaged dolls—all contribute to your understanding of the girls' experience and their attitudes toward it.

Figurative Language. Language can be literal or figurative. **Literal language** conveys the meaning of the words themselves (their denotations); **figurative language** conveys meaning that differs from the actual meanings of the words. The most important figurative language in literature is the *metaphor* and the *simile*. As you learned in Chapter 7, the heart of both these figures of speech is a comparison between normally unrelated things. Simile establishes its comparison by the use of *like, as,* or *as though*. Metaphor uses no such verbal clue. When Frost's speaker says of his old dog, "I can remember when he was a pup," you might think of the dog's life as a metaphor for the speaker's. Similarly, it's possible to read the dolls in "Barbie-Q" as a metaphor for the girls themselves.

SYMBOL

Symbols in literature are objects, actions, or events that convey a meaning beyond their literal significance. Yet how do you know if a detail is symbolic? Although you cannot always be certain about the symbolic significance of any detail, you can be alert to its possible symbolic overtones. Two questions can serve as guidelines for thinking about symbols in literary works.

1. *How important is the object, action, gesture, or dialogue?* Does it appear more than once? Does it occur at a climactic moment? Is it described in detail?

2. *Does a symbolic interpretation make sense?* Does it fit in with a literal or common-sense explanation?

Think about the dolls in "Barbie-Q." Can they be read as a symbol? Certainly they're important to the story: They appear throughout it; they are its subject, described in loving detail. Does a symbolic interpretation of them make sense? Possibly: They could be read as symbols of the girls' lives, as symbols of American consumer culture, or, perhaps, as symbols of class difference. All of those topics are important to the literal telling of the story, so it's reasonable to interpret the Barbies as symbols of those ideas.

THEME

A literary work's **theme** is its main idea, formulated as a generalization. The theme of a fable is its moral; the theme of a parable is its teaching; the theme of a novel or play is its implied view of life and conduct. Themes in fiction, poetry, and drama are most often presented indirectly rather than directly stated. More often than not, theme is less presented than implied. A possible theme of "The Span of Life" is that a life passes quickly. Another is that a life span can flash through a person's memory very fast. Different themes can also be expressed, such as that old age brings both backward glances and physical deterioration.

IRONY

Irony is not so much an element of literature as a pervasive quality in it. Irony may appear in literature in three ways: In a work's language (or style), in its incidents (or plot), or in its point of view. As you saw in Chapter 7, writers employ **verbal irony** to convey a character's limited understanding. They employ **situational irony** to reveal discrepancies between what seems to be and what is or between what is expected and what actually happens. Writers use **dramatic irony** to reveal the difference between what the characters know and what the readers or viewers know, sometimes directing our responses by letting us see things their characters do not.

Here is a poem by Theodore Roethke. Read it carefully and then answer the questions in the exercise that follows.

My Papa's Waltz

The whiskey on your breath
Could make a small boy dizzy;
But I held on like death:
Such waltzing was not easy.

We romped until the pans
Slid from the kitchen shelf;
My mother's countenance
Could not unfrown itself.

The hand that held my wrist
Was battered on one knuckle;
At every step I missed
My right ear scraped a buckle.

(continued)

> You beat time on my head
> With a palm caked hard by dirt,
> Then waltzed me off to bed
> Still clinging to your shirt.

Exercise 11-4

Answer questions about the elements of literature as they apply to the poem "My Papa's Waltz" by Theodore Roethke.

Example:

Who is the speaker of the poem?

an older male remembering himself as a small boy

1. The title of this poem is "My Papa's Waltz." What kind of "waltz" does the speaker remember? One that was graceful? Gentle? Smooth? Sober?

   The father is intoxicated and "waltzes" the child painfully around the

   room.

2. What is the setting of the poem?

   The speaker's childhood home, specifically the kitchen

3. Which words and images in the poem imply or refer to music, dance, or play?

   "waltz" (title); "waltzing"; "romped"; "every step"; "beat time"; "waltzed"

4. Which words and images imply or refer to pain, anger, hardship, or violence?

   "whiskey on your breath"; "dizzy"; "held on like death"; "Such waltzing

   was not easy"; "My mother's countenance / could not unfrown itself";

   "battered on one knuckle"; "ear scraped a buckle"; "palm caked hard by

   dirt"; "clinging"

5. What kinds of sentences does the poet use—long and complicated "adult" sentences or short and direct "child" sentences? Describe the punctuation of each stanza. How is the punctuation related to the subject matter of each stanza?

The sentences follow an easy, uncomplicated "child" structure. Each

stanza ends with a period, and there are no periods within stanzas. Each

stanza focuses on a different topic, and the period brings that topic to

an end.

6. Why is the poem titled "My Papa's Waltz," rather than "My Father's Waltz"? Although *papa* and *father* mean the same thing ("a male parent"), the connotations of the words are different. What is the difference? How does this work with the answer you gave to question 5?

The word "papa" is a more childish word than "father," thus reinforcing

the childlike style of the poem. Arguably, the word "papa" is a more

affectionate word than "father," and less formal.

7. By using the words "your" ("The whiskey on your breath") and "you" ("You beat time on my head"), the speaker seems to be talking directly to his father. What is the speaker's attitude to his father? Is the speaker angry, accusing his father of physical abuse? Is the speaker loving? Forgiving? Sad? Judgmental? Other?

Answers will vary.

8. The sound heard most often in the first stanza is something like a hissing noise, made by the consonants *s* and *z* in the words "whiskey," "small," "dizzy," "such," "waltzing," and "easy." What could that sound symbolize or represent?

Answers will vary. Possibilities: the child's breathlessness as he is

waltzed around the room; the father's labored breathing; the father's

breathlessness

9. What can you say about the theme of the poem?

   Answers will vary. Possibilities: We can look back with both pain and love

   at our parents' treatment of us. Parents can be told what living with

   them was like from a child's point of view. Childhood's song and dance

   can create today's poetry.

10. Some readers interpret the situation described in this poem as child abuse; others disagree, arguing that the speaker remembers the incident fondly, not with bitterness or anger. What do you think? Be sure to use details from the poem to support your interpretation.

   Answers will vary.

Applying the Skills

Reading the Parts

Edgar Allan Poe is considered one of the great masters of the American short story. Born in Boston, Massachusetts, in 1809, he was orphaned at the age of three and raised by tobacco merchant John Allan. Poe attended the University of Virginia but was forced to leave as a result of heavy gambling debts; he later attended West Point but was expelled and never finished his university education. Nonetheless, Poe made his living as an editor and a literary critic, writing his own stories and poems on the side. Edgar Allan Poe died a bizarre death in 1849: He was found unconscious in a Baltimore gutter—possibly drunk, possibly under the influence of opium (he was an addict), possibly, some scholars now believe, suffering from the end stages of rabies. He died four days later. The story that follows is one of Poe's best-known and most-loved works. As you read it, think carefully about the story's main character—its narrator—and consider his reliability and the story's point of view. Pay attention to details and make connections among them as you read. After you have read each section and answered the questions that follow it, move on to the next part. You will have the opportunity to read the story as a whole when you finish.

EDGAR ALLAN POE
The Tell-Tale Heart

True!—nervous—very, very dreadfully nervous I had been and am; but why *will* you say that I am mad? The disease had sharpened my senses—not destroyed—not dulled them. Above all was the sense of hearing acute. I heard all things in the heaven and in the earth. I heard many things in hell. How, then, am I mad? Hearken! and observe how healthily—how calmly I can tell you the whole story.

1

It is impossible to say how first the idea entered my brain; but once conceived, it haunted me day and night. Object there was none. Passion there was none. I loved the old man. He had never wronged me. He had never given me insult. For his gold I had no desire. I

2

think it was his eye! yes, it was this! One of his eyes resembled that of a vulture—a pale blue eye, with a film over it. Whenever it fell upon me, my blood ran cold; and so by degrees—very gradually—I made up my mind to take the life of the old man, and thus rid myself of the eye for ever.

Now this is the point. You fancy me mad. Madmen know nothing. But you should have seen *me*. You should have seen how wisely I proceeded—with what caution—with what foresight—with what dissimulation I went to work! I was never kinder to the old man than during the whole week before I killed him. And every night, about midnight, I turned the latch of his door and opened it—oh, so gently! And then, when I had made an opening sufficient for my head, I put in a dark lantern, all closed, closed, so that no light shone out, and then I thrust in my head. Oh, you would have laughed to see how cunningly I thrust it in! I moved it slowly—very, very slowly, so that I might not disturb the old man's sleep. It took me an hour to place my whole head within the opening so far that I could see him as he lay upon his bed. Ha—would a madman have been so wise as this? And then, when my head was well in the room, I undid the lantern cautiously—oh, so cautiously—cautiously (for the hinges creaked)—I undid it just so much that a single thin ray fell upon the vulture eye. And this I did for seven long nights—every night just after midnight—but I found the eye always closed; and so it was impossible to do the work; for it was not the old man who vexed me, but his Evil Eye. And every morning, when the day broke, I went boldly into the chamber, and spoke courageously to him, calling him by name in a hearty tone, and inquiring how he had passed the night. So you see he would have been a very profound old man, indeed, to suspect that every night, just at twelve, I looked in upon him while he slept.

Upon the eighth night I was more than usually cautious in opening the door. A watch's minute hand moves more quickly than did mine. Never before that night had I *felt* the extent of my own powers—of my sagacity. I could scarcely contain my feelings of triumph. To think that there I was, opening the door, little by little, and he not even to dream of my secret deeds or thoughts. I fairly chuckled at the idea; and perhaps he heard me; for he moved on the bed suddenly, as if startled. Now you may think that I drew back—but no. His room was as black as pitch with the thick darkness (for the shutters were close fastened, through fear of robbers), and so I

3

4

knew that he could not see the opening of the door, and I kept pushing it on steadily, steadily.

I had my head in, and was about to open the lantern, when my thumb slipped upon the tin fastening, and the old man sprang up in the bed, crying out— "Who's there?"   5

I kept quite still and said nothing. For a whole hour I did not move a muscle, and in the meantime I did not hear him lie down. He was still sitting up on the bed listening;—just as I have done, night after night, hearkening to the death watches in the wall.   6

1. What can you infer about the mental state of the narrator?

   a. He's happy.

   b. He's deranged.

   c. He's sullen.

   d. He's depressed.

2. What is the setting of the story in paragraphs 4–6?

   a. a haunted mansion

   b. the old man's kitchen

   c. the old man's bedroom

   d. a cemetery

3. To what does the narrator compare one of the old man's eyes?

   a. the eye of a vulture

   b. a billiard ball

   c. the moon

   d. the sea

4. Which of the following words best describes the language used by Edgar Allan Poe in this story?

   a. fanciful

   b. formal

   c. relaxed

   d. old-fashioned

5. By referring to the old man's eye as he does—for example, the "Evil Eye"—the narrator is trying to convince his readers that his murder of the old man was

   a. a sin.

  (b.) a justifiable act.

   c. a symptom of madness.

   d. a mistake.

Presently I heard a slight groan, and I knew it was the groan of mortal terror. It was not a groan of pain or of grief—oh, no!—it was the low stifled sound that arises from the bottom of the soul when overcharged with awe. I knew the sound well. Many a night, just at midnight, when all the world slept, it was welled up from my own bosom, deepening with its dreadful echo, the terrors that distracted me. I say I knew it well. I knew what the old man felt, and pitied him, although I chuckled at heart. I knew that he had been lying awake ever since the first slight noise, when he had turned in the bed. His fears had been ever since growing upon him. He had been trying to fancy them causeless, but could not. He had been saying to himself—"It is nothing but the wind in the chimney—it is only a mouse crossing the floor," or "it is merely a cricket which has made a single chirp." Yes, he has been trying to comfort himself with these suppositions; but he had found all in vain. *All in vain;* because Death, in approaching him, had stalked with his black shadow before him, and enveloped the victim. And it was the mournful influence of the unperceived shadow that caused him to feel—although he neither saw nor heard—to *feel* the presence of my head within the room.   7

When I had waited a long time, very patiently, without hearing him lie down, I resolved to open a little—a very, very little crevice in the lantern. So I opened it—you cannot imagine how stealthily, stealthily—until, at length, a single dim ray, like the thread of the spider, shot from out the crevice and full upon the vulture eye.   8

It was open—wide, wide open—and I grew furious as I gazed upon it. I saw it with perfect distinctness—all a dull blue, with a hideous veil over it that chilled the very marrow in my bones, but I could see nothing else of the old man's face or person: for I had directed the ray as if by instinct, precisely upon the damned spot.   9

And now have I not told you that what you mistake for madness is but over-acuteness of the senses?—now, I say, there came to my   10 ears a low, dull, quick sound, such as a watch makes when enveloped in cotton. I knew *that* sound well too. It was the beating of the old man's heart. It increased my fury, as the beating of a drum stimulates the soldier into courage.

But even yet I refrained and kept still. I scarcely breathed. I held the lantern motionless. I tried how steadily I could maintain the ray upon the eye. Meantime the hellish tattoo of the heart increased. It grew quicker and quicker, and louder and louder every instant. The old man's terror *must* have been extreme! It grew louder, I say, louder every moment!—do you mark me well? I have told you that I am nervous: so I am. And now at the dead hour of the night, amid the dreadful silence of that old house, so strange a noise as this excited me to uncontrollable terror. Yet, for some minutes longer I refrained and stood still. But the beating grew louder, louder! I thought the heart must burst. And now a new anxiety seized me—the sound would be heard by a neighbor! The old man's hour had come! With a loud yell, I threw open the lantern and leaped into the room. He shrieked once—once only. In an instant I dragged him to the floor, and pulled the heavy bed over him. I then smiled gaily, to find the deed so far done. But, for many minutes, the heart beat on with a muffled sound. This, however, did not vex me; it would not be heard through the wall. At length it ceased. The old man was dead. I removed the bed and examined the corpse. Yes, he was stone, stone dead. I placed my hand upon the heart and held it there many minutes. There was no pulsation. He was stone dead. His eye would trouble me no more.

11

6. By stating that "what you mistake for madness is but over-acuteness of the senses," the narrator indicates that he

   a.   thinks of himself as extremely frightened.

   b.   thinks of himself as a master manipulator.

   (c.) thinks of himself as extremely cunning.

   d.   thinks of himself as guilt-ridden and lacking in intellect.

7. What is the unstated main idea of paragraph 7?

   (a.) The old man is extremely frightened.

   b.   The old man is calm.

   c.   The old man is asleep.

   d.   The old man is lighthearted.

8. The first simile in paragraph 10, "such as a watch makes when enveloped in cotton," is used to describe
   a. the sound of the wind outside.
   b. the sound of the old man crying.
   c. the sound of the old man snoring.
   d. the sound of the beating of the old man's heart.

9. How does the narrator murder the old man?
   a. He smothers him with a pillow.
   b. He pulls the old man's bed on top of him, either suffocating or crushing him.
   c. He stabs him repeatedly in the heart.
   d. He stabs him in the eye.

10. What is the narrator's ultimate purpose in killing the old man?
    a. The old man killed the narrator's sister, so the narrator kills him to avenge her death.
    b. The old man has not paid his rent, and the narrator kills him out of rage.
    c. The narrator kills the old man so that he will no longer have to look at the old man's eye.
    d. The killing was an accident.

If still you think me mad, you will think so no longer when I describe the wise precautions I took for the concealment of the body. The night waned, and I worked hastily, but in silence. First of all I dismembered the corpse. I cut off the head and the arms and the legs.   12

I then took up three planks from the flooring of the chamber, and deposited all between the scantlings. I then replaced the boards so cleverly, so cunningly, that no human eye—not even *his*—could have detected anything wrong. There was nothing to wash out—no stain of any kind—no blood-spot whatever. I had been too wary for that. A tub had caught all—ha! ha!   13

When I had made an end of these labors, it was four o'clock—still dark as midnight. As the bell sounded the hour, there came a knocking at the street door. I went down to open it with a light   14 heart—for what had I *now* to fear? There entered three men, who introduced themselves, with perfect suavity, as officers of the police. A shriek had been heard by a neighbor during the night; suspicion of foul play had been aroused; information had been lodged at the police office, and they (the officers) had been deputed to search the premises.

I smiled—for *what* had I to fear? I bade the gentlemen welcome. The shriek, I said, was my own in a dream. The old man, I mentioned, was absent in the country. I took my visitors all over the house. I bade them search—search *well*. I led them, at length, to *his* chamber. I showed them his treasures, secure, undisturbed. In the enthusiasm of my confidence, I brought chairs into the room, and desired them *here* to rest from their fatigues, while I myself, in the wild audacity of my perfect triumph, placed my own seat upon the very spot beneath which reposed the corpse of the victim.   15

The officers were satisfied. My *manner* had convinced them. I was singularly at ease. They sat, and while I answered cheerily, they chatted familiar things. But, ere long, I felt myself getting pale and wished them gone. My head ached, and I fancied a ringing in my ears: but still they sat and still chatted. The ringing became more distinct:—it continued and became more distinct: I talked more freely to get rid of the feeling: but it continued and gained definitiveness—until, at length, I found that the noise was *not* within my ears.   16

No doubt I now grew *very* pale;—but I talked more fluently, and with a heightened voice. Yet the sound increased—and what could I do? It was *a low, dull, quick sound—much such a sound as a watch makes when enveloped in cotton*. I gasped for breath—and yet the officers heard it not. I talked more quickly—more vehemently; but the noise steadily increased. I arose and argued about trifles, in a high key and with violent gesticulations, but the noise steadily increased. Why *would* they not be gone? I paced the floor to and fro with heavy strides, as if excited to fury by the observation of the men—but the noise steadily increased. Oh God! what *could* I do? I foamed—I raved—I swore! I swung the chair upon which I had been sitting, and grated it upon the boards, but the noise arose over all and continually increased. It grew louder—louder—*louder!* And still the men chatted pleasantly, and smiled. Was it possible they heard not? Almighty God—no, no! They heard!—they suspected!—they *knew!*—they were making a mockery of my horror—this I thought, and this I think. But any   17

> thing was better than this agony! Any thing was more tolerable than this derision! I could bear those hypocritical smiles no longer! I felt that I must scream or die—and now—again!—hark! louder! louder! louder! *louder!*—
>
> "Villains!" I shrieked, "dissemble no more! I admit the deed!—tear up the planks—here, here!—it is the beating of his hideous heart!" 18

11. What does the narrator's use of the following words in paragraphs 13–15 convey: "cunningly," "cleverly," "audacity," "perfect triumph"?

    a. The narrator is smug and thinks that he will never be caught.

    b. The narrator is nervous and will probably leave town to avoid being caught.

    c. The narrator will probably commit suicide.

    d. The narrator feels remorseful about what he has done.

12. What is the author trying to convey in paragraphs 16–18?

    a. how devious the narrator is

    b. how stupid the police officers are

    c. the fact that the officers aren't really in the room with the narrator

    d. how insane the narrator really is

13. What was the author's purpose in writing this story?

    a. to inform

    b. to discuss the problem of mental illness

    c. to entertain

    d. to persuade

14. Why do you think the narrator sits directly above the buried corpse?

    a. He is so confident he won't be caught that he feels secure doing so.

    b. He wants to cover a bloodstain.

    c. He wants to cover a piece of the old man's clothing.

    d. He wants to distract the police officers from a bloodstain on the bed.

15. What does the beating heart symbolize in this story?

    a.   life

    b.   death

    (c.) guilt

    d.   remorse

Reading the Whole

Now that you've read Edgar Allan Poe's "The Tell-Tale Heart" in its parts and practiced making observations and interpreting its individual details, you're ready to read the story in its entirety. As you read the whole story, continue to apply your skills of critical reading and interpretive reading. Pay attention to the story's imagery, symbolism, pacing, and point of view. "The Tell-Tale Heart" is considered an early version of the modern horror story. Do you agree? Are you frightened by it? Why or why not? Think about your answers to those questions as you read.

EDGAR ALLAN POE
The Tell-Tale Heart

True!—nervous—very, very dreadfully nervous I had been and am; but why *will* you say that I am mad? The disease had sharpened my senses—not destroyed—not dulled them. Above all was the sense of hearing acute. I heard all things in the heaven and in the earth. I heard many things in hell. How, then, am I mad? Hearken! and observe how healthily—how calmly I can tell you the whole story.

It is impossible to say how first the idea entered my brain; but once conceived, it haunted me day and night. Object there was none. Passion there was none. I loved the old man. He had never wronged me. He had never given me insult. For his gold I had no desire. I think it was his eye! yes, it was this! One of his eyes resembled that of a vulture—a pale blue eye, with a film over it. Whenever it fell upon me, my blood ran cold; and so by degrees—very gradually— I made up my mind to take the life of the old man, and thus rid myself of the eye for ever.

Now this is the point. You fancy me mad. Madmen know nothing. But you should have seen *me.* You should have seen how wisely I proceeded—with what caution—with what foresight—with what dissimulation I went to work! I was never kinder to the old man than during the whole week before I killed him. And every night, about midnight, I turned the latch of his door and opened it—oh, so gently! And then, when I had made an opening sufficient for my head, I put in a dark lantern, all closed, closed, so that no light shone out, and then I thrust in my head. Oh, you would have laughed to see how cunningly I thrust it in! I moved it slowly—very, very slowly, so that I might not disturb the old man's sleep. It took me an hour to place my whole head within the opening so far that I could see him as he lay upon his bed. Ha—would a madman have been so wise as this? And then, when my head was well in the room, I undid the lantern cautiously—oh, so cautiously—cautiously (for the hinges creaked)—I undid it just so much that a single thin ray fell upon the vulture eye. And this I did for seven long nights—every night just after midnight—but I found the eye always closed; and so it was impossible to do the work; for it was not the old man who vexed me, but his Evil Eye. And every morning, when the day broke, I went boldly into the chamber, and spoke courageously to him, calling him by name in a hearty tone, and inquiring how he had passed the night. So you see he would have been a very profound old man, indeed, to suspect that every night, just at twelve, I looked in upon him while he slept.

Upon the eighth night I was more than usually cautious in opening the door. A watch's minute hand moves more quickly than did mine. Never before that night had I *felt* the extent of my own powers—of my sagacity. I could scarcely contain my feelings of triumph. To think that there I was, opening the door, little by little, and he not even to dream of my secret deeds or thoughts. I fairly chuckled at the idea; and perhaps he heard me; for he moved on the bed suddenly, as if startled. Now you may think that I drew back—but no. His room was as black as pitch with the thick darkness (for the shutters were close fastened, through fear of robbers), and so I knew that he could not see the opening of the door, and I kept pushing it on steadily, steadily.

I had my head in, and was about to open the lantern, when my thumb slipped upon the tin fastening, and the old man sprang up in the bed, crying out—"Who's there?"

I kept quite still and said nothing. For a whole hour I did not move a muscle, and in the meantime I did not hear him lie down. He was still sitting up on the bed listening;—just as I have done, night after night, hearkening to the death watches in the wall.

Presently I heard a slight groan, and I knew it was the groan of mortal terror. It was not a groan of pain or of grief—oh, no!—it was the low stifled sound that arises from the bottom of the soul when overcharged with awe. I knew the sound well. Many a night, just at midnight, when all the world slept, it was welled up from my own bosom, deepening with its dreadful echo, the terrors that distracted me. I say I knew it well. I knew what the old man felt, and pitied him, although I chuckled at heart. I knew that he had been lying awake ever since the first slight noise, when he had turned in the bed. His fears had been ever since growing upon him. He had been trying to fancy them causeless, but could not. He had been saying to himself—"It is nothing but the wind in the chimney—it is only a mouse crossing the floor," or "it is merely a cricket which has made a single chirp." Yes, he has been trying to comfort himself with these suppositions; but he had found all in vain. *All in vain*; because Death, in approaching him, had stalked with his black shadow before him, and enveloped the victim. And it was the mournful influence of the unperceived shadow that caused him to feel—although he neither saw nor heard—to *feel* the presence of my head within the room.

When I had waited a long time, very patiently, without hearing him lie down, I resolved to open a little—a very, very little crevice in the lantern. So I opened it—you cannot imagine how stealthily, stealthily—until, at length, a single dim ray, like the thread of the spider, shot from out the crevice and full upon the vulture eye.   8

It was open—wide, wide open—and I grew furious as I gazed upon it. I saw it with perfect distinctness—all a dull blue, with a hideous veil over it that chilled the very marrow in my bones, but I could see nothing else of the old man's face or person: for I had directed the ray as if by instinct, precisely upon the damned spot.   9

And now have I not told you that what you mistake for madness is but over-acuteness of the senses?—now, I say, there came to my ears a low, dull, quick sound, such as a watch makes when enveloped in cotton. I knew *that* sound well too. It was the beating of the old man's heart. It increased my fury, as the beating of a drum stimulates the soldier into courage.   10

But even yet I refrained and kept still. I scarcely breathed. I held the lantern motionless. I tried how steadily I could maintain the ray upon the eye. Meantime the hellish tattoo of the heart increased. It grew quicker and quicker, and louder and louder every instant. The old man's terror *must* have been extreme! It grew louder, I say, louder every moment!—do you mark me well? I have told you that I am nervous: so I am. And now at the dead hour of the night, amid the dreadful silence of that old house, so strange a noise as this excited me to uncontrollable terror. Yet, for some minutes longer I refrained and stood still. But the beating grew louder, louder! I   11 thought the heart must burst. And now a new anxiety seized me—the sound would be heard by a neighbor! The old man's hour had come! With a loud yell, I threw open the lantern and leaped into the room. He shrieked once—once only. In an instant I dragged him to the floor, and pulled the heavy bed over him. I then smiled gaily, to find the deed so far done. But, for many minutes, the heart beat on with a muffled sound. This, however, did not vex me; it would not be heard through the wall. At length it ceased. The old man was dead. I removed the bed and examined the corpse. Yes, he was stone, stone dead. I placed my hand upon the heart and held it there many minutes. There was no pulsation. He was stone dead. His eye would trouble me no more.

If still you think me mad, you will think so no longer when I describe the wise precautions I took for the concealment of the body. The night waned, and I worked hastily, but in silence. First of all I dismembered the corpse. I cut off the head and the arms and the legs. 12

I then took up three planks from the flooring of the chamber, and deposited all between the scantlings. I then replaced the boards so cleverly, so cunningly, that no human eye—not even *his*—could have detected anything wrong. There was nothing to wash out—no stain of any kind—no blood-spot whatever. I had been too wary for that. A tub had caught all—ha! ha! 13

When I had made an end of these labors, it was four o'clock—still dark as midnight. As the bell sounded the hour, there came a knocking at the street door. I went down to open it with a light heart—for what had I *now* to fear? There entered three men, who introduced themselves, with perfect suavity, as officers of the police. A shriek had been heard by a neighbor during the night; suspicion of foul play had been aroused; information had been lodged at the police office, and they (the officers) had been deputed to search the premises. 14

I smiled—for *what* had I to fear? I bade the gentlemen welcome. The shriek, I said, was my own in a dream. The old man, I mentioned, was absent in the country. I took my visitors all over the house. I bade them search—search *well*. I led them, at length, to *his* chamber. I showed them his treasures, secure, undisturbed. In the enthusiasm of my confidence, I brought chairs into the room, and desired them *here* to rest from their fatigues, while I myself, in the wild audacity of my perfect triumph, placed my own seat upon the very spot beneath which reposed the corpse of the victim. 15

The officers were satisfied. My *manner* had convinced them. I 16
was singularly at ease. They sat, and while I answered cheerily, they
chatted familiar things. But, ere long, I felt myself getting pale and
wished them gone. My head ached, and I fancied a ringing in my
ears: but still they sat and still chatted. The ringing became more
distinct:—it continued and became more distinct: I talked more
freely to get rid of the feeling: but it continued and gained definitiveness—until, at length, I found that the noise was *not* within my ears.

No doubt I now grew *very* pale;—but I talked more fluently, and 17
with a heightened voice. Yet the sound increased—and what could
I do? It was *a low, dull, quick sound—much such a sound as a
watch makes when enveloped in cotton*. I gasped for breath—and
yet the officers heard it not. I talked more quickly—more vehemently; but the noise steadily increased. I arose and argued about
trifles, in a high key and with violent gesticulations, but the noise
steadily increased. Why *would* they not be gone? I paced the floor
to and fro with heavy strides, as if excited to fury by the observation of the men—but the noise steadily increased. Oh God! what
could I do? I foamed—I raved—I swore! I swung the chair upon
which I had been sitting, and grated it upon the boards, but the
noise arose over all and continually increased. It grew louder—
louder—*louder!* And still the men chatted pleasantly, and smiled.
Was it possible they heard not? Almighty God—no, no! They
heard!—they suspected!—they *knew!*—they were making a
mockery of my horror—this I thought, and this I think. But any
thing was better than this agony! Any thing was more tolerable
than this derision! I could bear those hypocritical smiles no longer!
I felt that I must scream or die—and now—again!—hark! louder!
louder! louder! *louder!*—

"Villains!" I shrieked, "dissemble no more! I admit the deed!— 18
tear up the planks—here, here!—it is the beating of his hideous
heart!"

Integrated Skills

1. Why did Poe entitle this story "The Tell-Tale Heart"? Is this a
   good title? Why or why not?

2. Why does the narrator kill the old man? What is his motivation?

3. Why does the narrator get caught? Does he bring his capture
   on himself? How? Why?

4. To what extent is Poe's story about madness? To what extent is it about guilt?

5. How does Poe capture and keep his readers' attention and interest? Did he capture and keep yours? Why or why not?

Reading/Writing Connection

Edgar Allan Poe's "The Tell-Tale Heart" is a classic horror story. Write a paragraph in which you describe your response to Poe's story. Explain why you did or did not find it scary. You may wish to explain, as well, whether or not you enjoyed reading it, and why.

Reading Textbooks

Thematic Connections. You have just read Edgar Allan Poe's gothic horror story "The Tell-Tale Heart" and interpreted its meaning. You made observations about its details and drew conclusions from the connections among them. You also thought about whether or not it is scary and why. When questioning the story's ability to frighten readers, you may have thought about contemporary horror movies. Perhaps you even compared Poe's story to a horror movie that scared you. But did you know that movies are also subject to analysis and interpretation, just like literature is? The following passage from the introductory film textbook *Anatomy of Film* by Bernard F. Dick examines the genre of the horror movie. As you read it, think about how the elements of film are similar to—and different from—the elements of printed fiction.

Vocabulary Preview

Gothic (para. 1): in architecture, a style characterized by pointed arches, stained glass, and gargoyles; in literature, characterized by an emphasis on the eerie and the grotesque (adj.)

monochrome (para. 1): one color; in film, usually black and white, but sometimes sepia (a kind of brown) and white (adj.)

conducive (para. 2): favorable, able to bring about (adj.)

oedipal (para. 2): Generally used to describe a son's fixation on his mother; from the ancient Greek story of Oedipus, a man whose father was warned he would marry his mother (the father's wife) and kill the father. Despite the father's attempts to prevent the fate, the son does in fact marry his mother and kill his father, not realizing who they are. (adj.)

spawned (para. 4): created, given birth to (v.)

obligatory (para. 6): necessary, required, so common it becomes expected (adj.)

voyeurism (para. 6): the practice of getting pleasure from watching others (n.)

subjective (para. 6): Involved in the action. A subjective camera shows events to an audience from one character's point of view. (adj.)

codified (para. 7): established a working set of vocabulary and rules (v.)

film noir (para. 7): a style of film usually focused on a crime story and characterized by a dark, brooding feel (n.)

occasioned (para. 8): caused, brought about (v.)

trilogy (para. 9): series of three (n.)

The Horror Film

The basic types of horror films—ghost, creature, dual-personality, and mad scientist—had been established in the 1930s and 1940s along with the conventions of low-key lighting, shadowy surfaces, dissolve transformations, cellar laboratories with overflowing test tubes, fogbound woods, and Gothic mansions. While the musical and the western were photographed in either monochrome or color, the horror film was shot almost exclusively in black and white. In the 1950s, the use of color began with *House of Wax* (1953) and *Phantom of the Rue Morgue* (1954), but it was the British-made *Curse of Frankenstein* (1957), the first of Hammer Films' horror series, that set the trend toward the color horror film.

Although color and horror are not incompatible, as Roman Polanski's *Rosemary's Baby* (1968) and *Carrie* prove, color cannot capture the shadowy world of the unconscious as well as black and white, which is also more conducive to horror by suggestion. Color is suited to gore, the hallmark of the latest kind of horror film: the slasher film. Like every addition to a genre, the slasher film is not without precedent; its parent is *Psycho,* a genuine horror film with a subtle transformation. The oedipal Norman Bates becomes so closely identified with his mother that he assumes her personality, even to the extent of dressing in her clothes and murdering in her name. Significantly, Norman does not die at the end of *Psycho;* and as the years passed and *Psycho* became a classic, the need for sequels arose—*Psycho II* (1983), then *Psycho III* (1986). As long as there is an audience for horror, there will be a *Psycho* of some sort, although it is hard to imagine any of them surpassing or even equaling Hitchcock's.

2

The *Psycho* sequels illustrate a time-honored tradition in horror: the monster ceases to exist when the series or the cycle does. Even though it seems obvious that, at the end of *Frankenstein,* the monster dies in the fire that destroys the mill, he is discovered in the cellar at the beginning of *Bride of Frankenstein.* And even though the monster clearly perishes again in the inferno at the end of *Bride of Franken-stein,* he is resurrected for *Son of Frankenstein* (1939) four years later and paired with the Wolf Man in *Frankenstein Meets the Wolf Man* (1943) four years after he was revived by Frankenstein's son.

3

The same principle applies in the slasher film, the most popular being *Friday the 13th* (1980), although it is hardly the most inventive. Far more original is *Halloween* (1978), which introduced a plot device that *Friday the 13th* and similar films (e.g., *Prom Night* [1980]; *Terror Train* [1979]) imitated: a prologue depicting an earlier murder that bears heavily on the plot. *Halloween* led to three sequels (1981, 1983, 1988), but the public was more taken with *Friday the 13th,* which, within eight years after its release, had spawned seven films.

4

Like other horror cycles, the *Friday the 13th* spinoffs work from 5
the premise of the undying monster. In *Friday the 13th*, two teenage
camp counselors are killed because they were making love when
they should have been rescuing the drowning Jason. The killer is
Jason's mother, who is also killed at the end. The sequels feature
Jason himself, who emerges from the mud to continue his mother's
work.

In addition to the obligatory prologue, the slasher film practices 6
its own form of voyeurism: subjective camera. The camera is often
stationed outside a window, representing the point of view of someone looking in; it tilts up to a bedroom, as if someone were spying.
The slasher film also uses off-center compositions and framing that
exclude the killer, leaving only the victim in the frame. While the
slasher film may be a lesser form of horror, its use of subjective camera is a feature worth noting.

The slasher film, however, does not have a monopoly on subjec- 7
tive camera, a technique that has been used in movies as dissimilar
as *The Grapes of Wrath* and *Marnie*. Whether or not the slasher
film can be considered a genre or merely a subgenre of horror, as the
doomsday film is a subgenre of science fiction, is problematic.
Those who favor genre status argue that director Wes Craven
(Nightmare on Elm Street) in his *Scream* trilogy—*Scream* (1995),
Scream 2 (1997), and *Scream 3* (2000)—codified the conventions
of the slasher film, thereby suggesting that it constitutes a genre of
its own. Just as film noir and the musical have certain features that
distinguish them as genres, so does the slasher film: voyeuristic
camera, terrorized teens, the psychopathic phone caller, quick cuts
punctuated by ominous sounds, sex as a prelude to death, eerie
music with an echolike quality, the sudden appearances of a character at a window or doorway, the "everybody's a suspect" philosophy, a murder that occurred prior to the main action, the climactic
blood bath, the dead mother whose sins are visited upon her children, and the undying monster figure in the form of the killer(s),
who, even after they have apparently expired, get up on their feet
for one last charge.

What distinguishes the Craven trilogy from slasher films like 8
Prom Night (1980), which occasioned four sequels, and *Halloween*
(1978), which gave rise to seven, is its self-consciousness: not only
do the films reflect Craven's knowledge of the slasher conventions,
but the characters' knowledge of them as well. The teens in *Scream*
appear to have seen every horror movie ever made. There are refer-

ences to such films as *Nightmare on Elm Street, The Exorcist, Psycho, Silence of the Lambs,* and *Prom Night,* to mention only a few. The first victim (Drew Barrymore) is terrorized by a phone stalker who interrogates her by asking, among other questions, the identity of the killer in *Friday the 13th. Frankenstein* is on the screen in the local video store; in the knife-wielding finale, *Halloween* is on television. The teenage lovers, Billy Loomis and Sidney Prescott (Skeet Ulrich and Neve Campbell), characterize their relationship in terms of movie ratings (R, PG-13); later Loomis tells Sidney that life's "one great big movie, but you can't pick your genre." Loomis's knowledge, it turns out, is not restricted to movies; he knows a great deal about Sidney's mother, who was brutally raped and murdered a year earlier. But, as horror buff Randy Meeks (Jamie Kennedy) notes, in slasher films everyone's a suspect, and "sex is death" — particularly R-rated sex.

Just as *Scream* is conscious of being a slasher film, in which the characters are living out a slasher scenario (and in some cases know it), *Scream 3* is conscious of being the last installment of a trilogy. In *Scream 2,* the events depicted in *Scream* become the basis of a best-seller, "The Woodsboro Murders"; the book is made into a movie called "Stab," which becomes so popular that it spawns a trilogy of its own. *Scream 3* is about the making of "Stab 3," which, like *Scream 3,* is the last of a trilogy. By the end of *Scream 3* we realize that we have seen what would have been "Stab 3," if such a movie had ever been made. One of the *Scream 3* characters even states the three requirements of the finale: firing at the killer's heart is ineffective, since his bullet-riddled body will continue to lurch forward (hint: try another way or aim elsewhere); anybody can die, including those we would prefer to live; and finally, "the past will come back to bite you in the ass." 9

Although Craven's trilogy makes a good case for treating the slasher film as a genre, his films remain isolated examples of a form that has yet to show the range and depth of the horror film. 10

Thinking about the Textbook Selection

1. What are the main characteristics of a horror film?

2. Of the many films mentioned in this reading selection, which ones have you seen? Of these, which was the most terrifying for you? Why?

3. To what extent are slasher films horror films, and to what extent do they constitute a separate genre or type of film?

4. How do you think a film of Poe's "The Tell-Tale Heart" would create horror effects for viewers? Do you think that Poe's story would make a good horror film? A good slasher film? Why or why not?

Reading the Web

You're probably familiar with another popular form of storytelling—the urban legend, an often frightening story that is told as true with the aim of warning others but is almost always false. Well-known urban legends include stories of the killer who calls the babysitter from a phone extension inside the house, of the ax-wielding maniac hiding in the backseat of a woman's car, and of the business traveler who wakes up in the hotel bathtub surrounded by ice and missing his kidneys. You've probably heard, and maybe even told, some of these stories yourself. The Web site snopes.com, compiled and maintained as a hobby by urban legend enthusiasts Barbara and David P. Mikkelson, is devoted to collecting and debunking urban legends. The site is organized by themes, such as weddings, religion, sports, computers, history, and food. The page reproduced here is the table of contents for the "Horrors" section.

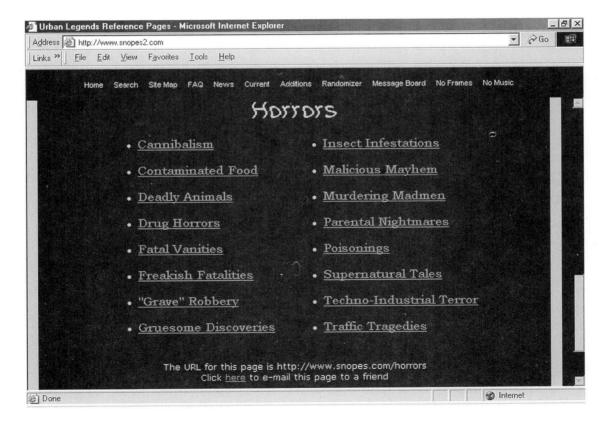

Thinking about the Web Page
. . . .

1. Which topic seems most likely to be related to Poe's "The Tell-Tale Heart"? Why?

2. Log on to the Web (snopes.com) and read one of the urban legends from the category (topic) you selected. To what extent is the urban legend like Poe's story? How does it differ? Which did you enjoy reading more? Why?

3. Urban legends seem to thrive even when people like the Mikkelsons make an effort to prove they're not true. What is it about these stories that makes people want to believe them?

Reviewing

**Recall /
Remember**

1. How is reading literature like reading an essay, an article, or a nonfiction book? How is it different?

2. What three basic things should you do when reading and interpreting a work of literature?

3. Where do you get the information and support you need to interpret a literary work?

4. Why is making inferences important to understanding poetry and short stories?

5. Identify and define four elements of literature.

**Chapter
Summary**

In this chapter you have learned how to read works of literature, such as short stories and poems, with understanding and pleasure. You saw that you can use the techniques of reading you learned earlier in this book — especially making careful observations, making inferences, and drawing conclusions based on those inferences — to read fiction and poetry with skill and confidence. You have used a focused process of interpretation throughout the chapter to read parables, poems, and short stories.

You have also been introduced to the special vocabulary used to discuss works of literature. You can use these terms and the concepts associated whenever you interpret literary works. These terms include plot and character, setting and point of view, irony, symbolism, speaker and situation, diction and imagery, figurative language, structure, sound, and theme. Looking carefully at these elements of literature helps you see how they are combined to convey the spirit and feeling of a work along with its theme, or meaning.

Chapter 12

Reading and Studying Textbooks

Getting Ready

This chapter applies what you have learned about reading to reading chapters in your college textbooks. It will help you understand the features and elements of your textbooks so you can read them more confidently.

As you have already discovered, a textbook differs from other kinds of books because it is specifically designed for study. A college textbook is typically written to introduce and define terms, explain and illustrate concepts, and demonstrate how to apply them in understanding the subject the textbook discusses. Textbooks are designed to be clear so that readers understand their content. Textbook authors try to be both informative and supportive in presenting their material.

Reading textbooks will bring together your reading skills, including understanding vocabulary, finding the main idea and supporting details, identifying patterns of organization, making observations and connections, developing inferences and drawing conclusions, and using techniques of critical reading. This chapter also introduces you to skimming for an overview and scanning for information—techniques for reading that are especially useful for reading college textbooks. In addition, you will find guidance for employing the study strategy known as **SQ3R** to help you learn and remember what you read.

You have already read excerpts from textbooks in previous chapters. This chapter includes an entire chapter from a textbook on the

Chapter Overview

429

subject of American history. The selection focuses on the Great Depression. We will work through the major elements of the textbook chapter so you can practice skills you have already learned.

Focusing
Questions

What is the first thing you do when you begin a reading assignment in one of your college textbooks?

How do you find specific information without reading a whole article, passage, or chapter?

Do you survey the chapter, quickly looking over its contents?

Do you skim the headings and subheadings in the chapter?

Do you look at the visual aids it contains, especially any pictures?

Do you read the captions that accompany diagrams, charts, tables, pictures, and other visual aids?

Do you read with a pen in hand, ready to annotate and jot quick notes?

What strategies do you use to help you understand and remember the information in a textbook passage or chapter?

What is the last thing you do when you complete a reading assignment?

Everyday
Reading

One of the ways you begin to read a textbook is to scan the table of contents or to skim a chapter. These ways of previewing material before reading it carefully are things we sometimes do in everyday life. When you pass a movie theater playing a dozen films, you quickly scan the titles. When you look up a restaurant's phone number in the phone book, you scan down to find the restaurant's name and number. You may skim the pages of the manual of your new radio alarm clock to find out how to set the time or the alarm. Or you may skim the junk mail that collects in your mailbox to see if anything interests you. Look for these and other opportunities to practice skimming and scanning in your everyday reading.

Learning the Skills

■ Understanding the Parts of a Textbook

To become an efficient reader, it is helpful to know the different parts of a book, what each part contains, and how it can help you in your reading and study.

THE TABLE OF CONTENTS

A **table of contents** lists the titles of a book's chapters. Most textbooks, including this one, also list chapter headings, subheadings, and other elements of the book. The table of contents provides an overview of the topics each chapter covers. The headings and subheadings identify more specifically each chapter's contents.

The headings and subheadings in the table of contents of a textbook make it easy for readers to locate information. One way you can make textbook headings work for you is to have some questions in mind when you look at a table of contents. You can then decide which chapters and sections are more likely to help answer your questions.

Exercise 12-1

Use the table of contents of this book to answer the following questions.

Example:

Which chapter contains a reading by Eric Schlosser?

Chapter 5

1. What are the three elements of critical reading?

   identifying a writer's purpose, distinguishing between facts and

   opinions, and determining an author's point of view

2. Where are implied ideas discussed?

   Chapter 3

3. Where can you learn how to develop your vocabulary?

   Chapter 2

4. Where can you find guidance in taking tests?

    Appendix C

5. Name four elements of literature.

    Answers will vary. Possibilities: plot, structure, setting, character,

    point of view, style, diction, imagery, figurative language, symbol,

    theme, irony

. . . .

THE INDEX

An **index** lists, in alphabetical order, the topics discussed in a book. A book's index is much more detailed than its table of contents. An index also provides references to individual pages, whereas a table of contents usually indicates only on what page a chapter or topic begins.

The index for *Making It Work* can be found on the inside of the book's back cover. Turn to it and look for the entry for "cause and effect." You will see that to learn or review cause and effect, you would turn to page 206.

Exercise 12-2
. . . .

Use the index at the back of this book to answer the following questions.

Example:

What kinds of sentence relationships are discussed in this book?

relationships between and within sentences

1. What two topics are listed under "conjunctions"?

    "coordinating" and "subordinating"

2. On which pages will you find information on implied main ideas?

    pages 78, 89, and 118

3. What kinds of supporting details are covered in this book?

   "major" and "minor"

4. Where in this book will you find information on using a dictionary?

   page 541

5. Does this book address the topic of reading literature?

   yes

. . . .

OTHER PARTS OF A BOOK

In addition to a table of contents and an index, a book may also include one or more of the following: a preface, an introduction, a glossary, an appendix, and a bibliography. College textbooks typically include all these features. Here is a description of what you can expect to find in each.

- **Preface.** A preface explains the author's reasons for writing the book. It may also include an overview of the book's contents. Some prefaces for college textbooks may include a section written "to the instructor" and another written "to the student."
- **Introduction.** A book's introduction identifies and explains the author's central ideas—the basic issue or concern of the book. It may also provide background information for understanding the book.
- **Glossary.** A glossary is an alphabetical list of terms that occur in the book. The terms are accompanied by definitions and sometimes also by examples or by page references to examples.
- **Appendix.** An appendix adds something extra to a book—for example, related information that did not fit easily into the book's chapters. Often appendices provide data in the form of charts, graphs, or statistics.
- **Bibliography.** A book's bibliography, sometimes under a heading such as "Works Cited" or "Additional Readings" or "Sources," identifies books and other sources the author consulted in writing the book. The sources are printed in alphabetical order, along with information including the name of the publisher and the place and date of publication.

Exercise 12-3

Using the table of contents and the index for one of your other textbooks, indicate or identify the following on the lines provided.

1. the book's major parts

    Answers will vary.

    _____

    _____

    _____

2. the titles of the chapters within one of those parts

    _____

    _____

    _____

    _____

3. whether the book includes an introduction, a preface, or both

    _____

4. whether the book includes an appendix, a glossary, or both

    _____

5. an important topic (one with many subdivisions) beginning with the letter *a, b,* or *c* and subtopics for the topic

    _____

    _____

    _____

■ Skimming for an Overview

Skimming, sometimes referred to as *previewing,* is a form of quick reading — reading only selected parts. Your goal is to read the essential parts and acquire a sense of the author's aim and idea. Previewing or skimming a reading selection prepares you to understand it better by helping you focus quickly on its main idea.

Follow the guidelines below when skimming or previewing an article or a chapter of a book.

Guidelines for Skimming

1. **Consider the title.** The title identifies the topic of the selection. It may also indicate the author's intended audience.

2. **Look for a subtitle or title heading.** Both of these provide additional, more specific information about the selection's topic.

3. **Glance at headings and subheadings.** These provide a breakdown of the topic discussed in the selection.

4. **Read the opening paragraph.** The first paragraph of a selection introduces the topic in some detail and often identifies the author's main idea.

5. **Read the first and last sentences of the remaining paragraphs.** These sentences usually contain the main point of each paragraph. They also identify connections among the selection's information and ideas.

6. **Look for boldface or italicized words.** Key words identify important concepts, which are generally illustrated and defined.

7. **Look at pictures, maps, charts, drawings, diagrams, or cartoons, and read the legend or caption for each.** The legend or caption explains each visual. A selection's visual information sometimes summarizes its written content.

8. **Read the concluding paragraph.** This last paragraph typically wraps up the selection by summarizing the main idea or by providing ways to think about its importance.

9. **Look for chapter summaries.** These highlight the central ideas of a chapter in concise form. In addition, answer any questions that appear at the end of the chapter. The questions are designed to cover the chapter's most important points.

■ Scanning for Information

Like skimming, **scanning** is a quick way of finding information. Scanning is useful for searching for specific information when you have a particular question in mind. The techniques of scanning complement and support those of skimming, which are useful for previewing a textbook chapter and for reviewing its content.

Scanning is particularly useful for finding specific inform3ation in a passage when no index or table of contents is available. Scanning is a type of quick reading—a form of searching.

Use the guidelines below to scan efficiently and effectively.

Guidelines for Scanning

1. **Scanning with specific questions in mind.** Write out your questions. Convert your search into the answer to a question.

2. **Look at the selection's organization.** If headings are included, note them. Copy down headings and subheadings in your notebook. Look for other breaks in the text that signal shifts of focus. If there are no breaks, look for signal words at the beginnings of paragraphs—transitional words such as *another instance, also, in addition, instead, on the other hand, a second reason,* and so on.

3. **Identify the most likely location for the information you are seeking.** Depending on what you are looking for, you might be more likely to find it near the beginning or end of a chapter. Or it might be the kind of information more likely to be buried in the middle of a passage.

4. **Check yourself once you find what you are looking for.** When you've found the information you are looking for, you will need to make sure it is accurate and useful. Perform a check by reading the context—the surrounding sentences—carefully.

■ Reading Graphics

Many types of visuals, or **graphics,** can accompany written material. In a single textbook alone, you may find photographs, maps, diagrams, charts, graphs, and tables that help illustrate what the textbook is teach-

Guidelines for Reading Graphics

1. Read the title and subtitle. The title and subtitle tell you what the graphic is about—the topic.

2. Read the caption or legend written beside or beneath the graphic. The caption or legend provides specific information about the content of the graphic.

3. Observe how the information in the graphic is organized—as a table, chart, map, and so on.

4. Observe the graphic's scale or units of measurement—whether its numbers represent thousands, for example, or percentages.

5. Determine the trend(s), pattern(s), and relationship(s) the graphic is designed to show. Look for connections among its data.

6. Read any explanatory notes (footnotes) the graphic includes. Notes might provide information about how the data represented in the graphic were collected or whether information is incomplete or out of date.

7. Check the source(s) of the information the graphic includes.

8. Make inferences and draw conclusions from the information or concepts presented in the graphic. Think about the significance of what the graphic shows.

9. Relate the graphic to the written text.

ing. Understanding the differences among the types of graphic material is the first step in understanding how that material helps illustrate the writing. Visuals serve the following important purposes:

- They clarify and illustrate key concepts.
- They summarize complex discussions in the written text.
- They provide additional information and examples.
- They add interest to written explanations and information.

Since graphics vary widely in form, appearance, and purpose, it is advisable to approach reading them systematically. Use the guidelines above, adapting them to the particular types of graphics you encounter in your reading.

Borne up by an alliance of diverse ethnic and racial groups that he called "the Rainbow Coalition," Rev. Jesse Jackson campaigned for the Democratic presidential nomination in 1984 and 1988. He and his family acknowledged a standing ovation after he addressed the 1988 Democratic convention.

Figure 12.1

PHOTOGRAPHS

Photographs are among the most common types of visual material. In textbooks, photographs create visual interest and direct readers' attention to important facts, issues, and ideas. Look, for example, at the photograph in Figure 12.1, from a textbook on American government. The caption explains the picture's significance.

MAPS

Maps depict physical locations and geographical areas. Geography books include maps that depict landmasses and bodies of water. Some maps show differences in elevation of the land as hills or mountains, plains, or deserts. Other maps may depict changes or trends — in weather patterns, for example, or in population density.

History books also tend to include many maps. A chapter on the American Civil War, for example, might have maps that show some of the following:

- the Union and Confederate states
- the railroad lines in the North and the South
- the movements of troops
- the locations of major battles
- the terrain of particular battle sites, such as Gettysburg

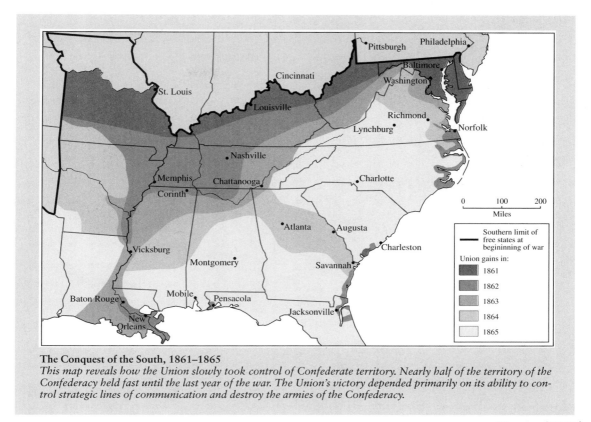

The Conquest of the South, 1861–1865
This map reveals how the Union slowly took control of Confederate territory. Nearly half of the territory of the Confederacy held fast until the last year of the war. The Union's victory depended primarily on its ability to control strategic lines of communication and destroy the armies of the Confederacy.

Figure 12.2

Figure 12.2, a map from the textbook *America's History* by James A. Henretta et al., shows how the Union took over more and more Confederate territory each year of the Civil War.

DIAGRAMS

Diagrams are drawings that show an object or a process by labeling its parts or its steps. Figure 12.3 on page 440, taken from the book *Exploring Psychology* by David G. Myers, depicts the autonomic nervous system and its connection to the organs of the body.

CHARTS

Three popular types of charts found in textbooks and in business materials are flowcharts, organizational charts, and pie charts.

Figure 12.3

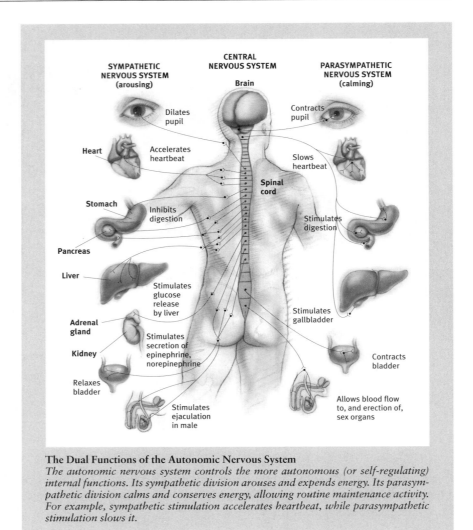

The Dual Functions of the Autonomic Nervous System
The autonomic nervous system controls the more autonomous (or self-regulating) internal functions. Its sympathetic division arouses and expends energy. Its parasympathetic division calms and conserves energy, allowing routine maintenance activity. For example, sympathetic stimulation accelerates heartbeat, while parasympathetic stimulation slows it.

Flowcharts. Flowcharts typically show how a process occurs or how a procedure works. Flowcharts include lines or arrows that indicate the direction, or flow, of the process portrayed. Because flowcharts are often used to summarize the accompanying text, they are particularly useful for review and study.

Figure 12.4, a flowchart from the textbook *Psychology* by David Myers, describes the steps involved in applying the scientific method. It also includes a specific example.

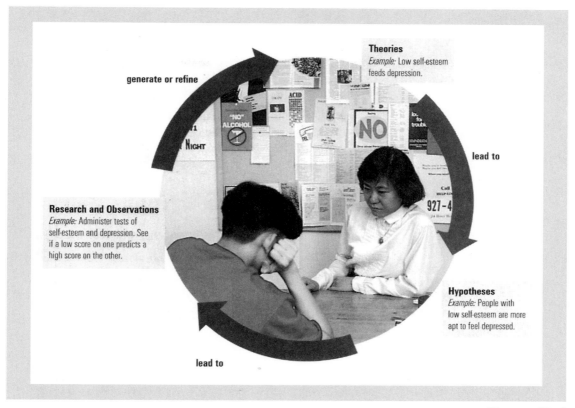

Figure 12.4

Organizational Charts. You will find organizational charts in business textbooks, in magazines devoted to business topics, and in corporate publications. Organizational charts are often used to show lines of authority, as illustrated by the chart in Figure 12.5 (page 442), from the textbook *Exploring the World of Business* by Kenneth Blanchard et al.

Pie Charts (Pie Graphs). Pie charts, also called pie graphs (and sometimes circle graphs), get their name from their shape. The circle of a pie chart or graph is "cut" into sectors, sliced by lines converging in the center. Each section represents a percentage of the pie. Pie charts show the relative size or importance of the various elements represented by the sectors.

The pie chart in Figure 12.6 (page 442) shows the types of ethnic groups entering the U.S. workforce in 2000. Notice how more than half of new workers were minority workers.

Figure 12.5

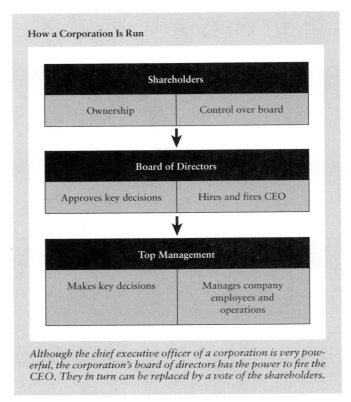

How a Corporation Is Run

Shareholders	
Ownership	Control over board

Board of Directors	
Approves key decisions	Hires and fires CEO

Top Management	
Makes key decisions	Manages company employees and operations

Although the chief executive officer of a corporation is very powerful, the corporation's board of directors has the power to fire the CEO. They in turn can be replaced by a vote of the shareholders.

Figure 12.6

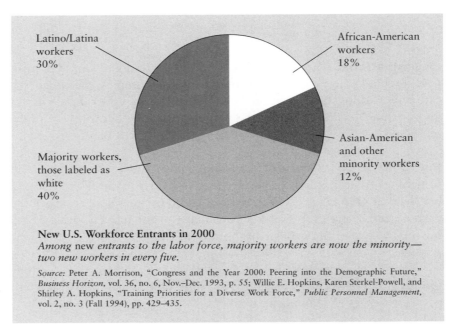

Latino/Latina workers 30%

African-American workers 18%

Asian-American and other minority workers 12%

Majority workers, those labeled as white 40%

New U.S. Workforce Entrants in 2000
Among new entrants to the labor force, majority workers are now the minority—two new workers in every five.

Source: Peter A. Morrison, "Congress and the Year 2000: Peering into the Demographic Future," *Business Horizon*, vol. 36, no. 6, Nov.–Dec. 1993, p. 55; Willie E. Hopkins, Karen Sterkel-Powell, and Shirley A. Hopkins, "Training Priorities for a Diverse Work Force," *Public Personnel Management*, vol. 2, no. 3 (Fall 1994), pp. 429–435.

GRAPHS

The two most common types of graphs are bar graphs and line graphs.

Bar Graphs. Bar graphs are used to compare amounts or quantities. Most often they show differences between items. The bar graph from *America's History* in Figure 12.7 shows how in 1860, at the start of the Civil War, the economy of the North was much stronger than that of the South.

Figure 12.7

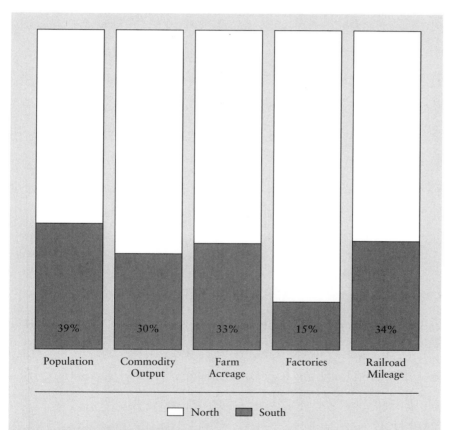

North ☐   South ■

Economies, North and South, 1860
The economic advantages of the North were even greater than this chart suggests because the population figures included slaves, commodity output was dominated by farm goods, farm acreage included unimproved acres (greater in the South), and southern factories were, on average, much smaller than northern factories.

Source: Stanley Engerman, "The Economic Impact of the Civil War," in Robert W. Fogel and Stanley L. Engerman, *The Reinterpretation of American Economic History* (New York: Harper & Row, 1971), 371; U.S. Census data.

Figure 12.8

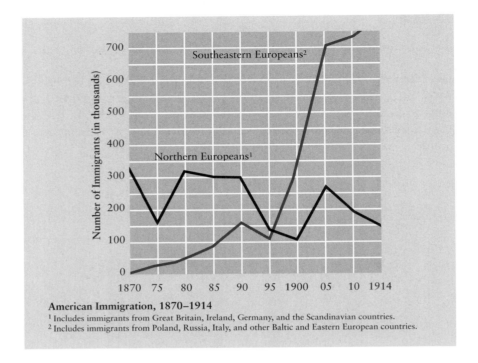

American Immigration, 1870–1914
[1] Includes immigrants from Great Britain, Ireland, Germany, and the Scandinavian countries.
[2] Includes immigrants from Poland, Russia, Italy, and other Baltic and Eastern European countries.

Line Graphs. Line graphs (also called linear graphs) are plotted or drawn on a horizontal and a vertical axis. Each axis represents a variable, or an item that varies in relation to the other. The line (or lines) of the graph allow viewers to compare the two items.

Figure 12.8, taken from the textbook *Politics in a Changing World* by Marcus Ethridge and Howard Handelman, shows changes in American immigration between 1870 and 1914. The vertical axis represents the number of immigrants in thousands, ranging from less than a thousand to nearly three-quarters of a million over the years shown. The horizontal axis represents the years from 1870 to 1914, in five-year increments. Notice that the graph contains separate lines representing two different immigrant populations, which are described in the graph's legend.

TABLES

Tables condense information. They provide a quick form of reference when you are reviewing facts. Tables typically present their information in orderly columns and rows. Columns are read from top to bottom; rows are read from left to right. When you look at a table, be sure you understand what is being represented in it. Read the table's title. Read the column and row headings. And look for changes or other patterns in the data.

Figure 12.9

Wind Speeds

	Wind Speed (km/hr)	Description	Effect of Wind on Sea Surface
	1	Calm	Minor surface
	1–19	Light to gentle breeze	Ripple and wavelets
Increasing Turbulence	20–49	Moderate to strong breeze	Moderate to large waves, whitecaps
	50–188	Moderate to strong gale	High waves, foam, spray
	89–117	Whole gale to storm	Very high waves, rolling sea
	117	Hurricane	Sea white with spray and foam, low visibility

Source: Modified from 1939 International Agreement and N. Bowditch, *American Practical Navigator*, U.S. Navy Hydrographic Office Publication 9, 1958.

The table in Figure 12.9, from the geology textbook *Understanding Earth* by Frank Press and Raymond Siever, describes the effects of increasing wind speed on water.

UNDERSTANDING TEXT AND GRAPHICS TOGETHER

In reading graphic visual materials in your textbooks, you'll need to connect not only the visual part of the graphic and its caption but also the entire graphic with the written text it illustrates or supplements.

When you read a textbook that includes visual materials and written text, use the guidelines below.

Guidelines for Linking Graphics and Written Text

- Preview the chapter by looking through it for graphics.

- Read the graphics and their accompanying captions to gain a preliminary overview.

- Read the textbook written material until you come to a reference to a graphic, often "see Figure X."

- Look at the graphic and read its caption.

- Think about the relation between the visual material and the written explanation.

- Return to your reading of the written text, moving back and forth between it and any visual materials it directs you to.

Keep in mind that the graphic materials included in college textbooks are visual aids, that is, a supplementary visual means to present information and concepts. Although you can never grasp a book's central ideas by looking at its visuals, you can use the graphics in a textbook to help you do several things: (1) zero in on key ideas and concepts; (2) preview a chapter or section; and (3) review a chapter or section.

Visual aids in textbooks perform a valuable function by enabling readers to "see" the material in another format. Graphics also provide visual aid for readers by summarizing essential information and concepts. In addition, graphic visual aids sometimes provide additional or supplementary material that is not specifically discussed in the text.

Figure 12.10

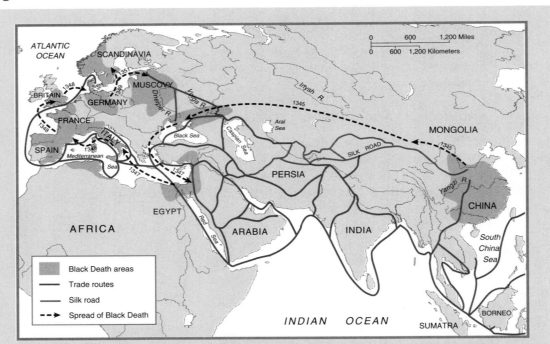

The Spread of Black Death, around 1350
The occurrence of the plague and its spread from town to town along the trade routes of Asia, Africa, and Europe alerted scholars to the connection between trade and the spread of disease. Disease-carrying hosts traveled the great intercontinental roads, infecting other people as they passed from China through Central Asia and on to Europe and Africa.

Exercise 12-4

Closely examine the graphics on pages 446 and 448, from *The Global Past* by Lanny B. Fields et al. and *Abnormal Psychology* by Ronald J. Comer. Then answer the questions that follow.

Example:

> Where and when, according to the map in Figure 12.10, did the Black Death (also known as the bubonic plague) first appear?
>
> *It first appeared in China around 1345.*

1. How long did it take for the Black Death to spread from China to Italy?

   two years

2. What is the relationship between trade routes and the spread of the bubonic plague in the middle of the 1300s?

   It appears that the plague followed trade routes.

   What can you infer from this relationship?

   Traders became infected with the disease and carried it with them

   across Asia and Europe.

3. According to the diagram in Figure 12.11 on page 448, which region of the human brain controls a person's sex drive?

   the hypothalamus

4. Where is the medulla?

   in the hindbrain, between the pons and the spinal cord

   What does it do?

   It controls heartrate, breathing, and digestion.

5. What part of the brain connects the two halves of the cerebral hemisphere?

   the corpus callosum

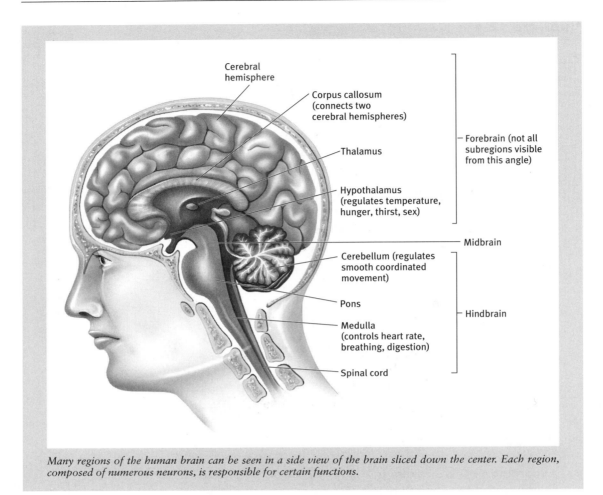

Many regions of the human brain can be seen in a side view of the brain sliced down the center. Each region, composed of numerous neurons, is responsible for certain functions.

Figure 12.11

Exercise 12-5

Closely examine Figure 12.12 (opposite), a line graph from the textbook *Media and Culture: An Introduction to Mass Communication* by Richard Campbell. Then answer the questions that follow.

Example:

How do sales of music tapes compare with sales of records from 1970 to 1975?

About twice as many records were sold as tapes. Sales of both

increased at about the same rate.

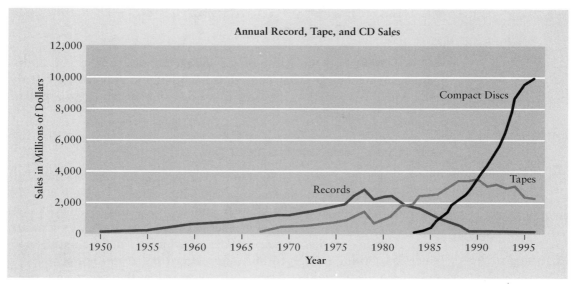

Figure 12.12

1. When were music tapes first introduced to the market?

   around 1967

2. At what point did music tapes start outselling records?

   around 1983

3. Approximately how many dollars' worth of compact discs were sold in 1995?

   about ten billion dollars

4. How do compact disc sales compare with record and tape sales?

   Compact discs have greatly outsold both records and tapes.

5. What can you infer about the effect of tapes and compact discs on record sales from this graph?

   Record sales started to drop about ten years after tapes were

   introduced and have disappeared almost entirely since the introduction

   of the compact disc around 1983.

■ SQ3R: Survey, Question, Read, Recite, Review

SQ3R is a method consisting of specific techniques to help you understand and remember what you read. Each letter stands for part of the technique: *S* is for survey, *Q* for question, and the three *R*s are read, recite, and review.

SURVEYING A READING SELECTION

There are four steps to surveying a reading selection, as shown in the box below. First, read the headings and subheadings. This will give you an outline of the article or chapter and help you understand what its main points are. After you have a sense of the big picture, look at any accompanying graphics to get an idea of which points the author considers important enough to illustrate. After that, read the opening and concluding paragraphs. These usually provide the selection's thesis statement and a summary of its major points. Finally, read any questions that accompany the selection; you can use them to focus your attention as you read.

The Four Steps of Surveying a Reading Selection

1. Read the headings and subheadings.

2. Look at accompanying illustrations.

3. Read the opening and concluding paragraphs.

4. Read any questions that accompany the selection.

Exercise 12-6

Survey the selection, from the textbook *Health in the New Millennium* by Jeffrey S. Nevid, Spencer A. Rathus, and Hannah R. Rubenstein. Then answer the questions.

Infectious Diseases

infectious diseases: diseases caused by direct or indirect contact with an infectious agent.

Infectious diseases are also referred to as *communicable diseases*. Infectious diseases are caused by contact with pathogens that multiply within the body. Pathogens are disease-causing organisms, including bacteria, viruses, fungi (yeasts and molds), and parasites such as insects and worms. Most pathogens are **microorganisms**—entities capable of carrying on life processes but too small to be seen by the naked eye. Infectious organisms reproduce within a **host**—a plant or animal that unwillingly provides them with a fertile breeding ground. Pathogens enter the body through ports such as tiny pores or sores in the skin, or through oral or nasal cavities. Unchecked, they can establish beach-heads within the body. They can use the body's own resources to reproduce and multiply and produce illness. Infectious organisms are transmitted in a number of ways, including contact with infected people or animals, insect bites, and contaminated food, air, soil, or objects (see Figure 12.13).

microorganism: any microscopic entity capable of carrying on life processes

host: person, plant, or animal that provides a hospitable environment for a pathogen

Figure 12.13

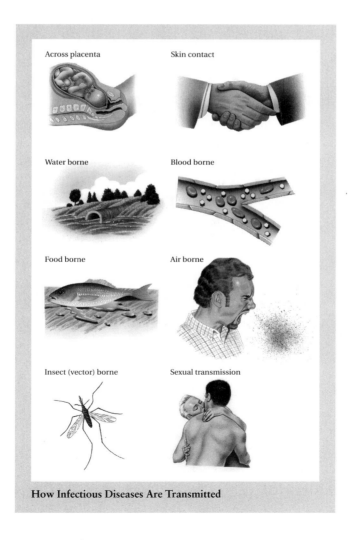

Across placenta

Skin contact

Water borne

Blood borne

Food borne

Air borne

Insect (vector) borne

Sexual transmission

How Infectious Diseases Are Transmitted

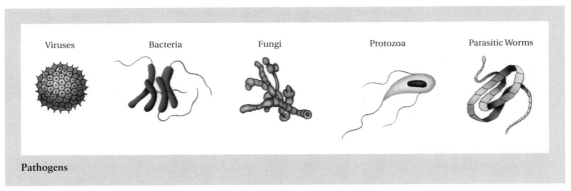

Pathogens

Figure 12.14

pathogenic: disease-causing

Some microorganisms are normally found in the body. They become infectious or **pathogenic** only when they "overgrow," or sprout colonies in parts of the body where they are not normally found. Figure 12.14 illustrates some of the more troublesome pathogens.

TYPES OF INFECTION

Infectious diseases may be *localized,* or restricted to a particular area or part of the body, as in some skin infections, or they may be *generalized* or *systemic,* involving many body organs and systems. We can distinguish too between **acute infections**, which hit us with an immediate wallop by producing fever and assorted unpleasant symptoms, and **chronic infections,** which develop slowly and produce less dramatic but longer-lasting symptoms. Acute infections are usually short-term, like the common cold or the flu, which run their course in a matter of days or weeks as the body destroys the invading pathogens. Some acute infections, like bacterial meningitis, can overcome the body's ability to defend itself, leading in some cases to death. Moreover, some chronic infections can turn into acute infections, while some acute infections may progress to chronic infections.

acute infection: infection in which pathogens cause an immediate set of symptoms; usually short-term

chronic infection: long-term infection

Still other infections can take months or even years between the time pathogens enter the body and the time any symptoms occur. These so-called **latent** ("hidden") **infections** are symptom-free but can become suddenly active, especially when the person's physical health is compromised by stress, other diseases, or emotional disorders. The virus that causes genital sores (*herpes simplex II*) can lie dormant after its initial outbreak for long periods before producing a recurrence; HIV can remain in the body for years before producing symptoms.

latent infection: "hidden" or inactive infection in which pathogens are not active enough to produce symptoms

THE COURSE OF INFECTIONS—
WHAT HAPPENS WHEN WE GET SICK

Whether you suffer a common cold or a life-threatening illness, infections progress through a sequence of common stages leading (hopefully) to recovery. Some fast-acting infections pass through each stage in a matter of days. Others take longer to run their course.

Incubation Period

The time between the entry of a pathogen into the body and the development of initial symptoms is called the **incubation period.** Though the pathogens are not yet producing symptoms, they begin multiplying during the incubation stage. Some fast-acting pathogens, like the viruses that cause the flu, take as little as one to two days to incubate. Others, such as the virus that causes rubella (German measles), incubate for two or three weeks before any symptoms appear.

incubation period: the time between the entrance of the pathogen and the first symptoms

Prodromal Stage

The period when symptoms first appear is called the **prodromal stage.** At first, symptoms are largely nonspecific and could be due to many kinds of infectious diseases. Common symptoms are low-grade fever, fatigue, and generalized aches and pains. The prodromal stage is the time at which we are generally most **contagious.**

prodromal stage: the initial stage of a disease before the onset of acute symptoms

contagious: describes a person who harbors an infectious organism and is capable of transmitting it to others

Clinical Stage

The development of full-blown symptoms characterizes the clinical stage. Symptoms specific to the infection appear. For rubella, for example, a characteristic red rash appears.

Decline Stage

Though some infections can be disabling or even fatal, most eventually run their course once the immune system gains the upper hand. The infection declines and symptoms subside. Though we feel better, we are not yet 100%.

Convalescence and Recovery Stage

Convalescence is the period between the end of the disease state and the return to health. Though the infection no longer rages, the pathogen has not necessarily been eliminated from the body. In some infections, such as herpes, hepatitis, and syphilis, some of the pathogen remains in the body in a dormant or latent state. **Passive carriers** are persons who are currently symptomless but harbor a latent or chronic infection.

passive carriers: persons who harbor infectious organisms, do not exhibit symptoms, but are capable of infecting others

Though they are free of symptoms, they may be capable of passing along the pathogen to others.

Always consult a health care provider if you suspect that you may not be fully recovered from an infection. For many kinds of infections, a simple culture, stain, or blood test can verify whether you remain infected.

Smart Quiz: *Think about It!*

- Why do you think it is important to understand what the incubation period of an infectious disease is?
- **Critical Thinking** Some infections are *latent,* or hidden. Why is it useful to know if you are infected with them?
- **Critical Thinking** Why do you think it is important to consult a health care provider if you suspect that you may not be fully recovered from an infection?

Example:

What is the major heading of this selection? (What can you expect the selection to be about?)

"Infectious Diseases"

1. Considering the two major subheadings, what do you expect will be covered in this selection?

   types of infections and the course of infections

2. Considering the minor subheadings, what do you expect to learn about the course of an infectious illness?

   It goes through five stages: an incubation period, a prodromal stage,

   a clinical stage, a decline stage, and a convalescence and recovery stage.

3. Look at Figure 12.13. What is it about?

   how infectious diseases are transmitted

4. List the ways in which infectious diseases are transmitted.

   across the placenta, by skin contact, water borne, blood borne, food

   borne, air borne, insect borne, and by sexual transmission

5. Look at Figure 12.14. What types of pathogens are shown?

   viruses, bacteria, fungi, protozoa, and parasitic worms

6. Read the opening paragraph of the selection. What are pathogens?

   "disease-causing organisms"

7. What are microorganisms (first paragraph)?

   "entities capable of carrying on life processes but too small to be seen

   by the naked eye"

8. What is a host (first paragraph)?

   "a plant or animal that unwillingly provides [infectious organisms] with

   a fertile breeding ground"

9. Read the last paragraph. What tests can show whether someone without symptoms might still be carrying an infection?

   "a simple culture, stain, or blood test"

10. Read the questions at the end of the selection. What is a latent infection?

    an infection that is hidden

. . . .

QUESTIONING A READING SELECTION

As a way to focus closely on what you read and to remember what you learn from it, ask yourself questions as you read.

One way to do this is to convert the reading selection's headings and subheadings into questions. Your questions can employ the standard question words: *who, what, when, where, why,* and *how.* The last two are the best kinds of questions for thinking about reasons and explanations.

For example, a textbook chapter about the process of ending relationships might have these major headings:

Why Break Up?

Confronting Relational Unhappiness: The Phases of Disengagement

Methods Used in Relational Disengagement

The Consequences of Relationship Disengagement

The first heading is already phrased as a question, which makes it easy to know what you should be asking as you read that section. The other three headings can be converted into questions: What are the steps of breaking up? How do people disengage from each other? What happens when a relationship ends?

You should also make a point of looking at a chapter's introduction and conclusion to see if the authors have provided focusing questions for you. As in *Making It Work,* textbooks often include these kinds of questions to help students understand the most important points of a chapter.

Exercise 12-7

Go back to the selection you surveyed on infectious diseases (pages 450–54). Turn the headings in the selection into questions. (Be creative! Don't start every question with *What.*)

Example:

How do we get infectious diseases?

1. *Sample answers follow. What is the difference between types of infections?*

2. *How long is the course of infections?*

3. *When does the incubation period start?*

4. *What is the prodromal stage?*
   _____

   _____

5. *How is the clinical stage different from the prodromal stage?*
   _____

   _____

. . . .

READING, RECITING, AND REVIEWING

In using the SQ3R method, you do not read an entire chapter all at once. Instead you **read** from one heading to another, looking for the answers to the questions you constructed in the questioning stage. Use the time between reading parts of the selection to **recite** aloud the answers to your questions. This recitation aspect of SQ3R is a kind of self-test you give yourself as you read.

To **review** means to re-see or to look again. In reviewing a reading selection, you should not reread it completely. Instead, reread the titles, headings, opening and concluding paragraphs, and the first sentence of each of the other paragraphs. You should also look again at any visuals, summaries, or questions.

In reviewing a reading selection you should repeat your questions and see if you can answer them. If you find any you cannot answer, reread that portion of the reading selection.

Applying the Skills

Reading Textbooks

Unlike the other chapters in *Making It Work,* the textbook reading reprinted here is an entire chapter. Taken from *America: A Concise History* by James A. Henretta, David Brody, and Lynn Dumenil, the chapter discusses something that you have most likely heard referred to in the news but may not know a lot about — the stock market crash of 1929 and the extended period of financial hardship that followed it.

Use the textbook reading to practice the SQ3R techniques you have just learned. Before you read the chapter, survey its pages to get a sense of what it covers. Ask yourself some questions about the topic. For example, what caused the stock market crash? How did it affect people? What was life like in the 1930s? As you read the chapter, take note of all the different parts of the chapter and be aware of how information is organized. What features present information, and what other features help you understand that material and put it in context? Notice also how the authors use photographs to provide or illustrate information. Annotate the chapter as you read and pay attention to how your own ideas grow as you go through the chapter — that is, pay attention to your own learning and how the chapter helps you with that. Once you have finished reading, review the chapter and recite the answers to your questions.

Approach the chapter as if you were in a history course. Read it as if you were going to be tested on the material, and, most important, read it to learn the material.

Vocabulary Preview

flappers (p. 461): young women in the 1920s whose distinctive clothing (such as beaded short dresses and feathered headbands) and behavior showed rebellion against convention (n.)

hapless (p. 461): unlucky (adj.)

vaunted (p. 461): praised, bragged about (adj.)

unabated (p. 462): without slowing or weakening (adj.)

precipitating (p. 462): bringing about, leading up to, causing (v.)

aggregate (p. 463): combined (adj.)

protracted (p. 464): taking place over a long period of time (adj.)

dissemination (p. 469): distribution, spread (n.)

supplanted (p. 472): replaced, overtaken (v.)

egalitarianism (p. 472): belief in equal rights (n.)

machinations (p. 474): plots, unethical plans (n.)

status quo (p. 478): Latin for "state in which" — the way things are (n.)

transient (p. 479): temporary, moving frequently (adj.)

moratorium (p. 481): temporary halt (n.)

Allied debts and reparations (p. 481): costs incurred by the United States, the United Kingdom, and France in World War I

watershed (p. 483): key moment, point of change (n.)

agitated (p. 485): attempted to arouse public feeling (v.)

foreshadowed (p. 485): hinted at, suggested (v.)

Twentieth Amendment (p. 486): the part of the U.S. Constitution that established January 20 as the date for presidential inaugurations (n.)

Chapter 24

THE GREAT DEPRESSION

Mass unemployment is both a statistic and an empty feeling in the stomach. To fully comprehend it, you have to both see the figures and feel the emptiness.

—CABELL PHILLIPS

Our images of the 1920s and the decade that followed are polar opposites. Flappers and movie stars, admen and stockbrokers, caught up in what F. Scott Fitzgerald called the "world's most expensive orgy"—these are our conceptions of the Jazz Age. The 1930s we remember in terms of bread lines and hobos, dust bowl devastation and hapless migrants piled into dilapidated jalopies. Almost all our impressions of that decade are black and white, in part because widely distributed photographs taken by Farm Security Administration photographers etched this dark visual image of depression America on the popular consciousness.

But this contrast between the flush times of the 1920s and the hard times of the 1930s is too stark. The vaunted prosperity of the 1920s was never as widespread or as deeply rooted as many believed. Though America's mass-consumption economy was the envy of the world, many people lived on its margins. Nor was every American devastated by the depression. Those with a secure job or a fixed income survived the economic downturn in relatively good shape. Yet few could escape the depression's wide-ranging social, political, and cultural effects. Whatever their personal situation was, Americans understood that the nation was deeply scarred by the pervasive struggle to survive and overcome "hard times."

The Coming of the Great Depression

Booms and busts are a permanent feature of the business cycle in capitalist economies. Since the beginning of the Industrial Revolution early in the nineteenth century, the United States had experienced recessions or panics at least once every twenty years. But none was as severe as the Great Depression of the 1930s. The country would not recover from the depression until World War II put American factories and people back to work.

691

692   THE GREAT DEPRESSION

CAUSES OF THE DEPRESSION

The downturn began slowly and almost imperceptibly. After 1927 consumer spending declined, and housing construction slowed. Soon inventories piled up; in 1928 manufacturers began to cut back production and lay off workers, reducing incomes and buying power and reinforcing the slowdown. By the summer of 1929 the economy was clearly in recession.

Yet stock-market activity continued unabated. By 1929 the stock market had become the symbol of the nation's prosperity, an icon of American business culture. In a *Ladies' Home Journal* article titled "Everyone Ought to Be Rich," the financier John J. Raskob advised that $15 a month invested in sound common stocks would grow to $80,000 in twenty years. Not everyone was playing the market, however. Only about 4 million Americans, or roughly 10 percent of the nation's households, owned stock in 1929.

Stock prices had been rising steadily since 1921, but in 1928 and 1929 they surged forward, rising on average over 40 percent. At the time market activity was essentially unregulated. Margin buying in particular proceeded at a feverish pace, as customers were encouraged to buy stocks with a small down payment and finance the rest with a broker loan. But then on "Black Thursday," October 24, 1929, and again on "Black Tuesday," October 29, the bubble burst. On those two bleak days, more than 28 million shares changed hands in frantic trading. Overextended investors, suddenly finding themselves heavily in debt, began to sell their portfolios. Waves of panic selling ensued. Practically overnight stock values fell from a peak of $87 billion (at least on paper) to $55 billion.

The impact of what became known as the Great Crash was felt far beyond the trading floors of Wall Street. Commercial banks had invested heavily in corporate stock. Speculators who had borrowed from banks to buy their stocks could not repay their loans because they could not sell their shares. Throughout the nation bank failures multiplied. Since bank deposits were uninsured, a bank collapse meant that depositors lost all their money. The sudden loss of their life savings was a tremendous shock to members of the middle class, many of whom had no other resources to cope with the crisis. More symbolically the crash destroyed the faith of those who viewed the stock market as the crowning symbol of American prosperity, precipitating a crisis of confidence that prolonged the depression.

Although the stock-market crash precipitated the Great Depression, long-standing weaknesses in the economy accounted for its length and severity. Agriculture, in particular, had never recovered from the recession of 1920 and 1921. Farmers faced high fixed costs for equipment and mortgages, which they had incurred during the inflationary war years. When prices fell because of overproduction, many farmers defaulted on their mortgage payments, risking foreclosure. Because farmers accounted for about a fourth of the nation's gainfully employed workers in 1929, their difficulties weakened the general economic structure.

THE COMING OF THE GREAT DEPRESSION   693

Certain basic industries also had economic setbacks during the prosperous 1920s. Textiles, facing a steady decline after the war, abandoned New England for cheaper labor in the South but suffered still from decreased demand and overproduction. Mining and lumbering, which had expanded in response to wartime demand, confronted the same problems. And the railroad industry, damaged by stiff competition from trucks, faced shrinking passenger revenues and stagnant freight levels, worsened by inefficient management. While these older sectors of the economy faltered, newer and more successful consumer-based industries, such as appliances and food processing, proved not yet strong enough to lead the way to recovery.

The unequal distribution of the nation's wealth was another underlying weakness of the economy. During the 1920s the share of national income going to families in the upper- and middle-income brackets increased. The tax policies of Secretary of the Treasury Andrew Mellon contributed to a concentration of wealth by lowering personal income tax rates, eliminating the wartime excess-profits tax, and increasing deductions that favored corporations and the affluent. In 1929 the lowest 40 percent of the population received only 12.5 percent of aggregate family income, while the top 5 percent of the population received 30 percent. Once the depression began, this skewed income distribution left the majority of people unable to spend the amount of money that was needed to revive the economy.

The Great Depression became self-perpetuating. The more the economy contracted, the longer people expected the depression to last. The longer they expected it to last, the more afraid they became to spend or invest their money, if they had any. The economy showed some improvement in the summer of 1931, when low prices encouraged consumption, but plunged again late that fall.

The nation's banks, already weakened by the stock-market crash, contributed to the worsening contraction. When agricultural prices and income fell more steeply than usual in 1930, many farmers went bankrupt, causing rural banks to fail. By December 1930 so many rural banks had defaulted on their obligations that urban banks too began to collapse. The wave of bank failures frightened depositors, who withdrew their savings, deepening the crisis.

In 1931 a change in the nation's monetary policy compounded the banks' problems. In the first phase of the depression, the Federal Reserve System had reacted cautiously. But in October 1931 the Federal Reserve Bank of New York significantly increased the discount rate—the interest rate charged on loans to member banks—and reduced the amount of money placed in circulation through the purchase of government securities. This miscalculation squeezed the money supply, forcing prices down and depriving businesses of funds for investment. In the face of the money shortage, the American people could have pulled the country out of the depression only by spending faster. But because of falling prices, rising unemployment, and a troubled banking system, Americans preferred to keep their dollars, stashing them under the mattress rather than depositing them in the bank, further limiting the amount of money in circulation. Economic stagnation solidified.

694   THE GREAT DEPRESSION

THE WORLDWIDE DEPRESSION

President Hoover later blamed the severity of the depression on the international economic situation. Although domestic factors far outweighed international causes of America's protracted decline, Hoover was correct in surmising that economic problems in the rest of the world affected the United States, and vice versa. Indeed, the international economic system had been out of kilter since World War I. It functioned only as long as American banks exported enough capital to allow European countries to repay their debts and to buy U.S. manufactured goods and foodstuffs. By the late 1920s European economies were staggering under the weight of huge debts and trade imbalances with the United States, which effectively undercut their recovery from the war. By 1931 most European economies had collapsed.

In an interdependent world, the economic downturn in America had enormous repercussions. When U.S. companies cut back production, they also cut their purchases of raw materials and supplies abroad, devastating many foreign economies. When American financiers sharply reduced their foreign investment and consumers bought fewer European goods, debt repayment became even more difficult, straining the gold standard, the foundation of international commerce in the interwar period. As European economic conditions worsened, demand for American exports fell drastically. Finally, when the Hawley-Smoot Tariff of 1930 went into effect, raising rates to all-time highs, foreign governments retaliated by imposing their own trade restrictions, further limiting the market for American goods and intensifying the worldwide depression.

No other nation was as hard hit as the United States. From the height of its prosperity before the stock-market crash in 1929 to the depths of the depression in 1932 and 1933, the U.S. gross national product (GNP) was cut almost in half, declining from $103.1 billion to $58 billion in 1932. Consumption expenditures dropped by 18 percent, construction by 78 percent; private investment plummeted 88 percent, and farm income, already low, was more than halved. In this period 9,000 banks went bankrupt or closed their doors, and 100,000 businesses failed. The consumer price index (CPI) declined by 25 percent, and corporate profits fell from $10 billion to $1 billion.

Most tellingly, unemployment rose from 3.2 percent to 24.9 percent, affecting approximately 12 million workers. Statistical measures at the time were fairly crude, so the figures were probably understated. At least one in four workers was out of a job, and even those who had jobs faced wage cuts, work for which they were overqualified, or layoffs. Their stories put a human face on the almost incomprehensible dimensions of the economic downturn.

Hard Times

"We didn't go hungry, but we lived lean." That statement sums up the experiences of many families during the Great Depression. The vast majority of Americans were neither very rich nor very poor. For most the depression did not mean losing thousands of dollars in the stock market or pulling children out of boarding school; nor did it mean going on relief or living in a shantytown. In a typical family in the 1930s the husband still had a job, and the wife was still a homemaker. Families usually managed to "make do." But life was far from easy, and most Americans worried about an uncertain future that might bring even harder times into their lives.

THE INVISIBLE SCAR

"You could feel the depression deepen," recalled the writer Caroline Bird, "but you could not look out the window and see it." Many people never saw a bread line or a man selling apples on the corner. The depression caused a private kind of despair that often simmered behind closed doors. "I've lived in cities for many months broke, without help, too timid to get in bread lines," the writer Meridel LeSueur remembered. "A woman will shut herself up in a room until it is taken away from her, and eat a cracker a day and be as quiet as a mouse."

Many variables—race, ethnicity, age, class, and gender—influenced how Americans experienced the depression. Blacks, Mexican Americans, and others already on the economic margins saw their opportunities shrink further. Hard times weighed heavily on the nation's senior citizens of all races, many of whom faced total destitution. Many white middle-class Americans now experienced downward mobility for the first time. An unemployed man in Pittsburgh told the journalist Lorena Hickok, "Lady, you just can't know what it's like to have to move your family out of the nice house you had in the suburbs, part paid for, down into an apartment, down into another apartment, smaller and in a worse neighborhood, down, down, down, until finally you end up in the slums." People like this, who strongly believed in the Horatio Alger ethic of upward mobility through hard work, suddenly found themselves floundering in a society that no longer had a place for them. Thus, the depression challenged basic American tenets of individualism and success. Yet even in the midst of pervasive unemployment, many people blamed themselves for their misfortune. This sense of damaged pride pervaded letters written to President Franklin D. Roosevelt and his wife Eleanor, summed up succinctly in one woman's plea for assistance: "Please don't think me unworthy."

After exhausting their savings and credit, many families faced the humiliation of going on relief. Seeking aid from state or local government hurt their pride and disrupted the traditional custom of turning to relatives, neighbors, church, and mutual-aid society in time of need. Even if families endured the demeaning process of certification for state or local relief, the amount they received was a pittance. In New York State, where benefits were among the highest in the nation, a family on relief received only $2.39 a week. Such hardships left a deep wound: Caroline Bird described it as the "invisible scar." For the majority of Americans, even those who were not forced onto the relief rolls, the fear of losing control over their lives was the crux of the Great Depression.

The Bread Line

Some of the most vivid images from the depression were bread lines and men selling apples on street corners. Note that all the people in this bread line are men. Women rarely appeared in bread lines, often preferring to endure private deprivation rather than violate standards of respectable behavior.

(Franklin D. Roosevelt Library, Hyde Park, NY)

FAMILIES FACE THE DEPRESSION

Sociologists who studied family life during the 1930s found that the depression usually intensified existing behavior. If a family had been stable and cohesive before the depression, then members pulled together to overcome the new obstacles. But if a family had shown signs of disintegration, the depression made the situation worse. On the whole, far more families hung together than broke apart.

Men and women experienced the Great Depression differently, partly because of the gender roles that governed male and female behavior in the 1930s. From childhood men had been trained to be breadwinners; they considered themselves failures if they could no longer support their families (see American Voices, "A Working-Class Family Encounters the Great Depression"). But while millions of men lost their jobs, few of the nation's 28 million homemakers lost their positions in the home. In contrast to men, women's sense of self-importance increased as they struggled to keep their families afloat. The sociologists Robert and Helen Lynd noticed this phenomenon in their follow-up study of *Middletown* (Muncie, Indiana), published in 1937:

> The men, cut adrift from their usual routine, lost much of their sense of time and dawdled helplessly and dully about the streets; while in the homes the women's world remained largely intact and the round of cooking, housecleaning, and mending became if anything more absorbing.

Even if a wife took a job when her husband lost his, she retained almost total responsibility for housework and child care. To economize women sewed their own clothes and canned fruits and vegetables. They bought day-old bread and heated several dishes in the oven at once to save fuel. Women who had once employed servants did their own housework. Eleanor Roosevelt described the stressful effects of the depression on these women's lives: "It means endless little economies and constant anxiety for fear of some catastrophe such as accident or illness which may completely swamp the family budget." Housewives' ability to watch every penny often made the difference in a family's survival.

Despite hard times Americans as a whole maintained a fairly high level of consumption. As in the 1920s households in the middle-income range—in 1935 the 50.2 percent of American families with an income of $500 to $1,500—did much of the buying. Several trends allowed those families to maintain their former standard of living despite pay cuts and unemployment. Between 1929 and 1935 deflation lowered the cost of living almost 20 percent. And buying on the installment plan increased in the 1930s, permitting many families to stretch their reduced incomes.

Americans spent their money differently in the depression, though. Telephone use and clothing sales dropped sharply, but cigarettes, movies, radios, and newspapers, once considered luxuries, became necessities. The automobile proved one of

AMERICAN VOICES

A Working-Class Family Encounters the Great Depression

LARRY VAN DUSEN

*A*lthough many families endured the privations of the Great Depression with equanimity, others, like Larry Van Dusen's family, experienced tremendous strains. In this passage from his oral history account to journalist Studs Terkel, he describes the pressures on male wage earners and their children.

My father led a rough life: he drank. During the Depression, he drank more. There was more conflict in the home. A lot of fathers—mine among them—had a habit of taking off. They'd go to Chicago to look for work. To Topeka. This left the family at home, waiting and hoping that the old man would find something. And there was always the Saturday night ordeal as to whether or not the old man would get home with his paycheck. Everything was sharpened and hurt more by the Depression.

Heaven would break out once in a while, and the old man would get a week's work. I remember he'd come home at night, and he'd come down the path through the trees. He always rode a bicycle. He'd stop and sometimes say hello, or give me a hug. And that smell of fresh sawdust on those carpenter overalls, and the fact that Dad was home, and there was a week's wages. . . . That's the good you remember.

And then there was always the bad part. That's when you'd see your father coming home with the toolbox on his shoulder. Or carrying it. That meant the job was over. The tools were home now, and we were back on the treadmill again.

I remember coming back home, many years afterwards. Things were better. It was after the Depression, after the war. To me, it was hardly the same house. My father turned into an angel. They weren't wealthy, but they were making it. They didn't have the acid and the recriminations and the bitterness that I had felt as a child.

SOURCE: Studs Terkel, *Hard Times* (New York: Pantheon Books, 1986), pp. 107–08.

the most depression-proof items in the family budget. Though sales of new cars dropped, gasoline sales held stable, suggesting that families bought used cars or kept their old models running longer.

Another measure of the impact of the depression on family life was the change in demographic trends. The marriage rate fell from 10.14 per thousand persons in 1929 to 7.87 per thousand in 1932. The divorce rate decreased as well because couples could not afford the legal expense of dissolving failed unions. And between 1930 and 1933 the birth rate, which had fallen steadily since 1800, dropped from 21.3 live births per thousand to 18.4, a dramatic 14 percent decrease. The new level would have produced a decline in population if maintained. Though it rose slightly after 1934, by the end of the decade it was still only 18.8. (In contrast, at the height of the baby boom following World War II, the birth rate was 25 per thousand.)

The drop in the birth rate during the Great Depression could not have happened without increased access to effective contraception. In 1936, in *United States v. One Package of Japanese Pessaries,* a federal court struck down all federal restrictions on the dissemination of contraceptive information. The decision gave doctors wide discretion in prescribing birth control for married couples, making it legal everywhere except the heavily Catholic states of Massachusetts and Connecticut. While abortion remained illegal, the number of women who underwent the procedure increased. Because many abortionists operated under unsafe or unsanitary conditions, between 8,000 and 10,000 women died each year from the illegal operations.

Margaret Sanger played a major role in encouraging the availability and popular acceptance of birth control. Sanger began her career as a public health nurse

Women Face the Depression

Most information for the 1930 census, conducted just as the depression gripped the nation, was gathered in personal interviews. This well-dressed census taker, Marie Cioffi, was probably lucky to get the job. The woman she is interviewing on East 112th Street in New York City, Margaret Napolitana, was likely a homemaker and, from her attire and expression, a struggling one. Meanwhile her daughter is not quite sure what to make of the two women's conversation.

(Corbis-Bettmann)

700   THE GREAT DEPRESSION

in the 1910s in the slums of New York City. At first she joined forces with socialists trying to help working-class families to control their fertility. In the 1920s and 1930s, however, she appealed to the middle class for support, identifying those families as the key to the movement's success. Sanger also courted the medical profession, pioneering the establishment of professionally staffed birth control clinics and winning the American Medical Association's endorsement of contraception in 1937. As a result of Sanger's efforts, birth control became less a feminist issue and more a medical question. And in the context of the depression it became an economic issue as well, as financially pressed couples sought to delay or limit their childbearing while they weathered hard times.

One way for families to make ends meet was to send an additional member of the household to work. At the turn of the century that additional member was often a child or a young, unmarried adult. The married working woman was most likely to be an African American, employed in domestic service. In the 1930s the most striking changes were that married white women expanded their presence in the labor market and the total number of married women employed outside the home rose 50 percent. The 1940 census reported almost 11 million women in the workforce—approximately a fourth of the nation's workers—and a small increase over 1930.

Working women, especially white married women, encountered sharp resentment and outright discrimination in the workplace. After calculating that the number of employed women roughly equaled total unemployment in 1939, the editor Norman Cousins suggested this tongue-in-cheek remedy: "Simply fire the women, who shouldn't be working anyway, and hire the men. Presto! No unemployment. No relief rolls. No depression." Many people agreed with the idea. When asked in a 1936 Gallup poll whether wives should work when their husbands had jobs, 82 percent of those interviewed said no. Such public disapproval encouraged restrictions on women's right to work. From 1932 to 1937 the federal government would not allow a husband and a wife to hold government jobs at the same time. Many states adopted laws that prohibited married women from working.

Married or not, most women worked because they had to. A sizable minority were the sole support of their families because their husbands had left home or lost their jobs. Single, divorced, deserted, or widowed women had no husbands to support them. This was especially true of poor black women. A survey of Chicago revealed that two-fifths of adult black women in the city were single. These working women rarely took jobs away from men. "Few of the people who oppose married women's employment," observed one feminist in 1940, "seem to realize that a coal miner or steel worker cannot very well fill the jobs of nursemaids, cleaning women, or the factory and clerical jobs now filled by women." Custom made crossovers from one field to another rare.

The division of the workforce by gender gave white women a small edge during the depression. Many fields where they had concentrated—including clerical, sales, and service and trade occupations—reinforced the traditional stereotypes of female work but suffered less from economic contraction than heavy industry, which employed men almost exclusively. As a result unemployment rates for white women, although extremely high, were somewhat lower than those for their male counterparts. This small bonus came at a high price, however. When the depression ended, women were even more concentrated in low-paying, dead-end jobs than when it began. White women also benefited at the expense of minority women. To make ends meet white women willingly sought jobs usually held by blacks or other minority workers—domestic service jobs, for example—and employers were quick to act on their preference for white workers.

White men also took jobs once held by minority males. Contemporary observers' concerns about the crisis of the male breadwinner or married women in the workforce rarely extended to blacks. Most commentators paid scant attention to the impact of the depression on the black family, for example, focusing instead on the perceived threats to the stability of white households. As historian Jacqueline Jones explains it, few leaders worried "over the baneful effects of economic independence on the male ego when the ego in question was that of a black husband."

During the Great Depression there were few feminist demands for equal rights, at home or on the job. On an individual basis, women's self-esteem probably rose because of the importance of their work to family survival. Most men and women, however, continued to believe that the two sexes should have fundamentally different roles and responsibilities and that a woman's life cycle should be shaped by marriage and her husband's career.

The depression hit another segment of the family—the nation's 21 million young people—especially hard. Though small children often escaped the sense of bitterness and failure that gripped their elders, hard times made children grow up fast. About 250,000 young people became so demoralized that they took to the road as hobos and "sisters of the road," as female tramps were called. Others chose to stay in school longer: public schools were free, and they were warm in the winter. In 1930 less than half the nation's youth attended high school, compared with three-fourths in 1940, at the end of the depression. College, however, remained the privilege of a distinct minority. About 1.2 million young people, or 7.5 percent of the population between eighteen and twenty-four, attended college in the 1930s. Forty percent of them were women. After 1935 college became slightly more affordable when the National Youth Administration (NYA) gave part-time employment to more than 2 million college and high school students. The government agency also provided work for 2.6 million out-of-school youths.

College students worked hard in the 1930s; financial sacrifice encouraged seriousness of purpose. Interest in fraternities and sororities declined as many students became involved in political movements. Fueled by disillusionment with World War I, thousands of youth took the "Oxford Pledge" never to support United States involvement in a war. In 1936 the Student Strike Against War drew support from several hundred thousand students across the country.

Although many youths enjoyed more education in the 1930s, the depression damaged their future prospects. Studies of social mobility confirm that young men who entered their twenties during the depression era had less successful careers than those who came before or after. After extensive interviews with these youths all over the nation, the writer Maxine Davis described them as "runners, delayed at the gun," adding, "The depression years have left us with a generation robbed of time and opportunity just as the Great War left the world its heritage of a lost generation."

POPULAR CULTURE VIEWS THE DEPRESSION

Americans turned to popular culture to alleviate some of the trauma of the Great Depression. In June 1935 a Chicago radio listener wrote station WLS, "I feel your music and songs are what pulled me through this winter." She explained that "Half the time we were blue and broke. One year during the depression and no work. Kept from going on relief but lost everything we possessed doing so. So thanks for the songs, for they make life seem like living." Mass culture flourished in the 1930s, offering not just entertainment but commentary on the problems that beset the nation. Movies and radio served as a forum for criticizing the system—especially politicians and bankers—as well as vehicles for reaffirming traditional ideals.

Despite the closing of one-third of the country's theaters by 1933, the movie industry and its studio system flourished. Sixty percent of Americans—some 60 to 75 million people—flocked to the cinema each week, seeking solace from the pain of the depression. In the early thirties moviegoers might be titillated or scandalized by Mae West, who was noted for her sexual innuendos: "I used to be Snow White, but I drifted." But in response to public outcry against immorality in the movies, especially from the Protestant and Catholic churches, the industry established a means of self-censorship, the Production Code Administration. After 1934 somewhat racy films were supplanted by sophisticated, fast-paced, screwball comedies like *It Happened One Night,* which swept the Oscars in 1934. The musical comedies of Fred Astaire and Ginger Rogers, including *Top Hat* (1935) and *The Gay Divorcee* (1934), in which the two dancers seemed to glide effortlessly through opulent sets, provided a stark contrast with most moviegoers' own lives.

But Hollywood, which produced 5,000 films during the decade, offered much more than what on the surface might seem to be escapist entertainment. Many of its movies contained complex messages that reflected a real sense of the societal crisis that engulfed the nation. The cultural historian Lawrence W. Levine has argued that depression-era films were "deeply grounded in the realities and intricacies of the Depression" and thus offer "a rich array of insights" into the period. Even if they did not deal specifically with the economic or political crisis, many films reaffirmed traditional values like democracy, individualism, and egalitarianism. They

HARD TIMES   703

Dancing Cheek to Cheek

During the Great Depression, Americans turned to inexpensive recreational activities such as listening to the radio and going to the movies. One of the most popular attractions in Hollywood movies was the dance team of Fred Astaire and Ginger Rogers, who starred together in ten movies.
(Steve Schapiro)

also contained criticisms—suggestions that the system was not working or that law and order had broken down. Thus, popular gangster movies, such as *Public Enemy* (1931), with James Cagney, or *Little Caesar* (1930), starring Edward G. Robinson, could be seen as perverse Horatio Alger tales, in which the main character struggled to succeed in a harsh environment. Often these movies suggested that incompetent or corrupt politicians, police, and businessmen were as much to blame for organized crime as the gangsters themselves.

Depression-era films repeatedly portrayed politicians as cynical and corrupt. In *Washington Merry-Go-Round* (1932), lobbyists manipulated weak congressmen to undermine democratic rule. The Marx Brothers' irreverent comedies more humorously criticized authority—and most everything else. In *Duck Soup* (1933) Groucho Marx played Rufus T. Firefly, president of the mythical Freedonia, who sings gleefully:

> The last man nearly ruined this place,
> He didn't know what to do with it.
> If you think this country's bad off now,
> Just wait till I get through with it.

Few filmmakers left more of a mark on the decade than Frank Capra. An Italian immigrant who personified the possibilities for success the United States offered, Capra made films that spoke to Americans' idealism. In movies like *Mr. Deeds Goes to Town* (1936) and *Mr. Smith Goes to Washington* (1939), he pitted the virtuous small-town hero against corrupt urban shysters—businessmen, politicians, lobbyists, and newspaper publishers—whose machinations subverted the nation's ideals. Though the hero usually prevailed, Capra was realistic enough to suggest that the victory was not necessarily permanent and that the problems the nation faced were serious.

Radio occupied an increasingly important place in popular culture during the 1930s. At the beginning of the decade about 13 million households had radios; by the end 27.5 million owned them. Listeners tuned in to daytime serials like *Ma Perkins*, picked up useful household hints on the *The Betty Crocker Hour*, or enjoyed the Big Band "swing" of Benny Goodman, Duke Ellington, and Tommy Dorsey. Weekly variety shows featured Jack Benny; George Burns and Gracie Allen; and the ventriloquist Edgar Bergen and his impudent dummy, Charlie McCarthy. And millions of listeners followed the adventures of the Lone Ranger (with his cry "Heigh-ho, Silver"), Superman, and Dick Tracy.

Like movies, radio offered Americans more than escape. A running gag in comedian Jack Benny's show was his stinginess; audiences could identify with an unwillingness—or inability—to spend money. Even more relevant was Benny's distrust of banks. He kept his money in an underground vault guarded by a pet polar bear named Carmichael—presumably a more reliable place than the nation's financial institutions. *Amos 'n' Andy* (see Chapter 23) is remembered primarily for its racial stereotyping. But the exceptionally popular show also dealt with hard times, often referring explicitly to the depression. A central theme was the contrast between Amos's hard work and Andy's more carefree approach to life. Amos, tending to believe that the nation's economic crisis had been brought about by the extravagant spending of the 1920s, criticized his friend's fiscal irresponsibility. As the historian Arthur Frank Wertheim notes, "The way that the characters' hopes for monetary success were turned into business failures mirrored the lives of many Americans." Though *Amos 'n' Andy* reinforced racial stereotypes, it also reaffirmed the traditional values of "diligence, saving, and generosity."

Mr. Smith Goes to Washington

In director Frank Capra's classic 1939 film *Mr. Smith Goes to Washington,* actor Jimmy Stewart plays an idealistic young senator who exposes the unscrupulous political machine that dominates his home state. In response, the machine frames Senator Smith for corruption. Although he is eventually vindicated, in this scene the despairing Smith encounters the avalanche of hostile mail generated against him by his crooked opponents. (MOMA-Film Stills Archive)

Americans did not spend all their leisure time in commercial entertainment. In a resurgence of traditionalism, attendance at religious services rose, and the home again became a center for pleasurable pastimes. Amateur photography and stamp collecting enjoyed tremendous vogues, as did the board game Monopoly. Reading aloud from books borrowed from the public library was another affordable diversion. But Americans bought books, too. Taking advantage of new manufacturing

706   THE GREAT DEPRESSION

processes that made books cheaper, they made best sellers of Margaret Mitchell's *Gone with the Wind* (1936), James Hilton's *Lost Horizon* (1933), and Pearl Buck's *The Good Earth* (1932). Finally, "talking was the Great Depression pastime," recalled the columnist Russell Baker. "Unlike the movies, talk was free."

Harder Times

Much writing about the 1930s has focused on white working-class or middle-class families caught suddenly in a downward spiral. For African Americans, farmers, and Mexican Americans, times had always been hard; during the 1930s they got much harder. As the poet Langston Hughes noted, "The depression brought everybody down a peg or two. And the Negroes had but few pegs to fall."

AFRICAN AMERICANS IN THE DEPRESSION

The African American worker had always known discrimination and limited opportunities and thus viewed the depression differently from most whites. "It didn't mean too much to him, the Great American Depression, as you call it," one man remarked. "There was no such thing. The best he could be is a janitor or a porter or shoeshine boy. It only became official when it hit the white man." The novelist and poet Maya Angelou, who grew up in Stamps, Arkansas, recalled, "The country had been in the throes of the Depression for two years before the Negroes in Stamps knew it. I think that everyone thought the Depression, like everything else, was for the white folks."

Despite the black migration to northern cities, which had begun before World War I, as late as 1940 more than 75 percent of African Americans still lived in the South. Nearly all black farmers lived in the South, their condition scarcely better than it had been at the end of Reconstruction. Only 20 percent of black farmers owned their own land; the rest toiled at the bottom of the South's exploitative agricultural system as tenant farmers, farm hands, and sharecroppers. African Americans rarely earned more than $200 a year, less than a quarter of the annual average wages of a factory worker. In one Louisiana parish black women averaged only $41.67 a year picking cotton.

Throughout the 1920s southern agriculture had suffered from falling prices and overproduction. The depression made an already desperate situation worse. Some black farmers tried to protect themselves by joining the Southern Tenant Farmers Union (STFU), which was founded in 1934. The STFU was one of the few southern groups that welcomed both blacks and whites. Landowners, however, had a stake in keeping sharecroppers from organizing, and they countered the union's efforts with repression and harassment. In the end the STFU could do little to reform an agricultural system that depended on a single crop—cotton.

All blacks faced harsh social and political discrimination throughout the South. In a celebrated 1931 case in Scottsboro, Alabama, two white women who had been riding a freight train claimed to have been raped by nine black youths, all under twenty years old. The two women's stories contained many inconsistencies, and one woman later recanted. But in the South when a white woman claimed to have been raped by a black, she was taken at her word. Two weeks later juries composed entirely of white men found all nine defendants guilty of rape; eight were sentenced to death. (One defendant escaped the death penalty because he was a minor.) Though the U.S. Supreme Court overturned the sentences in 1932 and ordered new trials on grounds that the defendants had been denied adequate legal counsel, five of the men eventually were reconvicted and sentenced to long prison terms.

The hasty trials and the harsh sentences, especially given the defendants' young age, stirred public protest, prompting the International Labor Defense (ILD), a labor organization tied closely to the Communist Party, to take over the defense. Though the Communist Party had targeted the struggle against racism as a priority in the early 1930s, it was making little headway recruiting African Americans. "It's bad enough being black, why be red?" was a common reaction. White southerners resented radical groups' interference, noting that almost all those involved in the Scottsboro defense were northerners and Jews. Declared a local solicitor, "Alabama justice cannot be bought and sold with Jew money from New York."

The Scottsboro case received wide coverage in black communities across the country. Along with an increase in lynching in the early 1930s (twenty blacks were lynched in 1930, twenty-four in 1933), it gave black Americans a strong incentive to head for the North and the Midwest. Harlem, one of their main destinations, was already strained by the enormous influx of African Americans in the 1920s. The depression only aggravated the housing shortage. Residential segregation kept blacks from moving elsewhere, so they paid excessive rents to live in deteriorating buildings where crowded living conditions fostered disease and premature death. As whites clamored for jobs traditionally held by blacks—as waiters, domestic servants, elevator operators, and garbage collectors—unemployment in Harlem rose to 50 percent, twice the national rate. At the height of the depression, shelters and soup kitchens staffed by the Divine Peace Mission, under the leadership of the charismatic black religious leader Father Divine, provided 3,000 meals a day for Harlem's destitute.

In March 1935 Harlem exploded in the only major race riot of the decade. Anger about the lack of jobs, a slowdown in relief services, and economic exploitation of the black community had been building for years. Although white-owned stores were entirely dependent on black trade, store owners would not employ blacks. The arrest of a black shoplifter, followed by rumors that he had been severely beaten by white police, triggered the riot. Four blacks were killed, and $2 million worth of property was damaged.

There were some signs of hope for African Americans in the 1930s. Partly in response to the 1935 riot but mainly in return for growing black allegiance to the

Lynching

The threat of lynching remained a terrifying part of life for African Americans in the 1930s, and not just in the South. Artist Joe Jones set this canvas in 1933, perhaps influenced by the fact that twenty-four blacks were lynched that year. He gave it the ironic title of *American Justice, 1933 (White Justice).* (Collection of Philip J. and Suzanne Schiller)

Democratic Party (see Chapter 25), the New Deal would channel significant amounts of relief money toward blacks outside the south. And the National Association for the Advancement of Colored People (NAACP) continued to challenge the status quo of race relations. Though calls for racial justice went largely unheeded during the depression, World War II and its aftermath would further the struggle for black equality.

DUST BOWL MIGRATIONS

A distressed agricultural sector had been one of the causes of the Great Depression. In the 1930s conditions only got worse, especially for farmers on the Great Plains. In the semiarid states of Oklahoma, Texas, New Mexico, Colorado, Arkansas, and

Kansas, farmers had always risked the ravages of drought (see Chapter 16), but the years 1930 to 1941 witnessed the worst drought in the country's history. Low rainfall alone did not create the Dust Bowl, however. National and international market forces, like the rising demand for wheat during World War I, had caused farmers to push the farming frontier beyond its natural limits. To capture a profit they had stripped the land of its natural vegetation, destroying the delicate ecological balance of the plains. When the rains dried up and the winds came, nothing remained to hold the soil. Huge clouds of dust rolled over the plains, causing streetlights to blink on as if night had fallen. Dust seeped into houses and "blackened the pillow around one's head, the dinner plates on the table, the bread dough on the back of the stove."

The ecological disaster prompted a mass exodus from the plains. Their crops ruined, their lands barren and dry, their homes foreclosed for debts they could not pay, at least 350,000 Okies (so-called whether or not they were from Oklahoma) loaded their belongings into beat-up Fords and headed west, encouraged by handbills distributed by growers that promised good jobs in California. Some went to metropolitan areas, but about half settled in rural areas where they worked for low wages as migratory farm laborers. John Steinbeck's novel *The Grapes of Wrath* (1939) immortalized them and their journey. In the novel the Joads abandon their land not only because of drought but also as a result of the economic transformation of American agriculture that had begun during World War I. By the 1930s large-scale commercialized farming had spread to the plains, where family farmers still used draft animals. In Steinbeck's novel, after the bank forecloses on the Joads' farm, a gasoline-engine tractor, the symbol of mechanized farming, plows under their crops and demolishes their home. Though it was a powerful novel, *The Grapes of Wrath* did not convey the diversity of the westward migration. Not all Okies were destitute dirt farmers; perhaps one in six was a professional, a business proprietor, or a white-collar worker. For most the drive west was fairly easy. Route 66 was a paved two-lane road; in a decent car, the journey from Oklahoma or Texas to California took only three to four days.

Before the 1930s Californians had developed a different type of agriculture from that practiced in the Southwest and Midwest. Basically industrial in nature, California agriculture was large-scale, intensive, and diversified, ironically requiring a massive irrigation system that would lay the groundwork for serious future environmental problems. The key crops were specialty foods—citruses, grapes, potatoes—whose staggered harvests required a great deal of transient labor during short picking seasons. A steady supply of cheap migrant labor provided by Chinese, Mexicans, Okies, Filipinos, and, briefly, East Indians made this type of farming economically feasible.

The migrants had a lasting impact on California culture. At first they met outright hostility from old-time Californians—a demoralizing experience for white native-born Protestants, who were ashamed of the Okie stereotype. But they stayed, filling important roles in California's expanding economy. Soon some

710   THE GREAT DEPRESSION

communities in the San Joaquin Valley—Bakersfield, Fresno, Merced, Modesto, and Stockton—took on a distinctly Okie cast, identifiable by southern-influenced evangelical religion and the growing popularity of country music.

MEXICAN AMERICAN COMMUNITIES

As Okies arrived in California, many Mexican Americans were leaving. In the depths of the depression, with fear of competition from foreign workers at a peak, perhaps a third of the Mexican American population, most of them immigrants, returned to Mexico. The federal government's deportation policy—fostered by racism and made feasible by the proximity of Mexico—was partly responsible for the exodus, but many more Mexicans left voluntarily when work ran out and local relief agencies refused to assist them. Los Angeles lost approximately one-third of its Mexican community of 150,000—the largest concentration of Mexicans outside Mexico—during the deportations, which separated families, disrupted children's education, and caused extreme financial hardship during the worst years of the depression. Although forced repatriation slowed after 1932, for those who remained in America deportation was still a constant threat, an unmistakable reminder of their fragile status in the United States.

Discrimination and exploitation were omnipresent in the Mexican community. The harsh experiences of migrant workers influenced a young Mexican American named César Chávez, who would become one of the twentieth century's most influential labor organizers. In the mid-1930s, Chávez's father became involved in several bitter labor struggles in California's Imperial Valley. Thirty-seven major agricultural strikes occurred in California in 1933 alone, including one in the San Joaquin Valley that mobilized 18,000 cotton pickers—the largest agricultural strike to date. All these strikes failed, but they gave the young Chávez a background in labor organizing, which he would use to found a national farm workers' union in 1962.

Not all Mexican Americans were migrant farm workers. Many worked as miners; others held industrial jobs, especially in steel mills, meat-packing plants, and refineries, where they established a vibrant tradition of labor activism. In California, Mexican Americans also found employment in fruit- and vegetable-processing plants. Young single women especially preferred the higher-paying cannery work to domestic service, needlework, and farm labor. In plants owned by corporate giants like Del Monte, McNeill, and Libby, Mexican American women earned around $2.50 a day, while their male counterparts received $3.50 to $4.50. Labor unions came to the canneries in 1939 with the formation of the United Cannery, Agricultural, Packing, and Allied Workers of America, an unusually democratic union in which women, the majority of the rank-and-file workers, played a leading role.

Activism in the fields and factories demonstrated how a second generation of Mexican Americans, born in the United States, had turned increasingly to the struggle for political and economic justice in the United States rather than retaining primary allegiance to Mexico. According to the historian George Sánchez, they were creating "their own version of Americanism without abandoning Mexican culture." Joining American labor unions and becoming more involved in American politics (see Chapter 25) were important steps in the creation of a distinct Mexican American ethnic identity.

Herbert Hoover and the Great Depression

Had Herbert Hoover been elected in 1920 instead of 1928, he probably would have been a popular president. As the director of successful food conservation programs at home and charitable food relief abroad during World War I, he was respected as an intelligent and able administrator. Although Hoover's name frequently emerged as a possible candidate in 1920, he did not run for president until the end of the decade. Timing was against him. Although his optimistic predictions in the 1928 campaign—that "the poorhouse is vanishing from among us" and that America was "nearer to the final triumph over poverty than ever before in the history of any land"—reflected beliefs that many Americans shared, that prosperity and Hoover's reputation were soon to be dramatically undermined. When the stock market crashed in 1929, he stubbornly insisted that the downturn was only temporary. In June 1930 he greeted a business delegation with the words "Gentlemen, you have come sixty days too late. The Depression is over." As the country hit rock bottom in 1931 and 1932, the president finally acted, but by then it was too little, too late.

HOOVER RESPONDS

Hoover's approach to the Great Depression was shaped by his priorities as secretary of commerce. Hoping to avoid coercive measures on the part of the federal government, he turned to the business community for leadership in overcoming the economic downturn. Hoover asked business executives to maintain wages and production levels voluntarily and to work with the government to build people's confidence in the economic system.

Hoover did not rely solely on public pronouncements, however; he also used public funds and federal action to encourage recovery. Soon after the stock-market crash he cut federal taxes and called on state and local governments to increase their expenditures on public construction projects. He signed the 1929 Agricultural Marketing Act, which gave the federal government an unprecedented role in stabilizing agriculture. In 1930 and the first half of 1931 Hoover raised the federal budget for public works to $423 million, a dramatic increase in expenditures not traditionally considered to be the federal government's responsibility. Hoover also eased the international crisis by declaring a moratorium on the payment of Allied debts and reparations early in the summer of 1931. The depression continued, however. When

AMERICAN VOICES

Public Assistance Fails a Southern Farm Family

*W*hen times were bad, even public assistance could be bad for a family in dire straits. Here a young mother living in the farming community of Commerce, Georgia, relates how relief efforts ironically proved to be a burden to her family of eight.

I've just met with a problem I cannot solve alone. I am a Mother of six children the oldest is only 11 years old the youngest 18 months and I'm expecting another in March. We couldn't get any crop for 1936 because we could neither furnish ourselves or had any stock. So here we are having made out on a little work once in a while all summer. And then in Aug I had to have a serious operation and now I'm not able to feed & clothe our six children as my husband couldnt find anything at all to do was compelled to get on relief job at $1.28 a day 16 days a month. Well you take 8 meals 3 times a day out of $1.28 and what will you have left is 24 meals and what kind of meals do you have? We have to buy everything we eat. We have nothing except what we buy. Our bedclothes are threadbare our clothes the same. No shoes and no money to buy yet the relief say that cant help us as he is working. Can he work naked. Can he sleep cold. I don't know of any one at all that can help me and I know we cant go on like this. . . .

I hate to be like this but can a person that is willing to work for a living and that honest and disable to help themselves sit idle and see their small children suffer day after day without enough food or clothes to keep their bodies warm when there are thousands of people with plenty to give if they knew your need.

How it hurts to know that you are almost starving in the land of plenty.

SOURCE: Julia Kirk Blackwelder, "Letters from the Great Depression," in *Southern Exposure* 6, no. 3 (Fall 1978), p. 77.

the president asked Congress for a 33 percent tax increase to balance the budget, the ill-advised move choked investment and, to a lesser extent, consumption, contributing significantly to the continuation of the depression.

Hoover's most innovative program—one the New Deal would later draw on—was the Reconstruction Finance Corporation (RFC), approved by Congress in January 1932. Modeled on the War Finance Corporation of World War I and developed in collaboration with the business and banking communities, the RFC was the first federal institution created to intervene directly in the economy during peacetime. To alleviate the credit crunch for business, the RFC would provide federal loans to railroads, financial institutions, banks, and insurance companies in a strategy that has been called *pump priming*. In theory, money lent at the top of the economic structure would stimulate production, creating new jobs and increasing consumer spending. These benefits would eventually "trickle down" to the rest of the economy.

Unfortunately, the RFC lent its funds too cautiously to make a significant difference. Nonetheless, it represents a watershed in American political history and the growth of the federal government. When voluntary cooperation failed, the president had turned to federal action to stimulate the economy. Yet Hoover's break with the past had clear limits. In many ways, his support of the RFC was just another attempt to encourage business confidence. Compared with previous chief executives—and in contrast to his popular image as a "do-nothing" president—Hoover responded to the national emergency on an unprecedented scale. But the nation's needs were also unprecedented, and Hoover's programs failed to meet them (see American Voices, "Public Assistance Fails a Southern Farm Family").

In particular, federal programs fell short of helping the growing ranks of the unemployed. Hoover remained adamant in his refusal to consider any plan for direct federal relief to those out of work. Throughout his career he had believed that privately organized charities were sufficient to meet the nation's social welfare needs. During World War I he had headed the Commission for Relief of Belgium, a private group that distributed 5 million tons of food to Europe's suffering civilian population. And in 1927 he had coordinated a rescue and cleanup operation after a devastating flood of the Mississippi River left 16.5 million acres of land under water in seven states. The success of these and other predominantly voluntary responses to public emergencies had confirmed Hoover's belief that private charity, not federal aid, was the "American way" of solving social problems. He would not undermine the country's hallowed faith in individualism, even in the face of evidence that charities and state and local relief agencies could not meet the needs of a growing unemployed population.

RISING DISCONTENT

As the depression deepened, many citizens came to hate Herbert Hoover. Once the symbol of business prosperity, he became the scapegoat for the depression. "In Hoover we trusted, now we are busted," declared the hand-lettered signs carried by the down and out. New terms entered the vocabulary: Hoovervilles (shantytowns where people lived in packing crates and other makeshift shelters), Hoover flags (empty pockets turned inside out), Hoover blankets (newspapers). Hoover's declarations that nobody was starving, that hobos were better fed than ever before, seemed cruel and insensitive. His apparent willingness to bail out businesses and banks while leaving individuals to fend for themselves added to his reputation for cold-heartedness.

As the country entered the fourth year of depression, signs of rising discontent and rebellion emerged. Farmers were among the most vocal protestors, banding together to harass the bank agents and government officers who enforced evictions and foreclosures and to protest the low prices they received for their

714   THE GREAT DEPRESSION

Hoovervilles

By 1930 shantytowns had sprung up in most of the nation's cities. In New York City squatters camped out along the Hudson River railroad tracks, built makeshift homes in Central Park, or lived in the city dump. This scene from the old reservoir in Central Park looks east toward the fancy apartment buildings of Fifth Avenue and the Metropolitan Museum of Art, at left.
(Grant Smith/Corbis)

crops. Midwestern farmers had watched the price of wheat fall from $3 a bushel in 1920 to barely 30 cents in 1932. Now they formed the Farm Holiday Association, barricaded local roads, and dumped milk, vegetables, and other farm produce in the dirt rather than accept prices that would not cover their costs. Nothing better captured the cruel irony of maldistribution than farmers destroying food at a time when thousands were going hungry.

Protest was not confined to rural America, however. Bitter labor strikes occurred in the depths of the depression, despite the threat that strikers would lose their jobs. In Harlan County, Kentucky, in 1931 miners struck over a 10 percent wage cut. Their union was crushed by mine owners and the National Guard. In 1932 at Ford's River Rouge factory outside Detroit a demonstration provoked violence from police and Ford security forces; three demonstrators were killed, and fifty more seriously injured. Later some 40,000 people viewed the coffins under a banner charging that "Ford Gave Bullets for Bread."

In 1931 and 1932 violence broke out in the nation's cities. Groups of the unemployed battled local authorities over inadequate relief, staging rent riots and

HERBERT HOOVER AND THE GREAT DEPRESSION   715

hunger marches. Some of these actions were organized by the Communist Party—still a tiny organization with only 12,000 members—as a challenge to the capitalist system, such as "unemployment councils" that agitated for jobs and food and a hunger march on Washington, D.C., in 1931. Though the marches were well attended and often got results from local and federal authorities, they did not necessarily win converts to communism.

Not radicals but veterans staged the most publicized—and most tragic—protest. In the summer of 1932 the "Bonus Army," a ragtag group of about 15,000 unemployed World War I veterans, hitchhiked to Washington to demand immediate payment of their bonuses, originally scheduled for distribution in 1945. While their leaders lobbied Congress, the Bonus Army camped out in the capital. "We were heroes in 1917, but we're bums now," one veteran complained bitterly. When the marchers refused to leave their Anacostia Flats camp, Hoover called out riot troops to clear the area. Led by General Douglas MacArthur, assisted by Major Dwight D. Eisenhower and Major George S. Patton, the troops burned the encampment to the ground. In the fight that followed, more than a hundred marchers were injured. Newsreel footage captured the deeply disturbing spectacle of the U.S. Army moving against its own veterans, and Hoover's popularity plunged even lower.

THE 1932 ELECTION: A NEW ORDER

Despite the evidence of discontent, the nation overall was not in a revolutionary mood as it approached the 1932 election. Having internalized Horatio Alger's ideal of the self-made man, many Americans initially blamed themselves rather than the system for their hardship. Despair and apathy, not anger, was their mood. The Republicans, who could find no credible way to dump an incumbent president, unenthusiastically renominated Hoover. The Democrats turned to Governor Franklin Delano Roosevelt of New York, who won the nomination by capitalizing on that state's reputation for innovative relief and unemployment programs.

Roosevelt, born into a wealthy New York family in 1882, had attended Harvard College and Columbia Law School. He had served in the New York State legislature and as assistant secretary of the navy in the Wilson administration, a post that had earned him the vice-presidential nomination on the Democratic ticket in 1920. Roosevelt's rise to the presidency was interrupted in 1921 by an attack of polio that left both his legs paralyzed for life. But he fought back from illness, emerging from the ordeal a stronger, more resilient man. "If you had spent two years in bed trying to wiggle your toe, after that anything would seem easy," he explained. His wife, Eleanor Roosevelt, strongly supported his return to public life and helped to mastermind his successful campaign for the governorship of New York in 1928.

The 1932 campaign for the presidency foreshadowed little of the New Deal. Roosevelt hinted only vaguely at new approaches to alleviating the depression: "The country needs and, unless I mistake its temper, the country demands bold, persistent experimentation." He won easily, receiving 22.8 million votes to Hoover's 15.7

million. Despite the nation's economic collapse, Americans remained firmly committed to the two-party system. The Socialist Party candidate, Norman Thomas, got fewer than a million votes, and the Communist Party candidate, party leader William Z. Foster, drew only 100,000 votes.

The 1932 election marked a turning point in American politics, the emergence of a Democratic coalition that would help to shape national politics for the next four decades. Roosevelt won the support of the Solid South, which returned to the Democratic fold after defecting in 1928 because of Al Smith's Catholicism and his views on Prohibition. Roosevelt drew substantial support in the West and in the cities, continuing a trend first noticed in 1928, when the Democrats appealed successfully to recent immigrants and urban ethnic groups. However, Roosevelt's election was hardly a mandate to reshape American political and economic institutions. Many people voted as much against Hoover as for Roosevelt.

Having spoken, the voters had to wait until Roosevelt's inauguration in March 1933 to see him put his ideas into action. (The four-month interval between the election and the inauguration was shortened by the Twentieth Amendment in 1933.) In the worst winter of the depression, Americans could do little but hope that things would get better. According to the most conservative estimates, unemployment stood at 20 to 25 percent nationwide. The rate was 50 percent in Cleveland, 60 percent in Akron, and 80 percent in Toledo—cities dependent on manufacturing jobs in industries that had essentially shut down. The nation's banking system was so close to collapse that many state governors closed banks temporarily to avoid further panic.

By the winter of 1932 to 1933 the depression had totally overwhelmed public welfare institutions. Private charity and public relief, both of whose expenditures had risen dramatically, still reached only a fraction of the needy. Hunger haunted cities and rural areas alike. When a teacher tried to send a coal miner's daughter home from school because she was weak from hunger, the girl replied, "It won't do any good . . . because this is sister's day to eat." In New York City hospitals reported ninety-five deaths from starvation. This was the America that Roosevelt inherited when he took the oath of office on March 4, 1933.

For Further Exploration

The 1930s are particularly rich in document collections of oral histories and other primary sources. Robert S. McElvaine's *Down and Out in the Great Depression* (1983) offers poignant letters written by ordinary people to the Roosevelts, Herbert Hoover, and other government officials. Studs Terkel's *Hard Times: An Oral History of the Great Depression* (1970) is an invaluable collection, as is Ann Banks, ed., *First-Person America*. See also Russell Baker's memoir about his depression-era childhood, *Growing Up* (1982). Similarly, there is much to choose from in the literature of the decade. The most familiar novel is John Steinbeck's *The Grapes of Wrath* (1939), but see also the radical novel *Pity Is Not Enough* (1933) by Josephine

FOR FURTHER EXPLORATION   717

T I M E L I N E			
1929	Stock market crash		Franklin Delano Roosevelt is elected president.
1930	Midwestern drought (through 1941)		
	Hawley-Smoot Tariff slashes demand for U.S. imports.	1933	Unemployment rises to its highest level.
			Birth rate drops to its lowest level.
1931	Scottsboro case		Marx Brothers' *Duck Soup*
	Hoover declares a moratorium on Allied war debts.	1934	Southern Tenant Farmers Union founded
	Miners strike in Harlan County, Kentucky.		*It Happened One Night* sweeps the Oscars.
	Communist-led hunger marches		
1932	Reconstruction Finance Corporation created	1935	National Youth Administration created
			Harlem race riot
	Bonus Army war veterans dispersed by U.S. Army troops	1936	Margaret Mitchell's *Gone with the Wind*
	Height of deportation of Mexican migrant workers		Birth control legalized
	Pearl S. Buck's *The Good Earth*	1939	John Steinbeck's *The Grapes of Wrath*
	Farm Holiday Association founded		Frank Capra's *Mr. Smith Goes to Washington*
	Violent strike at Ford's River Rouge plant in Michigan		

Herbst and Richard Wright's *Native Son* (1940), his classic novel about Bigger Thomas, a young African American man in Chicago mired in a life of poverty and violence. A haunting account of southern poverty is *Let Us Now Praise Famous Men* (1940) by James Agee, with photographs by Walker Evans. For a collection of poetry, fiction, and nonfiction writing, see Harvey Swados, *The American Writer and the Great Depression* (1966).

The University of Virginia's "America in the 1930s" is a comprehensive site. See especially "On the Air," which offers audio clips of *Amos 'n' Andy* and other series at <http://xroads.virginia.edu/~1930s/home_1.html>. Much valuable material can be found on the University of Utrecht's "American Culture in the 1930s" site at <http://www.let.ruu.nl/ams/xroads/1930proj.htm>, which in turn points to other sites dealing with literature, film, and other aspects of American culture during the depression. The Library of Congress's American Memory collection has extensive material on the Depression, including a multimedia presentation, "Voices from the Dust Bowl: The Charles L. Todd and Robert Sonkin Migrant Worker Collection, 1940–41," at <http://lcweb2.loc.gov/ammem/afctshtml/tshome.html>.

Thinking about the Textbook Selection

Answer the following questions about Chapter 24, "The Great Depression," from *America: A Concise History*.

1. Why do you think the authors begin the chapter with the quote by Cabell Phillips?

2. In a brief paragraph, summarize the major causes of the Great Depression.

3. How do the examples of 1930s movies, radio shows, books, and popular games illustrate how Americans experienced the depression?

4. What is the Scottsboro case? What does it tell you about race relations in the 1930s?

5. In the two "American Voices" feature boxes, the textbook chapter reprints excerpts from primary sources, or firsthand accounts, about what life was like during the depression. How do these passages differ from the regular textbook narrative?

6. Look closely at the photograph on page 484. Which of the authors' major points does it illustrate? What can you infer from it about New York City in 1930?

Reading the Web

Most introductory-level textbooks, like *America: A Concise History,* are supported by a companion Web site. Textbook sites are designed to help students better understand the course material and might include—among other things—questions, chapter outlines and summaries, study aids, additional readings, self-tests, links to related Web pages, bulletin boards, and advice on researching and writing papers. The following Web page shows part of the results of a student's assessment test for Chapter 24, "The Great Depression," in *America: A Concise History.*

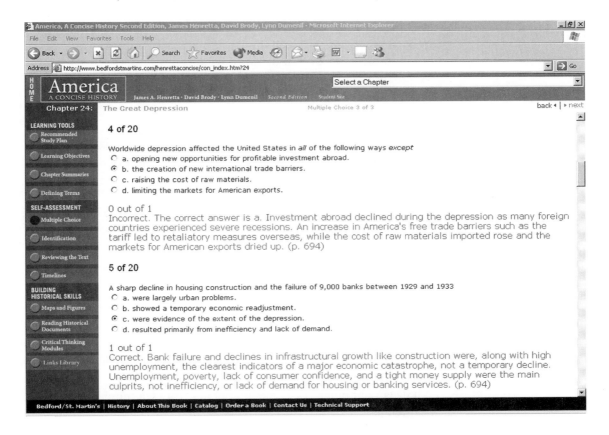

Thinking about the Web Page

1. How could the student use the feedback for her answers to improve her understanding of the textbook chapter's content? Where in the book could she find extra help?

2. What kinds of study aids can a student access on this Web site?

3. What could a student do if he had trouble accessing content on this site?

4. The resources on this companion Web site are available free to anybody who visits it. Go to bedfordstmartins.com/henrettaconcise and test your understanding of Chapter 24, "The Great Depression," by taking one of the self-assessment quizzes.

Reviewing

Recall / Remember

1. Why is it important to preview a textbook chapter before beginning to read it?

2. What are some things you can do in prereading a textbook or a textbook chapter?

3. Identify the major parts of a textbook and explain how you can use them to see what the book contains.

4. What are some of the elements typically included in textbooks? Choose three and explain how they can aid your reading comprehension.

5. What is skimming? List the guidelines for skimming a textbook chapter.

6. What is scanning? List the guidelines for scanning a textbook chapter.

7. Identify four common types of graphic material and explain what kinds of information they provide and how they visualize that information.

8. What is SQ3R? Explain how it works and how it can improve your reading comprehension and memory.

In this chapter you have practiced the reading strategies explained throughout this book. You have learned how to approach your college textbooks for careful reading and study. You have used vocabulary strategies to learn new terms, and you have used your skills to understand an author's main ideas and the details that support them. You have also made observations, connected them, drawn inferences from them, and arrived at conclusions that reflect your understanding of the chapter.

You also learned some new skills and strategies for understanding textbook materials, including interpreting visuals and using the SQ3R study method. These will help you get the most from your college reading materials.

In employing the reading strategies you have learned throughout this book to the sample textbook chapter, you should gain confidence that you can master college textbook material. Your confidence in being able to do this comes from the competence you have achieved in developing your reading skills. This competence and confidence improve not only your reading and study habits but also your ability to succeed in your academic work. In addition, you can apply your reading and study strategies to the reading you do in your everyday life and to the reading and study requirements you face at work.

Chapter
Summary

An Anthology of Readings

MAYA ANGELOU
Living Well. Living Good.

Maya Angelou, one of the best-known and most-respected writers of our day, is the author of a number of autobiographical books and collections of poetry, including *I Know Why the Caged Bird Sings,* the Pulitzer Prize–nominated *Just Give Me a Cool Drink of Water 'Fore I Die,* and her most recent, *A Song Flung Up to Heaven.* In 1993 Angelou recited her poem "On the Pulse of Morning" commissioned for Bill Clinton's presidential inauguration, becoming the second person to receive such an honor. "Living Well. Living Good." is a chapter from her best-selling 1993 book *Wouldn't Take Nothing for My Journey Now,* a collection of Angelou's essays and inspirational thoughts. In it, she remembers a story told her by her Aunt Tee, drawing from it an important life lesson.

Vocabulary Preview

incurred (para. 1): brought upon themselves (v.)

doilies (para. 2): small mats or strips of lace used to decorate or protect the surface of a piece of furniture (n.)

tautly (para. 2): tightly (adv.)

meticulous (para. 3): careful, nearly perfect (adj.)

melba toast (para. 5): very thin, dry crackers made of toasted bread (n.)

bid whist (para. 7): a card game played by two teams of two (n.)

trumps (para. 9): winning cards (n.)

convivial (para. 14): friendly (adj.)

Aunt Tee was a Los Angeles member of our extended family. She was seventy-nine when I met her, sinewy, strong, and the color of old lemons. She wore her coarse, straight hair, which was slightly streaked with gray, in a long braided rope across the top of her

1

head. With her high cheekbones, old gold skin, and almond eyes, she looked more like an Indian chief than an old black woman. (Aunt Tee described herself and any favored member of her race as Negroes. *Black* was saved for those who had incurred her disapproval.)

She had retired and lived alone in a dead, neat ground-floor apartment. Wax flowers and china figurines sat on elaborately embroidered and heavily starched doilies. Sofas and chairs were tautly upholstered. The only thing at ease in Aunt Tee's apartment was Aunt Tee.

I used to visit her often and perch on her uncomfortable sofa just to hear her stories. She was proud that after working thirty years as a maid, she spent the next thirty years as a live-in housekeeper, carrying the keys to rich houses and keeping meticulous accounts.

"Living in lets the white folks know Negroes are as neat and clean as they are, sometimes more so. And it gives the Negro maid a chance to see white folks ain't no smarter than Negroes. Just luckier. Sometimes."

Aunt Tee told me that once she was housekeeper for a couple in Bel Air, California, lived with them in a fourteen-room ranch house. There was a day maid who cleaned, and a gardener who daily tended the lush gardens. Aunt Tee oversaw the workers. When she had begun the job, she had cooked and served a light breakfast, a good lunch, and a full three- or four-course dinner to her employers and their guests. Aunt Tee said she watched them grow older and leaner. After a few years they stopped entertaining and ate dinner hardly seeing each other at the table. Finally, they sat in a dry silence as they ate evening meals of soft scrambled eggs, melba toast, and weak tea. Aunt Tee said she saw them growing old but didn't see herself aging at all.

She became the social maven. She started "keeping company" (her phrase) with a chauffeur down the street. Her best friend and her friend's husband worked in service only a few blocks away.

On Saturdays Aunt Tee would cook a pot of pigs' feet, a pot of greens, fry chicken, make potato salad, and bake a banana pudding. Then, that evening, her friends—the chauffeur, the other housekeeper, and her husband—would come to Aunt Tee's commodious live-in quarters. There the four would eat and drink, play records and dance. As the evening wore on, they would settle down to a serious game of bid whist.

Naturally, during this revelry jokes were told, fingers snapped, feet were patted, and there was a great deal of laughter.   8

Aunt Tee said that what occurred during every Saturday party startled her and her friends the first time it happened. They had been playing cards, and Aunt Tee, who had just won the bid, held a handful of trumps. She felt a cool breeze on her back and sat upright and turned around. Her employers had cracked her door open and beckoned to her. Aunt Tee, a little peeved, laid down her cards and went to the door. The couple backed away and asked her to come into the hall, and there they both spoke and won Aunt Tee's sympathy forever.   9

"Theresa, we don't mean to disturb you…" the man whispered, "but you all seem to be having such a good time…"   10

The woman added, "We hear you and your friends laughing every Saturday night, and we'd just like to watch you. We don't want to bother you. We'll be quiet and just watch."   11

The man said, "If you'll just leave your door ajar, your friends don't need to know. We'll never make a sound." Aunt Tee said she saw no harm in agreeing, and she talked it over with her company. They said it was OK with them, but it was sad that the employers owned the gracious house, the swimming pool, three cars, and numberless palm trees, but had no joy. Aunt Tee told me that laughter and relaxation had left the house; she agreed it was sad.   12

That story has stayed with me for nearly thirty years, and when a tale remains fresh in my mind, it almost always contains a lesson which will benefit me.   13

My dears, I draw the picture of the wealthy couple standing in a darkened hallway, peering into a lighted room where black servants were lifting their voices in merriment and comradery, and I realize that living well is an art which can be developed. Of course, you will need the basic talents to build upon: They are a love of life and ability to take great pleasure from small offerings, an assurance that the world owes you nothing and that every gift is exactly that, a gift. That people who may differ from you in political stance, sexual persuasion, and racial inheritance can be founts of fun, and if you are lucky, they can become even convivial comrades.   14

Living life as art requires a readiness to forgive. I do not mean that you should suffer fools gladly, but rather remember your own shortcomings, and when you encounter another with flaws, don't be eager to righteously seal yourself away from the offender forever.   15

Take a few breaths and imagine yourself having just committed the action which has set you at odds.

Because of the routines we follow, we often forget that life is an ongoing adventure. We leave our homes for work, acting and even believing that we will reach our destinations with no unusual event startling us out of our set expectations. The truth is we know nothing, not where our cars will fail or when our buses will stall, whether our places of employment will be there when we arrive, or whether, in fact, we ourselves will arrive whole and alive at the end of our journeys. Life is pure adventure, and the sooner we realize that, the quicker we will be able to treat life as art: to bring all our energies to each encounter, to remain flexible enough to notice and admit when what we expected to happen did not happen. We need to remember that we are created creative and can invent new scenarios as frequently as they are needed. 16

Life seems to love the liver of it. Money and power can liberate only if they are used to do so. They can imprison and inhibit more finally than barred windows and iron chains. 17

Thinking about the Selection

1. Use context clues to determine the meanings of the following words: *sinewy* (paragraph 1), *maven* (paragraph 6), and *beckoned* (paragraph 9).

2. Use word analysis to determine the meanings of the following words: *commodious* (paragraph 7), *comradery* (paragraph 14), and *founts* (paragraph 14).

3. Who is Aunt Tee, and what did she do for a living?

4. What is Aunt Tee's attitude toward herself and toward her work?

5. What kind of person is Aunt Tee? What details of the selection characterize her?

6. How did Aunt Tee's employers respond to her Saturday night parties?

7. Why didn't they ask to join in the fun?

8. What kind of relationship does Angelou have with her aunt?

9. What is the meaning of the last sentence of paragraph 13? What is the "lesson" that benefits Angelou?

10. Did you find this reading selection interesting or enjoyable? Why or why not?

NATALIE ANGIER
When (and Why) Dad Has the Babies

Natalie Angier is a Pulitzer Prize–winning science writer who currently reports for the *New York Times.* She has also written for *Discover, Time,* the *Atlantic, Parade,* and the Fox television network and taught for a while at New York University's Graduate Program in Science and Environmental Reporting. Her first book, *Natural Obsessions,* about cancer research, was listed as a notable book of the year by the American Association for the Advancement of Science; *The Beauty of the Beastly* has been translated into five languages. She has also written a book, *Woman,* about the female body. In this article about sea horses, which originally appeared in the *New York Times* (October 28, 1997), Angier reports a scientist's recent findings and describes the animals' unique ways of fertilizing, incubating, and caring for babies.

Vocabulary Preview

gestating (para. 3): transforming from fertilized eggs into beings that can survive outside the womb (v.)

in toto (para. 5): Latin for "on the whole," completely (adv.)

verities (para. 5): truths (n.)

viscous (para. 5): flowing slowly (adj.)

amalgam (para. 8): combination, mixture (n.)

cloacal (para. 14): related to a chamber that stores reproductive fluids (adj.)

epithelial (para. 15): tissue that encloses and protects internal organs (adj.)

fry (para. 17): offspring, babies (n.)

1   Many working mothers will attest to this: When a woman does the laundry and cooking, she gets clean clothes and food on the table. When a man does the housework, he gets a standing ovation. A good mother is natural, a good father divine.

2   And so it is that the male sea horse has long been viewed with awe, as a kind of submarine saint. Not only does he look like a Gothic hallucination, with his horse's head, anteater's snout and spiraling dragon's tail; he also behaves like a fantasy. As scientists discovered many decades ago, the male sea horse is the one that becomes pregnant, carries the young in his belly and gives birth. He is such a flamboyant specimen of devotion, such an exemplary parent, that the female sea horse is easily forgotten. How does that deadbeat mom spend her time, anyway?

Doing most of the work, it turns out, but behind the scenes and   3
without making a fuss. In results that shatter a staple of sea horse
lore, Dr. Heather Masonjones of Amherst College in Massachusetts
has determined that despite appearances, the female sea horse con-
tributes more effort and energy to the welfare of her young than the
male does, and that, therefore, sea horses are not quite the procre-
ational iconoclasts they were assumed to be. Dr. Masonjones has
found that although the male does carry the gestating embryos in a
brood pouch, he does not transfer nourishment to them through a
placenta-like organ as had been thought; instead, the embryos feed
off nutrients in the egg—food they had received beforehand from
their hard-working mother. Dad operates essentially like an incuba-
tor—a great guy, yes, but not a martyr to his children.

Dr. Masonjones studies dwarf sea horses, one of about 35   4
species of the fish found worldwide, and though she suspects her
findings are applicable to other types of sea horse, she has yet to
prove it. Her new results are part of her recently completed doc-
toral dissertation and are now being submitted for publication. She
presented some of the work at a recent meeting of the Animal
Behavior Society at the University of Maryland.

In tandem with being less motherly than legend has it, male sea   5
horses turn out to be less brotherly as well. Scientists had thought
that given the considerable commitment of male sea horses to child
care, sex roles would be swapped in toto, and the males would sit
back peacefully while the females thrashed it out with one another
over the right to mate with them. But as Dr. Amanda Vincent of
McGill University in Montreal, and Dr. Masonjones have shown,
some of the old verities of the animal kingdom apply: put a few
females together with a male, and not much happens. Put two or
more bachelor males in with a female, and the males go at it, inter-
locking their tails, extending their lower jaws and snouts, and jab-
bing at each other as they might at food. It is an odd, mannered,
viscous performance, the Jets and the Sharks[1] by way of molasses,
but the surliness is clear. "You can hear them snapping at each
other," Dr. Masonjones said. "It sounds like the snapping of fingers."

The latest insights into one of nature's most eccentric specimens   6
demonstrate once again the danger of making simplistic, overarch-
ing assumptions about reproductive behavior and the ever-shifting

---

[1]The Jets and the Sharks are rival street gangs in the musical *West Side Story*, a modern retelling of *Romeo and Juliet*.

dialectic between male and female. And though the results strip some of the sentimental gauze from the male's reputation, they enhance the sea horse's status as one of the most compelling and complex creatum, gilled or otherwise. Sea horses are fish, but they are not cold fish; they are great romantics. In a world where infidelity is almost universal, sea horses pair up and seem to be unerringly faithful to their mates, reaffirming their bond each day through elaborate courtship rituals. They are great pretenders, able to blend in with their surroundings so convincingly that they are nearly impossible to investigate. Dr. Vincent, considered the world's leading expert on sea horses, is one of the few people to study them in their native habitats, and even laboratory investigations of the creature are rare.

Sea horses may be too ethereal for their own good. Nobody knows how many sea horses swim the world's waters, and few countries bother regulating or tracking them. Dr. Vincent estimated that in the last five years, sea horse populations have plunged by 15 percent to 50 percent, depending on the species. The animals are harvested by the tens of thousands for use in traditional Chinese medicine, and demand for them has surged along with the boom in the Chinese economy. Sea horses are also gathered to supply the aquarium trade, although they fare poorly in captivity. They are sold as "curiosities," made into key rings, paperweights and mobiles. Their marine habitats are threatened by agricultural runoff, sewage, overfishing, boat traffic and a variety of other human activities.

"We need to put the brakes on now, before there's a catastrophic collapse," Dr. Vincent said. "You can't afford to lose 50 percent of a population in five years." She and a global network of activists and scientists are struggling to devise an amalgam of solutions to ease the pressure on sea horses. They are working to establish small-scale aquaculture programs in places like the Philippines and Vietnam, where the fish would be reared for trade rather than plundered from the wild; they are consulting with practitioners of Chinese medicine to learn how sea horse extracts are used, and what ingredients might serve as substitutes; and they are lobbying for the enactment of regulations to monitor and control the international trade in sea horses.

In September, the Australian Government responded by announcing that it would regard the family of fishes that includes sea horses, pipefishes and sea dragons as a form of wildlife. "They're the first marine fishes in Australia to be considered wildlife, rather than just food," Dr. Vincent said. "That means exports of them will be controlled and documented."

Sea horses may be poorly understood, but they have been   10
known, and exploited, since antiquity. They are pictured on Greek
vases, for they were thought to be the offspring of the stallions that
carried the god Poseidon's chariot across the waves. The Roman
naturalist Pliny wrote that ashes of sea horse could cure baldness,
impotence and rashes. By the 18th century, scientists realized that
sea horses are fish, though highly modified ones. Unlike most fish,
they wear their bones on the outside, as an exoskeletal armor that
offers considerable protection against predation. Their genus nomen-
clature, Hippocampus—hippo meaning horse, and campus, worm—
was used to name the sea horse–shaped structure in the brain
responsible for memory.

Sea horses range in size from half an inch to more than a foot in   11
length, and they are found in coastal waters throughout the world,
congregating in sea grasses, mangrove swamps and coral reefs. Like
chameleons, sea horses can change color to match their surroundings, going from drab to psychedelic in a matter of moments, and
they can even grow skin filaments to better mimic algae or coral.
The camouflage is both defensive and offensive. Sea horses are
ambush hunters, wrapping their tails around a strand of seaweed
and waiting for a small crustacean or other live prey to swim by, at
which point they lunge forward and suck the meal in through their
trunk-like snouts.

In love, sea horses are thoroughbreds. Once they have chosen a   12
partner, they have eyes for no other. A married sea horse of either
sex cannot be persuaded to cheat on its mate even when presented
with a tankful of willing singles. The pair reaffirm their bond each
morning through a courtship ritual of quivering, tail-wrapping, and
dancing round and round a blade of sea grass like figurines on a
music box. The female roams farther afield than the male, ever on
the lookout for better feeding grounds. She needs the calories to
generate a clutch of eggs. And when her eggs are ripe, the tango
begins. She approaches her mate and raises her head upward in a
slow arc. He quivers in response. She nods more emphatically, and
he nods in refrain.

Facing each other swan-style, they entwine their tails and rise   13
upward in the water. They disengage and do it again, 5, 10, 50
times, for hours and hours. "They're trying to line their bodies up
perfectly," said Dr. Masonjones, "so the female can insert her
ovipositer into the male's brood pouch."

Eventually, their bodies harmonize, and she transfers her eggs into his womb. As she does so, the male releases a burst of sperm from a cloacal opening above the pouch, fertilizing the eggs internally. Here Hippocampus stands alone. In many species of fish, males tend to the eggs and even brood live embryos in their mouths, but nowhere else in the animal kingdom is fertilization known to occur within the male's body. The eggs seeded, a sphincter muscle snaps the brood pouch shut, and a membranous seal forms behind it. **14**

Throughout the 10 or 12 days of gestation, the fluid within the pouch is completely insulated from the external environment, its salinity oxygen maintained at constant levels. Placenta-like epithelial tissue extends from the pouch lining to surround each embryo. That tissue was thought to permit the transfer of calories from the father's bloodstream to the young, but Dr. Masonjones has concluded that the placenta serves mainly as a waste-removal and gas-exchange system. **15**

Her experiments with dwarf sea horses, which are about two inches long, show that all the protein, fats and carbohydrates needed to feed the infants are derived from the meat of the mother's eggs. The role of the brood pouch, she says, is to act as a safe and predictable haven, a shelter from the fickle seas, so that the young need not devote egg energy to regulating salt and oxygen concentrations, but instead can spend it all on getting bigger faster. "At this point, it doesn't look like there are many energetic costs of brooding to the male," Dr. Masonjones said. **16**

Once the two dozen or so fry are sufficiently baked, the father goes into labor, which can last up to two days. Eventually the seal is broken, the pouch reopens, and a stream of fully developed, but very tiny, sea horses comes trotting out. Now they are on their own and must begin hunting immediately. Most die of starvation. **17**

There is no respite for the parents either. While the father was brooding, the mother was feasting, and making a new batch of rich, yolky eggs. The day after the male gives birth, his mate returns with the new clutch of ova to be fertilized and incubated. Throughout the seven-month breeding period, the male sea horse may become pregnant a dozen times, giving birth to more than 300 young. **18**

It is because the partners must be in perfect procreative synchrony, the mother ready with new eggs at exactly the moment when the father's pouch is open for business, that infidelity, nature's favorite ploy, becomes almost impossible. There is nothing to do but stay true, and start each morning with a twirl through the grass. **19**

Thinking about the Selection

. . . .

1. Before you read this article, how much (or little) did you know about sea horses?

2. Did you find this article interesting, entertaining, informative? Why or why not?

3. Use word analysis to determine the meanings of *dialectic* (paragraph 6), *ethereal* (paragraph 7), *exoskeletal* (paragraph 10), *ovipositer* (paragraph 13), and *membranous* (paragraph 14).

4. Use context clues to determine the meanings of *iconoclasts* (paragraph 3), *aquaculture* (paragraph 8), *psychedelic* (paragraph 11), *camouflage* (paragraph 11), *crustacean* (paragraph 11), and *synchrony* (paragraph 19).

5. Why are sea horses valued in Asian cultures?

6. What is unusual about the sexual behaviors of sea horses, especially male sea horses?

7. According to Heather Masonjones's research, how and where are sea horse eggs fertilized?

8. Why is Masonjones concerned about the various species of sea horses that exist today?

9. What is Natalie Angier's point of view toward Masonjones and her work with sea horses?

10. What is Angier's point of view toward sea horses themselves? What does she suggest about the relationship between and the responsibilities of male and female sea horses?

YOGI BERRA

When You Come to a Fork in the Road, Take It!

Hall of Famer and fifteen-time All Star Yogi Berra played baseball for the New York Yankees for nearly twenty years before becoming their manager for one season. He coached, then managed, the New York Mets for six years, returned to the Yankees as a coach and was promoted to manager, and then coached the Houston Astros from 1986 until he retired from baseball in 1992. Berra is known for his sayings—known as "Yogi-isms"—almost as much as he is for his record-setting baseball career. Famous quotes include "It ain't over 'til it's over," "It's déjà vu all over again," "The future ain't what it used to be," and "It gets late early out here." Berra has a number of books to his credit, including *It Ain't Over* and *When You Come to a Fork in the Road, Take It! Inspiration and Wisdom from One of Baseball's Greatest Heroes*, from which this selection is taken. In it, Yogi Berra reflects on the choices he's made in his life and offers decision-making advice to his readers.

Vocabulary Preview

remiss (para. 6): regretful, neglectful (adj.)

1 Throughout life you come to serious forks in the road—decisions. Which path do you choose? Sometimes it's tough. People are always afraid of making the wrong choice. But no matter what decision you make—taking a job, getting married, buying a house, whatever it is—you shouldn't look back. Trust your instincts.

2 The beauty of baseball is that you always have forks in the road—decisions that could mean the difference between winning and losing. If you're a manager, when do you take a pitcher out if he's tiring? Do you hit and run with slow runners on base? Like they say, decisions, decisions. Joe Torre does a great job as the Yankee manager; it always seems he makes the right decision. He trusts his instincts.

3 But he also trusts his bench coach, Don Zimmer, to bounce ideas off of. Zim has a lot of experience. He's Joe's security blanket. Between them, the Yankees are always on the right road.

4 I've always done things that *feel* right. I've also been lucky. Throughout my life, I've always had my family behind me, helping

me make the right choices. My first big life decision was at age fourteen, when I wanted to quit school after eighth grade to go to work. My parents, the principal, and the parish priest all had a conference and tried to talk me into continuing, but I was a lousy student and pretty stubborn and felt I was wasting my time. I remember a teacher once asking me, "Don't you know anything?" and I said I don't even suspect anything.

They finally all agreed I'd be just as well off working and handing over what I made to Mom. I realize now this was a major turning point in my life, and I was fortunate. Education is a necessary part of a young person's life. Very few who quit school early on ever wind up successful when they get older. 5

But the decision was for my own good, and it wouldn't have been made without Mom and Pop's approval. Also, without my parents—and my three older brothers—I wouldn't have been allowed to pursue my dream of playing baseball. Things worked out well, because if not for baseball, I might still be in the shoe factory. So I didn't have regrets about taking that fork in the road to leave school. Except, looking back now, I do feel a little remiss about not finishing. It's a void in my life, and it's why Carm and I arranged trust funds for our three sons, Larry, Tim, and Dale, to guarantee them a college education. Because of my situation, I was very anxious they get as much schooling as they could. 6

One of my biggest decisions ever was over fifty years ago, asking a beautiful waitress at Biggie's restaurant in St. Louis out on a date—then eventually asking her to marry me. I didn't have much confidence back then. I was bashful, nervous, and not good-looking. I could hardly believe my luck that Carmen liked me as much as I liked her. I soon knew as sure as anything that I wanted to spend the rest of my life with her. 7

After marrying Carm in 1949, we came to a few forks in the road—tough life decisions. At the time, I was making only $12,000 a year with the Yankees. After the season, we lived in St. Louis where I grew up (although Carm grew up in Salem, Missouri) and where we had real tight-knit families. Everything and everybody we knew were there. I even worked at nearby Ruggeri's restaurant as a head waiter in the off-season. 8

But we were kind of torn. There were more opportunities in the East. My baseball career was there. We wanted to start a family. Believe me, it was tough leaving everything behind when we finally decided to move to the New York area in 1951. But it was the right 9 thing for us, because we made a good new life, and got more comfortable financially. I doubt the same could've happened back home.

Carm and I talk over everything. The decision to leave St. Louis was ours. The big decision to become a coach with Casey Stengel and the Mets, and not stay with the Yankees in another job after being let go as manager in 1964, was ours. As it turned out, things were good coaching with the Mets. It was the right move, secure and safe. That's why Carm didn't want me to become their manager when Gil Hodges died in 1972. But I was at a crossroads—another fork in the road. I was forty-six years old and wanted to manage again, to prove I could. I didn't think I'd ever get another chance. Carm and my old pal Joe Garagiola thought I was foolish, and tried to talk me out of it. They thought I had a great job, since coaches last forever and managers don't. But I had a strong desire to take the Mets job, and did. I relished the challenge and never looked back. A year later, we won the National League pennant.

I think that's what all these graduation speakers mean when they quote me, "When you see the fork in the road, take it." Make a firm decision. Make sure it feels right. Learn from the choice you make. Don't second-guess yourself—there's no need to give yourself ulcers. But my advice on big life decisions is to get advice if you can. Talk it over with a parent, a mentor, a teacher, or a coach. They've had more life experience. They've got more miles on them, they can help you get on the right path. When I see my grandchildren choosing colleges and graduating from them and looking for the right job, I'm very proud. I see them making informed choices. They're coming to the fork in the road, and they know what to do.

Thinking about the Selection

1. What is unusual about the title of this selection? What sense does it make to you?

2. What does Yogi Berra mean by a "fork in the road"? What examples does he provide to illustrate what he means?

3. What "forks in the road" have you come to in your own life? What "forks" lie ahead for you?

4. What do you think of Yogi Berra's advice about not looking back once you have made a decision? Why?

5. What is Berra's attitude toward education? What education decision did he make for himself? What did he encourage his children and grandchildren to do? Why?

6. How does Berra portray his wife and marriage? Why do you think he mentions them?

7. What does Berra have to say about taking advice from others? What do you think of his advice about advice?

8. What does Berra mean when he says he "relished" the challenge of managing the Mets? What does "relish" mean in this context?

9. What does Berra mean when he says that parents, mentors, and teachers have "got more miles on them"? What implied analogy is he making?

10. If you could ask Yogi Berra one question, what would it be? Why?

BEN CARSON
Gifted Hands

The first surgeon to successfully separate twins joined at the head without losing either one, Ben Carson is the director of pediatric neurosurgery at Johns Hopkins University Hospital. Raised under difficult circumstances in Detroit's inner city, Carson decided when he was eight that he wanted to be a doctor and relied on faith and hard work to reach his goal. His philosophy—that all people can achieve what they want—is outlined in his book *Think Big.* He founded the Carson Scholars Fund in 1994 to help disadvantaged but academically gifted middle school and high school students save for college. In the following selection from *Gifted Hands,* Carson's autobiography, he describes his gift and explains how he used it and his creativity to make improvements to a medical procedure while he was still a student.

Vocabulary Preview

encompassing (para. 1): including (v.)
aptitude (para. 2): ability, talent (n.)
neurosurgeon (para. 6): brain surgeon (n.)

probe (para. 10): search blindly (v.)
radiology technician (para. 14): x-ray technician (n.)

1 It's my belief that God gives us all gifts; special abilities that we have the privilege of developing to help us serve Him and humanity. And the gift of eye and hand coordination has been an invaluable asset in surgery. This gift goes beyond eye-hand coordination, encompassing the ability to understand physical relationships, to think in three dimensions. Good surgeons must understand the consequences of each action, for they're often not able to see what's happening on the other side of the area in which they're actually working.

2 Some people have the gift of physical coordination. These are the people who become Olympic stars. Others can sing beautifully. Some people have a natural ear for languages or a special aptitude for math. I know individuals who seem to draw friends, who have a unique ability to make people feel welcome and part of the family.

3 For some reason, I am able to "see" in three dimensions. In fact, it seems incredibly simple. It's just something I happen to be able to do. However, many doctors don't have this natural ability, and

some, including surgeons, never learn this skill. Those who don't pick this up just don't develop into outstanding surgeons, frequently encountering problems, constantly fighting complications.

I first became aware of this ability when a classmate pointed it out at Yale. He and I used to play table soccer (sometimes called fussball), and, although I had never played before, almost from the first lesson I did it with speed and ease. I didn't realize it then, but it was because of this ability. When I visited Yale in early 1988, I chatted with a former classmate who is on staff there. He laughingly told me that I had been so good at the game that afterward they named several plays "Carson shots." 4

During my studies at medical school and the years afterward I realized the value of this skill. For me it is the most significant talent God has given me and the reason people sometimes say I have gifted hands.... 5

There ought to be an easier way, I thought as I watched my instructor. A skilled neurosurgeon, he knew what he was doing, but he had difficulty locating the foramen ovale (the hole at the base of the skull). The woman on whom he was operating had a condition called trigeminal neuralgia, a painful condition of the face. "This is the hardest part," the man said as he probed with a long, thin needle. "Just locating the foramen ovale." 6

Then I started to argue with myself. *You're new at neurosurgery, but already you think you know everything, huh? Remember, Ben, these guys have been doing this kind of surgery for years.* 7

Yeah, answered another inner voice, *but that doesn't mean they know everything.* 8

Just leave it alone. One day you'll get your chance to change the world. 9

I would have stopped arguing with myself except I couldn't get away from thinking that there must be an easier way. Having to probe for the foramen ovale wasted precious surgery time and didn't help the patient either. 10

OK, smart man. Find it then. 11

And that's just what I decided to do. 12

I was doing my clinical year at the University of Michigan's School of Medicine and was in my neurosurgery rotation. Each of the rotations lasted a month, and it was during this period that the surgeon commented on the difficulty of finding the little hole at the base of the skull. 13

After arguing with myself for some time, I took advantage of the friends I had made the previous summer when I worked as a radiology technician. I went to them and explained what was worrying me. They were interested and gave me permission to come into their department and practice with the equipment.

14

After several days of thinking and trying different things, I hit upon a simple technique of placing two tiny metal rings on the back and front of the skull, and then aligning the rings so that the foramen ovale fell exactly between them. Using this technique, doctors could save a lot of time and energy instead of poking around inside the skull.

15

I had reasoned it this way: Since two points determine a line, I could put one ring on the outside surface of the skull behind the area where the foramen ovale should be. I then would put the other one on the front of the skull. By passing an X-ray beam through the skull, I could turn the head until the rings lined up. At that point, the foramen falls in between.

16

The procedure seemed simple and obvious—once I'd reasoned it out—but apparently no one had thought of it before. Fact is, I didn't tell anyone either. I was thinking of how to do a better job and wasn't concerned with impressing anybody or showing my instructors a new technique.

17

For a short time I tormented myself by asking, *Am I getting into a new realm of things that others haven't yet discovered? Or am I just thinking I've figured out a technique no one else has considered before?* Finally I decided that I had developed a method that worked for me and that was the important thing.

18

I started doing this procedure and, from actual surgery, saw how much easier it was. After two such surgeries, I told my neurosurgeon professors how I was doing it and then demonstrated for them. The head professor watched, shook his head slowly, and smiled. "That's fabulous, Carson."

19

Fortunately, the neurosurgery professors didn't resent my idea.

20

Thinking about the Selection

1. What special gift does Ben Carson have? Why does he believe he has this gift? What does he do with it?

2. What are some other kinds of gifts Carson mentions?

3. Use context clues to determine the meanings of *foramen ovale* and *trigeminal neuralgia.*

4. What stories does Ben Carson tell about himself? What point does he use them to make?

5. How does Carson show his thinking process?

6. What were some of Carson's concerns as he discovered a simpler way to perform a difficult surgical operation?

7. How did Carson's professors respond to his discovery? How might they have responded?

8. Did you find this piece of writing interesting or engaging? Why or why not?

9. What can you learn from Carson's experience?

10. If you could speak with Carson, what would you say to him? Why?

PICO IYER

The Necessity of Travel

Born in England to Indian parents and currently living in California and Japan, Pico Iyer is a prolific travel writer. He works primarily as an essayist for *Time* magazine, which he credits with allowing him plenty of time off for exploring the world—Iyer travels constantly and has been to some of the remotest spots on the planet. In addition to writing frequent magazine columns and articles that have appeared in such publications as *Harper's, Sports Illustrated, Salon.com,* and the *New Yorker,* Iyer has published a novel and half a dozen books about his travel experiences, including *Video Night in Katmandu* and *Falling Off the Map.* His second novel is *Abandon* (2002). He wrote "The Necessity for Travel" for *Time* magazine, where it originally appeared on May 27, 2002. In it, this most experienced of travelers argues that in the wake of the tragic events of September 11, 2001, Americans must travel more—not less—to gain a greater understanding of the world beyond U.S. borders.

Vocabulary Preview

clamor (para. 1): loudly and publicly show a desire for (v.)

Pashtu (para. 2): the official language of Iran and Afghanistan, also spoken in parts of Pakistan (n.)

Other (para. 3): when capitalized, refers to persons who are perceived as foreign and different from oneself (n.)

holiday (para. 4): British term for vacation (n.)

The images, of course, will not go away: the planes exploding in flames, bodies falling through the air. And in their wake, more mundane but still disquieting pictures—endless lines in the airports, armed guards watching as shoeless innocents empty their pockets (while across the world people clamor for America's humiliation). To many of us, as the peak vacation season draws near, travel may seem a less appealing prospect than it has ever been.

And yet, I would argue, travel has never been so urgent, even necessary, as it is today. To at least a small extent, the horrors of last fall seem to have arisen from people knowing dangerously little about the far side of the world: Islamic radicals tilting[1] against an

---

[1] Iyer is referring to novelist Miguel Cervantes's romantic hero Don Quixote, whose deluded efforts to attack windmills in the belief that they were monsters has come to be called "tilting at windmills."

America they associate only with its economic and political might (or the pop-cultural blast of its images) and cruelly ignoring the human reality that is the true America; and, later on, Washington responding through a President who had seldom been abroad, and a CIA that by some accounts did not have a single Pashtu speaker in Afghanistan. Caught in the middle, as ever, were those ordinary, open-minded souls who might have harbored subtler and more enlightened thoughts about what Islam means, and America.

Travel is how we put a face and a voice to the Other and step   3
a little beyond our secondhand images of the alien. It is, in fact, how we learn about the world and come to terms (and sometimes peace) with it. All the information in the world on our flashing or high-definition screens cannot begin to convey the feel and smell, the human truth, of another culture. And all of us are lucky enough to live at a time when the far corners of the world are more accessible physically than ever before. The minute I got off the plane in Yemen last summer, I could see how everything I thought I knew about that country was wrong and how far most of its people lived emotionally from, say, the October 2000 bombing of the U.S.S. *Cole* in Southern Yemen. Likewise, the minute a Yemeni sets foot in New York City, she sees it as quite different from the lawless jungle of gun-toting druglords and prostitutes she may have imagined. Most people in the developing world, though, do not have the opportunity or resources to come and see us. It is therefore up to us—at least those of us with the time and money—to go and see them.

The principle applies, of course, even if we go no farther than   4
Washington or the Lebanese restaurant on the other side of town; we have the chance at any moment to walk outside our prejudices. Those who stay home may think the outside world is dangerous (and the more they stay home, the more dangerous it will seem). Yet as soon as we travel, we are reminded that, for example, during the 1980s when war was tearing apart Beirut, San Salvador and Kabul, Washington had a higher murder rate than any of them. Last year, when I took my 70-year-old mother on holiday to Syria, she quickly saw that its people were much friendlier than the country's dictatorship suggested, that the roads were clean and that (for a visitor in any case) life was in most respects as safe as in the affluent California town where she lives. Insofar as such places are difficult, traveling abroad allows us to appreciate better all the opportunities and freedoms of home that we otherwise take for granted.

In the wake of the 9/11 violence, most Americans were wise   5
enough to realize that the terrorist atrocities had nothing to do with
Hamid, in his skullcap, who runs the grocery store around the corner, while all the Muslims I knew grieved as if the losses were their
own. Yet many people wondered why America had provoked such
animosity. Traveling to Bolivia, Vietnam, India and many other
countries in the months since the attacks, I have been sobered to see
the words U.S. OUT OF AFGHANISTAN! scrawled across the walls of
an elegant colonial building in the Andes (while a shoeshine boy
down the street told me he longed to come to America to help fight
terrorists). In many closed or impoverished countries, meeting
Americans is the only way the people can learn that America is not
the "axis of evil"—a George W. Bush phrase that some foreigners
have turned back on the U.S.

In some ways, Sept. 11 was a harrowing reminder of how truly   6
we all live in the same neighborhood now, even if the differences
and distances between us remain as great as ever. In any neighborhood, it is the people who keep their doors locked and their curtains drawn who are the truly menacing ones. One of the difficult
things about the events of last fall was how powerless most people
felt as they watched the destruction onscreen. Many of us, in fact,
do have the power, however small, to take the first step toward real
communication—by going to Beijing, or Mexico City, or, best of
all, Damascus.

Thinking about the Selection

1. Iyer begins his essay with a series of details. What kinds of
   details does he select, and what is their collective impact?
   How do they relate to the final sentence (the topic sentence) of
   the opening paragraph?

2. Why does Iyer argue that "travel has never been so urgent,
   even necessary, as it is today"? What is his reasoning for this
   claim?

3. Use the context of the essay to infer the meanings of *harbored*
   (paragraph 2), *atrocities* (paragraph 5), *animosity* (paragraph 5),
   and *harrowing* (paragraph 6).

4. What reasons does Iyer suggest are partly responsible for the September 11 attacks?

5. What positive effects does Iyer see in travel, especially to places very different from where we live?

6. Do you agree with Iyer's argument that it is the responsibility of Americans to travel to other places, rather than for others to travel here? Why or why not?

7. Why does Iyer mention "Hamid, in his skullcap, who runs the grocery store around the corner"?

8. What is the point of Iyer's stories about his trips to Yemen and Syria?

9. What does Iyer convey through his comment about "the feel and smell, the human truth, of another culture"? How does Iyer think that we can acquire this understanding?

10. Do you find Iyer's argument persuasive? Why or why not?

LARA MARGOLIS
Chicken Scratch and E-Hugs

Lara Margolis grew up in a small town in central Pennsylvania and describes herself as having "intense fears of rabid birds, spaghetti, and my legs suddenly disappearing." A prize-winning chemistry major who graduated Phi Beta Kappa in 2002, she wrote frequent articles for the *College Dispatch,* the online student magazine for Franklin and Marshall College, and was head writing assistant in the college writing center. Margolis has also published a chemistry paper in the *Journal of Chemical Education.* "Chicken Scratch and E-Hugs" was written for the *Dispatch* when she was a college senior. In it, she describes her "addiction" to Instant Messaging and warns readers not to let new communication technologies weaken their writing and social skills.

Vocabulary Preview

replicate (para. 2): duplicate, reproduce, copy (v.)

ritual (para. 3): established series of behaviors, often used for religious ceremonies (n.)

I'll readily admit it: I was an Instant Messenger addict. My first encounter with Instant Messenger was in my senior year of high school, and by sophomore year of college, I couldn't live without it. Even though the constant little noises got annoying at times, I could chat with my friends without having to walk the dreaded hundred yards across campus, and my fear of phones became a dim memory. After every class, I made a beeline to my computer to see who was on, knocking out anyone or anything that dared get in my way, and my eyes took on a permanent glazed look of reflected computer glare. It was only when I found myself writing to my roommate six feet across the room that I realized I had a problem.

As much as we might gain in speed and convenience, technology, especially as a form of communication, certainly has its downsides. Despite little options like buddy icons and different colors and styles of font, neither Instant Messengers nor email really has much personality. A handwritten letter might be neatly penned on personal stationery or quickly jotted on a page torn from an assignment book; seeing a loved one's chicken scratch creates a feeling of warmth no neatly typed email could ever replicate. In computer-ese, the chuckles your stories produce in person are reduced to "lol's," less rewarding even when capitalized for emphasis. And nothing could ever convince me that at the end of a rough day, what I really need is an e-hug.

Although I think my typing speed has more than doubled with the aid of IM, internet communication allows me to commit less time and attention to my communication efforts. Instead of being fully intent on talking with someone on the phone or over coffee, I split my attention between four or five IM conversations, my biggest focus on not writing a response to the wrong person. Even my writing style has gone downhill as a result of my internet dependence. When I write letters, I go through a full-blown ritual, often writing several drafts to make sure I express everything just so; when I write emails, I often don't even bother to use capitalization. By using technology to communicate, I stop thinking of keeping in touch with friends as an opportunity to express my thoughts and personality, and begin to think of it as another daily chore that I should finish as quickly as possible.

The use of email has allowed me to not only become lazier about communication, but it has also allowed me to take the easy way out of uncomfortable situations. For the past few years, I have been able to mask my shyness behind the safety of the typed word. And although the site of a dialpad still sends shivers down my spine, I now realize the importance of developing good phone skills. After using the computer to avoid phone use for several years, I have found that I am at a distinct disadvantage when late night pizza cravings hit, as well as in my hunt for jobs and as I need to do phone interviews in my search for a job. But even for those without my personal phone-phobia, email allows us as students to avoid the uncomfortable situation of explaining, in person, why we have to miss a class or a job, ultimately making it easier to wimp out on our responsibilities.

I am not recommending that we all give up technology—I still become antsy when the campus email goes down for a day or two. But I think we spend so much time praising the new forms of communication that we forget the advantages of the old ones. Yes, through the campus internet connection, email and IM are nearly free, but then again, so are local phone calls, and for the price of a new iMac to provide your internet fix, you could buy more than 4000 stamps or make over 200 hours of long-distance calls. So next time you decide to contact an old friend, think of all of your options: the fastest isn't always the best.

Thinking about the Selection

1. What is the author's point of view regarding the use of new technologies for communicating? What, for example, is her attitude toward e-mail and instant messaging?

2. Identify the topic sentence of each paragraph. What kinds of evidence does Margolis provide to support each of them? Do you think the essay would benefit from other supporting details? Why or why not?

3. When did Margolis realize that she had a "problem" with using the new technologies to communicate with her friends?

4. To what extent do you share Margolis's experiences about using instant messaging, or e-mail, or the telephone?

5. What advantages and disadvantages does she identify for e-mail and old-fashioned letter writing?

6. How does the title of Margolis's essay relate to the point she makes about writing letters versus sending e-mails?

7. Margolis describes her fear of using the telephone. What effect has using e-mail had on her phobia?

8. Does Margolis express a preference for one kind of communication over another?

9. Are you persuaded by Margolis's arguments? Why or why not?

10. Did you find this essay interesting or entertaining? Why or why not?

TODD MCCARTHY
Anti-Smokers Ought to Butt Out of Movies

Todd McCarthy is the chief film critic and editor in chief of *Variety,* Hollywood's daily industry newspaper. In addition to penning hundreds of movie reviews, McCarthy is a respected writer and director of documentaries about film. His credits include *Forever Hollywood,* a celebratory retrospective of American movies that plays daily for tourists at Hollywood's Egyptian Theater; the PBS documentary *Preston Sturges: The Rise and Fall of an American Dreamer,* for which he won an Emmy in 1990; and *Visions of Light: The Art of Cinematography,* the Oscar winner for best documentary in 1993. McCarthy has also published a biography of film director Howard Hawks and acted in bit parts in the action movies *Grand Theft Auto* and *Cannonball.* The following article first appeared in *Variety*'s online edition on March 14, 2002. In it, McCarthy describes the current campaign to eliminate the depiction of smoking in movies and argues that the attempt is misguided and silly.

Vocabulary Preview

on par (para. 4): the same as (adj.)

garroting (para. 4): strangulation (n.)

disembowelment (para. 4): the removal of internal organs (n.)

zealots (para. 5): fanatics (n.)

brethren (para. 5): members of a group (n.)

emulate (para. 5): try to be like (v.)

cohorts (para. 7): members of a group (n.)

empirically (para. 8): through observation (adv.)

disposition (para. 11): attitude toward (n.)

In a Brave New World[1] being proposed by a fellow who obviously embraces the role of censor and enforcer of the rewriting of history, kids of all ages would be able to attend a biographical film about Adolf Hitler. But no one under 17, unless accompanied by an adult, would be allowed to see a similar picture about two of the world leaders most responsible for halting the career of the vegetarian teetotaling Nazi, Winston Churchill and Franklin D. Roosevelt. 1

If this self-appointed regulator has his way, many of the most beloved films of all time not set in the ancient world or outer 2

---

[1]McCarthy is referring to Aldous Huxley's novel *Brave New World,* about a future society in which everyone's behaviors and feeling are controlled by the government.

space—*Gone with the Wind, Citizen Kane, Titanic, The Sound of Music, Shane, Some Like It Hot, A Hard Day's Night, Breakfast at Tiffany's, Casablanca, Rio Bravo,* or just about anything starring Humphrey Bogart or John Wayne, not to mention Bette Davis, Gary Cooper, Frank Sinatra or the Marx brothers—will be automatically slapped with retroactive R ratings.

And if this single-issue crusader actually gets somewhere with his campaign, which already has convinced some people in Hollywood to take him seriously and has received amazingly sympathetic treatment in major publications in the past two weeks, we will soon be seeing a new warning line attached to the Motion Picture Assn. of America's Restricted rating that would read something like this: Danger—The Smoking You See in This Film Could Be Hazardous to Your Health.   3

Now that smoking has effectively been banned from all offices, restaurants, sporting venues and public places, with open-air parks looking like the next target, the banner is clearly being taken up for the next frontier of prohibition, for what I'll call third-hand smoke, stuff you can't actually inhale or even smell but that evidently can pollute you all the same. The charge is being led by one Stanton Glantz, a UC San Francisco School of Medicine professor, who, through his org Smoke Free Movies, has been taking ads, appearing on talkshows and lobbying industryites on behalf of his idea that smoking should be considered on par with graphic garroting, disembowelment, chainsaw dismemberment, decapitation, torture, machine gun massacres and all other manner of splatter-film violence, along with full-frontal nudity and a cascade of f-words, as far as film ratings are concerned.   4

If common sense prevailed in such matters, such a proposal would be laughed off or filed away deep in a don't-bother-to-reply drawer. But zealots gripped by a cause, no matter how nonsensical, won't go away quietly, so they must be addressed, albeit, one hopes, from a more logical mindset and in a less emotional tone than they employ. Where Glantz and his brethren, including Rob Reiner, who is apparently already trying to snuff out smoking in pictures at Castle Rock, score the most points is in their charge that onscreen smoking glamorizes the habit, that the sight of beautiful young people puffing away will encourage kids to emulate their idols.   5

It is certainly true that movie stars, from Marlene Dietrich and Lauren Bacall to James Dean and Jean-Paul Belmondo, have always made smoking look cool. But the allure of watching Bogart con-   6 stantly smoking while smoldering in *Casablanca,* Cooper wilting Dietrich in clouds of smoke in *Morocco* or Wayne lighting up as he bested his enemies in almost anything is undercut by the knowledge that these three most macho of stars actually died from a lifetime of chain-smoking, which presents anyone with a clear-cut choice for making up one's own mind.

Much more to the point, however, is that there are numerous other activities routinely, and attractively, shown onscreen that are considerably more dangerous statistically than smoking, particularly to younger people. When you roll together all the negative effects of drinking—auto accidents, physical abuse, reckless behavior, irresponsibility, waste of time and lives—they are infinitely more damaging than the effects of smoking, which usually take decades to accumulate into serious illness and even then negatively effect only about one-third of those who do it. But Glantz and cohorts, medical and otherwise, have expressed no outrage at the drinking shown, not only in movies, but still promoted via ads all over the media.

And how about the health hazards posed by obesity, which, according to major studies published last year, now represents a more serious problem in the United States than does anything to do with smoking. By rights, any motion picture showing people eating at McDonald's or Kentucky Fried Chicken, or chowing down on fatty foods or big desserts should automatically be rated R, since the long-term consequences are dire in a nation where, per a Rand report, three out of five Americans are overweight, a fact that can be empirically confirmed by a quick visit to Disneyland or Las Vegas.

Since we're not likely to see Budweisers and Big Macs banned from the bigscreen anytime soon, it's plausible to ask why the pit bulls of political correctness have decided to demonize smoking and ignore other much less normal aspects of life; to become incensed, for example, by the aggrieved Sissy Spacek's utterly understandable smoking in the already R-rated *In the Bedroom* or the constant cloud of smoke through which the aristocrats carry on, with absolute cultural and period accuracy, in *Gosford Park,* and turn a blind eye to the precarious driving in the PG-13-rated *The Fast and the Furious* or unsafe sex and wanton violence in countless movies. The reason can only be hatred of the tobacco companies, an attitude legitimized by the courts with their outrageous bequests to people who blame corporations for their own lifetimes of indulgence and lack of personal responsibility, and by the tobacco companies themselves for their history of deceit.

I am personally disgusted when I see a movie like *Saving Private Ryan* or *Pearl Harbor* that rewrites history by showing virtually no one (including FDR in the latter) smoking at a time when cigarettes were actually included in the military's C rations; so poisonous is the stance toward smoking now that I was actually thrilled to see the habit properly and proportionately represented in *Band of Brothers*. Glantz is so off-base on the issue of the logical, historical and normal depiction of smoking in motion pictures that, when challenged about whether any film showing Churchill or FDR (or so many others) would deserve an R rating, he dismisses such works as "documentary." In fact, if the anti-smoking adherents are interested in making a documentary promoting their cause, their most logical choice as a director might be Leni Riefenstahl who at 99 is presumably available and, as the creator of *Triumph of the Will*,[2] might know very well how to propagandize on behalf of a cause—anti-smoking—that was almost as dear to the heart of the fuhrer as it is to them. Glantz also vehemently denies that he's calling for censorship, which of course is the first tip-off that it is exactly what he's interested in.

To an industry (and a country) that likes to congratulate itself for its devotion to freedom of expression, it should be apparent that Glantz's movement, which is obviously gathering some steam, represents antidemocratic social engineering of the first order and should be resisted on principle regardless of one's personal disposition toward smoking.

10

11

---

[2]A Nazi propaganda film.

Thinking about the Selection

1. What is the author's main point in this article? Where does he express his idea most clearly in a single sentence?

2. What is McCarthy's purpose in naming specific films and film stars in paragraph 2?

3. How many paragraphs make up the introduction for this article? How many paragraphs constitute the author's conclusion?

4. Use word analysis to determine the meanings of *teetotaling* (paragraph 1), *retroactive* (paragraph 2), and *aggrieved* (paragraph 9).

5. What does Todd McCarthy think of the ideas advocated by Stanton Glantz? Where does he explicitly express his point of view about Glantz's ideas?

6. Why does McCarthy bring up the topics of drinking and obesity?

7. What purpose is served by his mention of Budweisers and Big Macs, along with the movies *Gosford Park* and *The Fast and the Furious*?

8. Why does McCarthy object to the movies *Pearl Harbor* and *Saving Private Ryan*?

9. Why does he praise the HBO movie *Band of Brothers*?

10. How persuasive is McCarthy in this piece? Do you agree or disagree with his point of view? Why?

KATHERINE ANNE PORTER

Rope

Before establishing her career as an acclaimed short story writer in the 1930s, Katherine Anne Porter was a newspaper reporter in Chicago and Denver. She grew up poor in Texas and Louisiana and noted that the majority of her energy in her early career "went to keeping my head above water." At one point a Communist sympathizer, she spent three years involved in revolutionary politics in Mexico, her "much-loved second country," while she earned a living writing and teaching. Her *Collected Stories* won the Pulitzer Prize in literature and the National Book Award in 1966. She died in 1980 at the age of ninety. "Rope," first published in 1928, reflects Porter's preference for character study over plot. The story's depiction of an argument between a young married couple has little action, but Porter manages to reveal depths of the character's emotions and their reactions to each other and the situation they're in.

Vocabulary Preview

borne (para. 10): past tense of the verb *to bear,* endured (v.)

forlorn (para. 15): sad (adj.)

craw (para. 19): stomach (n.)

melancholiac (para. 22): person who is constantly depressed and unjustifiably sad (n.)

uproarious (para. 28): hysterically funny (adj.)

1   On the third day after they moved to the country he came walking back from the village carrying a basket of groceries and a twenty-four-yard coil of rope. She came out to meet him, wiping her hands on her green smock. Her hair was tumbled, her nose was scarlet with sunburn; he told her that already she looked like a born country woman. His gray flannel shirt stuck to him, his heavy shoes were dusty. She assured him he looked like a rural character in a play.

2   Had he brought the coffee? She had been waiting all day long for coffee. They had forgot it when they ordered at the store the first day.

3   Gosh, no, he hadn't. Lord, now he'd have to go back. Yes, he would if it killed him. He thought, though, he had everything else. She reminded him it was only because he didn't drink coffee himself. If he did he would remember it quick enough. Suppose they ran out of cigarettes? Then she saw the rope. What was that for? Well,

he thought it might do to hang clothes on, or something. Naturally she asked him if he thought they were going to run a laundry? They already had a fifty-foot line hanging right before his eyes? Why, hadn't he noticed it, really? It was a blot on the landscape to her.

He thought there were a lot of things a rope might come in handy for. She wanted to know what, for instance. He thought a few seconds, but nothing occurred. They could wait and see, couldn't they? You need all sorts of strange odds and ends around a place in the country. She said, yes, that was so; but she thought just at that time when every penny counted, it seemed funny to buy more rope. That was all. She hadn't meant anything else. She hadn't just seen, not at first, why he felt it was necessary. 4

Well, thunder, he had bought it because he wanted to, and that was all there was to it. She thought that was reason enough, and couldn't understand why he hadn't said so, at first. Undoubtedly it would be useful, twenty-four yards of rope, there were hundreds of things, she couldn't think of any at the moment, but it would come in. Of course. As he had said, things always did in the country. 5

But she was a little disappointed about the coffee, and oh, look, look, look at the eggs! Oh, my, they're all running! What had he put on top of them? Hadn't he known eggs mustn't be squeezed? Squeezed, who had squeezed them, he wanted to know. What a silly thing to say. He had simply brought them along in the basket with the other things. If they got broke it was the grocer's fault. He should know better than to put heavy things on top of eggs. 6

She believed it was the rope. That was the heaviest thing in the pack, she saw him plainly when he came in from the road, the rope was a big package on top of everything. He desired the whole wide world to witness that this was not a fact. He had carried the rope in one hand and the basket in the other, and what was the use of her having eyes if that was the best they could do for her? 7

Well, anyhow, she could see one thing plain: no eggs for break-fast. They'd have to scramble them now, for supper. It was too damned bad. She had planned to have steak for supper. No ice, meat wouldn't keep. He wanted to know why she couldn't finish breaking the eggs in a bowl and set them in a cool place. 8

Cool place! if he could find one for her, she'd be glad to set them there. Well, then, it seemed to him they might very well cook the meat at the same time they cooked the eggs and then warm up the meat for tomorrow. The idea simply choked her. Warmed-over 9 meat, when they might as well have had it fresh. Second best and scraps and makeshifts, even to the meat! He rubbed her shoulder a little. It doesn't really matter so much, does it, darling? Sometimes when they were playful, he would rub her shoulder and she would arch and purr. This time she hissed and almost clawed. He was getting ready to say that they could surely manage somehow when she turned on him and said, if he told her they could manage somehow she would certainly slap his face.

He swallowed the words red hot, his face burned. He picked up the rope and started to put it on the top shelf. She would not have it on the top shelf, the jars and tins belonged there; positively she would not have the top shelf cluttered up with a lot of rope. She had borne all the clutter she meant to bear in the flat in town, there was space here at least and she meant to keep things in order.

10

Well, in that case, he wanted to know what the hammer and nails were doing up there? And why had she put them there when she knew very well he needed that hammer and those nails upstairs to fix the window sashes? She simply slowed down everything and made double work on the place with her insane habit of changing things around and hiding them.

11

She was sure she begged his pardon, and if she had had any reason to believe he was going to fix the sashes this summer she would have left the hammer and nails right where he put them; in the middle of the bedroom floor where they could step on them in the dark. And now if he didn't clear the whole mess out of there she would throw them down the well.

12

Oh, all right, all right—could he put them in the closet? Naturally not, there were brooms and mops and dustpans in the closet, and why couldn't he find a place for his rope outside her kitchen? Had he stopped to consider there were seven God-forsaken rooms in the house, and only one kitchen?

13

He wanted to know what of it? And did she realize she was making a complete fool of herself? And what did she take him for, a three-year-old idiot? The whole trouble with her was she needed something weaker than she was to heckle and tyrannize over. He wished to God now they had a couple of children she could take it out on. Maybe he'd get some rest.

14

Her face changed at this, she reminded him he had forgot the coffee and had bought a worthless piece of rope. And when she thought of all the things they actually needed to make the place

15

even decently fit to live in, well, she could cry, that was all. She looked so forlorn, so lost and despairing he couldn't believe it was only a piece of rope that was causing all the racket. What *was* the matter, for God's sake?

Oh, would he please hush and go away, and *stay* away, if he could, for five minutes? By all means, yes, he would. He'd stay away indefinitely if she wished. Lord, yes, there was nothing he'd like better than to clear out and never come back. She couldn't for the life of her see what was holding him, then. It was a swell time. Here she was, stuck, miles from a railroad, with a half-empty house on her hands, and not a penny in her pocket, and everything on earth to do; it seemed the God-sent moment for him to get out from under. She was surprised he hadn't stayed in town as it was until she had come out and done the work and got things straightened out. It was his usual trick.

It appeared to him that this was going a little far. Just a touch out of bounds, if she didn't mind his saying so. Why the hell had he stayed in town the summer before? To do a half-dozen extra jobs to get the money he had sent her. That was it. She knew perfectly well they couldn't have done it otherwise. She had agreed with him at the time. And that was the only time so help him he had ever left her to do anything by herself.

Oh, he could tell that to his great-grandmother. She had her notion of what had kept him in town. Considerably more than a notion, if he wanted to know. So, she was going to bring all that up again, was she? Well, she could just think what she pleased. He was tired of explaining. It may have looked funny but he had simply got hooked in, and what could he do? It was impossible to believe that she was going to take it seriously. Yes, yes, she knew how it was with a man: if he was left by himself a minute, some woman was certain to kidnap him. And naturally he couldn't hurt her feelings by refusing!

Well, what was she raving about? Did she forget she had told him those two weeks alone in the country were the happiest she had known for four years? And how long had they been married when she said that? All right, shut up! If she thought that hadn't stuck in his craw.

She hadn't meant she was happy because she was away from him. She meant she was happy getting the devilish house nice and ready for him. That was what she had meant, and now look!

16

17

18

19

20

Bringing up something she had said a year ago simply to justify himself for forgetting her coffee and breaking the eggs and buying a wretched piece of rope they couldn't afford. She really thought it was time to drop the subject, and now she wanted only two things in the world. She wanted him to get that rope from underfoot, and go back to the village and get her coffee, and if he could remember it, he might bring a metal mitt for the skillets, and two more curtain rods, and if there were any rubber gloves in the village, her hands were simply raw, and a bottle of milk of magnesia from the drugstore.

He looked out at the dark blue afternoon sweltering on the slopes, and mopped his forehead and sighed heavily and said, if only she could wait a minute for *anything*, he was going back. He had said so, hadn't he, the very instant they found he had overlooked it? 21

Oh, yes, well . . . run along. She was going to wash windows. The country was so beautiful! She doubted they'd have a moment to enjoy it. He meant to go, but he could not until he had said that if she wasn't such a hopeless melancholiac she might see that this was only for a few days. Couldn't she remember anything pleasant about the other summers? Hadn't they ever had any fun? She hadn't time to talk about it, and now would he please not leave that rope lying around for her to trip on? He picked it up, somehow it had toppled off the table, and walked out with it under his arm. 22

Was he going this minute? He certainly was. She thought so. Sometimes it seemed to her he had second sight about the precisely perfect moment to leave her ditched. She had meant to put the mattresses out to sun, if they put them out this minute they would get at least three hours, he must have heard her say that morning she meant to put them out. So of course he would walk off and leave her to it. She supposed he thought the exercise would do her good. 23

Well, he was merely going to get her coffee. A four-mile walk for two pounds of coffee was ridiculous, but he was perfectly willing to do it. The habit was making a wreck of her, but if she wanted to wreck herself there was nothing he could do about it. If he thought it was coffee that was making a wreck of her, she congratulated him: he must have a damned easy conscience. 24

Conscience or no conscience, he didn't see why the mattresses couldn't very well wait until tomorrow. And anyhow, for God's sake, were they living *in* the house, or were they going to let the 25 house ride them to death? She paled at this, her face grew livid about the mouth, she looked quite dangerous, and reminded him that housekeeping was no more her work than it was his: she had other work to do as well, and when did he think she was going to find time to do it at this rate?

Was she going to start on that again? She knew as well as he did that his work brought in the regular money, hers was only occasional, if they depended on what *she* made—and she might as well get straight on this question once for all!

That was positively not the point. The question was, when both of them were working on their own time, was there going to be a division of the housework, or wasn't there? She merely wanted to know, she had to make her plans. Why, he thought that was all arranged. It was understood that he was to help. Hadn't he always, in summers?

Hadn't he, though? Oh, just hadn't he? And when, and where, and doing what? Lord, what an uproarious joke!

It was such a very uproarious joke that her face turned slightly purple, and she screamed with laughter. She laughed so hard she had to sit down, and finally a rush of tears spurted from her eyes and poured down into the lifted corners of her mouth. He dashed towards her and dragged her up to her feet and tried to pour water on her head. The dipper hung by a string on a nail and he broke it loose. Then he tried to pump water with one hand while she struggled in the other. So he gave it up and shook her instead.

She wrenched away, crying out for him to take his rope and go to hell, she had simply given him up: and ran. He heard her high-heeled bedroom slippers clattering and stumbling on the stairs.

He went out around the house and into the lane; he suddenly realized he had a blister on his heel and his shirt felt as if it were on fire. Things broke so suddenly you didn't know where you were. She could work herself into a fury about simply nothing. She was terrible, damn it: not an ounce of reason. You might as well talk to a sieve as that woman when she got going. Damned if he'd spend his life humoring her! Well, what to do now? He would take back the rope and exchange it for something else. Things accumulated, things were mountainous, you couldn't move them or sort them out or get rid of them. They just lay and rotted around. He'd take it back. Hell, why should he? He wanted it. What was it anyhow? A piece of rope. Imagine anybody caring more about a piece of rope

26

27

28

29

30

31

than about a man's feelings. What earthly right had she to say a word about it? He remembered all the useless, meaningless things she bought for herself: Why? because I wanted it, that's why! He stopped and selected a large stone by the road. He would put the rope behind it. He would put it in the tool-box when he got back. He'd heard enough about it to last him a life-time.

When he came back she was leaning against the post box beside the road waiting. It was pretty late, the smell of broiled steak floated nose high in the cooling air. Her face was young and smooth and fresh-looking. Her unmanageable funny black hair was all on end. She waved to him from a distance, and he speeded up. She called out that supper was ready and waiting, was he starved?   32

You bet he was starved. Here was the coffee. He waved it at her. She looked at his other hand. What was that he had there?   33

Well, it was the rope again. He stopped short. He had meant to exchange it but forgot. She wanted to know why he should exchange it, if it was something he really wanted. Wasn't the air sweet now, and wasn't it fine to be here?   34

She walked beside him with one hand hooked into his leather belt. She pulled and jostled him a little as he walked, and leaned against him. He put his arm clear around her and patted her stomach. They exchanged wary smiles. Coffee, coffee for the Ootsum-Wootsums! He felt as if he were bringing her a beautiful present.   35

He was a love, she firmly believed, and if she had had her coffee in the morning, she wouldn't have behaved so funny . . . There was a whippoorwill still coming back, imagine, clear out of season, sitting in the crab-apple tree calling all by himself. Maybe his girl stood him up. Maybe she did. She hoped to hear him once more, she loved whippoorwills . . . He knew how she was, didn't he?   36

Sure, he knew how she was.   37

Thinking about the Selection

1. How does Katherine Anne Porter portray the man in this story? How does she portray the woman?

2. Why do you think the author left the characters unnamed?

3. How would you describe the relationship between the husband and wife? How do they talk to each other? How do they act toward each other?

4. What does each of them seem to want? Why?

5. What is the significance of the rope? Do you think it symbolizes something? What can readers learn about the characters from their comments about the rope—and about the eggs?

6. At one point (paragraph 9), Porter makes an implicit analogy between the wife and a cat. What does this suggest about the woman at that moment?

7. What are the husband and wife arguing about? Whose side seems more persuasive? Why?

8. How do you interpret the ending of the story? What has happened between the couple?

9. What prediction would you make for this couple's future? Why?

10. Did you find this story interesting or enjoyable? Why or why not?

DAVID SEDARIS
Make That a Double

David Sedaris, one of the most popular commentators on National Public Radio, was *Time* magazine's Humorist of the Year in 2001. His essays are published regularly in the *New Yorker* and *Esquire*, and his books *Barrel Fever, The SantaLand Diaries*, and *Naked* were all best-sellers. He and his sister also co-produce a number of plays in New York City. Sedaris spent two years teaching writing at the Art Institute in Chicago, where he majored in painting as an undergraduate. His latest book, *Me Talk Pretty One Day*, is a collection of short essays about his experiences as an American living in Paris. "Make That a Double" describes his trouble learning French and a clever trick he discovered to hide his inability to remember the genders assigned to French nouns.

Vocabulary Preview

inevitably (para. 2): unavoidably, always (adv.)

perimeter (para. 6): edge, border (n.)

discretion (para. 6): individual decision (n.)

prescribed (para. 7): assigned (v.)

kilo (para. 10): a metric unit equivalent to a little over two pounds (n.)

1   There are, I have noticed, two basic types of French spoken by Americans vacationing in Paris: the Hard Kind and the Easy Kind. The Hard Kind involves the conjugation of wily verbs and the science of placing them alongside various other words in order to form such sentences as "I go him say good afternoon" and "No, not to him I no go it him say now."

2   The second, less complicated form of French amounts to screaming English at the top of your lungs, much the same way you'd shout at a deaf person or the dog you thought you could train to stay off the sofa. Doubt and hesitation are completely unnecessary, as Easy French is rooted in the premise that, if properly packed, the rest of the world could fit within the confines of Reno, Nevada. The speaker carries no pocket dictionary and never suffers the humiliation that inevitably comes with pointing to the menu and ordering the day of the week. With Easy French, eating out involves a simple "BRING ME A STEAK."

3   Having undertaken the study of Hard French, I'll overhear such requests and glare across the room, thinking, "That's *Mister* Steak

to you, buddy." Of all the stumbling blocks inherent in learning this language, the greatest for me is the principle that each noun has a corresponding sex that affects both its articles and its adjectives. Because it is a female and lays eggs, a chicken is masculine. *Vagina* is masculine as well, while the word *masculinity* is feminine. Forced by the grammar to take a stand one way or the other, *hermaphrodite* is male and *indecisiveness* female.

I spent months searching for some secret code before I realized   4
that common sense has nothing to do with it. *Hysteria, psychosis, torture, depression:* I was told that if something is unpleasant, it's probably feminine. This encouraged me, but the theory was blown by such masculine nouns as *murder, toothache,* and *Rollerblade.* I have no problem learning the words themselves, it's the sexes that trip me up and refuse to stick.

What's the trick to remembering that a sandwich is masculine?   5
What qualities does it share with anyone in possession of a penis? I'll tell myself that a sandwich is masculine because if left alone for a week or two, it will eventually grow a beard. This works until it's time to order and I decide that because it sometimes loses its makeup, a sandwich is undoubtedly feminine.

I just can't manage to keep my stories straight. Hoping I might   6
learn through repetition, I tried using gender in my everyday English. "Hi, guys," I'd say, opening a new box of paper clips, or "Hey, Hugh, have you seen my belt? I can't find her anywhere." I invented personalities for the objects on my dresser and set them up on blind dates. When things didn't work out with my wallet, my watch drove a wedge between my hairbrush and my lighter. The scenarios reminded me of my youth, when my sisters and I would enact epic dramas with our food. Ketchup-wigged french fries would march across our plates, engaging in brief affairs or heated disputes over carrot coins while burly chicken legs guarded the perimeter, ready to jump in should things get out of hand. Sexes were assigned at our discretion and were subject to change from one night to the next—unlike here, where the corncob and the stringbean remain locked in their rigid masculine roles. Say what you like about southern social structure, but at least in North Carolina a hot dog is free to swing both ways.

Nothing in France is free from sexual assignment. I was leafing   7
through the dictionary, trying to complete a homework assignment, when I noticed the French had prescribed genders for the various land masses and natural wonders we Americans had always

thought of as sexless. Niagara Falls is feminine and, against all reason, the Grand Canyon is masculine. Georgia and Florida are female, but Montana and Utah are male. New England is a she, while the vast area we call the Midwest is just one big guy. I wonder whose job it was to assign these sexes in the first place. Did he do his work right there in the sanitarium, or did they rent him a little office where he could get away from all the noise?

There are times when you can swallow the article and others when it must be clearly pronounced, as the word has two different meanings, one masculine and the other feminine. It should be fairly obvious that I cooked an omelette in a frying pan rather than in a wood stove, but it bothers me to make the same mistakes over and over again. I wind up exhausting the listener before I even get to the verb.   8

My confidence hit a new low when my friend Adeline told me that French children often make mistakes, but never with the sex of their nouns. "It's just something we grow up with," she said. "We hear the gender once, and then think of it as part of the word. There's nothing to it."   9

It's a pretty grim world when I can't even feel superior to a toddler. Tired of embarrassing myself in front of two-year-olds, I've started referring to everything in the plural, which can get expensive but has solved a lot of my problems. In saying *a melon,* you need to use the masculine article. In saying *the melons,* you use the plural article, which does not reflect gender and is the same for both the masculine and the feminine. Ask for two or ten or three hundred melons, and the number lets you off the hook by replacing the article altogether. A masculine kilo of feminine tomatoes presents a sexual problem easily solved by asking for two kilos of tomatoes. I've started using the plural while shopping, and Hugh has started using it in our cramped kitchen, where he stands huddled in the corner, shouting, "What do we need with four pounds of tomatoes?"   10

I answer that I'm sure we can use them for something. The only hard part is finding someplace to put them. They won't fit in the refrigerator, as I filled the last remaining shelf with the two chickens I bought from the butcher the night before, forgetting that we were still working our way through a pair of pork roasts the size of Duraflame logs. "We could put them next to the radios," I say, "or grind them for sauce in one of the blenders. Don't get so mad. Having four pounds of tomatoes is better than having no tomatoes at all, isn't it?"   11

> Hugh tells me that the market is off-limits until my French improves. He's pretty steamed, but I think he'll get over it when he sees the CD players I got him for his birthday. 12

Thinking about the Selection

1. What is unusual or different about the opening paragraph sentences that Sedaris places in quotation marks? Is this the "Hard" or "Easy" French he mentions in his first sentence?

2. What does Sedaris find most difficult or challenging about learning French?

3. What example does Sedaris use to illustrate his difficulties in learning French?

4. What connection is there between Sedaris's discussion of learning French words and his remarks about using everyday English with his friends and the games he played with his sisters at dinner?

5. What solution does Sedaris find for himself to overcome his failure to remember the appropriate gender markers for French nouns?

6. What is the effect of Sedaris's use of the plural when buying things in France? What is his purpose in telling us about the two kilos of tomatoes, the two chickens, and the two pork roasts?

7. What is Sedaris's purpose in writing this piece? What is his tone?

8. Did you find this piece interesting, entertaining, informative? Why or why not?

9. What are the meanings of *inherent* (paragraph 3) and *hermaphrodite* (paragraph 3)?

10. How does the title capture Sedaris's topic and his tone?

JOEL STEIN
Life after Oprah

Joel Stein is a staff writer and humor columnist for *Time* magazine. Before joining *Time* he was a writer and sports editor for *TimeOut New York,* a guide to events and entertainment in the city. He has worked as a researcher for *TV Guide* and a writer/researcher for Martha Stewart's television show and *Living* magazine; when he was twenty-two, he auditioned for MTV's *The Real World* but wasn't selected for the cast. Although Stein's humor is usually focused on himself, in "Life after Oprah," from the March 25, 2002, issue of *Time,* he takes aim at Oprah Winfrey, her fans, and daytime television talk shows in general.

Vocabulary Preview

succession (para. 10): follower (n.)
Darwinian (para. 10): derived from Charles Darwin's theory of the "survival of the fittest" (adj.)

1   This isn't the first time Oprah has teased us. Sure, last week Oprah Winfrey announced that she's going to stop hosting her talk show in 2006, but she says this every so often, like the astronomers do about an asteroid heading toward the earth. But people actually read the articles about Oprah.

2   Men get hopeful each time, because for nearly two decades Oprah has brought us nothing but pain and heartache. Oprah is the opiate of the female masses, teaching them to build self-esteem by confronting the past and setting goals instead of feeling good the old-fashioned way: by having casual sex. She encourages women to look inside and "find their passion" without once entertaining the possibility that this passion might be fed with lots of sleeping around. Worse yet, she sets all these ridiculous expectations about reading once a month.

3   The whole idea of talking openly and sharing your feelings is antithetical to the good old-time values of emotional repression on which this country was founded. Plus, Oprah is way too self-satisfied with the common sense she hands out. The current issue of O magazine has an article on coping that suggests that you "make prioritizing a priority." There's also an awful lot of talk about

angels. The only angels men want to see are in Victoria's Secret ads. And her solution to everything is telling you to tack a note to your mirror. Tacking a note to your mirror accomplishes nothing but blocking you from seeing your fat self.

Despite all the good things she may do for women's self-esteem, men can't help feeling about Oprah the same way that gold investors felt about William Jennings Bryan.[1] She's just not looking out for our best interests. The only men who will suffer from Oprah not being on the air are Wally Lamb and Stedman Graham.

Besides, men are frustrated that we don't have our own Oprah. Ours are all embarrassing flameouts like Robert Bly, or the Promise Keepers, or Al Gore the week that Naomi Wolf made him wear flannel. The best we have right now are Adam Carolla and Jimmy Kimmel of *The Man Show,* and those guys wouldn't even be able to fill out their live audience if they didn't liberally sprinkle the studio with pole dancers.

I have absolutely no idea why women so wholly embrace Oprah's sanctimonious declarations of common sense. So I grabbed a Mid-western phone book and selected a woman at random, much the same way Larry King seems to select wives. The first person I reached was Lisa Davis of Des Moines, Iowa. After I explained that I really wasn't selling anything, I had a nice conversation with Lisa, a 42-year-old grandmother of two and cashier at Casey's General Store. Like many Americans, Davis gets her news from *Time,* only this time she got it more directly than usual. "Oh, no!" she said when I told her *Oprah* is going off the air. "I love Oprah Winfrey. I watch her program daily." After calming her down ("2006 is a very long way away. I mean with terrorist threats the way they are, who knows if Des Moines will even be here then?"), Davis told me how much she likes both *Time* and *Life* magazines. This was going to be a long call.

After breaking her heart yet again with the news that the monthly version of *Life* was folded two years ago ("Oh, no! So is it just *Time* now?"), I asked Davis how she was going to fill the coming Oprah void. She said she guessed she would go to church more and get her spirituality that way. The last time the end of an entertainment program caused an uptick for the church was when the Romans canceled throwing Christians to the lions.

[1]A three-time candidate for the U.S. presidency and secretary of state from 1913 to 1915, Bryan pushed to make silver, not gold, the standard for American currency.

As for what she loves about Oprah, Davis talked about angels and being reminded of what's important in life and learning how to listen to others or something like that. I kind of tuned out around then. She said Oprah's show has helped, in particular, in communicating with her fiancé. I asked her if all the Oprahisms she uses in talking about their relationship ever annoys him. "Oh, no, I don't tell him what she says," Davis said. "I just think about it and use it on him."   8

She said the best advice actually comes from Dr. Phil, the psychologist who is Oprah's Oprah. That's when I asked her if she was looking forward to Dr. Phil's new syndicated show in the fall. "Dr. Phil is getting his own show in the fall!" she yelled to her daughter in the next room. "There you go. That's what I'll be watching in 2006. Dr. Phil."   9

But the post-Oprah world will not offer a succession that simple. The reality is that the next daytime guru is very likely to be even more coddling and touchy-feely than Oprah herself. Remember when Phil Donahue seemed really threatening to masculinity? Before that Merv Griffin seemed like a wimp. Daytime talk-show hosts follow some reverse Darwinian law whereby they get less and less threatening every generation. The next daytime guru is going to be either Elmo or Tinky Winky.   10

Thinking about the Selection

1. What is Joel Stein's attitude or point of view toward Oprah Winfrey and her show? Where does he reveal this attitude or point of view?

2. What question would you ask Stein about his piece, if you had a chance to talk with him or an opportunity to write him a letter? Why would you ask that question?

3. Identify two of the many people Joel Stein mentions in his article. Why do you think he mentions these people? How effective are his references to them?

4. What is the purpose of the comparison Stein uses in the first paragraph? What is the point of this comparison with the asteroid heading toward earth?

5. What particular aspects of Oprah's advice to women does the author criticize? How would you characterize his tone in referring to Oprah's advice to women?

6. Use the context of the article to determine the meanings of *antithetical* (paragraph 3) and *sanctimonious* (paragraph 6).

7. Why does the author include the phone interview with Lisa Davis, the grandmother from Des Moines, Iowa?

8. What is the author's main idea? How is the title of the piece related to its topic and main idea?

9. Did you find this piece persuasive? Why or why not?

10. Did you find this piece entertaining, informative, or interesting? Why or why not?

Using a College Dictionary

In the same way that a library is important to the intellectual life of a college, so is your college dictionary central to your academic work. If you have not already done so, you need to acquire a good college-level dictionary that includes between 150,000 to 200,000 words. One of the following would be fine in either a book or a CD-ROM version:

The American Heritage College Dictionary. 4th ed. Boston: Houghton Mifflin, 2002.

Random House Webster's College Dictionary. 2nd rev. ed. New York: Random House, 2000.

Webster's New World College Dictionary. 4th ed. New York: Hungry Minds, 1999.

■ Getting Acquainted with Your Dictionary

A dictionary is a mini-library of information, a mini-encyclopedia of knowledge. It includes information about history and geography, brief biographical identification of historical figures, and the names of country and state capitals. It typically includes weights and measures and a list of the world's currencies. However, dictionaries mostly contain information about words, including spelling, pronunciation, part of speech, meaning, and origin (also called *etymology*).

Usually dictionaries consist of a section for each letter of the alphabet; within each section, the words beginning with that letter are listed alphabetically. The entry for each word generally begins with the word itself, divided into its syllables, which are usually separated by a small dot. Following the word is a pronunciation guide that uses symbols to show how the word is spoken. After this guide is a notation listing which part of speech the word is (noun, verb, adjective, and so on). The word's definitions usually follow and are followed in turn by a notation about the word's origin. Look at the following entry for the word *marmoset*, taken from the *American Heritage College Dictionary*.

> **mar•mo•set** (mär′mə-sĕt′, -zĕt′) *n.* Any of various small, clawed monkeys of the genera *Callithrix* and *Cebuella* of the American tropics, having tufted ears and long tails. [ME *marmusette*, a small monkey < OFr. *marmouset*, grotesque figurine, alteration of *marmotte*, marmot. See MARMOT.]

In this definition, you may not recognize every symbol, but you can see the different parts of the entry. This appendix will help you understand these symbols and parts of dictionary definitions and will help you learn to use them as well.

■ Spelling

If you can't spell a word, how can you look it up? It's a logical question, and there are three good answers. First, of course, is that you often look up unfamiliar words that you encounter when you read, so the spelling is right in front of you. Second, problems with the spelling of words rarely involve their first three or four letters, which are all you usually need to find a word in the dictionary. Third, when a word has a complicated or unusual spelling, you can usually guess one or two different ways it might be spelled and try them both. Some words beginning with the *f* sound, for example, begin with *ph;* some words beginning with the *s* sound begin with *c,* and so on. Use what you already know about spelling rules in general, and in most cases you will be able to find the word.

The dictionary provides the correct spelling of words in English, as well as many commonly used foreign words and expressions such as *laissez-faire* and *faux pas.* It also indicates alternative spellings when more than one is acceptable. The word *marshal,* for example, can also be spelled *marshall.* When two spellings are indicated, often one is preferred. This preferred spelling is usually given first.

In addition, the dictionary will also indicate British spellings for words such as *color* (British: *colour*); *reflection* (British: *reflexion*); and *realize* (British: *realise*).

■ Pronunciation

One of the more immediately useful functions of a dictionary is to indicate how words are pronounced. When you learn a new word in your reading, you may want to use it in conversation—and you will want to pronounce it correctly.

Like other dictionaries, the *American Heritage College Dictionary* provides a pronunciation key on every page or two-page spread. This will help you understand what the symbols mean in the pronunciation guide for each word. If you look closely at the small print, you will see how each of the symbols listed next to the word should be pronounced. You can figure this out by looking first for the ′ mark, which indicates the syllable that is stressed or accented. Next take each vowel sound. Look at how it is configured with any marks and find the corresponding item in the pronunciation key.

ă	pat	oi	b**oy**
ā	pay	ou	**ou**t
âr	**care**	o͝o	t**oo**k
ä	father	ō͞o	b**oo**t
ĕ	p**e**t	ŭ	c**u**t
ē	b**e**	ûr	**ur**ge
ĭ	p**i**t	th	**th**in
ī	p**ie**	*th*	**th**is
îr	p**ier**	hw	**wh**ich
ŏ	p**o**t	zh	vi**s**ion
ō	t**oe**	ə	**a**bout, it**e**m
ô	p**aw**		

Stress marks: ′ (primary); ′ (secondary), as in **dictionary** (dĭk′shə-nĕr′ē)

This chart contains two kinds of information. First, each sound is indicated by a short word that shows how it should be pronounced. The vowel combination *oi*, for example, sounds like the *oy* in *boy*. Second, the example of the word *dictionary* is given at the base of the chart to indicate primary and secondary accents. These heavier and lighter accent marks indicate which syllables you should stress when saying the word and which syllable receives the strongest stress or accent.

If you come across the word *epitome,* for example, you might wonder how to pronounce it. Does its ending rhyme with *Rome?* Is it accented on the first, second, or third syllable? Are the vowels long or short? Does the *e* sound like the *e* in *me* or the *e* in *get,* or some other way? Does the *i* sound like the *i* in *line* or the *i* in *lit?* And what of the *e* at the end of the word? Is it pronounced or not?

Here is how the word is shown to be sounded in the *Random House Webster's College Dictionary:*

e•pit•o•me (ĭ-pĭt′ə-mē)

Notice the little swirled line above the first letter of the pronunciation guide. It indicates that the first *e* in *epitome* sounds more like an *i*— a short *i* sound like the one in the word *it.* This is the sound of the *i* in *pit* as well. Notice too that the accent falls on the *i*—the syllable *pit* is stressed when saying *epitome.* Look next to the end of the word, at the *e.* That sound is long, the *e* sound of *me.* Finally, look at the symbol designating the *o* sound in the word. This is a schwa, which looks like an upside down and backward letter *e.* The schwa is pronounced "uh"— the sound of *a* in *about.* It is never accented.

What you have been doing in breaking down the word *epitome* to understand how to pronounce it is similar to what you did earlier in breaking words down into their roots, prefixes, and suffixes to understand their meanings. In both types of learning you have been making careful observations about language. You also made connections between words that use similar roots, prefixes, and suffixes. In addition, you are connecting what you know about the sound values of short and long vowels to what you see provided in the dictionary pronunciation chart.

■ Part of Speech

Your dictionary will also indicate the part of speech for each word. There are eight parts of speech: noun, pronoun, verb, adjective, adverb, preposition, conjunction, and interjection. The following chart defines and illustrates each.

THE PARTS OF SPEECH

Part of Speech	Function	Example
verb	indicates action or state of being	*talk, think, care, seem, run*
noun	names a person, place, thing, concept, or quality	*George Washington, Shirley Jones, house, sister, dime, history, despair*
pronoun	takes the place of a noun	*I, you, he, she, it, us, her, they, ours, any-one, myself, himself*
adjective	describes (modifies or qualifies) a noun or pronoun	*handsome, tired, old, clever, desperate, clumsy*
adverb	describes a verb, adjective, or another adverb	*often, courteously, noisily, nevertheless, really*
preposition	indicates the relation-ship between a noun or pronoun and another word in a sentence	*to, from, with, behind, by, above, beyond, through*
conjunction	links or joins words, phrases, and clauses	*and, but, or, nor, for, so, yet*
interjection	expresses surprise or emotion	*Hey, Oh, Wow, Ah*

For words that can function as more than a single part of speech — such as *book,* which can be a noun *(I bought a book)* or a verb *(I need to book a room)* — dictionaries give separate meanings for each part of speech.

Dictionaries abbreviate the parts of speech. *Adjective,* for example, is usually abbreviated *adj.* to distinguish it from *adverb,* which is abbreviated *adv.* Nouns are abbreviated *n.,* and verbs are designated by *v.* If you are not sure what an abbreviation stands for, consult the glossary in the front or back of the dictionary, where all symbols are explained. If you're not sure what part of speech a word is, consult your dictionary.

■ Meanings

This section is entitled *meanings*, with an *s*, because many words have more than one meaning. Sometimes the meanings are very different. Sometimes the meanings can be so different as to be opposite. *Cleave*, for example, means both "to split or divide," as with a cleaver, and "to adhere closely, to cling," as in "a man should cleave to his wife."

Usually a word with multiple meanings will not contain opposite meanings, but rather a range of related meanings. The word *drum*, for example, means a musical percussion instrument, the act of playing on such an instrument, the sound of such an instrument, or the sound produced by striking a hollow tree or similar object — and so on. But there are also additional related meanings with the words *eardrum* and *drumfish*.

Chum offers a greater range of meanings, including these three very different ones: (1) a close companion or friend; (2) cut or ground bait dumped into the water to attract fish; and (3) a kind of salmon. The meanings for *chum* may be listed separately as *chum 1*, *chum 2*, and *chum 3*. Or the different meanings may be numbered in the same entry.

Here is how the *American Heritage College Dictionary* lists meanings for *chum*:

> **chum¹** (chŭm) *n.* An intimate friend or companion. *—intr.v.* **chummed, chum•ming, chums. 1.a.** To be an intimate friend. **b.** To display good-natured friendliness. **2.** To share the same room, as in a dormitory. [Perh. short for *chamber fellow*, roommate.]
> **chum²** (chŭm) *n.* Bait usu. consisting of oily fish ground up and scattered on the water. *—v.* **chummed, chum•ming, chums.** *—intr.* To fish with chum. *—tr.* To lure (fish) with chum. [?]
> **chum³** (chŭm) *n.* A chum salmon.

■ Related Words

Dictionaries typically list related forms of a word in a single entry. They do this to conserve space. But it is very helpful if you wish to increase your vocabulary. In looking up the word *astrology* in the *Random House Webster's College Dictionary*, for example, you will also find spellings and pronunciations for these related words: *astrologer*, *astrologist*, *astrological*, *astrologic*, *astrologous*, and *astrologically*. Only one meaning is given — the meaning for the main entry, *astrology*, because the related words share its meaning: "the study that assumes and attempts to interpret the influence of the heavenly bodies on human affairs." You may recognize the suffixes that end these related words (if you don't, refer back to Chapter 2). By applying your knowledge that *-ist* indicates a person, for example, you can determine that an astrologist is somebody who practices or studies astrology.

■ Synonyms and Antonyms

Synonyms are words with similar meanings, such as *mistake* and *blunder*. Antonyms are words with opposite meanings—*yes* and *no,* for example. Your dictionary will almost certainly list synonyms as part of the entry for a word and may also list antonyms, though not as frequently. Both the *Random House Webster's College Dictionary* and the *American Heritage College Dictionary* include brief synonym paragraphs in which they list a group of related words and explain their difference in meaning.

Here is an example from each dictionary. First, the *Random House, contemporary:*

> **con•tem•po•rar•y** (kən tem′pə rer′ē). *adj., n., pl.* **-rar•ies.** —*adj.*
> **1.** existing, occurring, or living at the same time; belonging to the same time. **2.** of the same age or date: *a Georgian table with a contemporary wig stand.* **3.** of the present time: *a lecture on the contemporary novel.* —*n.* **4.** a person or thing belonging to the same time or period with another or others. **5.** a person of the same age as another. [< LL *contempor-* (s. of *contempor(āre)* (to) be at the same time = *con-* CON- + *tempor-* (s. of *tempus*) time) + -ARY] —**con•tem′po•rar′i•ly,** *adv.* —**con•tem′po•rar′i•ness,** *n.* —**Syn. 1.** coeval, coexistent; concurrent, simultaneous.

And now the *American Heritage, discuss:*

> **dis•cuss** (dĭ-skŭs′) *tr. v.* **-cussed, -cuss•ing, -cuss•es. 1.** To speak with others about; talk over. **2.** To examine or consider (a subject) in speech or writing. [Middle English *discussen,* to examine,
>
> *(continued)*

from Anglo-Norman *discusser,* from Latin *discussus,* past participle of *discutere,* to break up : *dis-,* apart; see DIS– + *quatere,* to shake; see **kwēt-** in Appendix.] **—dis•cuss′a•ble, dis•cuss′i•ble** *adj.* **—dis•cuss′er** *n.*

SYNONYMS: *discuss, argue, debate, dispute, contend.* These verbs mean to talk with others in an effort to reach agreement, to ascertain truth, or to convince. *Discuss* involves close examination of a subject with interchange of opinions: *"Men are never so likely to settle a question rightly as when they discuss it freely"* (Macaulay). *Argue* emphasizes the presentation of facts and reasons in support of a position opposed by others: *"There is no good in arguing with the inevitable"* (James Russell Lowell). *Debate* involves formal, often public argument: *The candidates agreed to debate the campaign issues face to face. Dispute* implies differences of opinion and usually sharp argument: *members of the legislature disputing over increases in the military budget.* To *contend* is to strive in debate or controversy: *"Letting a hundred flowers blossom and a hundred schools of thought contend is the policy"* (Mao Zedong).

■ Origin

Your college dictionary also provides information about the origin, or etymology, of words. The word *dictator* derives from a Latin verb — *dicere,* meaning "to speak or tell.z" Your dictionary lists that derivation with the abbreviation *L.* for *Latin.* Other languages from which English words may be derived are also abbreviated, such as *OFr.* for *Old French* and *Gk.* for *Greek.*

Since English is a language with a rich history of derivation, you will find many words coming from other languages. From Italian, for example, English has taken *macaroni* and *volcano;* from French, *royal;* from Dutch, *easel, landscape,* and *cruise.* English has borrowed the words *alcohol* from Arabic, *coffee* from Turkish, *bazaar* from Persian, and *wampum* from Algonquian, to cite a few examples. A substantial portion of English words, however, derive from Anglo-Saxon, or Old English, and its later development into Middle English.

English actually was not the first language spoken in England. Celtic was apparently the native language there. But with the arrival of Germanic tribes — Angles, Saxons, and Jutes — who conquered the Celts, the earliest form of English emerged. This oldest form of English is designated *AS* for *Anglo-Saxon* and *OE* for *Old English*. Old English was written and spoken from about A.D. 400 to 1100, when Middle English emerged. During the period of Old English the language was enriched by words from Latin and Greek because those were the languages of scholarship in the Western world. During the Middle English period, English borrowed heavily from French, because the French conquered England in 1066, when William of Normandy won a major battle against the English. Middle English developed into the beginning of what we know as Modern English around 1500, half a century before the birth of Shakespeare in 1564.

With continued development of technology and increasing cultural exchange, English has borrowed a large number of words from many of the world's languages. At the same time, English has become one of the most important languages in the world, spoken not only in Great Britain and North America but also by people in Jamaica, South Africa, Australia, and New Zealand. English is also an officially recognized language in Kenya, Pakistan, Uganda, Liberia, India, and the Philippines.

When a word's dictionary definition includes information about the origin, or etymology, of a word, it will usually appear at the bottom of the definition. Look back at the definition of *marmoset* on page 542 for an example. The etymological information appears in brackets:

[ME *marmusette,* a small monkey < OFr. *marmouset,* grotesque figurine, alteration of *marmotte,* marmot. See MARMOT.]

This coded note lists the history of the word as it evolved over time. The codes differ slightly from dictionary to dictionary but are usually similar. To understand what you see in the etymological note, look for your dictionary's key to understanding the abbreviations and symbols—almost always in the first few pages of the book. In the case of *marmoset,* the abbreviation *ME* means *Middle English.* The Middle English version of the word, *marmusette,* changed into our modern word. The < that follows indicates that the Middle English version of *marmoset* came from the *OFr.,* or Old French, version, which didn't mean exactly the same thing as our current version. You can see here that it meant "grotesque figurine." Finally, the note indicates that more information can be found in the definition of *marmot.*

Studying and Taking Tests

Doing well on tests depends on being well prepared for them. But you can also use specific techniques and strategies to improve your performance. These techniques not only will improve your grades but also will help you better understand your course material and give you a stronger grasp of your subjects. In short, they will make you a better learner.

■ Being Prepared

LONG-TERM PREPARATION

Successful long-term preparation is essentially everything you can and should do in taking a course seriously. It includes faithful class attendance, careful preparation, thoughtful participation, regular reviewing, and judicious note taking. Long-term test preparation should include compensating for missed classes by talking with your instructors and by copying the notes of a classmate whose academic performance and abilities you respect. Further, long-term preparation may involve establishing a study group that meets regularly throughout the term (not just the night before a major exam) to discuss class lectures and meetings, to review assigned readings, to compare notes, and to do short-term test preparation.

Ideally, your long-term preparation should include reading and doing assignments before each class meets, attending class regularly, and following up with additional study and review. To succeed in test preparation, you need to take your work seriously, make a study schedule, and stick to it.

STUDYING FOR A TEST

Depending on how successful your long-term preparation has been and on how comfortable and confident you are with the course material, your short-term preparation can vary widely. For a course in which you have been doing the work consistently all along, you may need to do no more than a once-over lightly, perhaps a couple of hours of review. For a course in which you feel unsure and unsettled, even if you have been hardworking all along, you should devote more time: The added time and effort will increase both your confidence and your familiarity with the material.

Find a comfortable place to study—just not so comfortable that you find yourself lounging or dozing. Wherever you study best (your dorm room, the library, a vacant classroom, your kitchen, dining room, bedroom, outside), make sure the temperature is right. Hot, stuffy rooms put you to sleep. Cold ones may keep you from concentrating.

If you concentrate best at a desk, make sure that's where you seat yourself. If you need room to write, be sure you have it. Wherever you end up, make sure you won't be distracted by music, by other students or family members, or by other temptations to keep you from your work—unless music helps you study better or other people encourage you or answer your questions. Of course, some of this advice may be impossible for you to follow—at least some of the time. But do your best to find some disturbance-free space.

Avoid marathon study sessions, especially the night before a test: You'll tire out and won't remember as much as you need to. Instead, schedule a number of shorter study periods, spread out over the course of a week or two before your test. Set goals for your study sessions. Try to accomplish something specific at each one. Plan to outline a chapter or to memorize a set of formulas or to work a specific number of exercises. Plan to review your class notes or to reread and take new notes on a certain number of pages or chapters. If your overall goal for a session is too ambitious, cut it into several smaller segments. Tackle your smaller goals one at a time. Rather than fretting over the number of study hours ahead of you or the magnitude of your task, divide everything into manageable units and work on the small pieces. Before long they'll add up and you'll find yourself developing momentum.

Periodically, after accomplishing one of your goals, reward yourself. Take an ice cream or TV break. Chat for a few minutes with friends. Read an article in a popular magazine. But be strict with yourself. Set a limit for your break, then return to work. After you meet some of your longer, more ambitious goals, take a few hours off to watch a ball game or see a movie. Do some exercise or treat yourself to a special dinner. These breaks will keep you fresh and make your remaining study time more productive than if you try to plow through everything all at once.

Consider writing down notes and thoughts while you study. You can jot notes in the margins of your books. You can make a brief outline of what you've read. You can ask yourself questions that occur to you while you study. And you can make connections between what you are studying and what you remember from class discussions. If you are reviewing your notes, you can make additional notes in the margins or on facing pages of your notebook. Writing like this will engage you with the material you're studying and improve your comprehension. It will also make it more likely that you'll remember the information while you're taking the test.

STRATEGIES FOR REMEMBERING

Useful rules exist for remembering anything, whether you are learning it for the first time or relearning or reviewing it.

One: *focus*. Concentrate on what you are committing to memory. If it's a piece of music, listen with your full attention. If it's a sequence of biochemical processes, look at the whole sequence and then break it into parts. Focus on those small parts. Then put them back together. Analyze, or break the work down, into small pieces. It's easier to memorize something large by building your way piece-by-piece to the whole, rather than trying to swallow the whole thing in one mental gulp.

Two: *associate*. Try to connect what you are committing to memory with something else. You may recall learning the names of the musical staff (E-G-B-D-F) by associating those lines with the first letter of each word in this sentence: Every Good Boy Does Fine. You may have learned other things by means of rhyme, or you may have created a song of them.

The same SQ3R method you learned in Chapter 12 can help you study for a test successfully. Survey your notes and the book chapters that you need to know. Ask yourself questions about the material, or have someone else ask you questions. Note any you miss, and restudy (or reread) the material. Try saying aloud what you want to remember. You can tape important information and play it back so you hear it. Recite and repeat any information you need to know well. You can also walk around, from time to time, when you study, perhaps reciting aloud what you are trying to learn. The rhythm of your walking and the sound of your voice can increase your ability to absorb what you are studying.

One of the best ways to remember what you learn in your study sessions is to *review*. You should review immediately after you complete a study session. You can review again later after some time has elapsed. Try to review material from a previous study session at the beginning of the current one. In reviewing for a midterm exam, for instance, you might schedule four study sessions. You should review at the end of each session and at the beginning of the second, third, and last ones. By the time you reach the fourth study session in preparing for a midterm or final exam, you will have reviewed the fourth chunk of material once, the third session chunk twice, the second session material three times, and the first session material four times. In other words, you will be well prepared.

■ Answering Test Questions

A major test is sitting on your desk. What should you do? How should you proceed?

First, *collect yourself*. Don't let anxiety get the better of you. If you feel tense and nervous, breathe slowly and deeply for a few moments. Then spend a minute looking over the entire test to get a sense of the kinds of questions it contains. Make sure you know how much time you have overall and how much time you'll need for each part. Then set to work.

Second, *read the test instructions — and all of the questions — carefully.* Skim through the entire test before starting to answer the questions. Make sure you understand them. If you don't, ask for clarification.

Finally, *be methodical*. Answer the questions you're sure of first, then move on to the more difficult ones. If a test is challenging enough, you will come across questions that stump you. Rather than labor over them, skip them and return to them after you have answered the ones you know. Try to get into a rhythm of responding correctly. Your confidence will pick up. And in the course of answering the questions you do know, you may find yourself recalling other details that help you respond accurately to those you had at first skipped.

Different kinds of test questions require different approaches and answer strategies. Familiarizing yourself with these different strategies will help make you a more successful test taker.

TRUE/FALSE QUESTIONS

When taking true/false tests or test sections, mark first all the questions you are confident are either true or false. Then, for those statements you are unsure about, consider them true unless you can find a reason to think them false (more statements on such tests tend to be true than false). If you *must* guess, guess true.

A statement is false if *any* part of it is false or if it is only partly true. For example, the following statement is false because one part is false:

> John F. Kennedy, Richard Nixon, and Jimmy Carter were Democratic presidents.

Even though Kennedy and Carter were Democrats, Nixon was a Republican. Including him makes the overall statement false.

Be leery of absolutes, or questions that lack qualifiers. Questions that include words such as *always, never, all,* and *none* are usually — but not always! — false. In contrast, questions that include words such as *sometimes, frequently, some,* and *many* tend more often to be true. Consider the following two statements:

> All college courses can be taken on a pass/fail basis.
>
> Many college courses can be taken on a pass/fail basis.

The first statement is false. The second one is true. The difference in the statements is one small word that makes one big difference.

As a general rule, read true/false questions with extreme care. Look for single words that tip you off one way or another to the statement's truth or falsehood. You will usually find them.

MULTIPLE-CHOICE QUESTIONS

Multiple-choice questions may be incomplete statements followed by different ways to complete them. They may also be complete statements or questions followed by a series of possible answers. Only one of the answer choices is considered truly correct, or the "best" answer for the question. Multiple-choice questions can be tricky because often two answer choices seem to be correct. You can use a few basic strategies to sort these out.

First, eliminate the choices you know are incorrect. In a question with four possible answers, if you can eliminate two of them you have a 50 percent chance of getting the question right, even if you are unsure about the remaining answer options.

Second, before you decode an answer, analyze the remaining answer possibilities as if the completed statements were true/false questions. If an answer option gives you a false statement, it's almost definitely not the correct answer.

Finally, look for an answer meaning "all of the above." Inclusive answers like these usually offer the best choice. Consider this example:

> Silver is used to make
>
> a. jewelry.
> b. musical instruments.
> c. automobile equipment.
> d. all of the above.

The correct answer is *d*. If you know that silver is used to make jewelry and musical instruments, your choice should be "all of the above" even if you don't know that silver is used to make some automobile equipment.

Another type of inclusive answer for multiple-choice questions occurs in questions that do not include "all of the above" as an option. Consider the following example:

> Height is likely to vary most among which of the following groups?
>
> a. professional jockeys
> b. professional basketball players
> c. practicing dentists
> d. African Pygmies

The most inclusive group of the four is dentists, who are not typically short, like jockeys and Pygmies, or taller than average, like basketball players.

Other techniques for identifying correct multiple-choice options include being wary of extreme modifiers such as *always*, *never*, and *only*—just as when answering true/false questions. Also, avoid the temptation to choose answers with unfamiliar words, as test makers often introduce strange terms as distractors, or incorrect answers.

FILL-IN QUESTIONS

Fill-in questions ask you to complete a statement by supplying missing words or phrases. To answer fill-in questions you need to understand the type of answer required by the statement. Usually a word or phrase in the statement itself will provide a clue to the kind of answer you need to supply. The number of blanks always indicates the number of words in the correct answer. For example, the following statement requires the name of a professional basketball team:

> Before the Chicago Bulls broke the record for most wins in a National Basketball Association season, the _____ _____ held that record.

Notice that there are two blanks, one for the location name and one for the team name: the team name alone isn't a complete answer.

When answering fill-in questions, look closely at the article *a* or *an* before a blank. In the first case, you will need to supply a word that begins with a consonant; in the second, a word that begins with a vowel. Be aware, however, that some instructors will eliminate this clue by writing questions that use *a(n)* before the blank, indicating that the word to follow could begin with either a consonant or a vowel.

SHORT-ANSWER AND ESSAY TESTS

The test questions we have discussed so far generally require that you make a choice. But many, if not most, college-level tests expect more of you. Instructors give tests to assess how much you've learned and how well you can express your new knowledge. The tests, therefore, ask you to display your understanding, either with short, one-sentence-to-one-paragraph answers, or with longer, essay-length answers. Short-answer and essay exams typically require students to synthesize information gleaned from lectures and readings, to explain relationships among important events and ideas, and to evaluate them. Writing strong essay exam answers is essential for success in many college courses.

Let's assume that you've prepared yourself well. You've done the necessary studying. Let's also assume that you've read and understood the questions and that you are ready to get down to work. What do you do?

Budget Your Time. Answering an essay examination question poses a challenge because you are writing under the pressure of time. To write essay exam answers that demonstrate your grasp of a subject, you will have to write both effectively and efficiently. For example, if your exam includes two essay questions in a fifty-minute period and if the questions are equally weighted, plan to devote about twenty minutes to each, leaving yourself five minutes to plan your answers and five minutes to review them.

Interpret the Questions. Be sure you understand what you are being asked to do. Here are some examples of common types of essay exam questions and the key terms you should look for in responding to them.

Identify means to name, indicate, or specify. Some essay exams include *identify* as part of a question that asks you to "identify and explain" or to "identify and discuss."

> Identify three prominent African American scientists and explain their contributions to their respective fields.

An effective answer to this question will name the three scientists before explaining their contributions. It's not enough just to name them; nor would it be effective to discuss African American contributions to science without specifically listing the three scientists called for in the question.

Explain means to provide reasons for, to lay out causes, effects, or consequences. Explanations can be simple or complex, general or specific; they can include sparse or full detail. The time limit for an essay response will determine how much or how little explanation you should provide.

> Explain how a legislative proposal becomes a law.

A successful two-minute answer to this question would briefly outline the process. If the exam were structured in such a way that you have twenty minutes to answer, you would be expected to flesh out the outline with examples and details.

Discuss means to talk or write about. The instruction is not specific, and as a result it is important to know how much flexibility you have with your answer. *Discuss* is often used to mean *explain,* but it can also be used if the instructor wants you to provide your own opinion on an issue. Use your inference skills to assess what the instructor is likely to be looking for, or ask before you begin. Consider the difference between the following two similar questions:

> Discuss the philosopher Hugo Bedau's arguments against capital punishment.
>
> Discuss your response to Hugo Bedau's arguments against capital punishment.

In both cases, before you start writing about Bedau's arguments, you would have to list or identify them. Although the word *discuss* is used in the first question, it's a good bet that you're expected to explain what Bedau's arguments against capital punishment are, not what you think of them. In the second question, you are expected not only to explain Bedau's arguments but also to provide your own opinion of them. Be careful, though: When a test asks your opinion, you must provide evidence to support it.

Define means to explain what something is, to point out characteristic features, to identify limits, or to put something into a category. Definitions can be brief or extended. A short-answer or essay question that asks you to define a term or concept may also require that you examine, explain, elucidate, exemplify, characterize, list, or further discuss the various aspects or elements of your definition:

> Define the concept of multiculturalism. Discuss the social and political issues the debate about multiculturalism has raised.

To answer this question, you would first explain in a few words what multiculturalism is, perhaps something like "an effort to include people from a variety of ethnic and cultural backgrounds." After you have established what it is, you would then identify and discuss the issues that the effort has prompted. An answer that only discussed the issues, without a definition (and vice versa), would receive only partial credit.

Compare and **contrast** both mean to consider two things as they relate to each other. You may need to emphasize similarities or focus on differences, depending on the question.

> Compare Woody Allen's movie comedies with those of Mel Brooks.
>
> Contrast Woody Allen's movie comedies with those of Mel Brooks.
>
> Compare and contrast Woody Allen's movie comedies with those of Mel Brooks.

An answer to the first question would focus on the similarities between Allen and Brooks; an answer to the second would spend more time discussing how the two are different from each other. An answer to the third question requires a discussion of both similarities and differences.

Analyze means to break into parts in order to yield insight. To do an analysis of something involves looking at its details and at its component parts closely and carefully.

> Analyze the structure and function of the cell.

In answering this question, you would identify what a cell is made up of, how its parts work together, and what they do.

Evaluate means to assess or make a judgment about. You may be asked to evaluate the claims made by competing theories or to evaluate the performance of a stock. Evaluation often involves comparison and explanation.

> Evaluate the performance of Whitney Houston in the 1995 film *Waiting to Exhale.*

To answer this question, you might consider how Houston's performance compared with that of the other actresses. Perhaps you think her role in this later movie shows how much she's grown as an actress since appearing in *The Bodyguard.* You might bring in as evidence the opinions of professional movie critics or film criticism concepts you learned in the class. And, of course, you would say whether you liked or disliked her performance—as long as you provide examples and details to justify your evaluation.

Plan Your Answer. Once you have read the question and understand what you are being asked to do, allow yourself a few minutes to think before you begin writing your answer. Spend some time considering what you want to say and how you might go about using what you know to support your idea. You will find that you can remember quite a bit in even a few minutes of thinking—if you are well prepared. Collect your thoughts and begin to sort them. Consider too how much time you have to answer the question, and then plan your time sensibly.

Begin with some preliminary writing—jotting a few rough notes in no special order. You can arrange your notes later by simply numbering them as you prepare to write your full essay response. The very act of putting pen on paper should stimulate further thought and help you make connections among all that you have studied and learned. You can also order your notes in a scratch outline, noting how you can begin and end your essay and identifying some points to cover in between. By making a rough sketch of where you are heading and how you plan to get there, you will decrease the chances of forgetting something important. You will also enhance the organization and readability of your answer.

Try, even in your rough preliminary notes, to include a thesis statement that responds concretely and specifically to the question.

Write Your Answer. As you write, be sure to respond directly to the question. Avoid vagueness and bland generalizations. Also avoid trying to throw everything you can think of into your answer; instead, attack the question head-on.

Consider the following question:

> Discuss the political factors that led up to the American Revolution.

This very specific question requires an answer that addresses political factors only—not economic, military, or religious ones (unless you can show how these other kinds of factors directly relate to the political issues the question calls for).

You also do not want to answer a broad question too narrowly. Respond to a question that asks how divorce affects children in the United States by providing information, statistics, evidence, and arguments specifically about all kinds of effects of divorce on children (social and psychological effects as well as financial and other effects). You should not stray from the question, however, by discussing the causes of divorce or its effects on divorcing couples.

Blend your ideas with evidence. Use specific details to back up your general points. This is critical. Essays that omit specific references or concrete examples often reveal a lack of knowledge. Such answers may be superficial or vague. On the other hand, essay responses that contain only information and specific details may reveal a lack of understanding. You need both facts and explanations, specific details and the ideas they exemplify.

The most important thing you can do when writing an essay exam is to attend carefully to what the question asks for and then to be specific and thorough in providing an answer that demonstrates what you know. You will also want to write quickly. Although you may be more comfortable with slow, careful writing, in a timed test you simply do not have that luxury. Rapid writing may also help stimulate additional thinking. As you write out one detail or example, you may think of another.

Be sure to reserve a few minutes to review your test before considering it finished. As you review, you may discover that you overlooked a telling detail, an important issue, or a significant fact. Or you may find that you left out a word or phrase that would make a sentence clearer. You may even find that you wrote the opposite of what you intended.

If you find yourself running short of time in an essay exam, map out the direction your essay would have taken if you had time to complete it. Provide an outline for the instructor, showing what you intended to discuss. Depending on how specific you can make the outline and on how accurate and thorough you have been up to that point, you should receive a better grade than if you simply stop writing in midstream.

Acknowledgments (continued)

Natalie Angier, "When (and Why) Dad Has the Babies." Originally published in the *New York Times,* October 28, 1997. Copyright © 1997 The New York Times Company. Reprinted by permission.

Kara Baskin, "Latin American Music," *Arrive,* January/February 2002. Copyright © 2002 by Amtrak, Inc.

Yogi Berra, "When You Come to a Fork in the Road, Take It!" from *When You Come to a Fork in the Road, Take It! Inspiration and Wisdom from One of Baseball's Greatest Heroes* by Yogi Berra, with David Kaplan (contributor). Copyright © 2002 by Hyperion, a division of Random House, Inc. Reprinted by permission.

Kenneth Blanchard, Charles Schewe, Robert Nelson, and Alexander Hiam, excerpts from *Exploring the World of Business.* Copyright © 1996 Worth Publishers. Used with permission of Worth Publishers.

Richard Campbell, excerpts from *Media and Culture: An Introduction to Mass Communication,* 3rd ed. Copyright © 1998 St. Martin's Press. Used by permission.

Margaret Carlson, "The Case for a National ID Card," reprinted from *Time,* January 21, 2002. Copyright © 2002 Time, Inc. Reprinted by permission.

Ben Carson, "Gifted Hands" from *Gifted Hands* by Ben Carson. Copyright © 1990 by Zondevan Publishing House, a division of Random House, Inc. Reprinted by permission.

"Celebrity Sauces," *Consumer Reports,* June 2002, pp. 12–13. Copyright © Consumer's Union, Inc. Reprinted by permission. All rights reserved.

Sandra Cisneros, "Barbie-Q" from *Women Hollering Creek* by Sandra Cisneros. Copyright © 1991 by Sandra Cisneros. Published by Vintage Books, a division of Random House, Inc., and originally in hardcover by Random House, Inc. Reprinted by permission of Susan Bergholz Literary Services, New York. All rights reserved.

Mark Cloud, "Dirty Work," *Parents Magazine,* June 2002, p. 153. Reprinted by permission of the author.

Michael Cole and Sheila R. Cole, "Punishment" and untitled excerpt from *The Development of Children* by Michael Cole and Sheila R. Cole. Copyright © 2001 by Michael Cole and Sheila R. Cole. Used with permission of Worth Publishers.

Rachael Cowley, "King or Queen of the Road: A Girl's View" ["Women Stop for Directions"], *Spectrum,* Penn Valley College, December 8, 1999. Also located online at www.spectrum.kcmetro.edu/. Reprinted by permission of the author and *Spectrum.*

Craig Cox, "Livin' Large in America." Reprinted from the *Utne Reader,* December 2001. Copyright © Craig Cox. Reprinted by permission.

Bernard Dick, "The Horror Film" from *Anatomy of Film,* 4th ed., by Bernard F. Dick. Copyright © 2002 Bedford/St. Martin's. Reprinted by permission.

Ezra Dyer, "Ennui Weekend," *Improper Bostonian,* May 29–June 11, 2002. Copyright © 2002 by the author. Reprinted by permission.

Ed Eyestone, excerpt from "Head for the Hills," *Runner's World,* February 2002. Copyright © 2002 Rodale Inc. Reprinted by permission.

Ted C. Fishman, "A Simple Glass of Water." Originally published in the *New York Times,* August 23, 2001. Reprinted by permission.

Gary Gately, "The Counter Man," *Arrive,* January/February 2002. Copyright © 2002 by Amtrak, Inc. Reprinted by permission.

Henry Louis Gates Jr., "On Honoring Blackness" from *The American Enterprise: A Magazine of Politics, Business, and Culture* (www.TAEmag.com), September–October 1995, pp. 49–50. Copyright © 1995 by The American Enterprise Institute. Reprinted by permission.

Ellen Goodman, "What Matters," *Boston Globe,* April 7, 2002. Copyright © 2002 The Boston Globe, Inc. Reprinted by permission.

Sarah Greene, "Musical Lobsters," *Discover Magazine.* Available online at www.discover.com/aug_01/featlobster.html. Copyright © 2001 The Walt Disney Company. Reprinted by permission.

James A. Henretta, David Brody, and Lynn Dumenil, "The Great Depression," Chapter 24 of *America: A Concise History,* 2nd ed., *Vol. 2: Since 1865.* Copyright © 2002 Bedford/St. Martin's. Reprinted by permission.

Don H. Hockenbury and Sandra E. Hockenbury, "The Power of Touch" and "Forgetting: You *Forgot* the Plane Tickets?!" excerpted from *Psychology,* 3rd ed. Copyright © 1997 Worth Publishers. Used with permission.

Pico Iyer, "The Necessity of Travel," reprinted from *Time,* May 27, 2002. Copyright © 2002 Time, Inc. Reprinted by permission.

Wendy Kaminer, "The War on High Schools," *American Prospect,* Volume 11, Issue 3, December 20, 1999. Copyright © 1999 by Wendy Kaminer. Used by permission.

Bob Karwin, excerpt from "Fear Your Car," from "Just a Thought—The Monthly Humor Column" on bobkarwin.com (www.geocities.com/rkarwin/thought.html, October 17, 2002). Used by permission.

Joseph Kerman and Gary Tomlinson, "Instruments of the Orchestra" from *Listen*, Brief 4th Ed., by Joseph Kerman and Gary Tomlinson. Copyright © 2000 Bedford/St. Martin's. Reprinted by permission.

Mona M. Maisami, "Born in Amrika." Originally published in the *College Record* (Volume 4, Number 4) at Franklin and Marshall College. Reprinted by permission of Mona M. Maisami.

Malcolm X, "Coming to an Awareness of Language" from *The Autobiography of Malcolm X* by Malcolm X, with the assistance of Alex Haley. Copyright © 1964 by Malcolm X and Alex Haley. Copyright © 1965 by Alex Haley and Betty Shabazz. Reprinted by permission of Random House, Inc.

Lara Margolis, "Chicken Scratch and E-Hugs," reprinted from *College Dispatch* (www.fandm.edu/campusLife/Organizations/dispatch/archives/v4/v4n4/hugs.html), Volume 4, No. 4. Copyright © *College Dispatch* at Franklin and Marshall College. Reprinted by permission.

Todd McCarthy, "Anti-Smokers Ought to Butt Out of Movies," from Variety.com. Copyright © 2002 by Variety, Inc. Reprinted by permission.

David Myers, excerpts from *Psychology*, 5th ed. Copyright © 1987 Worth Publishers, Inc. Used with permission.

Jeffrey S. Nevid, Spencer A. Rathus, and Hannah R. Rubenstein, "Body Fat Distribution and Health" and "Viva Mexican Food!" from *Health in the New Millennium*. Copyright © 1998 Worth Publishers. Used with permission.

Alleen Pace Nilsen, from "Sexism in English: A 1990s Update." Copyright © Alleen Pace Nilsen. Reprinted by permission.

Dan O'Hair, Gustav W. Friedrich, John M. Weimann, and Mary Weimann, "Cultural and Relational Contexts" from *Competent Communication*, 2nd ed. Copyright © 1997 Bedford/St. Martin's. Reprinted by permission.

James L. Roark, Michael P. Johnson, Patricia Cline Cohen, Sarah Stage, Alan Lawson, and Susan M. Hartmann, excerpt from *The American Promise*, 2nd ed. Copyright © 2002 Bedford/St. Martin's. Reprinted by permission.

Ian Robertson, excerpt from *Sociology*, 3rd ed. Copyright © 1987 Worth Publishers, Inc. Used with permission.

Kim Stanley Robinson, "A Colony in the Sky," *Newsweek*, September 23, 1996. Copyright © Newsweek, Inc. Reprinted by permission.

Theodore Roethke, "My Papa's Waltz." Copyright © 1942 by Hearst Magazines, Inc. From *The Collected Poems of Theodore Roethke* by Theodore Roethke. Used by permission of Doubleday, a division of Bantam Doubleday Dell Publishing Group, Inc.

Deborah Rosenberg, "Fighting G-Force," *Newsweek*, June 10, 2002. Copyright © Newsweek, Inc. Reprinted by permission.

Eric Schlosser, "The Most Dangerous Job" from *Fast Food Nation: The Dark Side of the All-American Meal* by Eric Schlosser. Copyright © 2001 by Eric Schlosser. Reprinted by permission of Houghton Mifflin Company. All rights reserved.

David Sedaris, "Make That a Double" from *Me Talk Pretty One Day* by David Sedaris. Copyright © 2000 by David Sedaris. By permission of Little, Brown and Company, Inc.

Joel Stein, "Life after Oprah," reprinted from *Time*, March 25, 2002. Copyright © 2002 Time, Inc. Reprinted by permission.

Gloria Steinem, "The Importance of Work" from *Outrageous Acts and Everyday Rebellions* by Gloria Steinem. Published by Henry Holt and Company, Inc. Copyright © 1983 by Gloria Steinem. Copyright © 1984 by East Toledo Productions, Inc.

Dylan Thomas, excerpt from "Do Not Go Gentle into That Good Night" from *Poems of Dylan Thomas*. Copyright © 1939 by New Directions Publishing Corporation, 1945 and 1952 by the Trustees for the Copyrights of Dylan Thomas. Reprinted by permission of New Directions Publishing Corp.

Timothy Tregarthen and Libby Rittenberg, excerpt from *Economics*, 2nd ed. Copyright © 2000 by Worth Publishers. Used with permission.

John Updike, "Beer Can." Originally appeared in the *New Yorker*, Jan. 18, 1964. From *Assorted Prose* by John Updike. Copyright © 1964 by John Updike. Reprinted by permission of Alfred J. Knopf, Inc.

Margaret Walker, "Lineage." Copyright © the Estate of Margaret Walker. Reprinted by permission.

Illustrations

Page 35: "Welcome to U.S. English." Online. Internet. Available www.us-english.org/index2.htm. Copyright © U.S. English. Used by permission.

Page 66: "Racial Profiling." Online. Internet. Available www.civilrights.org/issues/cj/_profiling/. Copyright © Leadership Conference on Civil Rights. Used by permission.

Page 106: "Beyond the Veil." Online. Internet. Available www.pbs.org/visavis/women_mstr.html. Used by permission of Shiva Balaghi and Internews, Inc. Used by permission.

Page 139: "Losing My Tolerance for 'Zero Tolerance.'" Online. Internet. Available www.thisistrue.com/zt.html. Copyright © Randy Cassingham. Used by permission.

Page 172: "ConAgra Foods." Online. Internet. Available www.conagrabeef.com/. Copyright © ConAgra Foods, Inc. Used by permission.

Page 199: "Apples vs. Pears," illustration from *Health in the New Millennium* by Jeffrey S. Nevid, Spencer A. Rathus, and Hannah R. Rubenstein. Copyright © 1998 Worth Publishers. Used by permission.

Page 226: "About Goodwill." Online. Internet. Available www/goodwill.org/index_gii.cfm/530. Copyright © Goodwill, Inc. Used by permission.

Page 259: "Boyd Tinsley." Online. Internet. Available www.davematthews.com/. Copyright © Bama Rags, Inc. Used by permission.

Page 293: "Mars Project." Online. Internet. Available www.marsproject.com/tour.htm. Used by permission of Rob Martin.

Page 319: "Death Penalty Information Center." Online. Internet. Available www.deathpenaltyinfo.org. Copyright © 1998 Death Penalty Information Center. Used by permission.

Page 334: "Welcome to VZServe Express Customer Service." Online. Internet. Available www.verizonwireless.com/care/index_b.html. Copyright © 2002 Verizon Wireless. Used by permission.

Page 335: "Welcome WorldCom Wireless Customers." Online. Internet. Available wireless.wcom.com/index.asp. Copyright © 2002 WorldCom. Used by permission.

Page 384: "National Security: American Civil Liberties Union Freedom Network," this page last updated 1996. Online. Internet. Available www.aclu.org/issues/security.isns.html. Copyright © American Civil Liberties Union. Used by permission.

Page 427: "Horrors" from the Urban Legends Web page. Online. Internet. Available www.snopes2.com/. Used by permission of Barbara Mikkelson.

Page 438: Dennis Brack photograph, reprinted by permission of Black Star.

Page 439: "The Conquest of the South, 1861–1865," map from *America's History*, 2nd ed., by James A. Henretta, David Brody, and Lynn Dumenil. Copyright © 2002 by Bedford/St. Martin's. Used by permission.

Page 440: "The Dual Functions of the Autonomic Nervous System," illustration from *Exploring Psychology*, 5th ed., by David G. Myers. Copyright © 2002 by Worth Publishers. Used by permission.

Page 441: "Research and Observations," illustration from *Psychology*, 5th ed., by David G. Myers. Copyright © 1998 by Worth Publishers. Used by permission.

Page 442 (top): "How a Corporation Is Run" from *Exploring the World of Business* by Kenneth Blanchard, Charles Schewe, Robert Nelson, and Alexander Hiam. Copyright © 1996 by Worth Publishers. Used with permission.

Page 442 (bottom): "New U.S. Workforce Entrants in 2000," adapted from Peter A. Morrison, "Congress and the Year 2000: Peering into the Demographic Future," *Business Horizons,* Vol. 36, No. 6, Nov.–Dec. 1993, p. 55, and Willie E. Hopkins, Karen Sterkel-Powell, and Shirley A. Hopkins, "Training Priorities for a Diverse Work Force," *Public Personnel Management,* Vol. 2, No. 3 (Fall 1994), pp. 429–35.

Page 443: "Economies, North and South, 1860," Stanley Engerman, "The Economic Impact of the Civil War," in *The Reinterpretation of American History* by Robert W. Fogel and Stanley L. Engerman (New York: Harper & Row, 1971), p. 371; U.S. Census Data.

Page 444: "American Immigration, 1870–1914," from *Politics in a Changing World* by Marcus Ethridge and Howard Handelman. Copyright © 1994 by St. Martin's Press. Used by permission.

Page 445: "Wind Speeds," modified from 1939 International Agreement and N. Bowditch, *American Practical Navigator,* U.S. Navy Hydrographic Office Publication 9, 1958.

Page 446: "The Spread of Black Death, around 1350," map from *The Global Past* by Lanny B. Fields, Russell J. Barber, and Cheryl A. Riggs. Copyright © 1998 by Bedford/St. Martin's. Used by permission.

Page 448: "Regions of the Human Brain," illustration from *Abnormal Psychology* by Ronald J. Comer. Copyright © 2001 by W.H. Freeman & Co. Used by permission.

Page 449: "Annual Record, Tape, and CD Sales" from *Media and Culture: An Introduction to Mass Communication,* 3rd ed., by Richard Campbell, based on information from the Recording Industry Association of America. Used by permission.

Pages 451, 452: "How Infectious Diseases Are Transmitted" and "Pathogens," illustrations from *Health in the New Millennium* by Jeffrey S. Nevid, Spencer A. Rathus, and Hannah R. Rubenstein. Copyright © 1998 by Worth Publishers. Used by permission.

Page 466: "The Bread Line." Franklin D. Roosevelt Library, Hyde Park, NY. Used by permission.

Page 469: "Women Face the Depression." Corbis-Bettmann. Used by permission.

Page 473: "Dancing Cheek to Cheek." Steve Schapiro. Used by permission.

Page 475: "Mr. Smith Goes to Washington." MOMA-Film Stills Archives. Used by permission.

Page 478: "Lynching." Collection of Philip J. and Suzanne Schiller. Used by permission.

Page 484: "Hoovervilles." Grant Smith/Corbis. Used by permission.

Page 489: "America: A Concise History." Online. Internet. Available www.bedfordstmartins.com/henrettaconcise/con_index.htm?24. Copyright © 2002 Bedford/St. Martin's. Used by permission.